D1154256

Alienation and Charisma

ALIENATION and CHARISMA
A Study of
Contemporary American Communes

BENJAMIN ZABLOCKI

THE FREE PRESS
A Division of Macmillan Publishing Co., Inc.
New York

Collier Macmillan Publishers
London

The Free Press
A Division of Macmillan Publishing Co., Inc.
866 Third Avenue, New York, N. Y. 10022

Collier Macmillan Canada, Ltd.

Library of Congress Catalog Card Number: 79-55938

Printed in the United States of America

printing number
1 2 3 4 5 6 7 8 9 10

Library of Congress Cataloging in Publication Data

Zablocki, Benjamin David
    Alienation and charisma.

    Bibliography: p.
    Includes index.
    1. Communal living--United States--History.
2. Collective settlements--United States--History.
3. Communal living--History. 4. Decision-making,
Group. 5. Alienation (Sociology) 6. Leadership.
I. Title.
HQ971.Z3   307.7   79-55938
ISBN 0-02-935780-2

Copyright Acknowledgments

To the memory of my father,
Henry Zablocki

Contents

Preface

In 1965, when I began to study American communes, I was convinced, as I remain today, that communes constitute an important site for the exploration of fundamental sociological problems. This book is concerned primarily with collective decision making in communes and only secondarily with communal living as an alternative life-style. I have been particularly interested in the problems posed for decision making by the conflict between ideology (the collective manifestation of purposive goals and values) and social structure (the patterned regularities of human interaction).

Out of the early period of my research came *The Joyful Community* (1971), a case study of a single contemporary commune. That commune, the Bruderhof, was notable for its extraordinary structural stability, as well as for its capacity for repeated charismatic renewal. In this book I have undertaken to explore in breadth certain problems that were treated in the earlier work in depth. The research design is comparative, and the focus is now on a diversity of communal types—urban and rural, stable and unstable, successful and unsuccessful. Even charisma is treated in this book as a variable. The communes studied vary from the fully charismatic through a range of less charismatic, semicharismatic, and noncharismatic types.

The potential value of studying communes in comparative perspective was clear to me long before the Bruderhof study was begun. Noam Chomsky has argued that, "A serious study of morals or of social systems would . . . ask itself what kinds of social systems are conceivable. Then it would ask itself what kinds have actually been realized in history. . . ." (1969:32). I first began to think about the problem of discovering which, among all the conceivable social systems, are humanly attainable, while I was an undergraduate, taking Sidney Morgenbesser's course in the philosophy of the social sciences. Later, in a seminar in the comparative analysis of Latin American societies taught by C. Wright Mills, I began to think that it might be possible to make a small start at tackling this problem by carrying out a comparative study of what were then called utopian communities. Mills taught me always to sift my ethnographic research findings through a comparative data grid. This technique eventually helped make it possible to transform my early disconnected investigations of rural communes into the beginnings of the systematic longitudinal study of 120 contemporary American rural and urban communes which is reported in this book.

I took these general interests to graduate school where James Coleman challenged me to think about the deeper question of how there come to be in the first place social systems whose interests are not simple functions of their members' interests. This question has remained at the theoretical heart of my work ever since. Anyone who was lucky enough to be a part of the Johns Hopkins graduate department of social relations during its early years owes a considerable debt to those teachers and students who so roundly affirmed the value of sociological enterprise that one could muster the courage to undertake gargantuan research projects like this one, even in this present time of so-called sociological malaise. The work of James Coleman, Art Stinchcombe, James Davis, and Peter Rossi are and will probably always be my model for what a sociologist should be doing.

This book is part of a larger research project, other parts of which are still in progress. I was assisted in this work by a number of graduate students of exceptional ability: Craig Calhoun, Jane Ferrar, Greg Jirak, Michael Manhardt, Peter Messeri, Anita Micossi, Oto Okugawa, and Charles Sprague. Deserving of particular mention are the two of my students who helped to administer the urban commune project—Ray Bradley, now assistant professor of sociology at the University of Minnesota, and Angela Aidala, now assistant professor of sociology at Rutgers University. Ray Bradley worked closely with me on every part of the planning and execution of the urban phase of the data collection. His enthusiasm for sociology and his feel for the continuous interaction between theory and research were sources of inspiration for myself and everyone else associated with him. Bradley's dissertation, *Pyramids of Power and Communion: The Structural Properties of Charismatic Communes,* represents a significant forward step upon one of the paths of inquiry for which this book has provided only a rough initial sketch.

Angela Aidala arrived late on the project but also stayed late, and played a major role in keeping the data collection alive for two full years after the formal project termination date. Aidala's particular interest is in the components of ideological systems. Like Bradley's, her dissertation represents a significant part of the future of the larger research undertaking which this book has begun.

The constant encouragement and friendly guidance of Amitai Etzioni and Herb Gans at the Center for Policy Research helped get the later stages of this research off the ground. Of the many administrative staff members at CPR who were helpful, Stephanie Clohosey, Zoe Harrison, and Clara Shapiro are owed special thanks. As the scale and scope of the research increased beyond the capacities of one person, the task of coordinating many tasks fell increasingly to two able project administrators, Jane Kingston and Claudia Lawrence. Without the tact, organizing skill, and the energy, persistence, and attention to detail of these two women, the rest of us could never have accomplished so large a portion of our over-ambitious agenda.

All or parts of this book were read in manuscript by James Coleman, Sigmund Diamond, William J. Goode, Michael Inbar, Barbara McIntosh, Neil Smelser, Arthur Vidich, Lisa Wertheimer, and Christine Wright-Isak, as well as by my students, particularly Angela Aidala and Ray Bradley. The generous and copious comments and criticisms of these readers helped to shape the book's structure, tighten its argument, and enrich its exposition with detail. Discussions with Robert Bellah, Bennett Berger, Sarane Boocock, Fred Davis, Robert Fogarty, Rosabeth Kanter, Saul Levine, Gillian Lindt, Hyam Mariampolski, Barbara Myerhoff, Robert Nisbet, Charles Plott, Phil Selznick and Burt Singer, were also of great value to me during this stage of the work.

Various corporate entities were also of great help to me. The California Institute of Technology, where I spent one of the most stimulating years of my life, was the place where the form for this book first emerged. The first draft was written at the Bureau of Applied Social Research in New York. Seminars at Columbia, Caltech, Rutgers, The University of Chicago, and the Institute for Advanced Studies in Vienna provided me with many opportunities to try out emerging ideas and formulation. The Center for the Study of Law and Society at Berkeley, the Environmental Quality Lab at Caltech, and the Center for Policy Research in New York at various times provided homes for this research.

The field work for this research presented enormous obstacles and I owe a great debt to a dedicated and resourceful group of colleagues. Jeanette Alexander, Calvin DeFilipus, Nina Housman, Mimi Leonard, Joan Medlin, Michael Ort, Debbie Podus, Howard Schneider, Charles Smith, and Ernest Vollin did the field work, with Aidala, Bradley, Sprague and myself. Of course, none of this field work would have been possible had it not been for the openness and generous cooperation of many hundreds of commune members.

Important tasks of data management were performed by Wendy Bradley, Lee Cokorinos, Miriam Davis, Walt Harrison, Harriet Lightman, Pam Melvin, Milcha Mrema, James O'Toole, Betty Sheets, Angela Sinanian, Emily Singer, Betsy Stover, Jamie Sunderland, and Tom Thirlwall. The many hours of tape transcripts and the several drafts of the manuscript were typed by Jane Kingston and Claudia Lawrence. Dora Barbera, Nancy Fernandez, Jeanne Galaydick, and Nancy Lerner assisted with the typing.

The work presented in this book was supported by a number of grants. Major support was received in the form of a research grant from the National Institute of Mental Health (1 RO MH 25525-01MP). In addition to my obvious gratitude for the funding, I would particularly like to express my appreciation to Elliot Liebow and his staff at the Metro Center for going along with my hunch that the more expensive technique of network data gathering and analysis should be used rather than the cheaper and more conventional individual survey analysis, and for allowing me supplementary funds for this purpose. It will be obvious to the reader how many of the findings presented here could not have been discovered if the Metro Center had not allowed me to have my way in this matter. In addition, small grants from the Center for the Study of Law and Society, from the Columbia University Research Council, from the Haight-Ashbury Research Project (NIMH), and from the UCLA study of alternative childrearing patterns (NIMH), as well as Danforth and NSF predoctoral fellowships to two of my research assistants all helped to move the work along.

My family lived with this work in progress for a long time. Lewis Coser has classified communes among the "greedy institutions" because of the tremendous demands they make upon the time and energy of their participants. But the task of studying and writing about communes has proven no less greedy of my time and energy, and I want to thank my wife, Lisa Rossman Zablocki, and my children, Tom, Daniel, and Matthew, for going through this experience with me, and Lisa especially for repeatedly taking time from her busy medical training to help me with various creative and mundane tasks when I could con no one else into sharing them.

List of Tables

List of Figures

I suggest that there is little hope that we will get far in our efforts to develop and enrich sociological theory with such a blunt instrument as the concept of charisma as part of our theoretical tool-kit.

Had the concept not become, by now, all too often a substitute for serious research, and a barrier to thinking equalled by few other sponge-words of our time—notably 'alienation'—it would scarcely be worth devoting so much space to it. Thinking about its ambiguities, however, may help us clarify our minds.

Peter Worsley

Introduction

We live at a time in which the major practical problem facing society and the major theoretical problem facing sociology have become one and the same: the problem of collective decision making. We are faced with a society whose members' various interests do not converge, nor do they conflict according to any meaningful pattern. In such circumstances there can be no question of achieving or maintaining functional equilibrium; there can be no legitimate system of social control; there can be no grand dialectical conflict, but only piddling little conflicts. Equilibrium theory, social control, and conflict have been among the major traditional unifying perspectives within sociology. But all of them rest upon the assumption that groups of people (at least those with power) know how to decide what they want to achieve or preserve.

Within this broad problem area of collective decision making, we shall be concerned in this book with one important component: the question of consensus, how it gets lost, and how it gets regained. For such a task we need the concepts of alienation and charisma. Peter Worsley is right, in the excerpt quoted above, to dismiss these terms for the confusion and fuzziness they have brought with them. But the ability of these concepts to fascinate, even in their obscurity, has to do with the fact that they go to the heart of the matter. They need not to be dismissed but to be resurrected. We need to banish them as semi-mystical concepts dealing with intrinsically unobservable inner states of anguish and heroism, and at the same time to redefine them, closer to the spirit and intent of classical theory,

1

as reciprocal concepts dealing respectively with the observable ungluing and regluing of the decision making bond between the individual and the collectivity.

There are many ways of studying collective decision making. The subject has engaged some of the best minds in economics, political science, sociology, and psychology (e.g., Gary Becker, Mancur Olson, William Riker, James Coleman, R. Duncan Luce). Our strategy, in this book, will not be as ambitious as any of theirs. Instead, we shall attempt to get an elementary grasp on the subject by tackling it on the most favorable possible terrain, by studying collectivities whose entire existence revolves around the decision making function.

Communitarianism is a social movement whose very reason for being, as we shall see, can be traced in good part, to the breakdown of the decision making process in larger scale collectivities under the strain of rapidly multiplying choice alternatives. Communes are forms of social organization whose major locus of action tends to be the consensus seeking process. We shall see how difficult are the issues that get raised even when we confront this intrinsically difficult subject within such an ideally suitable context.

Why Study Communes?

In beginning a study of communes, it is easy to ask the wrong questions: Are they utopias? Are they on the increase? Do they lead to personal happiness? Are they viable substitutes for nuclear families? What proportion of the total population now lives in them? Although some of these questions will be addressed in this book, they are neither the most socially relevant nor the most sociologically interesting issues raised by the existence of communes.

An alternative perspective is to look at communes as decision making arenas within which human purposes dreams, and desires interact and contend with structural necessities. Viewed in this way, communes have much they can teach us about the fundamental nature of the social bond. Many communes are experimental attempts to build social order upon a basis of love. Others are attempts to live anarchistically, without any constraints on individual behavior. Still others are attempts to subordinate all individual will to a single general will. Most of these experiments fail; the few that succeed are usually drastically modified over time. For the systematic examination of these various ways of trying to modify social structure, communes, with their unambiguous definitions of purpose and membership, their intricate and involuted role sets, and their well-defined but volatile hierarchies, constitute a useful natural laboratory.

One way of getting into the basic questions is to ask why it is so difficult for people who share a clear idea about the values that should guide their social relationships to build a stable social system reflecting these values. This is not to say that the values of the members of any actual commune are always all that clear in their own minds to begin with. But lack of decisiveness or clarity on the individual level, as we shall see, contributes to but is not at the root of the problem. There seem to be deterministic social forces that prevent such groups of kindred spirits from pooling their resources for joint enterprises requiring social partnership, even when they possess resourses adequate to the goals of economic partnership. For reasons not primarily economic, communitarian enterprises rarely reach a stable equilibrium.

The obstacle is not, however, simply one of longevity. Although few communal experiments last longer than a few years, their mortality rate does not differ by all that much from that of other radical voluntary organizations. But comparison with the achievements of small cooperative business enterprises, for example, leads to the conclusion that even under optimal conditions communal partnership is far more difficult to sustain than economic partnership. Some small cooperative businesses do succeed, against the odds, in reaching a stable equilibrium with stated goals achieved. It is rare to find even such a basic accomplishment among communes.

The communal experiments discussed in this book are different from one another in many ways. But they are alike in that they have set themselves against one or more of the mastering social trends of our time—be it individualism, secularism, urbanism, industrialism, capitalism, or the increasing specificity of family roles. Both the technological and the political conditions of our times seem to hold out the promise that such trends can be resisted, that lifestyles can be chosen. But is this true for collectivities of shared purpose or only for individuals? Can it be that the same society that offers the individual such an unprecedented and bewildering array of choices creates collective patterns for structured roles and statuses that are strictly determined within narrow limits? We shall attempt to discover, through a longitudinal investigation of the 120 contemporary communes studied in this book, what margins for choice, if any, really exist in the selection of a communal program of action and way of life.

Background of the Research Tradition

Historical records tell us of communes, utopian communities, mutualistic societies, or intentional communities dating as far back as 1663 in the United States (Bestor, 1950). But most communes have been short-lived, and even the most successful have been marginal to the development of American culture. As a result, American sociologists, while sometimes acknowledging their theoretical importance, have rarely considered communes worth the effort of empirical research.

A review of the ethnographic literature indicates that prolonged exposure to a given commune has often been more helpful than sociological sophistication. Houriet (1971), although a journalist, was able to write one of the more scientifically valuable descriptions of about a dozen hippie communes because he spent a great deal of time totally immersing himself in the life of each. On the other hand, a well known and experienced sociologist published a study of the Morningstar Ranch commune, based on a very short visit, which was worse than useless. This sociologist was misled (perhaps maliciously) by his "guide" and his informants into believing that the immediately visible guest and transient area of the commune was the entire commune. He spent his time scrutinizing this relatively unpopulated public area as if it were a commune while all the while, less than a hundred yards away, a rich and varying drama of communal relationships was being enacted, hidden behind a veil of trees.

While the above example is extreme, the case study phase of commune research has been responsible for a number of persistent myths in the literature. One of these myths is that more communes have been reported on than is, in fact, the case. What Rosabeth Kanter has called "the old standbys," twenty or so unusually accessible and friendly communes, have kept on creeping into the literature under a variety of pseudonyms, giving rise to the impression that they represent well over a hundred discrete cases. Another persistent myth, with a similar source, is that commune membership is almost exclusively middle class in background. This is certainly not the case, as we shall see in Chapter 3, except in the sense that anyone who is young, white, and functionally literate is labeled middle class. Part of this problem stems from a sampling bias. Predominantly middle-class communes tend to be much more accessible to the researcher than are predominantly working-class communes.

There have also been practical research problems. Communes have been hard to locate, hard to gain access to, and appallingly evanescent as compared with the highly structured kibbutzim. Ethnographic data have had to accumulate for over a decade before we reached the point of being ready to take off into the domain of systematic comparative research.*

By the mid-1960s, an accumulation of studies of the Israeli kibbutzim had demonstrated the rich potentialities for sociology in the existence of discrete, well-bounded, natural social experiments. In America, communes were attracting attention if for no other reason than that they were playing a prominent role in the interesting and bewildering youth "counterculture." In the renascent subdiscipline of collective behavior, a theoretical justification for the study of intense, but short-lived, social phenomena was beginning to emerge.[†] It was in this context that this research was begun.

Significance of the Research Perspective

Some of the most basic questions asked by sociology—Why is there not a war of all against all? Why do people seek collective restraints on their personal freedom? What are the forces that attract and repel the members of a collectivity from one another?—may be profitably studied at the commune level. Normative explanations of social control and relational equilibrium beg the question of how normative systems get started and become legitimate in the first place. When we try to answer these questions by looking directly at society, we find ourselves stumped by the confounding effects of tradition and law. The study of communes, however, gives us the opportunity to look at social groups as normative

---

*Not all research on communes is or should be comparative. Intensive participant observation of single cases continues to go on at the present time and properly so. Every commune is a social world, and the opportunities for new discovery by perceptive observers will never be exhausted. However, the case study method is inherently limited, and, especially since 1970, work on communal organizations by Berger (1972, 1974), Kanter (1972, 1973b, 1974), and Zablocki (1972a, 1973) in America and by Rabin (1965) and Talmon (1972) in Israel has proceeded in comparative perspective.

[†]The period 1965-1975 was also a time of continuing intense interest in the topic of community in general. See Coleman, 1971; Gans, 1967, Goren, 1970; Laumann, 1973; Liebow, 1967; Moynihan, 1969; Rossi et al., 1974; Suttles, 1972; Tilly, 1974.

systems *in statu nascendi,* when the legitimating power of tradition and law are still at their minimum.* The instability of communes presents us with the opportunity to watch the process of social change speeded up, while their intentionality provides an unusual degree of freedom from determination by the past.

The significance of social movements, argues Killian (1964), "lies not in their careers but in their consequences for the larger society and its culture." To the extent that this means that the sociological importance of a phenomenon is always to be measured by its social importance, we believe this to be an error in judgment. Sociologists have been in a position analogous to that of chemists prior to the nineteenth century, constrained by external forces, or by their own misguided sense of duty, to study structures and processes on grounds other than the internal logic of their own discipline. Thus, we now realize that chemists should not be required to study the properties of gold because it is valuable, or of oxygen because it is common, or of iron because it is useful but, rather, need to be brought by the internal logic of their own investigations into studying such elements as radium, which is difficult to find and difficult to study but provides a key to more of the secrets of the periodic table than all the other elements combined. In the case of radium, that element's very instability, the rate of its decay, determined its usefulness to the discipline.

Sociologists have been similarly constrained by an ethic that confounds the social relevance of a phenomenon with its sociological relevance. The most widespread forms of human collective life are not necessarily the most strategic areas for sociological investigation. The persistence of tradition and the ramification of law, to take two examples, are both important phenomena. But both miss the opportunity to get to the heart of human collective experience—the actual emergence of consensus out of the raw stuff of relational conflict and coalition. The study of communes provides us with opportunities to be present at the births and deaths of collective order, consensus, and legitimacy.

The Commune as a Research Site

Aside from their intrinsic interest, communes also have certain general properties that help to facilitate research. Sociology has a need to study processes whose natural time scales mesh with the time scale of research. For the most part, societies and cultures change all too slowly for their consequences to be observed in their entirety by any single piece of research. Dramatic instances of social change, on the other hand, such as mob behavior and crisis decision making, occur too rapidly. The changes in both social structure and personality structure that occur within communes follow a time scale intermediate between that of the larger society and that of the various mass phenomena. Significant structural transformations often occur within a single year's time in communes. These same communes have nevertheless maintained enough of a common thread of identity to be recognizable as continuous social systems. Transitions from anarchism to totalitarianism, schisms, purges, revolutions, and reconstitu

*This is especially true for a study that chooses, as we have done, to look at a sample of communes, most of which are in the early years of their development.

tions are some examples of such conveniently timed social events. Furthermore, the short lifespan of many communes enables us to observe them through all stages of their growth and decay.

Communes are as discrete, explicit, and purposive as formal organizations. At the same time, they are as natural, pervasive, and diffuse as ordinary communities. As bounded organizations, the dynamics of their integrations and disintegrations are more open to study than are those of ordinary communities. As communities, on the other hand, communes provide a site for research on areas of human relationship (e.g., sex, child rearing) that cannot be studied in formal organizations.

Communes are better than nuclear families as research sites for many kinds of sociological problems. Whereas nuclear families share many of the same characteristics, they lack full intentionality. As traditional entities, they do not articulate a great proportion of the motivations for the interactions of their members. Communes, being ideological entities, are forced to do so. Communes are also forced to try to justify discrepancies between attitudes and behavior, as the family unit is not. For all of these reasons, we have come to view the commune as a significant research site for the investigation of the search for consensus in social systems.

A Commune Is Not a Microcosm

An appreciation of the many advantages of the commune as a research site should not lead us to the error of thinking that communes may be viewed as microcosmic reflections of the larger society. People do not behave the same way in small face to face groups as they do in large relatively impersonal societies. In particular, networks of strong direct relationships, which we are going to see play a major role in determining the fate of communes, cannot possibly play nearly as important a role in the dynamics of large societies, or even of natural communities.

With regard to the problem of collective decision making, however, the differences between communes and societies do not pose a problem. If we were going to argue that communes have found the way to make collective decisions successfully, and that larger societies should either emulate them or disaggregate themselves into small like-minded communities, we would be falling prey to the microcosmic fallacy. But, in fact, what we shall be arguing is that the problems of collective decision making run far deeper than what might have been imagined. Unless we can understand why small groups of likeminded individuals find it so hard to achieve and maintain consensus without taking totalitarian shortcuts we will have little hope of understanding the far more complex difficulties faced by larger and more heterogeneous collectivities.

Definitions of Terms

For the most part, we can define our terms as we go along. However, there are several terms that have multiple meanings in sociological literature that we wish to use in somewhat more precise ways. These terms are: commune, aliena-tion, charisma, self, and investment of self. For two of these terms, alienation and charisma, our definitions at this point will have to be tentative and provi-sional, since this entire book, on a certain level, may be seen as an effort to rede-fine these terms. For the others, however, there is merely the matter of specify-ing exactly what we do and do not mean.

Commune

Our definition of commune will refer both to the individual and to the rela-tional level of analysis. Let us define a commune as any group of five or more adult individuals (plus children if any), the majority of whose dyads* are *not cemented by blood or marriage,* who have decided to live together, *without com-pulsion, for an indefinite period of time,* primarily for the sake of an *ideological goal,* focused upon the *achievement of community,* for which a collective house-hold is deemed essential. This definition does not necessarily imply a utopian program,† community of property, communal childrearing, or egalitarianism, although these characteristics are often associated with communal living. The frequency with which these characteristics are found in communes is treated, rather, as a subject for investigation. The proposed definition is strictly induc-tive, having to recommend it only the fact that it seems to distinguish those collectivities that are generally thought of as communes from those that are not.

Two further conditions were imposed upon the communes to be studied in this book. First, they had to include either representatives of both sexes or else one sex plus children. The primary reason for this condition was to eliminate Christian monastic communities from consideration,‡ not because monasteries

---

*Throughout this book we will be treating communes at times as networks of relationships and at times as groups of individuals. This will entail shifts in the unit of analysis. A *dyad* is defined as the unit of analysis formed by the arbitrary bracketing of any pair of individu-als. We will think of a dyad as existing regardless of whether there is any *social* relationship between the individuals. Thus a group of four people will alternatively be described as a group of six dyads, a group of five people as a group of ten dyads, and, in general, a group of N people as a group of $(N)(N - 1)/2$ dyads.

†Most communitarians explicitly reject utopian imagery, choosing instead to stress their experimental openmindedness; and we shall not use the term in discussing contemporary communes, except where drawing historical connections. Utopias have come in three forms: exhorted, imposed, and communitarian. Exhorted utopias are those proposed with no practical plan for implementation. Examples are Plato's *Republic,* Augustine's *City of God,* Thomas More's *Utopia,* Samuel Butler's *Erewhon,* and most recently B. F. Skinner's *Walden II.* Imposed utopias differ from exhorted utopias in that they constitute attempts of sovereign powers to provide their citizenry with a better, more perfect communal struc-ture. Calvin's City of Geneva, the Jesuit order of seventeenth-century Paraguay, the New Town movement in England and America in this century, and, most recently and ambi-tiously, the Chinese communes constitute examples of imposed utopias. As interesting and important as these phenomena are, they do not fall within the scope of the book. We shall be concerned here only with what may be called the communitarian utopias. communal experiments that arise from the voluntary, deliberate intentions of the participants.

‡An unintended consequence of this definition was the elimination of most homosexual communes from the sample. One of the more surprising results of the urban stage of the field work was the great number of homosexual communes (both male and female) to be found in most large American cities.

are not true communes, but because they constitute so vast and specialized an area of interest that it is best not to treat them in a study emphasizing the contemporary communal movement.

The second condition was that the commune had to have a public identity— a name or a function by which the group was collectively known to the larger society. This restriction was imposed reluctantly for methodological reasons. Without some sort of enumeration of the national population of communes, one cannot make even the crudest inferences from the sample to the population of all American communes. In the absence of a full household census, such an enumeration was made possible only by excluding from the study by definition all secretive communes. Some of the most interesting of the revolutionary political communes in America and some of the more esoteric religious cults were thereby excluded.

Alienation

We make use of two quite different definitions of alienation in this book—a traditional one in Part I and our own definition, based specifically on the decision making function, in Part II. The term alienation as used by sociologists has been much criticized for its lack of precision (Feuer, 1962; Worsley, 1968; Schacht, 1971). Microsociological investigators of alienation, with Melvin Seeman (1972) leading the way, have pinned their hopes for the concept upon multidimensional scaling. Anywhere from five to eight "dimensions" of alienation (Neal and Rettig, 1967; Allardt, 1971; Seeman, 1972) have been identified by various authors, the most thoroughly studied of which seem to be *normlessness* and *powerlessness*. However, attempts to validate scales of measurement along these dimensions have not been successful. This should not surprise us. The experience of psychologists with the concept of intelligence should have taught us that, if a concept does not first have a well-understood unitary function, dimensionalization itself, however sophisticated, will not provide one. Nevertheless, Seeman's definition is the best available and will serve to launch our investigations.

Seeman (1972) defines alienation in terms of six dimensions of socially learned expectation:

> Alienation refers to six related but distinguishable notions, and these six varieties of alienation can be rather sharply defined in terms of the person's expectancies or his values. Thus, to be alienated means to be characterized by one or several of the following:
> 1. a sense of *powerlessness:* a low expectancy that one's own behavior can control the occurrence of personal and social rewards; for the alienated man, control seems vested in external forces, powerful others, luck, or fate.
> 2. a sense of *meaninglessness:* a sense of the incomprehensibility of social affairs, of events whose dynamics one does not understand and

whose future course one cannot predict (more formally, a low expectancy that satisfactory predictions about future outcomes can be made).

3. a sense of *normlessness:* a high expectancy that socially unapproved means are necessary to achieve given goals; the view that one is not bound by conventional standards in the pursuit of what may be quite conventional goals (e.g., position, wealth).

4. *value isolation* (or *cultural estrangement*): the individual's rejection of commonly held values in the society; the assignment of low reward value to goals or behaviors that are highly valued in the given society (e.g., alienated artist or intellectual).

5. *self-estrangement:* the individual's sense of a discrepancy between his ideal self and his actual self-image and the failure to satisfy certain postulated inherent human needs. Borrowing heavily from classic descriptions of *the worker who is estranged* when carrying out unfulfilling and uncreative work; to be self-estranged is to be engaged in activities that are not rewarding in themselves.

6. *social isolation:* the individual's low expectancy for inclusion and social acceptance, expressed typically in feelings of loneliness or feelings of rejection or repudiation (found, for example, among minority members, the aged, the handicapped, and various kinds of less visible strangers).

These definitions are operational in the sense that one can then develop questionnaires or observational plans that have specific instructions for measuring the degree to which people are experiencing alienation. Operationalizing the definition of a concept, however, is a necessary but not sufficient condition for rendering it well formulated. It is still not clear what these putative dimensions have in common. Why are they dimensions of a single variable rather than of six distinct variables? Seeman's response to this question is that each dimension undermines one or more of the core values of Western democratic society (e.g., powerlessness undermines the values of mastery and autonomy; normlessness, the values of order and trust; value isolation undermines consensus; and social isolation undermines the values of egalitarianism and individual worth).

Seeman's definition, in an effort to cover all the territory, is forced to lump together a number of different kinds of complaints that would probably be better treated separately. Rather than setting off the concept crisply, it invites confusion with such related concepts as anomie and dispair. Perhaps the most serious problem with this definition, however, is that it gives us alienation without an object, that is, it doesn't specify, *alienation from what?*

Despite these difficulties, it is Seeman's definition of alienation that we will use throughout the first part of this book, until we are ready to present our own alternative definition in Part II. Its disadvantages are outweighed by the advantage of being able to contrast the kinds of alienation (in Seeman's terms) experienced by commune members with the kinds that receive most attention in the larger social world. We shall see that, whereas powerlessness and normlessness have been the forms of alienation most endemic to Western democratic societies, meaninglessness and value isolation are the forms that most plague commune members.

In Part II of this book, beginning in Chapter 6, we use our findings concerning the communal decision making process to develop an alternative definition of alienation. This definition is based upon the postulate that all alienation has to do in essence with loss of the ability to make or help make choices. It further requires that alienation have a subject and an object, the subject always being a person and the object being that same person (self-alienation) or a collectivity (social alienation). We break down the decision making process into five stages or levels, each of which is associated with a form of alienation. These levels are: meanings, goals, strategies, norms, and comparisons with alternatives. They represent not five distinct dimensions of alienation but five ordered levels along a single dimension. These range from the most encompassing level of alienation, in which the participants cannot achieve consensus even on the meanings of jointly experienced events, to the least encompassing level, in which the participants are in full consensus with respect to internal matters of the collectivity, but lack consensus on the conditions for the continuance of the collectivity itself.

Charisma

We are going to propose and argue for a fairly unusual definition of charisma in this book. Initially, this will probably take some willing suspension of disbelief on the part of the reader. Charisma has been defined as a form of authority (Weber, 1947, p. 358ff), as a pattern of social structure (Parsons, 1937, p. 567), as a pattern of readiness to be led (Friedland, 1964, p. 18), as a shared system of beliefs (Turk, 1971, p. 122), and as a form of interpersonal influence (Etzioni, 1975, p. 305). All of these perspectives contain valuable insights about charisma, but none of them seem to get to the essence of the phenomenon as we have observed it in communes.

We wish to define charisma as a collective state resulting from an objective pattern of relationships in a specific collectivity that allows the selves of the participants to be fully or partially absorbed into a collective self. Moreover, we shall argue that this absorption (charisma) is both real and primordeally social, that it can be perceived directly and not merely deduced from its consequences, and that it is based upon the human capacity to invest the self into other persons or larger collectivities. The objective pattern of relationships that allows charisma to emerge we shall call *charismatic potential*. A person whose authority is based on the widely shared belief that he or she is an embodiment of the collective self we shall call a *charismatic leader*. Belief alone, without actual widespread self investment cannot, by this definition, produce charismatic authority.

The concept of charisma, as so defined, cannot be separated from the concept of alienation. The two are reciprocal. Charisma overcomes alienation by allowing people to identify their own interests with those of the collectivity to a sufficient degree that consensus can be reached on important collective decisions. Naturally, groups will vary in the extent that they need to evoke this identification, but it should be clear that we are arguing, in opposition to many theorists (e.g., Shils, 1965; Worsley, 1968; Bensman and Givant, 1975), that charisma is potentially a characteristic of any collectivity.

In order to be able to see that charisma is at bottom a relational characteristic, one must first of all be able to see relationships as they function in the collective decision making process. One must be able to see that there are always not one but two worlds of collective decision making: an overt, formal, and often highly ritualized collective search for consensus; and, at the same time, a covert, informal, and continuous process of relational decision making in which people are constantly being accepted or rejected, dominated or deferred to, courted or ignored.

Much otherwise very fine research on sects, cults, coalitions, and communes has lacked one important set of technical ingredients, the analytic tools for examining relational structure in its full complexity. The research reported in this book, although it also falls far short of this goal, has benefited in this regard from many recent advances in the techniques of network data collection and analysis. We are thus able to show, although often with only very crude measures, what other studies of similar phenomena have had to ignore—a strong and pervasive covariation between interpersonal relationship networks and patterns of organizational decision making.

Charisma is a rather widespread phenomenon in communes. Often it is embodied in a single charismatic leader, but sometimes the collectivity itself (or some portion of it) is the charismatic factor. From a systems perspective, charisma is a self-corrective device in a social system that halts and reverses a slide into alienation (inability to achieve consensus) often by changing the very beliefs and preferences of the participants. This persuasive ability of the charismatic leader is what Amitai Etzioni has defined as charisma itself (1975, pp. 305ff):

> the ability of an actor to exercise diffuse and intense influence over the normative orientations of other actors. . . . But whereas authority, as usually understood, implies only that the subject holds in abeyance his own criteria for decision and action, and accepts as legitimate the directives of his superiors, *charisma implies that the subject has been influenced to modify some of his own criteria* . . . (emphasis added)

In extreme forms, its manifestations are so visible and dramatic that it is easy to understand why most observers have assumed that none other than the leader could be the root cause of the phenomenon.

A related issue is the question of how charismatic a leader must be to be considered a charismatic leader. There has been a sentiment within sociology opposed to sullying some of the grander historically pregnant concepts of social theory by identifying them too readily with everyday counterparts. This makes about as much sense as refusing to use the concept of mass to describe a pebble after it has been used to describe mighty Jupiter in its orbit. Is it not more useful to think of concepts as having many attributes, including magnitude and scope? To say that the charismatic leaders discussed in this book are not in the same league with Moses, Napoleon, or Mao is certainly an understatement. However, the charismatic attributes on which they differ are primarily those of magnitude and scope. A difference in degree, no matter how vast, does not automatically qualify as a difference in kind. The point is that they do not differ from these great men in the relational and collective properties they allow to flourish. It is these common fundamental properties, not the place of their propagators in history, that are of interest here.

The notion of alienation and charisma as reciprocal concepts is not new to sociology. It is at least implicit in Max Weber's discussion of the differential susceptibility of various societal subgroups to prophetic (i.e., charismatic) influence. Parsons discusses this connection explicitly in his "Introduction to Max Weber's *The Sociology of Religion*" as follows (1974, p. 54):

> It seems to be almost a truism that different societies, and different structural elements within each, will have different sensitivities to the same stimulus to break with the established order. This sensitivity is perhaps the same thing as what is now called "alienation." The alienated elements are those which are relatively "available" to be stirred by prophetic movements.

A similar point is made by Turk (1971, p. 127):

> Closely related to this idea is Eisenstadt's view of the charismatic leader's role in producing new combinations of meanings. In our terms, such innovation would either reconcile variously valued matters or fill a value vacuum; both instances would lead to the bestowal of charisma—at least according to the discussion thus far. Parsons moved closely toward this viewpoint in his discussion of Nazism as a charismatic response to alienation.

However, neither Parsons nor Turk develops a framework in which charisma, as a countervailing force to the decision making inertia brought about by alienation, can be studied. An aim of this book is to begin to develop the theoretical relationship to the point where, eventually, given data on a group's degree of alienation, social structure, and network of relationships, one may hope to be able to predict with what probability charismatic events will occur and charismatic leaders arise.

Self and Investment of Self

Let the self be defined, operationally, as that entity on behalf of which choices are made. The individual can identify with larger social entities wholly or in part. We shall refer to such identifications as "investments of self." An investment of self into a collectivity shall be considered an assignment to that collectivity (or some agent thereof) of some degree of power to shape the preferences of the given individual.

An individual invests some portion of his or her resources (time, land, knowledge, or money) into a collectivity in the hope that the collectivity will then be able and willing to take actions benefiting the individual more than the individual could have been benefited by using these resources in his or her own behalf. Similarly, an individual invests some portion of himself or herself into a collectivity in the hope that the collectivity will then be in a position to use these preference-shaping powers to achieve the consensus necessary for some collective action that will benefit the individual more than the individual could have been benefited by retaining preference autonomy and taking action on his or her own. Investment of resources invariably involves risk which thereby justifies the profits that then accrue. However, investment of self involves even greater risks, is therefore a less common and more poorly understood investment process, and quite often requires the "other worldly" or mystical justifications of a prophet or charismatic leader, or situations in which life and death are at stake.

Alienation, charisma, and investment of self are mutually related. Alienation consists of an inability to make collective decisions. Investment of self is an action that can be taken by an individual in the attempt to overcome this inability. Charismatic influence refers to the process whereby the collectivity makes use of, so to speak, the "self" that various of its members have invested in it to bring their preference sets into sufficient coherence for collective decision making to occur. There is nothing, of course, in this definition to preclude the possibility of a nonalienated individual investing of himself or herself in the collectivity and thus being subject to charismatic influence, but there is no reason why he or she should be motivated to do so. In general we should expect to find charismatic influence operating only in collectivities in which there is alienation, and we can state as a general proposition to be tested that the probability of charismatic influence occurring in a group is directly proportional to the degree of alienation that that group is experiencing.

The definitions of alienation and charisma used in this book require, of course, a relaxation of the economist's key assumption of preference invariability. From an econometric point of view, this opens up a can of worms. Kenneth Arrow (1972) rightly cautioned against the admissibility of what an economist would call "short-run" preference variability:

> . . . We will also assume in the present study that individual values are taken as data and are not capable of being altered by the nature of the decision process itself. This, of course, is the standard view in economic theory (though the unreality of this assumption has been asserted by such writers as Veblen, Professor J. M. Clark, and Knight) and also in the classical liberal creed. If individual values can themselves be affected by the method of social choice, it becomes much more difficult to learn what is meant by one method's being preferable to another.

But it may be the case that certain well-formulated propositions about collective choice in the absence of fixed individual preferences can be made and furthermore can be made without recourse to the need, as has been suggested by Gary Becker (1976), for a psychological theory of taste formation. We shall argue that, under certain not uncommon circumstances, individual preferences in a collective situation do change in a manner that is lawlike, empirically observable, and explainable in terms not of psychological process but of social interaction and structure.

Aims and Limitations

This is a study of contemporary American communes in their formative years. The point at which we begin to observe them is not at their very births (except occasionally and coincidentally), but it is, in all but a few cases, close enough to the beginning of each commune's history for us to be able to see the groups in their preinstitutional states. The overall aim of this research is to understand more clearly how consensus is gained and lost among groups of people striving for similar ideological goals.

A sample of 120 communes was studied during the period 1965–1978. The first phase of the research, carried out between 1965 and 1974, involved the study of clusters of rural communes. All communes included in this phase were followed over a long period of time. Almost all were visited at least twice, with a one-year interval separating the two visits, for periods varying from one week to four months. A limited amount of systematic, individual-level data was also collected during this period through interviews. The communes were followed at yearly intervals thereafter to determine which of them were still in existence, but no other systematic data were collected beyond the second visit.

The second phase of the study, conducted between 1974 and 1975, consisted of a panel study of sixty urban communes in six large American cities. A complete two-wave survey of the communes was conducted in 1974 and repeated in 1975. A limited amount of third-wave data on some of the communes was also then collected in 1976. As with the rural communes, the urban communes were then followed at one-year intervals through 1978 to determine, each year, which had survived.

The rural and urban phases of this research developed from designs that only partially overlap. The rural phase depended more upon participant observation techniques and selected in-depth interviews. The urban phase also made use of these techniques, but in a more cursory fashion. A major data collection instrument of the urban phase was the self-administered questionnaire. The rural data base is richer in the minutiae of communal life, but it lacks extensive systematic data on the individual commune members. The urban data base is poorer in depicting process, but richer in multilevel perspective. It allows us to look at the mutual interplay of individual, dyad, and group. This multimethod approach can be confusing at times. It certainly imposes a burden on the reader to keep track of whether we are discussing the urban, the rural, or the full sample. It is hoped, however, that the strengths of each of the research approaches used will also serve to compensate for the weaknesses of the other.

At certain points in the study, a choice had to be made between breadth and depth of approach. Where forced to choose, this study aims for breadth. Ethnographic descriptions have been used to establish settings and provide examples, not, in general, to advance an argument. For example, this book does not focus on the collective decision making process itself, as was done in *The Joyful Community*. Instead it focuses on the problem of abstracting the dimensions of consensual decision making that are relevant to communal survival and achievement. In line with this strategy, it was decided to treat the major variables in this book: stability, ideological intensity, alienation, and charisma as if they were continuous, rather than treating them as categories that can only either be present or absent.

Although the primary aim of this book is to study the phenomenon of collective decision making in communal settings, there are several subsidiary aims. Two of these aims, in particular, should be mentioned here because they help to account for the specific structure of presentation in the rest of the book.

First, and most obviously, this is a study of communes in general. Although major attention has been reserved for an analysis of choice and decision making functions, we have also sought to include in the book any information needed for a general understanding of the contemporary communitarian phenomenon. Although not all topics could receive the attention they deserve in a single book, an obligation was assumed, in what is probably the most wide ranging investigation of the subject to be undertaken, to touch as many bases as possible.

Second, this is a study of an entire social movement. We were fortunate in being able to span with this research the entire history of communitarianism as a social movement in America during the 1960s and 1970s. It is rare to have an opportunity to study a movement that is both over and done with so quickly and whose members, at the same time, hold still long enough to be studied repeatedly over time, as individuals. This book may be considered either a comparative study of many communes or a case study of a single social movement or both.

There is, however, an important historical limitation on the data used for this study that must be borne in mind. The data collection for the urban phase of the study was carried out in 1974 and 1975 and, to some extent, in 1976. These were declining years for the communitarian movement. Because all the systematic data on individual change came from the urban subsample, it is impossible to say which individual-level patterns that were observed are generalizable to communal living groups in all times and which are specifically associated with movement decline. But this is part of the price we must pay for attempting to move the laboratory out into the real world.

Another limitation has to do with the piecemeal way in which this research was carried out. This book brings together research done at various times over a ten-year interval (1965–1975), using a wide variety of data gathering techniques. It represents among other things an attempt to apply some of the methodology used in the comparative study of formal organizations to the traditionally softer field of social movements. The goal has been to blend statistical and sociometric inferences with findings drawn from ethnographic and interview data.

The book reflects both the strengths and the weaknesses of a multimethod approach. Frequently it is possible to improve validity by bringing several approaches to bear simultaneously on the same problem. But frequently also the basis of evidence will shift one or more times during an argument as we move, for example, from questions that have been addressed largely with qualitative data to questions that have been addressed largely with quantitative data. This imposes inevitable burdens on the reader. These would not be necessary if the method-trait matrix were complete, so to speak. But, especially when the argument shifts from commune to the individual as the unit of analysis, there is also a shift in data base brought about by the absence of systematic individual-level data from the rural communes.*

Natural social experiments have certain bothersome design properties as compared with laboratory experiments. A critical limitation, from the point of view of classical experimental design (Campbell and Stanley, 1963), is that members are assigned to groups by self-selection. Nonrandom selection complicates the task of making causal inferences, even from panel data. Another design limitation which may, however, as we shall see, be turned into an advantage is that communes generally have very high membership turnover. One may legitimately ask whether a commune revisited after a one-year interval, which has experienced a 70 percent membership turnover, should still be considered the same commune. But the study of social structure is the study of relational invariance in the face of component variation; of the degree to which, while content changes, form persists. To look at membership turnover as indicating social triviality, therefore, misses the point. If it were not for the ephemerality of communal persons, the endurance of communal statuses and roles would not be ascertainable.

Membership turnover in groups can be, and has been, systematically varied in the laboratory; but this again misses the point of the current investigation. It is difficult to simulate purposive action in the laboratory. But social structures —especially deviant social structures—must mobilize desire to survive in order to survive. Nor is there a simple, direct, linear relationship between survival and commitment to survival. The topic is complex, greatly in need of investigation, and most amenable to investigation in the context of natural social experiments.

The study of communes thus represents both an opportunity and a challenge. There is opportunity to study purposive group phenomena with an unusual degree of data completeness. The challenge is to devise methods of analysis that take advantage of the power of experimental design over survey design, while safeguarding against the inevitable effects of unmeasured influences outside the laboratory.

---

*It is not only the rural-urban distinction that creates these problems. Communes differed in the level of access that they allowed (some allowed group- and individual-level data but not sociometric data to be collected, for instance, and one urban commune allowed only taped interviews and not questionnaires). After the first wave, this problem is exacerbated by sample attrition and differential quality of later-wave data.

PART I

Incidence, Participation,
and Stability

This book is divided into two parts of four chapters each. In Part I, the emphasis is upon the objective analysis of observable events. We pay particular attention to status transition events: communes being founded, communes disintegrating, people joining, people leaving, marriages, divorces, changes in leadership, and so on. Discussion of the meanings of the events to the participants, especially the ideological meanings, is postponed, in so far as possible, until Part II.

This organizing principle works well in all respects except one. Because communes are so thoroughly ideological entities, we are forced to postpone detailed descriptions of the communes themselves until Chapter 5, the first chapter of Part II. This will not matter so much for readers who are primarily interested in following the logic of an unfolding set of arguments. However, some readers will wish to have concrete mental pictures of the entities being studied available to them as early as possible. For these readers, we advise that Chapter 5 be read out of sequence, between Chapter 2 and Chapter 3.

In the four chapters of Part I, we look at communitarianism as if through four different lenses. We start out, in Chapter 1, at a great distance and each successive lens allows us to zoom in on the phenomenon and see it at closer range. In the first chapter, we are too far away to see communes themselves, but can only see communitarian movements as they are unevenly distributed across the continents and across the centuries. In Chapter 2, we look at a single decade (1965 to 1975) and a single communitarian movement in greater detail, and are also introduced to the specific 120 communes that comprise our sample. In Chapter 3, we come close enough to the specific communes to see them not only as communes but also as aggregates of individual people. In Chapter 4, we come close enough to see not only the individual members of each commune but the form and content of the relational bonds that link the members of a commune together.

*However hazardous it may be to pursue the causation of
social phenomena in a society which cannot itself be directly observed, the incidence . . . is here far too clearly defined,
both in space and in time, to be without significance . . .
the social situations in which outbreaks of revolutionary
millenarianism occurred were in fact remarkably uniform;
and this impression is confirmed when one comes to examine particular outbreaks in detail.*

Norman Cohn

CHAPTER 1

The Distribution of
Communitarian Movements

Communes are treated in this book primarily as research sites. It would be an error, however, to investigate them in isolation from their specific geographical and
historical contexts. The natural experiment, as opposed to the laboratory experiment, is always part of a larger social fabric. Because communes are unevenly
distributed across continents and centuries, it is reasonable to begin this investigation with an attempt to answer the question: Why do communes appear in
some places and times and not others?

There are two reasons for beginning with a discussion of the ecological and
historical forces that have engendered communitarianism. First, this will provide
a frame for some of our later analyses. Second, precisely because the argument
of the book comes to rest heavily upon field observation and quantitative analysis of survey data, the very different kind of evidence presented in this chapter
can serve as a cross-validating check. Although the criteria of evidence must be

19

considerably less rigorous and the dependence on secondary sources greater in such an approach, the problem of interpreting respondents' meanings is not faced because the analysis is based upon the relative frequency of events. The strengths of these approaches serve to compensate for each other's weaknesses.

A Worldwide Contemporary Phenomenon

All industrialized nations in the world today have engendered communes. Although widespread research on communes outside the United States is available only for Israel (Talmon, 1972; Spiro, 1956; Rabin, 1965; Blasi, 1978), scattered studies of considerable value have been made of Canadian, English, Indian, Japanese, Scandinavian, and German communes, both urban and rural (Bennett, 1967; Rigby, 1974; Plath, 1971; Dorner, 1977; French and French, 1975; Delespesse and Tange, 1967, 1971). Urban communes have been reported in Budapest, Copenhagen, Geneva, Hiroshima, Mexico City, Montreal, Paris, Prague, Rome, Stockholm, Tokyo, Vienna, Wellington, and many other cities. Rural farming communes are to be found on every continent: Auroville in India, Aiyetoro in Nigeria, the Quaker Monteverde in Costa Rica, L'Arche in France, Riverside in Australia, and Beeville in New Zealand are only a few scattered examples.

In keeping with the self-imposed definitional limitations outlined in the introduction, there will be no discussion of the government-initiated and -sponsored collective farms in the Soviet Union or the "communes" in China. These are, of course, important phenomena, but they lie outside the scope of this study. But the existence of communes not under government sponsorship has been documented in Iron Curtain countries, such as Hungary, Czechoslovakia, and Poland.* This suggests that communitarianism can occur even without the widespread opportunities for youth rebellion that have been associated with the United States, Japan, and Western Europe.

The withdrawal of youth from conventional forms of social participation can best be described as a worldwide social movement. Communitarianism, of course, is only one of the many forms this has taken. But it is a form that very well reflects the movement's spirit: the quest for authenticity through reduction of scale.† As with any social movement, it has attracted members not only from its youthful base but from among utopian dreamers and discontented drifters of all ages. Although this worldwide movement has taken on various

---

*The Polish weekly newspaper *Kultura* reports on what is said to be the first "hippie commune" in Poland. The newspaper says that it consists of five men, three women, a donkey and a dog. *Kultura's* report is believed to be the first public acknowledgment of hippies in communist countries.

The leader of the commune, a 30-year-old former television mechanic identified only as "Witek," explains that members abandoned city life because they couldn't take the pressure or the drinking. Witek adds that the commune allows its members to "do their own thing." The newspaper says the police have the community under observation. *Communities* 17 (November 1975): 56.

†For examples of other types of responses in the same vein see, e.g., P. Berger et al. (1973); Lipset (1975).

distinctive nationalist characteristics (e.g., among the kibbutzim in Israel, the Yamagists in Japan), its international cultural similarities outweigh these differences.

It is difficult to say just when in recent times this movement from large scale to small scale commitments began. Nietzsche commented upon it very early. Max Weber foresaw its coming as long ago as 1918 (1946a, p. 155):

> The fate of our times is characterized by rationalization and intellectualization and, above all, by the "disenchantment of the world." Precisely *the ultimate and most sublime values have retreated from public life either into the transcendental realm of mystic life or into the brotherliness of direct and personal human relations.* It is not accidental that our greatest art is intimate and not monumental, nor is it accidental that today only within the smallest and intimate circles, in personal human situations, in *pianissimo,* that something is pulsating that corresponds to the prophetic *pneuma,* which in former times swept through the great communities like a firebrand, welding them together. [emphasis added]

The movement surfaced in Central Europe after World War I and again in North America, Europe, and Japan in the mid-1960s. Elements of the earlier manifestation later contributed to the rise of fascism in Europe. Not surprisingly, the fascist period was followed by a period of disillusionment with all social movements (Lipset 1975, p. 193):

> . . . [This occurred] in the two decades following World War II when the belief in diverse forms of charismatic *Wertrationalität* in the religious, economic, and political orders broke down in part because the various ideologies and utopias became routinized operational realities. Protestantism and Catholicism, fascism, capitalism, communism, and social democracy all lost their power to inspire men to work hard, to live morally, or to change the world.

But by 1965 in the West, slightly earlier in Japan, the enthusiasm of youth for utopian dreams and communal relationships had once again revived to the level at which a small but vigorous communitarian movement could be sustained.

Most communes are to be found in those nations that industrialized early (England, Germany, France, the United States) and in those later-developing nations (Israel, Japan) that most fully and enthusiastically modeled themselves upon the Western European prototype. Lipset (1975, p. 195) traces the spread of the "youth movement" to fundamental cultural contradictions between postindustrial values and postindustrial means of achieving goals.

> The spread of contemporary youth rebellion is in part a consequence of the contradiction between the widespread diffusion of the goal of freedom as an absolute value and the emergence of *"a new type of social alienation* focused not only around the feeling of being lost in a maze of large-scale, anonymous organizations and frameworks, but also around the possibility of the loss of the meaning of participation in these political and national centers." This tension makes for intense frustration, *particularly among the*

educated young, who most accept the charismatic Wertrationalität of the social order. [emphasis added]

This new type of alienation of which Lipset speaks is really only a neglected type of alienation. Most studies of alienation (Seeman, 1975) have focused on the dimensions of powerlessness and normlessness. But, during communitarian periods, meaninglessness and estrangement from cultural values are the more salient dimensions. This can happen only in societies in which the problem of *getting what one needs* is overshadowed by the problem of *knowing what one wants* which typically happens whenever the future seems to open into a multiplicity of possible futures. Under such circumstances, a utopian vision, realized in the modest form of a small communal homestead, can easily seem a better bargain than a bloc of votes in the legislature or tactical control of the city streets.

Communes are not evenly distributed among the nations of the world. Whereas high concentrations of communes can be found in Israel, the United States, Japan, Canada, Denmark, Holland, England, and Germany, communes are relatively scarce in Latin America, Southern Europe, and the Arab world.* Moreover, although communitarianism is more likely to be found in affluent, industrialized, and urbanized nations than in less developed areas, modernization alone does not account for all this variation. The situation is complicated by the tendency of communitarians to emigrate. The large numbers of communes to be found in Canada, for example, have less to do with major contradictions in Canadian social structure than with the hospitality of Canada to dissident immigrant groups and the availability of cheap land.

Israel is another example of a nation whose communes were largely built by immigrants. However, although the original kibbutz ideologies were shaped in Central and Eastern Europe, Israel has thoroughly made them its own. Today, Israel is the nation with the greatest proportion of its population living in communes and the only nation in which these communes are central rather than marginal to the economic and political organization of the state.† The unique combination of military, agricultural, and cultural problems faced by European Jews in the settlement of Israel are, of course, well known. The kibbutzim are best seen as a uniquely creative response to these problems rather than as a manifestation of postindustrial alienation. The kibbutzim, therefore, stand some-

---

*According to Norman Cohn (1957), Arab Sufis lived in communitarian settlements in Spain in the twelfth century, and these exerted a significant influence on the later Brotherhood of the Free Spirit in Europe. But contemporary communitarianism has not manifested itself in the Arab world of the twentieth century. However, this may now be changing. A number of middle class members of the demodernizing movement known as the Muslem Brotherhood have recently turned to isolated communal living as a way of maintaining purity within the interstices of a rapidly secularizing Egyptian society (see Altman, 1979, p. 101).

†But the 2.7 percent of Israelis living in kibbutzim (*Statistical Abstract of Israel*, 1974, p. 35), although still a larger proportion than that of any other nation, has been steadily declining from its peak of 7.3 percent in 1947.

what apart from the rest of the world's communitarianism. Although they are in part a product of the "youth movement," it was the first (1920s) rather than the second (1960s) wave of this movement that gave them birth. The kibbutzim have remained relatively unaffected by the more recent communitarian enthusiasms of the 1960s and 1970s.

Even Japanese communitarianism, at first sight a clear example of a response to the bewildering rapidity of modernization, is said to have its own unique cultural roots that go back to the beginning of the Tokugawa era (Bikle, 1971). However, like its counterparts in America and Europe, communitarianism in Japan began to flourish only in the 1960s. The influential and proliferant Japanese Kibbutz Association was founded in 1962 and formally incorporated in 1967 (Fairfield, 1972b). The Japanese hippie communes, mostly short-lived, began to appear in the late 1960s. The religious Yamagists established themselves somewhat earlier, in 1953, but enjoyed a major growth spurt in the 1960s. The Kibbutz Association is particularly interesting in that it reflects an attitude toward commune building that is uniquely Japanese and that is remarkably similar to Japan's earlier attitude toward industrialization and Western technology. The Kibbutz Association has sent young volunteers to Israel to live on kibbutzim, find out how they work, and return to adapt these obviously successful forms to the needs of Japanese culture.

Most recent communitarian movements in continental Europe have been geographically concentrated in a narrow central corridor. This concentration—in Germany, Denmark, the Netherlands, northern Italy, Austria, and southern Sweden—runs along a north-south axis between the Western and the Soviet worlds. We may speculate that the people of Central Europe, living between two political cultures, are more likely to experience ambiguity of value and doubt concerning ultimate meanings than are other European populations.

Portuguese- and Spanish-speaking peoples are singularly noncommunitarian. Although American Catholics are drawn to communal living quite as often as would be expected by their relative representation in the national population, traditionally Catholic nations have always been characterized by comparatively little of the ideological proliferation that leads to communitarian withdrawal. Yet there are scatterings of communal groups in Ireland and Italy and a fair number in France. Very few are to be found in Spain, Portugal, or Latin America, the exceptions usually deriving from recent immigrant stock. The Bruderhof, during its long tricontinental hegira, picked up many recruits in the lands through which it passed. But no permanent Paraguayan families became part of its brotherhood (and not through lack of proselytizing) during its twenty-year stay in that country.

Joseph Love (1971, pp. 117ff.) has attempted to account for this phenomenon in terms of what he calls the "Luso-Hispanic frame of mind":

> Why have utopian thought and action been so negligible in Latin America?
> . . . the existence of latifundium-based societies with many of the members

of lower strata outside Western culture; ... the course of Latin American political history in which the problems of anarchy and tyranny absorbed the energies of the region's intellectuals; and perhaps a Luso-Hispanic "frame of mind," favoring doctrines in which social problems are placed in a cosmic frame of reference and for which utopian communities seem irrelevant—e.g., Thomism, Comptian positivism, and Marxism.

Love's argument is compelling, especially in that what we have earlier distinguished as imposed utopias (e.g., the Jesuit "Reductions" in seventeenth-century Paraguay) have been far from uncommon in Latin America*; and secret sectarian movements, from the Penitentes of Old and New Mexico to the Sabastianists of Brazil, have flourished from time to time, as have anarchist political followers of Bakunin and Malatesta. In most parts of the world, all these types of movements have furnished the stuff of communitarianism, but rarely so where Spanish or Portuguese is spoken.

If it were possible to plot the density of communitarian experiments on a map of the world, considerable variation would be observed. We have seen that this variation can be partly explained in terms of both the extent and the rapidity of modernization, although numerous historical, cultural, and ecological factors greatly complicate the picture. We have suggested that the operative causal element in modernization leading to communitarianism is the proliferation of choices and the concomitant loss of unambiguous sources of meaning. However, our confidence in this assertion must be limited because, in historical terms, we have examined only a single case. Let us therefore shift our attention from space to historical time in an effort to see more clearly the relation between choice proliferation and the communitarian impulse.

A Recurrent Social Phenomenon

Communes have been around for a long time. However, they have always been peripheral rather than central to any known civilization. For thousands of years, in both Asia and the West, the communitarian impetus has never succeeded in catching on or in dying out. John Bennett (1975, p. 63) calls it "the oldest 'new' and the most traditional 'experimental' social movement in the West."

Communitarianism as a strategy for social change differs fundamentally from revolution as a strategy for social change. Communitarianism is concerned with the *discovery or creation* of shared values. Revolution is concerned with the *achievement* of shared values. If this is true, we ought to find that the historical prerequisite for communitarianism is the rapid and discontinuous expansion of cultural alternatives and opportunities and that the historical prerequisite for revolution is the visible and acknowledged existence of a common enemy or obstacle.

*Note also the Saint Simonian influence on Argentine government in the early nineteenth century (Love, 1971, p. 118).

In Parsonian imagery, communitarianism may be thought of as revolution's latency phase. This is not to say that the two impulses never coexist in time or that they follow each other according to some patterned sequence. But, even when communitarian and revolutionary social movements occur together in time, as in the 1960s, they tend to go their own separate ways. Communitarian social movements share with revolutionary social movements the psychological symptoms of alienation. But the alienation of communitarian movements does not lead to class consciousness and class struggle. On the contrary, it is expressed as ideological confusion and is manifested at the individual level as the inability to make choices among a plethora of attractive action alternatives.

The communtarian strategy is to escape from alienation by achieving consensus within a circumscribed social microcosm. This strategy has continued to win adherents for over two thousand years. It is what Bennett (1975, pp. 63ff.) refers to when he speaks of "a persisting template of sharing and interacting that undergoes repeated revival as an alternative to the majority institutions."

This is correct, but more can be said. Communitarian history is continual, not continuous. The movement ebbs and then flows again. Communitarian revivals occur, not randomly, but in specific eras. If it were possible to graph the incidence of communitarianism as a function of time down through the centuries, and if it were also possible to graph, in a similar manner, the divergence of beliefs and standards of moral evaluation from a common source, a strong positive association would likely be found between these two variables. In the absence of the data for such a graph, the following descriptions will have to suffice.

The trajectory of Western history describes a monotonic progression in the complexity of cultural and social differentiation. This progression has not been smooth but discontinuous. It is at points of discontinuity, with the Roman unification of the Mediterranean world in the first century B.C. and the first century A.D., with the reestablishment of wide-ranging commerce in the twelfth and thirteenth centuries, with the discovery of new continents and the collapse of theological homogeneity in the sixteenth and seventeenth centuries, with the Industrial Revolution in the late eighteenth and early nineteenth centuries, and with the crises of internationalism and secularism in the latter part of the twentieth that we find an upsurge in both the longing for consensual community and the opportunity for communitarian experimentation. Each forced leap to greater plurality of values and fragmentation of roles brings with it a renewed longing for *Gemeinschaft* as well as the appearance of temporary cultural interstices in which significant numbers of people find themselves with the resources and the freedom to pursue this longing.

Historians have not been able to date, with any certainty, the earliest examples of communitarian experiments. Oriental communitarian history is based upon evidence clouded in myth. Some scholars believe that self-sufficient Taoist communes existed in China in the fifth century B.C. (Fogarty, 1972). If so, their appearance coincides with the breakdown of Chou feudalism and the beginning of the so-called "period of contending states." It is possible that communitarian ashram villages existed in India at an even earlier time. However, a well-substantiated Western tradition of communitarianism begins in the first century B.C. according to Bennett (1975), "with the Galilean withdrawal sectarians—the Essenes and others, who . . . sought to escape the alienation and corruption of Roman Palestine."

The Early Roman Empire

Communes, almost by definition, do not make history, and their traces disappear much more rapidly than the traces of dynasties and wars. We begin to hear about them, ordinarily, only when they abandon the purely communitarian impulse to take on revolutionary or institution-building roles. Therefore we know little about communes of the ancient world. But the sketchy evidence that has survived allows us tentatively to locate the earliest period of communitarianism in the Western World in the period roughly between 100 B.C. and A.D. 100.

The first communitarians of whom we have record are the withdrawal sectarians of Roman Palestine. Their appearance can be traced to the impingement of cosmopolitan Hellenistic values upon a local Judaic culture. Although the forced Hellenization of the Jews had been going on for two centuries by the time that Pompey brought Palestine into the Roman orbit, it was only at this time that the cultural threat became widely perceived as serious. As the sporadic and inefficient Seleucid Hellenization gave way to the seemingly invincible tide of Roman Hellenization, sectarian activity became more frantic and more desperate.

As in all other "communitarian epochs," only a small fraction of the population was motivated to communitarian withdrawal. But this fraction was influential. We see in this period a variety of sectarian responses to the threat of Roman culture. But, as compared with the rebellion of the Zealots, the ritualism of the Pharisees, or the theological innovation of the Sadducees, it is the withdrawal of the Essenes that shows the greatest fascination with and implicit respect for Hellenistic civilization. These sectarians had absolutely no confidence that their own pure and fragile world view could survive cultural interplay with Hellenism.

A communitarian impulse could also be found among the small, isolated Christian communities throughout the first century (A.D.). In Paul's letters and in *Acts*, we see emphasis on the collective possession of charismatic powers by small groups with well-defined boundaries. Often these were joint households having both a common purse and an ideological emphasis on the purity of internal unity (i.e., consensus). As both Empire and Church became more established, this communitarian impulse faded. After the fall of the Empire, what communitarian spirit there might have been was swept into monasticism.

The Twelfth and Thirteenth Centuries

Prior to the twelfth-century renaissance, we have over a thousand years with no nonmonastic documentation of communitarian experiments. The first well-substantiated evidence of widespread medieval communitarianism is of the heretical sect, the Brotherhood of the Free Spirit. Membership in Free Spirit communities was highly transitory (Cohn, 1957) but no more so than that of many modern communal federations. Along with the Cathari, Waldenses Albigenses, and numerous others,* these came to flower in Western Europe in the late twelfth and early thirteenth centuries.

In the millennium between the communal martyrs of the first century and the communal heretics of the twelfth and thirteenth, the Catholic church played a peculiar role in keeping the dormant communitarian tradition alive. According to Norman Cohn (1957, pp. 191ff.):

> At least by the Third Century A.D., Christian doctrine had assimilated from the extraordinarily influential philosophy of Stoicism the notion of an egalitarian State of Nature, which was irrecoverably lost . . . . It was agreed by most of the later Fathers that inequality, slavery, coercive government and even private property had no part in the original intention of God, and had come into being only as a result of the Fall. . . . Corrupted by Original Sin, human nature demanded restraints which would not be found in an egalitarian order; inequalities of wealth, status, and power were thus not only consequences of, but also remedies for sin.

Because the doctrine of the Fall can be made vivid only by way of contrast, Catholic theologians from St. Augustine and St. Ambrose on down, perhaps inadvertently, maintained and embellished soul-stirring legends of an earthly egalitarian utopia prior to the Original Sin. In every generation there must have been some who misconstrued this Eden lost as an Eden yet to be found and thus kept a coherent vision of a communitarian dream active in the culture even while dormant in society.

By the twelfth and thirteenth centuries, communitarianism could again be spoken of as an active social movement. These were the times when, according to Bennett, "the mountain paths and town ghettoes all over Europe were overrun from time to time by wandering fanatics, militants, flower people, most of whom preached brotherhood and poverty and were a thorn in the side of the Church." There is evidence (Cohn, 1957) that this communitarian movement was a response to a sudden influx of new wealth to Western Europe, bringing with it the alienation born of the rapid multiplication of choice alternatives, just like the most recent communitarian movement of the present day. Cohn (1957, p. 53) says:

*It is not known what proportion of the adherents of these sects actually lived together in communal households, but it is certain that some of them did.

The areas in which the age-old prophecies about the Last Days took on a new, revolutionary meaning and a new, explosive force were the areas which were becoming seriously over-populated and were involved in a process of rapid economic and social change.

We are not merely talking about a rise in some medieval analogue to the gross national product when we speak of the rapid multiplication of choice alternatives in Europe beginning in the twelfth century. What is striking is the sheer range of new goods and cultural symbols that became available to Western Europe at this time. The revival of trade between Italy and the Near East; the opening of the Rhone as a reliable route for goods from the Orient to flow into France and Germany; the appearance of fairs at which Italians and Northern merchants could foster regular business contacts for the first time—all contributed to a sense, reflected in the literature of the time, of the kaleidoscopic reordering of possibilities and prospects.*

The thirteenth century was the century of monasticism in Europe. The heretical sects continued to flourish, but the spirit that impelled them was now matched by a counterpart within the Church, leading to the establishment at this time of the great mendicant orders: Franciscan (1210), Dominican (1215), Carmelite (1245), and Augustinian hermits (1256); as well as by a growth in numbers and an increase in vigor and confidence within the older Benedictine order. By the end of the thirteenth cenutry, however, this spirit had largely dissipated. A growing secularism within the Church and the corruption inherent in the system of commendation of monastic revenues did much to destroy the idealism of this communitarian movement. Outside the Church, meanwhile, the mood of those heretical sects that survived became less communitarian, more class-conscious, and more revolutionary, as "consider the lilies" gave way to "drive out the money changers."

In the fourteenth and fifteenth centuries there was a relative decline of communitarian experiment in most parts of Europe. Although the communal Brethren of the Free Spirit were active well into the fourteenth century, and the year 1420 was the peak of the mass Taborite offshoot of the Hussite movement in Bohemia, these were exceptions to the general rule.

These exceptions point to an instructive paradox. History records more about the Brotherhood of the Free Spirit in the fourteenth than in the preceding two centuries. And no more dramatic and well-documented episode of voluntary communitarianism may be found in medieval history than in the Taborite movement. How can these phenomena be dismissed as exceptions?

The answer is to be found in the ideologies of the movements themselves. The well-publicized fourteenth century assault of the Brotherhood of the Free Spirit

*It is interesting to note that, in a more primitive context, the cargo cults (Worsley, 1968; Thrupp, 1962) arise in response to similar discontinuities in the expansion of choice. These intensely charismatic religious movements provide nothing more valuable to their members than value consensus in the face of powerful outside pressures toward dissensus.

on the institution of private property reflects a growing politicization and the growth of a rudimentary class consciousness (Mannheim, 1936). Similarly, the Taborite common purse was the instrument of a mass political movement drawing upon the symbolism of an older and underlying communitarian ideology. Like the Paris Commune of 1871, it shared with communitarianism only a name. Its ideology was one of revolution.

The twelfth and thirteenth centuries stimulated communitarianism with the beginning of trade with Asia. The sixteenth century stimulated communitarianism with the beginning of the age of exploration and discovery. But the intervening two centuries are marked by a dip, at least according to the records now available to us, in the incidence both of communitarianism and cultural discontinuity.

The Sixteenth and Seventeenth Centuries

With the coming of the Protestant Reformation we again find proper conditions for the nurturance of a communal movement. The sixteenth century saw the beginnings of the radical reformation that was to be the seedbed not only of most of the subsequent communitarianism in both Europe and America, but also of many of the significant noncommunitarian social movements of modern times. As can be seen from Figure 1-1, communitarianism in this epoch did not blossom randomly throughout Europe but came from what Bestor (1950, p. 20) has called "a restricted zone of religious radicalism that stretched from central Europe to the British Isles."*

The communitarian movements of the sixteenth and seventeenth centuries were densely clustered in space. This becomes interesting theoretically when we reflect that the area north of this "commune belt" was uncontested Protestant territory and the area south of the region was largely uncontested Catholic territory. Once again we see communitarianism arising in just those areas where consensus had been lost and opposing ideological perspectives contended. The absence of a single dominant ideology created both an opportunity and a need. The opportunity was the freedom to choose; the need was to find a collectivity within which consensus among free choices was attainable. The absence of consensus on meanings and values brought about by ideological fragmentation created pockets of longing for communities of belief, while, at the same time, making grander, society-wide factions, denominations or parties appear unachievable.

We are speaking here in broad generalities. Regional differences throughout

*Note the similarity with the contemporary European zone of communitarianism discussed earlier. Although one runs east-west and the other north-south, both buffer the major ideological empires of their time: Catholicism versus Protestantism and communism versus capitalism.

FIGURE 1-1.   Marchlands of European Religious Wars (Sixteenth to Early
               Eighteenth Centuries) from Which the Western Tradition of Sectarian
               Communitarianism Derived

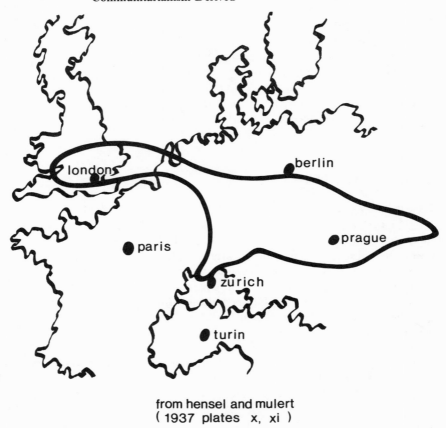

from hensel and mulert
(1937 plates x, xi)

Europe in the incidence of communitarianism were far more pronounced than
we can do justice to in this brief exposition. The time spans in question would be
quite different, for example, if we were focusing solely on Southern Germany,
where communitarianism developed relatively early, then if we were focusing
solely on Holland, where it developed somewhat later. The precision in our
counting, however, does not really justify greater detail in these matters than we
have been giving them.

The seventeenth century was a period of geographical transition for communitarianism. While retaining strong roots in the Old World, it took new roots in
the Americas. By the beginning of the eighteenth century, North America had
become the center stage for communitarian experiments. This transition to America coincides with an improvement in the quality of the historical data available to

us. Therefore, as we move on now to examine America's contribution to the communitarian history, we will also be able to zoom in a bit closer to look at the actual rise and decline of specific communitarian movements.

A Venerable American Tradition

For three centuries there has not been a single year without at least one historically documented communitarian organization in the United States. However, that portion of the national population involved has never much exceeded one per one thousand (10^{-3}), and communitarianism has never succeeded in becoming more than a minor part of American life and culture. It has always functioned as a deviant, radical, or otherworldly fringe, drawing off idealists, social malcontents, and dreamers rather than finding, as for instance in Israel, a place for itself within the structure of societal institutions.

As in Europe, American communes have appeared not at a constant rate but, rather, in waves (very much like epidemics), occurring once every forty or fifty years or so for the past two hundred years.

Communes in America flourished neither on the frontier itself, where the intensity of the struggle for survival was its own talisman against alienation, nor along the settled coast, where the expanding institutions of a new society still seemed capable of providing a portion and place for most everyone. Instead they clustered in that zone that had been the frontier a generation earlier and that now offered too many choices and less-than-encompassing social controls. The so-called burned-over district of western New York State in the first half of the nineteenth century (Cross, 1965) is an example of such a region.*

Communal incidence rates fluctuate rapidly. Figure 1-2 shows that there have been five sharp peaks of commune building in American history, the current one being the greatest in magnitude. We have been locating communitarian movements in time in terms of their rates of incidence (new starts) rather than their prevalence (the number existing at any given time). This has not made much difference as long as we have been talking in terms of centuries. But now that we are moving to a historical period for which we have data at five-year intervals, our choice of definition becomes significant.

As Okugawa (1974) has pointed out, any attempt to describe a communitarian movement in terms of its incidence alone is bound to be misleading because it ignores the fact that a constant level of interest in communal living should be expected to coincide with a decreasing level of incidence to the extent that stable groups come into existence and satisfy their members' needs for communal living over a long period of time. Or, to put it another way, to the extent that communal groups have been formed in the past and continue to exist, there is a decrease in need for new ones to be created unless the number of people

---

*See Okugawa (1974) for a complete state-by-state breakdown of the prevalence of communitarianism behind the moving American frontier in the period 1787–1919.

FIGURE 1-2. Incidence: Logarithm of the Number of Communitarian Experiments Founded per Five-Year Period (1787 to 1975)[1]

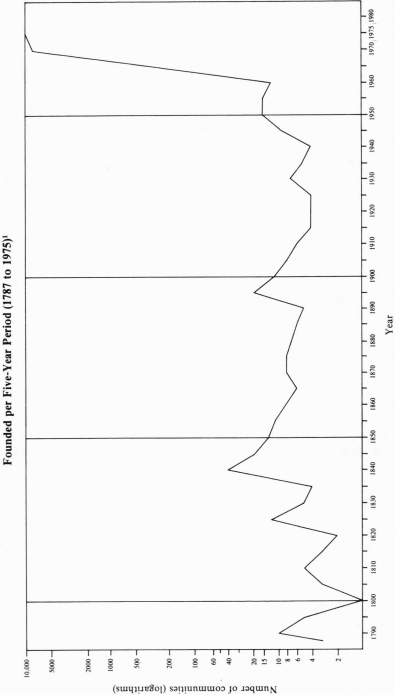

Year

Number of communities (logarithms)

[1]Compiled from the following sources: Albertson, 1936; Bestor, 1950; Bushee, 1905; Deets, 1942; Hayden, 1976; Hostetler, 1974a; Kanter, 1972; Kephart, 1976; Kramer, 1955; Okugawa, 1974, 1980; Williams, 1939; Wooster, 1924; Zablocki, 1972a.

desiring to live communally is also constantly increasing. As Figure 1-3 illustrates, prevalence rates tend to be similar to rates of incidence but with smoother gradations of change and fewer sharp fluctuations.

We shall, nevertheless, continue to describe the duration of communitarian movements in terms of their rates of incidence. It is only by doing so that we can convey an accurate picture of the ebb and flow of communitarian enthusiasm as a response to social opportunities and cultural contradictions. But it should be borne in mind that, when dates are given for the birth and death of a communitarian movement, the first date corresponds to the observable appearance of a new phenomenon, whereas the second corresponds to a much less clear perception of the movement's loss of vitality, not of membership. Indeed, it sometimes happens that the actual number of participants in a social movement (be it civil rights, antiwar, feminist, or communitarian) peaks after the movement itself has ceased to be a dynamic force in the society.

The Colonial Period (1620–1776)

The very earliest communes in America were tentative religious experiments, undertaken by Protestant dissenters seeking freedom in the New World from the religious turmoil and persecution of seventeenth-century Western Europe.

It is not often remembered that Massachusetts itself experimented briefly (and disastrously) with communitarianism. In 1623 William Bradford, governor of the Plymouth Colony, wrote (in disgust) that the colony's abortive attempt at community of property should serve to illustrate (Diamond, 1963, p. 46):

> the vanitie of that conceite of Platos & other ancients, applauded by some of later times;—that the taking away of propertie, and bringing in communitie into a comone wealth, would make them happy and flourishing; as if they were wiser than God.

In 1663, Plockhoy's Commonwealth, which lasted only one year, was founded in Delaware—then part of New Netherlands. Plockhoy's Commonwealth was plundered by the English conquerors, in the words of a historian of the time, "to a very naile" (Bestor, 1950, p. 27).

The Labadie Community, founded in 1683, was somewhat more successful, lasting for forty two years until it disbanded. The members of the community met and decided that the spirit that had led them to live communally had somehow departed. Rather than perpetuate an institution that had lost its meaning, they preferred, with regret, to disband.

By the eighteenth century, the communitarian tradition in America had taken root if not fire. The arrival of the Amish in 1727, the establishment of an important Moravian colony at Bethlehem, Pennsylvania, in 1741 (with a communal economy instituted in 1744), and the arrival of Ann Lee and the first of the Shakers in America in 1774 were events that permanently influenced the religious and social character of the nation.

FIGURE 1-3. Prevalence: Logarithm of the Number of Communitarian Experiments Existing from 1787 to 1975 Grouped by Five-Year Averages[1]

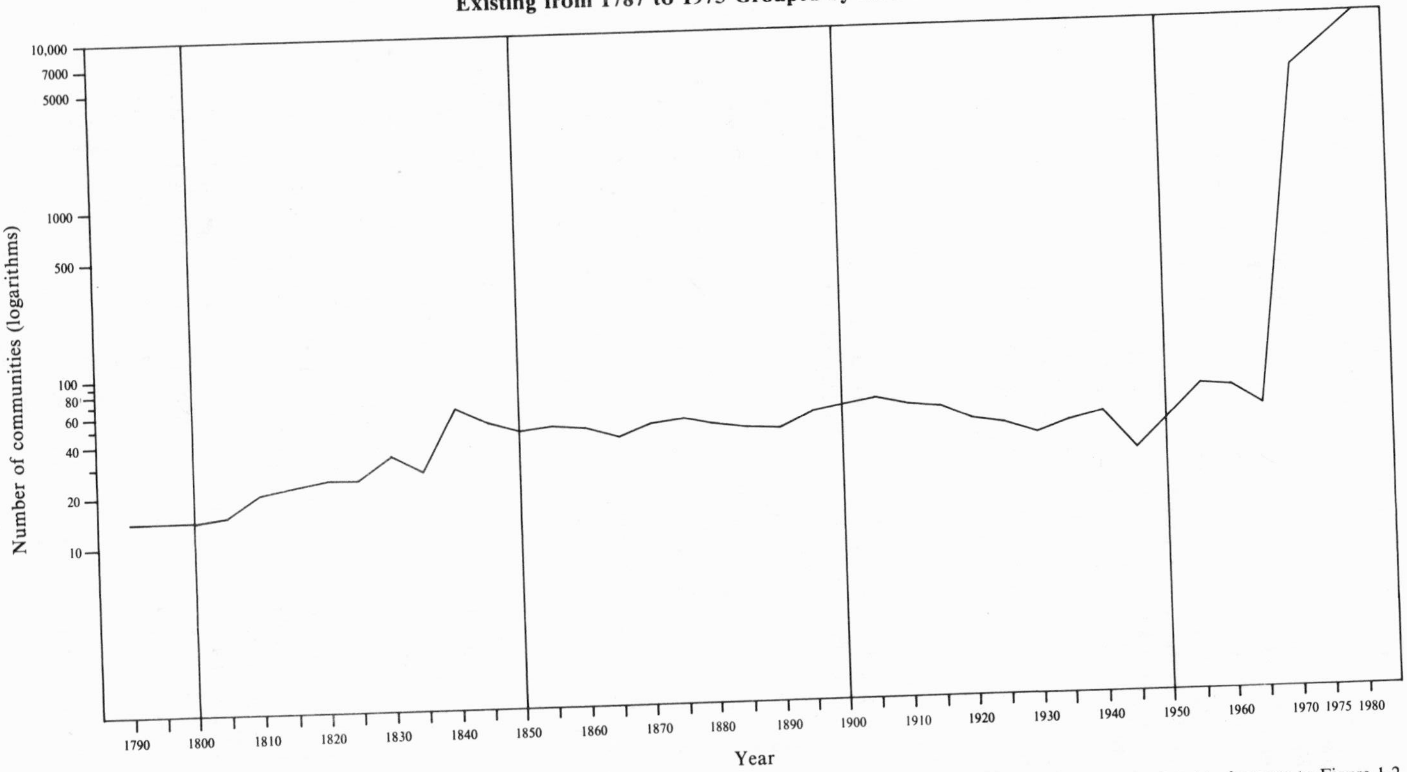

[1]Compiled from same sources listed in footnote to Figure 1-2.

Number of communities (logarithms)

Year

One might ask, nevertheless, why the Great Awakening in midcentury did not engender more communitarian spirit. No indigenous communitarian movement occurred in America in the eighteenth century, despite the successful transplantation of those communitarian colonies from Europe already mentioned. It might be argued that the American colonists of the eighteenth century lacked the resources for commune building. But we would argue that they also lacked the consciousness of meaning and value heterogeneity that would motivate them to seek to congregate with selected others on the basis of shared ideology. Certainly awareness of ideological differences (especially those based on class and regional lines) was present in the eighteenth century. But it was paradoxically that great unifying achievement, the constitutional convention and ratification, at the end of the century that made citizens of the new nation aware of the limitations of their actual consensus on fundamental values.

The Shaker Influx (1790–1805)

Even the Shakers, although they arrived in numbers toward the end of the eighteenth century, did not capture the imaginations of significant numbers of American recruits until the first decade of the nineteenth century. Nordhoff (1875, pp. 131ff.) describes how this transformation from colony to movement took place:

> Meantime, in the first year of this century [nineteenth] there broke out in Kentucky a remarkable religious excitement . . . . *Camp-meetings were held in different counties, to which people flocked by the thousands; and here men and women and even small children, fell down in convulsions, foamed at the mouth, and uttered loud cries.* . . . To these encampments the people flocked by thousands. . . .
>
> Hearing of these extraordinary events, the Shakers at New Lebanon sent out three of their number . . . to "open the testimony of salvation to the people." . . . They set out on New Year's Day, 1805, and traveled on foot about a thousand miles. . . . They made some converts in Ohio and Kentucky and *were, fortunately for themselves, violently opposed and in some cases attacked by bigoted or knavish persons; and with this impetus they were able to found at first five societies, two in Ohio, two in Kentucky, and one in Indiana.* [emphasis added]

For about twenty years (1805-1824) the communitarian impetus slowed down as the nation turned its attention to national matters. The Shakers, however, continued to thrive for the rest of the century, only diminishing the rate at which they formed entirely new colonies in favor of the expansion of existing ones.

The historical perspective increases the stature of these early Shakers to the point where they hardly seem cast from the same mold as our present-day scruffy communitarians. But it would be incorrect to ascribe to the individual biographies of the rank-and-file Shakers a uniform measure of the prestige that rightly accrues to the Shakers as a whole. As close historical scholarship has revealed, there were many paupers, losers, and drifters among the stock of early Americans conscripted for Shakerdom (Andrews, 1953). The genius of the movement consisted not in its gathering together the cream of American social and technical inventive talent, but in its creation of an environment that fostered such invention in the few that were capable of it.

But it was not only the Shakers who were actively building communes during this period. Among others, all of which were religious and sectarian, Jemima Wilkinson's Jerusalem (Hinds, 1908) and George Rapp's Harmony (Noyes, 1870; Young, 1945) are two prominent examples. The wilderness-seeking communitarian sects of this period are in some ways reminiscent of the withdrawal sects of Roman Palestine. As offshoots of the vaguely bounded religious movement known as Pietism, they feared confrontation with the rational spirit of the enlightenment in much the same way that the ancient pious Jews had been afraid to encounter the rationalism of Hellenic civilization. In the semisettled places just east of the moving American frontier, groups of Christians felt that it was still possible to await the end of the world in some semblance of piety and wholeheartedness.

There were no secular communitarian ideologies at this time, and it was only through the vector of religious revivals that communal groups could congeal. Yet it is important to note that the periods of commune building did not usually coincide with the peaks of revivalist fervor but, instead, seemed to alternate with them (Noyes 1870, p. 25). Once again we see evidence of the latency function played by communitarianism. The times when Christian millenarianism gripped masses of people were not the same times that people chose to band together communally on the basis of their shared millenarian faith.* Where a system of belief, however ephemeral, is experienced in the society, it will not be sought with such fervor in the community.

With the coming of the administrations of James Madison and James Monroe, communitarianism went into a temporary eclipse. The Shakers continued growing and Joseph Bimeler founded his Separatist Society of Zoar in Ohio during this period, but there was not the same general fascination with the idea of retreat into the wilderness to await the Second Coming. Perhaps the mood of the nation had turned more secular. Certainly it had turned more nationalistic. In the light of our theory of communes and value consensus, it should be noted that the one brief disappearance of party politics from American life—the "era of good feeling"—occurred during this period.

The Utopian Socialist Period (1824—1848)

The farcical presidential election of 1824 reflected the fact that the era of good feeling was over in America, and the enthusiastic reception given to the

---

*This may also help to explain why the earlier Great Awakening in the 1730s was not more productive of communes.

utopian socialist ideas of Robert Owen, who came to this country in that same year, indicated that large numbers of people were once again considering the alternative of dropping out of mainstream society. The quarter century of Owenism and Fourierism was a period of unprecedented commune building. Although not as many communes were built as during the 1965–1975 decade, never before or since this utopian socialist period did American society as a whole take the movement so seriously. In 1840, Ralph Waldo Emerson wrote in a letter to Carlyle: "We are all a little wild here with numberless projects of social reform. Not a reading man but has a draft of a new community in his waistcoat pocket . . ." (Holloway, 1966, p. 19).

This was the first great period of secular communitarianism. Religious communes continued to prosper as well, but the locus of confusion and dread of contamination had shifted from rationalist philosophy and theology to capitalist economics. Aside from the Shakers, the few communes that have achieved a lasting place in American history (New Harmony, Brook Farm, the North American Phalanx, Oneida) all were founded during this period. Much has been written about the Owenite and Fourierist movements,* but this is not the place to attempt to recapitulate their fascinating histories. It should be noted, however, that all the secular communes of this period had short lifespans. The longest-lived was thirteen years. By way of contrast, a fair number of religious communes from this and the earlier communitarian era were able to survive anywhere from twenty-five years to over a century. Despite their ambitious socialist ideologies, none of these communes made an economic impact upon the larger society, although most managed to scratch out adequate livings and a few even became moderately prosperous.

In the year 1848, Europe exploded into revolution, and the epoch of modern socialism, as a full-fledged international movement, was begun. It would be difficult to overestimate the effect of these unsuccessful revolutions upon the political consciousness of the century. Utopian socialism, already ailing from its many practical failures on American soil, was virtually blown away with the times (Hobsbawm, 1975, pp. 158ff.):

> In a sense all the theories of revolution at the time were, and had to be, attempts to come to terms with the experience of 1848. . . . This applies to Marx as well as to Bakunin, to the Paris Communards as well as to the Russian populists. . . . The major utopian currents had ceased to exist as such. Saint-Simonianism had cut its links with the left. . . . Robert Owen's (1771–1858) followers had turned their intellectual energies to spiritualism and secularism, their practical energies to the modest field of collective stores. Fourier, Cabet and the other inspirers of communist communities . . . were forgotten. Horace Greeley's (1811–72) slogan "Go West Young Man" proved more successful than his earlier Fourierist ones. Utopian socialism did not survive 1848.

---

*Bestor (1950) has the definitive bibliography on Owenism, and Manuel (1966) has one on Fourierism.

From about 1848 to about 1890 communitarianism in America went into eclipse. This, of course, was an eclipse of incidence not of prevalence. A few communes were founded during this period, and a fair number of those already in existence continued to survive. As evidence for this, Noyes and Nordhoff, both writing in the 1870s, could speak of "socialism," as they called it, as a living movement. Noyes's own commune, Oneida, was founded in 1848 and enjoyed the whole of its prosperous thirty-three-year existence during this period of eclipse.

In Chapter 2 we will see the same phenomenon repeated with respect to the movement of 1965-1975. Oneida was, in a sense, the heir to the utopian social-ist movement. Some of its most productive and influential members were refugees from failed communes of this period, just as, today, the Farm in Ten-nessee derives much of its membership from the failed communes of 1965-1975. The principle of survival of the fittest ensures that a few of the strongest com-munes will outlast by many years the movement that gave them birth. Further-more, the principle of cultural diffusion ensures that the movement will not flourish in all places simultaneously. We thus should expect, and do find, that new communal starts appear in cultural backwaters for a few years after the movement has run out of steam in the areas of its first growth.*

The Turn of the Century (1890–1915)

Each communitarian movement examined thusfar can be associated with a major social or cultural innovation which fragmented prevailing systems of meaning and value. In the early part of the nineteenth century, the bugaboo was the rational philosophy and theology of the enlightment. In the 1830s and 1840s it was capitalism. As the nineteenth century drew to a close, technology was the disruptive force that helped to spawn yet another communitarian move-ment.

Edward Bellamy, Lawrence Grönlund, Henry George, and William Dean Howells were among the intellectual progenitors of this movement. Unlike Owen, Brisbane, and Greeley, of the utopian socialist period, these men did not take active leadership roles in the movement. It seems to have been largely trade union leaders and moderate socialist theorists who, horrified at some of the excesses of radical Marxism, attempted to blend the communitarian ideal with

*Fourierism is a good case in point. Although the movement had thoroughly lost its social force by 1848, new starts continued to occur for a few years more. An effective charis-matic leader like Josiah Warren was able to bend the moribund movement to his own pur-poses until well into the next decade. But the communes that he founded were dependent solely on his charismatic will, not on an underlying Fourierist movement to hold together. And, finally, in a few culturally remote places (e.g., Perth Amboy, New Jersey, and Cement City, Texas), Fourierist phalanxes were still being founded as late as 1853 (Raritan Bay Union) and 1855 (Réunion).

utopian technological principles to produce a form of socialism less destructive of American cultural values (Hayden, 1976, p. 289ff).*

For the first time during this period communitarianism became a truly nationwide social movement. Socialist and anarchist communes appeared in California (Hine, 1966), the Northwest (Le Warne, 1975), and the Deep South (Alyea, 1956), as well as the more traditional East and Midwest. The period also produced the earliest documented evidence of urban communitarianism (Bennett, 1975). From the Home Colony, Equality, and Freeland on Puget Sound, to Fairhope on Mobile Bay in Alabama, to Stelton Farm in New Jersey, the common theme of labor etherialized through technology was working itself out.

By far the most significant communitarian experiment of this period was Llano Del Rio, founded in Los Angeles by Job Harriman, defeated candidate for mayor on the Socialist ticket. This commune endured for almost a quarter of a century, from 1914 to 1938, first in Southern California and then in Louisiana. A cornerstone of its ideology was the notion of the labor saving device. Probably no commune before or since has ever placed quite so much emphasis on the ability of sheer technique to free labor from the evils of drudgery and exploitation. The commune could find no way, however, to stabilize its power relationships and it eventually succumbed to one of a long series of factional disputes.

After 1915, commune building in America went into a fifty-year decline, but at no point did it completely stop.† There was a brief revival of communitarian interest after World War II, particularly among Quaker and Brethren conscientious objectors. About a dozen communes founded in the 1930s, 1940s, and 1950s still exist today. But nothing approximating a communitarian social movement on a national scale occurred again until about 1965. In the following chapter, we shall examine this most recent outburst of communitarian interest in considerably greater detail.

Conclusions

Our survey of the geographical and historical distribution of communes and communitarian movements has had to rely on data of very uneven quality, especially for the years prior to 1800. Nevertheless, certain empirical regularities cannot be dismissed. One is that the distribution of communes both spatially and

---

*The communitarian ideology of this period was not uniformly socialist. Anarchist communitarian experiments were also to be found in all parts of the country as were a scattering of new religious communitarian ventures. The Quakers exhibited a renewed interest in communitarianism during this period. However as has been typical of this sect, Quaker interest was expressed not so much in doing it as in helping others do it. During the 1890s, the Quakers were instrumental in facilitating the migration of the communitarian Doukhabor sect from Russia to North America.

†Father Divine's Peace Mission Movement in the 1930s is the most well known of those communal movements that continued to appear during this ebb. Father Divine's movement was also exceptional, as we shall see in Chapter 3, in that it appealed primarily to Blacks.

temporally, is patterned. Another is that there appears to be a correlation between the incidence of communitarian movements and the breakdown of traditional meaning and value systems. Viewed from such a great distance, there appears to be some evidence that communitarianism is, as we have hypothesized, a social response to the loss of larger-scale consensus brought about by the cultural proliferation of choice alternatives.

The "Great Awakening" phenomenon is endemic in Amer-
ica, and it is probable that, however atypical, our period is
another example of it.... Even if we have become "post-
American" or "post-Puritan," it is still, we would suggest,
in a most American and Puritan way.

Robert Bellah

CHAPTER 2

American Communitarianism
as a Social Movement

In this chapter we move from the general to the specific. We have scanned the
continents and the centuries using sparse data to compile a perspective on the
incidence of communitarianism. We shall now restrict ourselves to a single country (the United States) and a single decade (1965-1975) in which a particular
communitarian movement can be examined more comprehensively. But even
one entire social movement is too complex to be systematically analyzed. We
shall restrict ourselves in the final sections of the chapter, to a sample of communes drawn from the larger social movement population. This sample of 120
communes, and the participants therein, will serve as the objects of investigation
in all subsequent chapters of this book.

Profile of a Social Movement

We shall conceive of a social movement, following Heberle (1951, pp. 23ff),
as a collectivity, not as a process. But the collectivity making up a social movement at any moment cannot be understood without reference to the larger pub-

41

lic in which the movement is embedded, a public animated by such similarity of aspiration and/or discontent that it provides a steady source of recruits and ensures that the continuity of the movement will be independent of the loyalty of those people who happen to be its current members.

As Killian (1964, p. 431) has pointed out, social movements can and frequently do contain within them many smaller and more precisely organized groups. As in the current work, these groups may come to be the objects of investigation instead of the larger collectivity of which they are a part. But to better understand the behaviors of these communal groups, we must first look at them in the context of the larger social movement that gave them life and the still larger public that was their lifeblood.

A communitarian social movement, roughly between the years 1965 and 1975, fostered the creation of tens of thousands of (mostly ephemeral) communes and led to a general interest in communal living as a revolutionary force and alternative life-style. Like its utopian predecessors, this social movement has had little direct effect on the society of which it was a part. Some might argue that it is thus hardly worthy of investigation. But our concern is to study, not deeds, but intentions. We are therefore just as interested in failures as in successes and just as interested in the movement's decline as in its rise.

Let us now look at three aspects of this contemporary communitarianism: (1) its similarity to and differences from other communitarian movements in American history, (2) its own rise and decline and (3) the rise and decline of the larger public that supported it.

Historical Differences and Similarities

As we saw in Chapter 1, the communitarian movement of 1965–1975 was only the most recent of a recurring series in America since the earliest colonial times. But more communes were begun in this one recent decade than in all previous American history. Even taking into account the tendency of historical distance to understate the frequency of events, the most recent period of commune building eclipsed all previous ones. Whereas each of the other communitarian movements produced fewer than a hundred communes of which we have record, the most recent one produced tens of thousands.

However, if we look not at numbers of communes but rather at numbers of communitarians as a function of the total American population, we find more constancy. An order of magnitude of 10^{-3} (no greater precision is possible) of the American population became involved in communal living in each of its peak periods.* But this constancy masks certain changes that tend (roughly) to

---

*The 1890–1915 period, about which relatively little information is available, probably fell short of this level.

cancel each other out. The population of the United States has, of course, gone up steadily during all of this period. At the same time, there has been a tendency for the average population of communes to decline. Before 1820 the average commune had over one hundred adult members. After 1820, the average population fell to somewhere between fifty and one hundred adults. In the recent period, the average commune had about twenty-five adult members.

When a rare phenomenon becomes relatively common, it is reasonable to ask whether it is still the same phenomenon or a new one using an old name. Although such taxonomic decisions are always somewhat arbitrary, it would seem that the evidence favors continuity over distinctiveness. The most recent movement is unique in ways other than its high incidence rate and low mean population. But it is no more different from those of past centuries than the communitarian movements of past centuries were from one another, a fact that historical distance tends to obscure.* The basic theme of retreat from disorder and incoherence of the *Gesellschaft* to the order and coherence (at least ideologically if not in practice) of the *Gemeinschaft* has remained the same. And fragility of structure and elusiveness of utopian goals have continued to characterize communitarian efforts.

There is surprisingly little awareness among present-day communitarians of their historical forebears. Few communes set out deliberately to emulate admired communal experiments of the past or to avoid repeating the mistakes of those that failed. Table 2-1 shows the proportion of urban commune members in a 1974 survey who indicated an awareness of certain selected communes of the past and present. The only names of communal movements that were recognized by a majority are those that exist at the present time. The names of communes that existed prior to 1965, even the distinguished Brook Farm, were unfamiliar to most. Although comparable data were not obtained from rural communitarians, there is reason to believe that their historical ignorance is less pronounced. Many rural communes at least possess the classics of utopian and communitarian literature in their libraries. A Walden Two commune called Twin Oaks has even named its buildings in honor of significant communal experiments of the past.

Location. Geographically, the location of communes has shifted to accommodate shifts in the American population. The constant factor, however, has been the search for cheap land not too isolated from markets and people. Now, as in earlier times, rural communes are often found in geographical clusters. The new development has been the advent of the urban commune. We have

---

*To cite only one very obvious example, the American communes of the colonial period and even the early Shakers were able to exist as semisovereign "island" utopias in a manner inconceivable to all but the most remote nineteenth-century communes. For an example of the importance of this historical difference, compare the early with the late Oneida (Carden, 1969) to see the effects upon a commune that bridged both these worlds.

TABLE 2-1. Proportion of Urban Commune Members Who Have Heard
of Selected Historical and Contemporary Communes

Commune Name	Lifespan	Proportion Who Have Heard of	Number of Respondents[1]
Kibbutz	1909–	79%	220
Walden Two[2]	(1948)[2]	71	218
Synanon	1959–	71	214
Oneida	1848–1880	39	213
Brook Farm	1841–1847	29	215
Bruderhof	1920–	29	214
New Harmony	1826–1827	27	215
New Buffalo	1967–	13	216
Llano Del Rio	1914–1935	7	214

[1] This question was asked of about half of the respondents ($N = 220$) in the first wave of the urban commune study (1974).
[2] Walden Two, itself, is a fictional commune described in a novel by B. F. Skinner published in 1948. However, a number of real communes have been patterned after this fictional utopia. These are sometimes called "Walden Two communes" or "Walden Two-type communes."

almost no record of urban communes in the nineteenth century, but today they are more prevalent than the rural.*

Bennett Berger et al. (1972, p. 3) see urban communes as a less pure form of the essentially rural ideal:

. . . urban communes represent a less thorough commitment to serious communal experiment than rural communes do, because choosing to live in an urban commune is not so profoundly consequential a choice; it does not necessarily involve isolation from or inaccessibility to one's former milieu, a radical change in the structure of one's daily life, and engagement in unfamiliar forms of work which may require the development of new skills which present a deep challenge to one's very identity.

. . . a recurrent topic of discussion in urban communes [is] whether to get some land and move to the country, while rural communes almost never talk about collectively moving back to the city . . . .

But Rosabeth Kanter (1974) and Saul Levine (1972) have argued convincingly that the urban commune must be considered as a unique phenomenon on its own terms. If less radically sectarian and institutionally complete, it may never-

*The reason for the common misconception that communes are primarily a rural rather than an urban phenomenon, a manifestation of the youthful flight from the cities, is that during the 1960s rural communes tended to be larger, more radical, and certainly more vocal than their urban counterparts. Some excellent case studies (Gardner, 1970; Diamond, 1971; Kinkade, 1973; Beame et al., 1973; Sundancer, 1973) have been written by commune members themselves about their own communal experiences. These have all been rural. Sociological surveys (Roberts, 1971; Zablocki, 1971, 1972a; Kanter, 1972) have also tended to stress the rural over the urban. Urban communes have been represented in the literature by the more recent works of Kanter (1974, 1975) and by the writings of two psychiatrists (Speck, 1972; Levine, 1972).

theless be the more adaptive and ultimately, perhaps, the more significant response to alienation from contemporary society. At any rate, in their internal dynamics, discussed in later chapters, rural and urban communes display few major differences.

Communal forms are shaped by ecological and architectural possibilities. Until recently there seemed to be neither reason nor opportunity for communal living groups to exist with an urban base. But it is possible, although unlikely, that significant numbers of urban communes existed in the past and vanished leaving no historical trace. The ecological niche filled by urban communes (the large homes of the affluent who have fled the cities) has no counterpart in early generations.

Economics. The condition of communes relative to the larger national economy is the same as it has almost always been—marginal but not desperate. Few communes have ever succeeded in carving out comfortable and secure niches for themselves within the larger economy or apart from it. But even fewer, in the past as now, could trace their disintegrations to economic difficulties. In fact, except during the period 1824–1848, economic goals and strategies have seldom been the central issues of communitarian ideology. Only a minority of communes in any historical period ever practiced full economic communism.

There is, however, one economic distinction, related to the advent of the urban commune, that does sharply differentiate contemporary communes from those of times past. Never before, at least in American history, have large numbers of communes subsisted on the wages earned by members at outside jobs.* Communes have hitherto gotten their livelihoods in a great variety of ways. It is not the addition of wage earning itself (always present as a supplemental or emergency source of income in the past) that makes the great difference. Rather, it is that many of these jobs are actually careers, demanding a loyalty at least equal to the loyalty demanded by the commune. The presence of multiple outside careers among commune members creates strains similar to those raised by the presence of two careers within a family. Conflicting career responsibilities do not negate, and may even strengthen, the commune. But their presence is a fact that radically changes the structure of the traditional commune just as it has changed the structure of the traditional family.

Membership. When we compare the kinds of people who joined the communes of past times with those that join today, we again see more similarities than differences. Then, as now, people joined for a wide variety of reasons under a wide variety of circumstances. Then, as now, alienated majorities had to be inspired by charismatic minorities. Religious and secular approaches contended with each other. Some people made lifetime commitments, whereas

---

*Even this distinction becomes blurred if we are willing to go back as far as sixteenth-century Europe. Many of the Anabaptist communes were made up principally of wage earners, as, of course, were many of the early Christian church communities of the first century A.D.

others were just passing through. Some were interested in changing the world, whereas others, often within the same commune, wanted only to retreat from the world.

The process of joining a commune, however, has changed. It has been easy to join a contemporary commune. In the nineteenth century, Robert Owen's virtually open admission policy was the exception rather than the rule. The Shakers, Rappites, and even Brook Farm adopted generally stringent policies limiting recruitment and membership. In the period 1965–1975, completely unrestricted admission was, at least during the early years, the moral (if not the statistical) norm. It is significant that communes restricting membership or screening members have felt defensive about the practice and have felt the need to justify their restrictions. Long trial memberships and novitiates, relatively common in the nineteenth century, were quite rare in the most recent period.

Stability. Rosabeth Kanter (1972) has shown, and this study confirms, that stringency of admission standards is directly correlated with commune stability. The greater ease of admission among the contemporary groups would thus lead us to predict low longevity and great membership turnover, a fact we find to be true. But it is important to recognize that communes have always been unstable ventures. Multicentury enterprises such as the Hutterians and the Shakers are the glamorous exceptions that blind us to the great numbers of six-month, one-year, and two-year "flops." Historically, of course, such ephemeral communes leave few if any traces and cannot readily be studied. Working with contemporary data, we have the opportunity to correct the biased historical tendency to overemphasize success and deemphasize failure to survive.

It would be interesting to know whether communes of the present survive or fail to survive for the same reasons as those of the past. We know that in one respect they do. Long-term stability, then as now, is correlated with the presence of religion, charismatic leadership, and the involvement of the specific commune in a larger federation of communes. But we cannot compare epochs with respect to short-term stability. As we shall see in Chapters 3 and 4, the stability of contemporary communes has most to do with certain patterns of interpersonal relationship. But such relational patterns rarely leave historical traces.* We cannot, therefore, be sure that this was equally true in the past. However, Gillian Lindt† has suggested that, at least for the eighteenth-century Moravian communes, untenable relationship networks were probably a well-hidden major cause of dissolution.

Authority. Contemporary communes have been, on the whole, less authoritarian than communes of earlier centuries. There is a tendency in all communes, however, both now and in former times, to gravitate to increasing authoritarianism as a function of time. And the form which this authoritarianism invariably

---

*With the burning of the Oneida diaries, in recent years, one of the few possible exceptions to this rule was unfortunately eliminated.
†Personal communication.

takes is charismatic. The charismatic poppa, the wise old guru, the political fire-brand, all have been familiar figures throughout communitarian history and con-tinue to be so today.

Legislative assemblies have always been rare among communes. Voting has never been a popular way of deciding the outcome of divisive issues. Consenual meetings of the whole, seeking to come to a common mind, have been the norm. This process, of course, lends itself well to charismatic influence. Anarchism has also been a perennially favorite philosophy among communitarians, and this form of organization too, by creating a power vacuum, has lent itself to the emergence of charismatic leaders.

We know little about the actual workings of authority relations in former times. But the historical record gives us overwhelming evidence that these rela-tionships were highly troublesome and frequently led to breakups and schisms, perhaps even more frequently than is the case today. No commune has ever succeeded in completely suppressing relationships of subordination and super-ordination as far as we know. Communes of every era have been aware of the need to consciously strive to prevent these inequalities from being exploited for personal advantage.

Ideology.   Rosabeth Kanter (1972, p. 8) has discerned a three-stage historical evolution within American communitarianism:

> Thus, the initial impetus for the building of American communes has tended to stem from one of three major themes: a desire to live according to religious and spiritual values . . . a desire to reform society by curing its eco-nomic and political ills . . . or a desire to promote the psychosocial growth of the individual by putting him into closer touch with his fellows. . . . These three threads vaguely correspond to the three historical waves of American utopian communities: the first lasted from early days to about 1845, when religious themes were prominent; the second, stressing economic and poli-tical issues . . . in the 1840's; and the third psychosocial period . . . became especially important in the 1960's.

Our findings support this set of distinctions but suggest that it is more one of ideological flavor than ideological type. Religious communes are now, and have always been, the predominant ideological category among communes. And all communes, whether religious or secular, have been by their very nature con-cerned with economic and political change. Even waiting for the imminent millenium implies a certain radical perspective toward the economy and the state.

The basic types of communes have not changed much, at least since the nineteenth century. There are now, as there were then, mystical cult communes, traditional religious (Christian) communes, communes interested in political change, communes interested in cultural change, groups formed simply for the purposes of cooperation, and others to help other people address their personal problems.

What has changed—and it is probably the most significant way in which contemporary communes differ from their historical ancestors—is that all these ideological perspectives have come to be skewed in the direction of promoting the interests of the individual. Even the religious groups, although less so than the secular communes, stress the importance of the self-actualizing experience far more often than did the religious communes of the past.

John Bennett, who has studied both the Hutterians and contemporary communes, ascribes the distinctive character of the latter to an unusual emphasis on the value of individualism and individual freedom (1975, pp. 82ff):

> We have then the two objectives of the contemporary commune: one, to restore the integrity of the small groups, the primary socializing units of society . . . and second, to provide a sense of identity, a full and satisfying personality for the individual members. . . .
> The second objective is, I believe, an essentially contemporary one. I can find no emphasis on individuality in the literature on the early movements with the exception of some of the utopian communitarian schemes of the late eighteenth and nineteenth centuries. . . .

This emphasis on the individual has many structural consequences for the contemporary commune. One of the most important has to do with commitment. In another context, Morris Janowitz (1953) coined the term "community of limited liability" to connote changes in the modern natural community in the direction of lessened commitment. Many contemporary communes are "communes of limited liability." Both the individual and the collectivity are constantly aware of the ever-present option to leave if the costs of continued participation come to outweigh the benefits. Now, as in the past, charismatic leaders have been instrumental in provoking the willing suspension of such awareness. However, all but a few of these contemporary charismatics have felt the need to justify this willing suspension in terms of its ultimate benefit to the individual.

With respect to location, economic life, membership criteria, stability, authority, and ideology, we have seen that there is no consistent pattern of differences between contemporary communes and those of previous times great enough to justify our using a new generic term for the contemporary phenomena that we are investigating. The differences that do exist, on the whole, are no greater than the differences among themselves of the various communitarian movements of the past.

The Rise and Decline of a Social Movement

Potential charismatic leaders, eager followers, and independent community seekers sprang up in abundance in the summer of 1965. A great many people, unbeknownst to one another, had independently rediscovered the communitarian response and were mulling over its applicability. Communes made their reentrance into American society not only in Cambridge or Berkeley, Greenwich Village or the Haight-Ashbury, but in all these and many other places at about the same time.

The American communitarian movement of 1965–1975 started at the Atlantic and Pacific coasts and moved inland. At first it moved out of the cities and into the countryside. Later, in part, it returned to the cities. As with any blanket statements about the origin of a social movement, these are only partial truths. Communal survivals from earlier in the century still were to be found in the Sierra Nevadas, the Appalachians, the Ozarks, and the northern Great Plains in the early 1960s. Records exist of hippielike communes in San Francisco and New York as early as 1963, although even in these cities nothing approximating a social movement began until 1965.

The growth of communitarian interest was discontinuously rapid beginning in 1965. Rural communes reached a peak of new development between 1969 and 1971, with a tapering off in new starts thereafter. Urban communes reached a later peak, with new starts not tapering off until 1976. In general, however, the demarcation of the end of the movement was less precise (and certainly less dramatic) than its beginning. Only with several years' hindsight can we say with some confidence that, by the end of 1975 (or certainly no later than 1976), the communitarian movement had been absorbed into a communitarian alternative life-style. The communal zeal that has lived on, in isolated pockets, is both serious and intense. But it resembles the idiosyncratic communitarianism of 1850–1890 or of 1946–1964 more than the sweeping social movement of 1965–1975.

Many writers have commented upon the distinctiveness of the 1965–1975 decade. Herman Kahn (1977) has called it a decade of social malaise and educated incapacity. Robert Havighurst (1975) has referred to it as a decade of demographic indigestion. It does, of course, and not coincidentally, correspond closely to the period of American involvement in the war in Vietnam. Let us discuss the commune movement in terms of the social and cultural temper of its times and then go on to discuss it in demographic terms.

The prior years (1960–1964) set the stage. The 1960s began on notes of idealism and self-determination. The exploration of outer space had begun. Young people were beginning to use mind-altering drugs in what they came increasingly to refer to as the exploration of inner space. The kaleidoscopic reordering of possibilities and prospects recalled other earlier eras of rapid change in consciousness. The civil rights movement was racking up a steady string of successes and serving, for many people, as a model of orderly revolution, American style. Contradictions were appearing but not yet rending the social fabric. In 1962, the Students for a Democratic Society met and drafted what came to be known as the Port Huron Statement defining the position of the New Left (Hayden, 1977, p. 70):

We took it to the Port Huron convention, which turned out to be a very euphoric communal experience. It was a beautiful setting, right on Lake Huron. We had one large meeting room, which could comfortably accommodate a plenary session and there were lots of little cabins. . . . It was amazing. In five days we had a finished version. . . .

The Port Huron Statement might not seem so radical today, but for 1962 it was a pretty advanced document. *It began by stating the need for values rather than immediately offering political programs and making legislative demands.* [emphasis added]

Meanwhile, the Food and Drug Administration was permitting the public sale of birth control pills for the first time and the National Council of Churches was agreeing that it was morally justified to use them. But it had not yet become evident that these little pills, even more than the notorious psychedelics, would spell the end of centuries'-old patterns of relationships between the sexes and between the generations.

In this predawn period (1960-1963), there were a few, scattered new commune starts. Tolstoy Farm was a prominent pacifist commune started in the state of Washington at this time. A few communes had sprouted up from the remnants of the old beat colony at Big Sur in California. A handful of others could be found in New England, in Appalachia, in Cambridge, in Berkeley, and in New York. But there was still very little sense of being part of a larger social movement.

By 1964, a shared sense of counterculture had begun to emerge among a generation that was beginning to become collectively conscious of itself as "youth." The Beatles craze and rock music in general were one symptom of this cohort consciousness. The Free Speech Movement at Berkeley was another. A third was drugs. Timothy Leary and Richard Alpert had been dismissed from Harvard the year before and were now actively promulgating their psychedelic philosophy. More and more people were experimenting with consciousness-altering drugs.

By this time communes were beginning to cluster in space, although settlements within clusters were still quite sparse. An area along the California coast, from the Russian River to Big Sur, was the first of these clusters to become visible to researchers. In other areas that would one day be dense communitarian regions, the ground was being prepared. In northern New Mexico, Tijerina's success in organizing the Hispanic community into an *Alianza Federal de Mercedes* was bringing young white radical allies and observers into the area. The civil rights movement was doing the same for southern Appalachia.

In August 1964, three blasts upon the trumpet of human events heralded the advent of a communitarian decade.* After long indecisiveness, the U. S. Senate passed the Gulf of Tonkin Resolution, effectively removing any remaining barriers to full-scale American participation in the war in Vietnam. After a long search, the bodies of three civil rights workers were found in the Mississippi

*These events heralded, more precisely, a decade of general radical and countercultural activity of which communitarianism is merely the aspect currently being investigated.

swamp. This and the less-than-sympathetic response of some radical blacks signaled a sharp change in mood within the civil right movement. Finally, after long debate, the antipoverty program including a food stamp bill was signed into law. This meant, among other more significant things, that one could drop out without danger of going hungry, for the first time in American history.

Movement Beginnings. With the coming of the year 1965, American youth culture experienced a sharp and unmistakable change in mood. A concrete response to the political events of the preceding year and the trends of the preceding five years or so suddenly jelled. Like all shifts in mood, this one is difficult to document specifically. One indicator, however, is popular music. The number one spot in the pop singles chart had been held in the previous two years by such songs as *Sugar Shack, Be My Baby, My Guy,* and *Do Wah Diddy Diddy* typical fare—as well as, starting in 1964, by many Beatles' songs. In 1965, the Beatles songs began to express the drug culture and, perhaps more significantly, the shared secret symbolism of the youth movement. Other top hit songs departed radically from the older formula. As the year drew on, the number one position was held at times by *Eve of Destruction, Get Off of My Cloud, Sounds of Silence, Mister Tambourine Man,* and *Can't Get No Satisfaction.*

A youth culture, on both coasts, had become fully aware of itself and was expressing itself, among other ways, by the widespread proliferation of communes. The formula of communes = hippies = drugs was becoming imprinted upon the public consciousness at this time, resulting in official and vigilante harrasment against even some of the older religious communes. But, as yet, such incidents were the rare exceptions. Most people had no opinion of communes or even knew that they existed. In San Francisco, Ken Kesey's acid tests were spreading the drug experience to a mass audience while maintaining a certain amount of symbolic unity in the interpretation of the drug experience. Many communes were begun in the San Francisco Bay Area at this time. Even such smaller cities as Atlanta were developing counterculture movements. In 1965, the Atlanta Walden Two Committee was formed, a group that would later be instrumental in founding the first successful rural commune based upon the utopian ideas of B. F. Skinner. At least one other urban commune, revolving around Atlanta's underground radio station, was founded at this time.

By 1966, the effects of the alienation of youth from virtually all social institutions could be felt. Church attendance among young people began to drop (especially for Catholics), a steady decline that was not to be reversed until 1976. The antiwar movement had now been mobilized at every major university in the country.

The year 1966 was one of mass "happenings" and "be-ins" in San Francisco and New York. Urban communes continued to proliferate during this year. Urban communes were still chiefly seen as way stations to eventual rural settlement.* However, two countertendencies foreshadowed the later develop-

*Some groups sought to have the best of both worlds. For example, the Zen Center of San Francisco purchased its rural retreat, Tassajara, in this year.

ment of urban communes as ends in themselves. The first was the crashpad phenomenon. In 1966, at the height of drug culture utopianism, the norm of free access to space inspired many individuals and groups in large cities to open their houses to all comers as places to "crash" for indefinite periods of time. The second was the appearance, again at the two coasts, of the first of the big national federations of Eastern religious urban communes (e.g., The International Society of Krishna Consciousness in New York).

The year 1966 also marked the appearance of rural open communes on a large scale for the first time. These flourished for several years mainly in California. Open communes follow the basic principle that there shall be no rules limiting admission or determining expulsion of members. All are free to come, none can be asked to leave, and only informal social and ecological pressures limit the freedom of each person there to do as he or she chooses. Many such communes rapidly reached the size of three or four hundred members, but they were subject to rapid fluctuations in population and extremely high membership turnover.

The open commune of 1966-1969 represents an early exuberant stage of the communitarian movement and played an important role in the dissemination of American communitarianism in the late 1960s. Although most members stayed for only short periods of time, they developed network affiliations and gained necessary experience both in communal living and rural enterprise that allowed them to graduate to the founding of communes with more structured membership policies. Because of their accessibility, some open communes were discussed extensively in the mass media. Thus, they came to represent, in the popular mind, an image of what all or most communes were like. Some of the larger open communes, such as Morningstar Ranch, Drop City, or Tolstoy Farm, remained the media stereotype of communitarianism even after this style gave way to more structured formats.

Movement Heyday.   The years 1967 and 1968 were the heyday of the rural communitarian movement. The mood in American cities grew ugly during this time, and the temper of the urban youth movement both on and off the campuses gravitated toward the revolutionary. By 1968, militant opposition to the war and rebellion against university authority were at their height. Those who had no stomach either for accommodation with the establishment or violent opposition were driven to the countryside in ever-increasing numbers. But such movement was not all politically neutral or escapist. Incipient guerrilla bands in the Sierra Nevadas and the Sangre de Cristo Mountains began to be formed in this period, with tactical links to urban revolutionary groups.

Christian communitarianism flourished during these years. As Catholic church attendance continued to decline sharply, alternatives were sought that would have greater appeal to the new generation. In Pittsburgh, in 1967, the Catholic-based Charismatic Renewal Movement was begun, a loosely federated organization that has since become a worldwide organization. Similar movements within evangelical Protestantism appeared at the same time throughout the Midwest and

South. Jewish *Chavarim* and mainstream Protestant "fellowships" and "living experiments" reflected similar impulses in the cities (Neusner, 1972).

These were years of massive cross-country migrations of young people traveling in large caravans and in small groups. Thousands of communitarians began arriving in northern New Mexico and the Pacific Northwest at this time. Most of them came by way of California, but many others were westward bound from the East and Midwest. Although urban communes were still largely confined to cities on the two coasts, the beginnings of a communitarian counterculture could be seen stirring in the inland cities of Houston, Chicago, Detroit, and Denver, to name a few. By late 1968, the urban communitarians were beginning to get a sense of themselves as distinctly urban rather than prerural. The crisis atmosphere in the cities inspired many to a service orientation among the communes choosing the urban alternative. Synanon transformed itself from drug rehabilitation center to commune at this time, and many other groups began to look for ways they could help the urban poor and hopeless.

By 1968, rural communes began to consolidate. Open community was still a strong norm, but enough commune disintegrations had by now occurred to produce a crop of second-timers anxious to avoid repeating past mistakes and eager to build more stable communes with more sophisticated authority structures. Naïve anarchism gave way to more complex ways to engender unity without voting.

Time of Troubles. The Nixon years began in 1969 and with them came a period of social reaction against communitarianism. The reaction was never very harsh because communes were generally perceived to be among the least of the problems posed by the youth rebellion. But communitarianism certainly did suffer its share of the repression of dissidence and social experiment that came to characterize the Nixon years.

However, in August 1969, the mood within the communitarian movement was one of optimism and exuberance. The music festival at Woodstock, New York, in that month became for many the high-water mark of the entire decade. Both rural and urban communes were being founded with greater frequency than ever before. Revolutionary youth leaders were taking the movement seriously for the first time and considering how they might coopt it. Even a nononsense political group like the Black Panthers experimented briefly (and unsatisfactorily) with communal living at this time. The Woodstock period stimulated the most serious of all attempts (none of which ever got off the ground) to organize the movement nationally via some sort of landholding trust, cooperative purchasing company, and recruitment-placement center. The would-be organizers failed to realize that communitarianism was flourishing to the extent that it was precisely because there was not the larger-scale value consensus necessary for that sort of central organization.

The year 1969 also marked the waning of the open commune ideal. All over the country the serious members of communes were closing ranks and throwing the freeloaders out. Occasionally violence or arson was used to get the nonproductive to leave. Where this was impossible, as in the famous Drop City, the productive members themselves left to form a closed commune, leaving their earlier creation in the hands of those who would not or could not measure up to standards.

Many open communes failed because of inadequate mechanisms for limiting population. Their very economic success brought about their downfall by making them more attractive to the multiplying horde of communitarian seekers on the roads by 1969. Disillusionment with the open communal ideal led to the creation of communes in which some restrictions were placed on membership, generally in the form of a limit on the number of people who could occupy the land at any given time, requirements for membership, or a statement of adherence to the ideology before being accepted as a member.

But, just as the established communes were taking steps to expel their lazy and incompetent members and to establish admission barriers to keep more of the same from joining, the federated national religious sects were proliferating in every area of the country, with economic organizations capable of motivating and using just about any warm body. The year 1969, therefore, also marks the beginning of the epoch of the absentee charismatic leader. Such leaders, frequently Eastern gurus, built lucrative communitarian empires using the dregs of the earlier commune movement and tapping into the continuing exodus of unskilled and disoriented young people from conventional society.

Some comparatively mild social persectuion was felt by communes in 1969. Space City Collective in Houston was attacked by the Ku Klux Klan. In various rural areas, merchants' boycotts of local communes were begun. Police raids for drugs or for building or zoning violations were the most common ways of expressing social hostility toward communes. Most people still did not know how to react to communes. It was still unclear at this time whether or not communes had an inalienable constitutional right to exist.

By 1970 there were full-scale efforts to break the radical youth movement, and communitarianism came in for its share of the hostility. The more general strategies were get tough (Kent State) and co-opt (lower the voting age to 18). The rural communes were more visible and thus more vulnerable than their urban counterparts so they bore the brunt of it. This was one factor leading to the shift within the movement, which occurred at about this time, toward an urban center of gravity. By 1970, there were at least a dozen communes in just about every major city in the country.

The attack on rural communes was marked by widespread violence in 1970. A spirit of vigilantism grew as court decisions made it increasingly clear that communes in and of themselves were not illegal and could not be banished from any given city or county without specific reasons established by due process. Olampali, the largest and most prosperous of the California communes, was burned to the ground by vigilantes. In 1970 there was conflict with the Chicanos in northern New Mexico. Many communitarians were beaten or shot at, and a few communes were looted or burned as the fragile alliance between "long hairs" and Chicanos broke down completely. There was violence also in California, and in northern California and central Oregon there were highly effective trade embargoes enforced by the local merchants.

Co-optation, of course, took a more subtle form. In 1970 government and foundation grants to set up or aid selected communes first became available. Political and labor organizations, taking their cue from the Eastern religion model, saw that nationwide federations of sponsored communes would provide a steady and substantial source of volunteer labor for "the cause." The huge pool of alienated youth was hungry for a cause outside itself that it could believe in. The charismatic organization that could supply such a cause, washed down with liberal doses of communal euphoria, would have a supply of reasonably intelligent, well-educated, energetic workers willing to accept long hours at tedious work and the wages of voluntary poverty.

By 1971 there was no longer any doubt that the movement had become more urban than rural. 1971 marked a demographic watershed. For the first time in the history of the United States (or of any other nation), more people lived in the suburbs (36 percent) than in either the central cities (29 percent) or the rest of the country (35 percent). This trend was given additional impetus in 1971 by the Supreme Court ruling that school busing for integration purposes was legal. White flight accelerated, leading to the increased availability of commune-suitable housing. Urban communes quickly moved in to fill the vacuum. Especially fortunate were the large multihousehold religious sects. Some religious sects were wealthy enough to select a neighborhood in the center of a city, buy up a block or more of cheap transitional housing, and more or less take over the neighborhood.

Rural communes in 1971 were busy consolidating and building bridges of communication with their neighbors after the debacle of 1970. A large number of rural communes with very strong charismatic leaders appeared at this time. For example, this was the year that Steve Gaskin and his followers settled at the Farm, in Tennessee.

Decline of The Movement. The year 1972 marked the beginning of the end of the rural communitarian movement as measured by new starts. Except in New England, the incidence of new communes decreased. Well-established groups dug in and applied themselves to the long and difficult task of becoming integrated into the local economy and the larger community. Urban communitarianism, in contrast, was just hitting its stride in 1972. Communal clearinghouses and placement centers were thriving in several major cities. All the mass religious sectarian commune federations continued to grow.

By 1973, the mood of youth in America observably changed once again. Political alienation was rampant. Optimism was rare. The nation was obsessed with Watergate and with the coming recession. The fertility rate hit rock bottom.

Rural communes continued to dig in. There were few new starts. Urban communes were beginning to feel the weight of a large number of accumulated disbandings and were becoming disillusioned. But there were still a fair number of new urban communal starts. Eastern religious and Christian groups did especially well. In 1973 there was a repeat of the massive be-ins of the 1960s, only now in the form of religious revival meetings. The Divine Light Movement, the Happy Healthy Holy Organization, the Hari Krishnas, the Christian Charismatics, and the Jesus freaks served as hosts for such activities.

The years 1974 and 1975 continued the negative social mood. There was a recession and Nixon resigned. Communes were coming to be widely thought of as alternative life-styles of mutual support and protection rather than as manifestations of a utopian social movement.

Communes were just one dramatic aspect of a generally heightened concern with community as a dimension of life-style during this period. Housing developers responded to this heightened concern by featuring community themes in their advertisements. In California, one advertised a new type of residence arrangement for young singles that he called the *"communium"* (cross between commune and condominium) and that featured a greater degree of collectivization, especially in kitchen and dining facilities, than had hitherto been available in the American rented housing market. In Tennessee, another clever builder reported that he had saved a considerable amount of money by developing an urban housing complex for upper-middle-class young marrieds around an organic farm. He pointed out that such a farm held greater cultural appeal for many of his prospective homebuyers than a golf course would, was no more expensive to build, and was considerably cheaper to maintain. It also provided the additional benefits of cheap, fresh vegetables and (optional) therapeutic manual labor for the young executive commuters for whom the project was designed.

By 1975, the war in Vietnam finally ended and the impetus for social change once again turned to political reform. Issues such as sexual equality in employment and energy conservation became more important than community to many. For the first time since 1965, it was necessary for communes to advertise for members. Supply of places had, for the first time in the decade, exceeded the demand for them. At the same time, the sheer number of communal households continued to rise. However, the ideologically intense communes, with the exception of some religious cults, dwindled for the first time.

The trend from 1965 to 1975 took the form of a shift from activist communitarianism to life-style communitarianism. Most communes founded in the 1960s emphasized ideological goals involving the revolutionary transformation of society, although it is true that most communes taught revolution by example rather than by force of arms. As the movement entered the 1970s, a greater emphasis on coexisting with the larger society or living in its interstices became apparent. By 1976, more people saw communal living as a viable temporary alternative life-style, whereas the number of those committed to lifetime communitarianism continued to decrease.

Alienation from ultimate meanings and cultural values did not, of course, disappear or even demonstrably diminish after 1975. What seemed to happen instead was an accommodation with the society through its institutions that ordinarily promote the search for value consensus. Both in politics and religion, 1976 marked a sharp turn toward the legitimate search for values within the established institutions. The presidential campaign of Carter and Mondale injected such concerns into the political arena. The Gallup Opinion Index meanwhile showed that the churches were starting to reverse a ten-year slide in the rate of church attendance of adults under 30 years of age. The character of the youth movement had clearly changed, not back to the optimism of the early 1960s, but at least to a resigned, if not cynical, reengagement with the larger social issues.

Rise and Decline of a Supporting Public

A social movement, as we have defined it, is a *collectivity* whose members are persons but whose survival is not dependent on the loyalty of *specific* persons. A social movement cannot exist in isolation but only when it is surrounded by a much larger pool of potential recruits. We use the term "public," taken from the collective behavior literature, to denote such a large subpopulation positively disposed toward, but not necessarily active in, a social movement.

A public, almost by definition, cannot be studied through its actions. We want to know why the communitarian public suddenly swelled during the decade 1965–1975. The political and cultural reasons are discussed in previous sections of this chapter. But demography also is significant in the rise and fall of publics.

The population explosion of the communitarian public beginning in about 1965 rested upon three demographic pillars: employment, marriage, and childbearing. Within each of these three domains of action, major demographic shifts, bearing particularly on youth, clearly differentiated the period 1965–1975 from the years before and (to a lesser extent) from the years after.* An intervening variable between each of these demographic shifts and susceptibility to communitarianism was the expansion of choice alternatives. In areas of life in which tradition had long sufficed, decision was now suddenly required. Many young people, poorly prepared to make momentous life-career decisions on their own and having no larger respected system of cultural values to look to for guidance, naturally banded into ideological groups for moral support, Demographic variables thus have had a dual effect on commune membership. They have had a direct effect upon factors of opportunity to join and an indirect effect, through choice proliferation, on felt need to join.

---

*As is typical in such cases, the public did not decline in size at the movement's end nearly so rapidly as it had increased at the beginning. Social accommodation and the divergence of prevalence from incidence rates make the decline of a social movement less sensitive to demographic shifts than the start of one.

In the decade we are discussing, the proportion of the population aged 15 to 24 bulged with respect to the older working years' population aged 25 to 64.* This glut, which had consequences for employment, was caused by an overadequacy of supply—a simple result of the baby boom of 1945-1960—and a more complex inadequacy of demand—having to do primarily with changes in the nature and composition of the American labor force. There is evidence that the cohorts of young people reaching age 15 after 1975 are sharply different from those born in the prior fifteen years in attitudes toward countercultural movements and toward the legitimacy of societal institutions.

A high degree of alienation from the world of work has sometimes been attributed to permissiveness in the theories of child rearing under which this youth cohort was raised. However, there is evidence that it may be, rather, a result of a large-scale rejection of willing recruits by the labor force itself. The American economy, even prior to the 1974-1975 recession, was not able to use more than half the young people aged 16 through 21 in productive jobs, and some of those youths could find only part-time jobs. This has been more true in American society than elsewhere (Havighurst, 1975, pp. 131ff):

> This phenomenon seems peculiar to the United States. Other modern industrialized societies, including western Europe, Australia, and Japan, absorb young people readily into the labor force. The difference is partly due to the fact that there are juvenile wage scales in these countries, while in the United States, minimum wage laws and labor union policies operate against the employment of youth.

The increased man-hour productivity of labor, the large number of youths seeking jobs, and the vastly increased pool of available labor due to the large-scale entrance of women into the labor force and the acceptance of blacks and other minorities in positions above the lowest levels have all contributed to a situation in which workers from the younger age pool are not being absorbed into the labor force to replace members of the older group (25 to 64 years old) who retire or die at anywhere near a sufficient level to accommodate job-seeking youth.

In situations in which boys can look forward to work but girls cannot, there is a natural early gravitation toward the formation of independent nuclear family units. Where neither boys nor girls can look forward to work (or where both can),† the isolated nuclear family may seem a more dubious model, although still attractive to the great majority. But a significant minority will consider other alternatives, including communes.

*This ratio, however, is not extraordinarily high in comparison with the ones of the early part of this century (primarily for reasons of increased life expectancy and a very high birth rate during the early part of the century), though it is quite a bit higher than those in the period both before and after.

†Note in this regard that the number of two-income households about doubled between 1965 and 1976. *U.S. News and World Report,* March 27, 1978, p. 46.

However, the real unemployables do not join communes. Communitarianism is an experiment with life, and such experimentation requires a certain amount of security. Quite a few people who try communal living are marginal to the American system of social stratification. Classless, white, urban, liberally but not professionally educated, they are insulated both from any real danger of slipping into poverty and from any real opportunity of becoming absorbed in demanding and worthwhile careers.

At the same time that a glut of youth was appearing on the labor market, a glut of women was appearing on the marriage market. These two phenomena are partly related. In 1965, it was still very much the norm that a male be secure in a job before considering marriage. Although the difficulty that young men found in entering the labor market in the late 1960s and early 1970s was not reflected so much in high levels of youth unemployment, at least for whites, it did cause many young people to take jobs without futures or security and to delay marriage for this reason.

But the major causes of the excess of marriageable women have to do with demography and war. On the average, men are about three years older than women when they begin to consider marriage seriously, and men tend to seek and find partners a few years younger than themselves. But, because of the baby boom, more women of, say, age 19 were arriving on the marriage market each year than were men of age 22 (Glick and Norton, 1977). To add to the imbalance, another 6 percent of all those males who became adults in the decade were sent to Vietnam, and an additional 0.5 percent went into exile abroad or into hiding at home to avoid the draft (Baskir and Strauss, 1978).

All this resulted in delayed marriage as measured by a sharp increase in the proportion of women still single at ages 20 to 24. It is impossible to say how much of this delay would have happened anyway especially because major changes in the attitudes and opportunities of women and in the moral constraints imposed by society were taking place concurrently. Although the comparable figures for the 25- to 30-year-old cohort indicate that a certain amount of this marriage delay is simply short-term postponement, there may be more to the picture than that. According to Glick (1975, p. 23):

> It is too early to predict with confidence that the increase in singleness among the young will lead to an eventual decline in life-time marriage [but], just as cohorts of young women who have postponed childbearing for an unusually long time seldom make up for the child deficit as they grow older, so also young people who are delaying marriage may never make up for the marriage deficit later on. They may try alternatives to marriage and they may like them.

To the extent that marriage in the past served as a stabilizing factor and socialized individuals into conventional adult roles, this means that there were increasing proportions of people not subject to these influences from 1965 to 1975.

TABLE 2-2. **Living Pattern Alternatives in Contemporary American Society**[1]

Living with	% of Total
Spouse and children	42%
Spouse and no children	37
Alone	12
Children only	4
Roommate of same sex	2
Roommate of opposite sex	2
Communal household[2]	1

[1] N = 120 million adults not in institutions in 1977.

[2] But note that most communal households do not meet the more stringent requirements of ideology and commitment necessary to classify them as communes according to the definition used in this book.

Instead of predictable life-cycle stages, youth in the decade we are discussing were faced with a bewildering array of possibly fateful choices. No one pattern of living characterized even a bare majority of adherents by the end of the decade (see Table 2-2). In a certain sense, communes served as tribal reservations for those whose adulthood was put on hold by the events of the decade. During more demographically normal times the cohorts of young people between the ages of 15 and 25 would be absorbed into society largely through participation in the labor force and through marriage and family formation. The communitarianism of 1965-1975 may be partially explained by the failure of the job market and the marriage market to cope with that decade's youth glut.

Two other factors should be mentioned as bearing upon the increase of candidates for communal living that began in about 1965. These are restrictions in the rate of childbearing and increases in the numbers of the unmarried. Lifetime births expected by wives aged 18 to 24 suddenly declined in 1965. After a long period of stability at slightly more than three children, it steadily decreased until about 1975, when it seemed to stabilize at a bit under two children. The decade also witnessed a sharp increase in the proportion of ever-married women under the age of 30 who had no children (Glick and Norton, 1977). As with marriage, some of this is postponement and some represents a decision not to have children at all. In either case, more potential recruits for communes resulted. The childless are more free to experiment, and those with only one child are more in need of extended family peers for their children.

Demographic arguments can be highly misleading if interpreted outside of the context of the given social expectations and social controls of a particular society. For instance, a number of the demographic statements made here apply even more to conditions in the Soviet Union than to those in the United States. And yet the Soviet Union experienced no great wave of commune building during this period. At the other extreme, the demographic profile of Israel seems less conducive to communitarianism than does that of the United States.

And yet Israel leads the world by far in the creation of communes. Demographic factors at best can measure only the communitarian potential of a society. This potential can either be strictly discouraged, as in the Soviet Union, or strongly encouraged and supported, as in Israel, or pretty much left alone to find its own level, as in the United States.

A Restrictive but Tolerant Social Climate

The general public is most aware of a social movement when it is making news. A movement makes news when it disrupts (or threatens to disrupt) the equilibrium of established social institutions. Thus, there is a bias in measuring a social movement's activities by the number of its media citations. As communes have become less radical in their programs, less threatening in their behavior, and less shocking in their morality, they have experienced a rapid decline in newsworthiness. This has led to the widespread impression that communitarianism, as a life-style, has dwindled. Yet there were probably more people living communally in 1979 than at any time in the previous 15 years. However, the virulence of the public response to the movement has declined greatly in these 15 years as communitarianism has evolved from radical social movement to acceptable alternative life-style.

Communitarianism has always had to contend with official rules and regulations and unofficial public reactions. In both these domains, the reception given to the movement has been more negative than positive. In a typically American pattern, the hostility of neighbors and unofficial citizens' groups has been greatest, that of public agencies notably milder, and that of the courts least hostile—at times even friendly. Without a doubt, individual communitarians have sometimes suffered cruelly for their standpoints, and entire communes occasionally have been forced out of existence. But, on the whole, the effect of American society upon communitarianism has been more one of restricting specific behaviors than of blanket prohibition.

Law and Public Policy

Courts and public agencies have made it very clear that communes have the right to exist. The Bill of Rights speaks so plainly on this subject and the historical record is so full of honorable communitarian prototypes that there can be no serious denial of the right of American citizens to assemble peacefully into communes. The situation in which this basic right has been questioned is in the recruitment practices of the mass religious cults. As of this writing, no high court decisions have been passed down pertaining to the right of parents to kidnap their unwilling "children" over the age of 18 from tightly guarded cultic fortresses. Decisions among lower courts have been mixed, depending much upon the philosophy of individual judges, but have tended to deny the rights of parents to conduct such seizures while being equally unwilling to prosecute the parents for kidnapping to anywhere near the full extent of the law. If there is such a thing as brainwashing, as we believe there is, the problems raised by this issue may become critical in the years to come. But, at present, only the plainly inadequate laws pertaining to mental competency are available for such cases, and they have generally been interpreted in favor of the communes.

Zoning. Whether communes have a right to reside in any specific place of their choosing has been open to considerably more question. Zoning laws have regulated land use and life-style in America for over half a century. The constitutionality of these laws has been well established. Although exclusionary zoning, aimed at protecting the class or racial character of a neighborhood, has come under partially successful attack in the 1970s (e.g., *Suburban Action Institute* v. *New Canaan, N. Y.,* 1971), the right of the larger community to designate certain geographical areas for exclusive residential use by families has not been denied.

For this reason, much of the zoning controversy over communes has focused on the legal definition of the family unit. Prior to 1965, religious orders, nursing homes, foster homes, and common-law marriages put forth legal arguments for inclusion within the definition of family, with mixed results. In 1966, a Connecticut court ruled that a Synanon (drug rehabilitation) commune with a population varying from eleven to thirty-four members did not constitute a family and thus was not entitled to occupy the property it had purchased in the town of Westport. The court sidestepped the issue of defining the family by arguing that a legitmate purpose of the local zoning law was to limit population density, so that it could rightfully exclude a commune whose membership fluctuated much more rapidly than did that of any family. But, when a middle-class commune with a stable population attempted to move into a mansion next door to the residence of the governor of Minnesota in 1973, its right to do so was upheld in court on the grounds that it functioned as a family.

In 1973, a California court (later upheld by the state court of appeals) began the task of creating legal distinctions between traditional and voluntary families (*Palo Alto Tenants Union* v. *Morgan*, reported in Henner, 1976):

> There is a long recognized value in the traditional family relationship which does not attach to the "voluntary family." The traditional family is an institution reinforced by biological and legal ties which are difficult, or impossible, to sunder. It plays a role in educating and nourishing the young, which, far from being "voluntary," is often compulsory. Finally, it has been a means, for uncounted millennia, of satisfying the deepest of physical and emotional needs of human beings.

By this time, the *de facto* right of communes to live unobtrusively in neighborhoods zoned for single-family housing had largely been accepted. The decisions cited here and later ones were aimed (defensively) at preventing this form of accommodation from becoming accepted as a fundamental right.

The U. S. Supreme Court issued two important rulings on this subject, one in 1974 and the other in 1977. The first was the famous Belle Terre decision, which affirmed the right of the village of Belle Terre, Long Island, to prohibit a group of six college students from calling themselves a communal family and renting a home. In the majority opinion, Justice William O. Douglas addressed the issue head on:

> A quiet place where yards are wide, people few, and motor vehicles restricted, are legitimate guidelines in a land use project addressed to family needs. . . . The police power is not confined to the elimination of filth, stench, and unhealthy places. It is an attempt to lay out zones where family values, youth values, and the blessings of quiet seclusion and clean air makes the area a sanctuary for people.

This ruling established the right of communities to restrict the use of dwellings by adults not related by kinship.

However, in a second ruling, the Supreme Court (1977) established that zoning regulations did not have the power to define family in such a way that extended kinship groupings were prohibited from occupying single-family dwellings:

> The law has consistently acknowledged a private realm of family life which the state cannot enter. . . . The tradition of uncles, aunts, cousins, and especially grandparents sharing a household has roots equally venerable and equally deserving of constitutional recognition. . . . The Constitution prevents East Cleveland from standardizing its children — and its adults — by forcing all to live in certain narrowly defined family patterns.

This ruling established, in the words of Justice William Brennan, that it is unconstitutional to define family as confined to parents and parents' own children.

A New Jersey Supreme Court ruling, in 1979, went still further in liberalizing the definition of what is meant by family. The court declared unconstitutional all zoning ordinances that set limits on the number of unrelated persons who could share a house. The majority opinion argued that "regulations based on biological or legal relationships of individuals in many cases do not reflect the real world . . . [and] that as long as a group bore the generic character of a family unit as a relatively permanent household, it should be equally as entitled to occupy a single family dwelling as its biologically related neighbors." (Sullivan, 1979, p. 1).

The many legal battles over zoning regulation of communes ended in a kind of stalemate. Many local jurisdictions ceased to care. Communes lost their battle to establish their unquestioned identities as families. On the other hand, it became clear that towns and neighborhoods wishing to exclude communes would have to show reasonable cause and often would have to be willing to endure lengthy legal disputes.

Communal Ownership of Property. All communes face the problem of property ownership. Although any commune may incorporate, communes, in and of themselves, do not have the legal standing that corporations have to act and be treated as economic persons. In fact, very few communes in America have chosen to incorporate (13 percent of those in the current study). Incorporation requires specification of lines of authority that many communes have felt to be antithetical to their ideological purposes. Also, corporations protect the rights of particular people, whereas it is often some abstract ideal that communitarians are concerned to protect. There is no way, however, in American law, for property to be owned by an ideal.

TABLE 2-3. Communes by Location and Means of Property Ownership

	Urban		Rural	
	Number	% of Total	Number	% of Total
Trusteeship	0	0%	7	12%
Corporate ownership	5	9	11	18
Other collective ownership	2	3	3	5
Owned by one or a few members	9	15	20	33
Rental	40	68	9	15
Squatting or mining claim	0	0	4	7
Outside agency	2	3	6	10
Other or mixed	1	2	0	0
Total	59	100%	60	100%

In this regard, the trusteeship form of ownership deserves specific comment. It is statistically rare among the communes we have studied (see Table 2-3), but it is the form that has been associated with some of the most successful communitarian ventures (e.g., Seventh-Day Adventist communes in the United States, kibbutzim in Israel). In a trusteeship, the title to one or more communes is vested in a board whose members may be legally obliged to assure that it be used for the attainment of some ideal. Communes generally lease their land from this board of trustees (which may or may not include members of the commune itself). Trustees then regulate the kinds of activities that occur on the land and, significantly, the amount of money the commune needs to pay to a departing member. This can be and frequently is considerably less than the member may have put into the commune. In some cases, boards of trustees have been able to purchase land at bargain prices before people were ready to move onto it and have been able to hold this land until a commune was ready for it. In other cases, communes turned the title of their own land over to a board of trustees, not wishing to be tempted to engage in real estate speculation.

The trusteeship is the only form of landholding currently recognized in

American law in which land or property does not ultimately belong to a specific individual or individuals. It comes closest to the notion of land or property held in trust for an ideal and thus seems particularly appropriate for groups whose structure revolves around the furtherance of ideals.*

Food Subsidies. In addition to their battle for zoning rights, communes fought and won the right to subsidized food. We have already seen that the beginning of the food stamp program, in 1964, was one of the events that ushered in the communitarian decade. Although the majority of communes studied never considered applying for or accepting food stamps, a significant minority did so and many more were concerned that mere commune membership not deprive them of the right. Furthermore, this effective national insurance against hunger provided a social climate very conducive to risky communal experimentation.

In 1971, Congress ammended the food stamp program to exclude from participation any household containing an individual who was unrelated to any other household member (Henner, 1976). Congressional debate over the bill made it clear that its purpose was to exclude hippie communes and thus mollify certain severe critics of the food stamp program as a whole. A federal district court immediately issued a restraining order against this legislation and, in 1973, the Supreme Court declared it unconstitutional:

> For if the constitutional conception of "equal protection of the laws" means anything, it must at the very least mean that a bare congressional desire to harm a politically unpopular group cannot constitute a *legitimate* government interest. As a result, [a] purpose to discriminate against hippies cannot, in and of itself and without reference to (some independent) considerations in the public interest, justify the 1971 amendment.

The right of commune members to participate fully in government welfare programs involving the distribution of food or other goods or services has by now been fully established.

Child Custody. Aside from shelter and food, the issue most threatening to communes in their relationship to the law has been child custody. Because many commune members are divorced men or women with children whose former spouses do not live in communes, the issue has been whether commune membership per se should be admissible evidence against the fitness of a parent to have custody. Many such cases have been decided in local courts.

---

*Lou Gottlieb, founder of Morningstar Ranch in California, undoubtedly had the same notion in mind when he deeded his own land to God, in trust for his commune. But this transfer was disallowed under California law.

Because few, if any, cases have been appealed, it is impossible to delineate a general legal position on this matter. However, the great majority of specific cases that have come to light have been ones in which commune mothers have lost custody of their children. In none of these cases was commune membership itself cited as a reason. Instead, various aspects of specific communes — high membership turnover, drug use, unsanitary living conditions, and so on — were cited. It should be noted, however, that, unlike zoning or food stamp decisions, custody decisions have only a specific reference. Because they do not make the news, such decisions will come to light only if they have a certain shock value. It may well be that the cases that have been publicized are sharply different from those cases in which custody was awarded to the communal parent.

Government Aid. We have been talking of hindrances to communes on the part of legal and administrative agencies. But, in a few cases, communes have been helped by the government as well. In the 1940s, the government supported collective farms as an aid to rural reconstruction after the Depression. In 1943, a bill before Congress to "prohibit the use of funds for carrying on any experiment in collective farming except the liquidation of any such project heretofore initiated" was defeated in Congress. But the fact that the bill even came to a vote reflects the suspicion with which America has always regarded anything communal. In 1970, the federal government briefly experimented with providing grants to communes for various purposes ranging from rural reconstruction to urban drug rehabilitation. But these were criticized and have since disappeared. In summary, it seems reasonable to say that the attitude of the government toward communes has hovered between mild restriction and benign neglect but that the federal court system has often had to intervene to prevent communes from receiving harsher treatment at the hands of local authorities and courts.

Public Opinion

The amount of public attention paid to communes and the virulence of society's reaction to them have far exceeded the attention given them by the courts and public agencies. Several communes were destroyed by arson during or after the period of the study. In one rural commune in Arizona, all members were severely beaten by hostile neighbors in a late night attack, and many other communes were threatened. Another commune in the Appalachia cluster was repeatedly dynamited. Many communitarians have been shunned, refused admission to local shops, or spat at during visits to nearby towns. Many urban communes have been sued for zoning violations, some have been threatened by neighbors, and one Houston commune was harassed by both the Ku Klux Klan and the local police in the same week.

FIGURE 2-1. **American Attitudes Toward Social Movements—Annually Since 1972: Proportion Favorable to Each Movement According to Yankelovich Annual Survey**

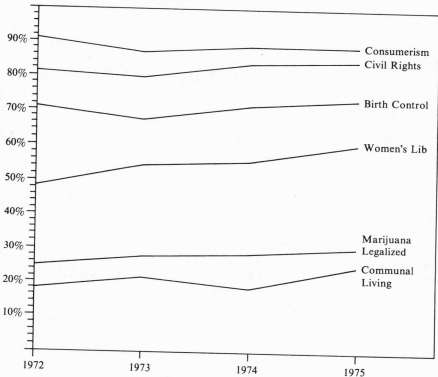

A study of the attitudes of a national sample of American adults* (18 years old and over) shows communitarianism to have been consistently unpopular among the public at large (Figure 2-1). The study, replicated annually between 1972 and 1975, measures American attitudes toward a variety of social movements.

Consumerism is and has remained the most popular of these movements, with about 90 percent of the population recording favorable attitudes. Consumerism is followed, in descending order of favor, by the civil rights movement, the birth control movement, women's liberation, the movement for the legaliza-

*The survey asks the following question: "Many changes have taken place in this country over the past ten years. These changes have frequently resulted from social movements of various kinds. Some of the movements and the issues raised by them have received wide support from the public. Others have been less popular. We are interested in your own opinions. For each of these movements and/or issues I mention, tell me whether you are completely for it, more for it than against, more against it than for it, or completely against it." *Current Opinion* 2 (September 1974): 98–99.

tion of marijuana, and, finally, communal living. The general pattern is stable, but the commune movement has experienced the greatest proportional increase, going from 14 percent approval to 21 percent approval during the years 1974–1975.

Communal living is looked on more favorably by males than by females and more favorably by the young than the old. For example, in 1975, 34 percent of those in the 18- to 24-year-old bracket were very much opposed to communal living, whereas 70 percent of those in the 45- to 54-year-old bracket were so opposed. In general, opposition to communal living increased steadily with increasing age. Surprisingly, in view of their virtual absence from the communal living scene, nonwhites have been more favorably disposed to communal living than whites. This, however, may reflect nonwhites' generally more positive attitude toward social movements and may be a spillover effect from their vastly more favorable attitude toward the civil rights movements in the four preceding years.

Attitudes toward communitarianism varied by region with familiarity breeding greater tolerance. By 1975, respondents living in the West showed by far the lowest degree of opposition to communal living, and those in the North Central states (where communes are relatively sparse) showed the greatest. In 1974, data were also available by urbanicity. They showed that 88 percent of all those living in nonmetropolitan areas were opposed to communal living as compared with only 75 percent in metropolitan areas opposed.

Communal living as a temporary life-style for unattached young people has generally received far more approval than communitarianism as a permanent commitment. In 1971 Yankelovich asked a national sample of college students whether they would be interested in living communally themselves (Havighurst, 1975, p. 219). Fifty-one percent said that they were not at all interested, 31 percent expressed interest in communal living for a short period of time, and only 5 percent expressed interest in communal living as a permanent style of life.

In general, since 1975, society has slowly come to a greater acceptance of communes. At the same time, the meaning of communitarianism has undergone change in the minds of the commune participants. As commune members themselves have come to look more benignly upon the larger society, the larger society has also come to look more tolerantly upon communes.

A Sample of American Communes

We come now to a major point of departure in our analysis. Thus far in this chapter, we have been standing off as if at a great distance and looking at the communitarian movement as a whole. It is now time to take a closer look at the communes themselves. To do so we must draw a relatively small but representative sample from the population of thousands of communes that existed in America during the period 1965–1975.

As we zoom in for a closer observation of commune life, it may be hard to avoid the impression that communes are isolated little worlds unto themselves. It should be clear from our discussion so far that they are not. Communes are born and die, commune members come and go, but they do so within the context of a larger social movement's interactions with a still larger society. For example, it should be useful to bear in mind that the urban subsample of the communes studied was investigated during the years 1974–1976 and beyond. While it is doubtful that our general findings would have been much different if the urban subsample had been as thoroughly dispersed over the decade as the rural subsample, it is possible that many specific details would have been different had the urban groups been studied during the movement's early years rather than during the years of its decline.

Twelve Geographical Areas

The choice of the twelve specific geographical areas to be studied was made according to an evolving plan: the goal was to capture in particular as much as possible of the unobservable whole. Six clusters of rural counties, densely settled with communes, were selected for analysis, and these were later matched by six large Standard Metropolitan Statistical Areas (SMSAs). As Figure 2-2 indicates, these geographical areas are widely distributed throughout the continental United States. Most of the rural field work was completed before the urban phase was begun, or even thought of, reflecting a historical change in the center of gravity of the communitarian movement as the decade wore on. (See Appendix A)

The areas of dense communal concentration in the United States are not haphazard. Regular patterns of settlement are to be found both within larger rural areas and among the neighborhoods within metropolitan areas. Contemporary communitarianism can be regarded, in part, as an ecological response to

FIGURE 2-2.   Urban SMSAs and Rural Clusters of Counties Where Research on Communes in This Book Was Carried Out

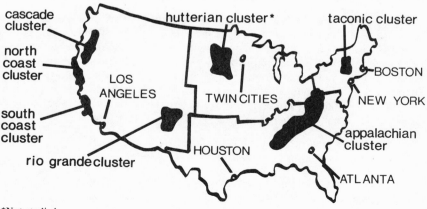

*Not studied.

demographic changes occurring in the composition and distribution of the American population. To simplify a complex phenomenon by stating it in terms of ecological causes alone, the placement of rural communes can be looked at as a response to the availability of marginal land caused by the transition from family farming to corporate farming. We should thus expect to find rural communes in places where more land is being withdrawn from agriculture than is the norm. Urban communes can be looked at as a response to the availability of marginal housing in big cities, caused by the suburbanization of the upper and middle classes and the diminishing proportion of families with more than two children. We should thus expect to find urban communes in the wake of the suburban exodus.

Figure 2-3 illustrates an attempt to test these ecological hypothesis with available census data. Figure 2-3A shows that, during the period under investigation, in all but one of the six regions, a good deal more land was withdrawn from farming than was withdrawn in the surrounding region of the country. The one exception is accounted for by noting that this is a cluster of counties directly south of San Francisco, which was largely exurbanized in the 1960s. Figure 2-3B shows that there is a much higher ratio of poverty to owner-occupied homes in census tracts in which communes have been located than in the SMSA as a whole. We take this ratio to be an indicator of decaying single-family housing. The hypothesis is substantiated for every city except Boston, a city in which communes are dispersed to an unusually great degree.

With the exception of Boston, each of the cities in our sample developed, during the decade 1965–1975, one or two areas of dense communitarian settlement. In Atlanta, first Tenth Street and later the Grant Park section became known for their communes. In Houston, Montrose and Houston Heights were the neighborhoods. Venice and parts of Santa Monica served this function in Los Angeles, as did the West Bank in Minneapolis, and the Lower East Side and the Upper West Side in New York. A long-time observer of the Twin Cities "hippie" scene reported the following rather typical occurrence:

> One "scene" on the West Bank revolved around a sort of legendary character named Red Nelson and an apartment house of twelve units. The building was torn down in 1965, but for about five to six years before demolition it served as an extended family for the residents. Red was somehow able to take charge of renting and rented to all his friends. So what followed was a period of people living in separate units, partying in Red's apartment, and sharing and building a minicommunity. People helped each other out, would just visit for breakfast, share problems. . . .

A Los Angeles field worker, on the other hand, reported the following about a very different face of communitarianism:

> I noticed, arriving at the commune, that the entire neighborhood that they lived in was an old, well-established area, previously very wealthy, with the older houses having finely manicured lawns, etc. The Georgian house was no

FIGURE 2-3. Testing Ecological Hypotheses About Communal Stability

A. Proportion of Land Withdrawn from Farming, 1964-1969, in National Regions Compared with Clusters of Counties within Those Regions with High Concentrations of Communes

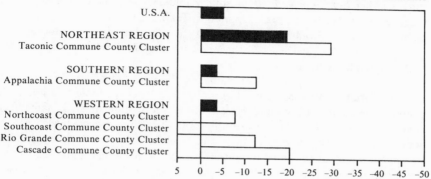

Proportional Difference Acreage in Farming 1969 as Compared with 1964

B. Ratio of Families below Poverty Level to Percentage of Homes That Are Owner Ocupied in SMSAs Compared with Clusters of Census Tracts in Which Identified Communes Are Located

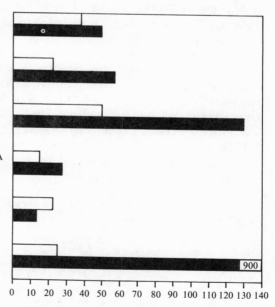

Ratio of Proportion of Families Below Poverty Line
to Proportion of Homes That Are Owner Occupied (1974)

exception to this. Perhaps one of the largest, it was built of wooden shingle construction, dark brown, with a well-tended front yard and flower bed surrounding the grass.

But, whether *lumpenproletariat* or solidly middle class, one ecological fact remains constant for most urban communes. Taking advantage of a general demographic shift away from large families and the need for very large houses, they were utilizing urban space which had become oversized for ordinary contemporary urban households.

By narrowing our study of communes to the places in which they are most densely scattered, we achieve what is probably the best possible solution to the dilemma posed by the boundlessness of the social movement. Isolated rural communes and small town and medium-sized city communes are neglected. But enough variation is preserved to maintain a feel for ecological variety within the movement while, at the same time, the density of clusterings allows us to train our attention on a reasonably large number of specific communes for a reasonably long period of time.

One Hundred and Twenty Communes

Ten communes were selected from each of the six rural clusters and ten from each of the six SMSAs to yield a total of 120 communes to be followed closely for at least one year.* The 120 communes chosen for close investigation do not constitute a probability sample of all communes generated by the communitarian movement in America between the years 1965 and 1975. Probability sampling requires the ability to enumerate all of the cases in the population from which the sample is to be drawn. But the difficulties involved in estimating the number of communes existing in the United States at any one time are well known and probably insurmountable. The Census Bureau, by its own admission, was not well prepared for the job of locating and identifying communal households in its 1970 census.† The absence of census data, and of any official federation of American communes, contributes to our lack of reliable statistical data concerning the commune movement.

---

*In fact, a third wave of data was collected from the urban communes (Aidala, 1976) two years after the initial contact. A basic core of information concerning communal survival, relocation, births, deaths, marriages, membership turnover, and leadership change has been updated at yearly intervals ever since the study formally ended, and this will probably continue until the sample is extinct.

†The U. S. Bureau of the Census has undertaken procedures to enumerate communal households. Field techniques are currently being pretested in anticipation of a full enumeration in 1980. The experience of 1970, however, should be taken as an important object lesson in the importance of informing even the most comprehensive of social data-collecting operations with a certain amount of sociological knowledge. Because the Census Bureau was officially ignorant of communes in 1970, it rarely found any, although there were thousands. I, myself, had the experience of seeing how this ignorance worked, firsthand. I was present at an urban commune in Berkeley in 1970, doing research, when the census taker arrived at the front door. The front door of this communal house opened directly

The study of sixty rural communes was begun in 1965 and was carried out in intermittent stages until 1975. The study was not pursued in all six rural areas simultaneously. The Taconic and the Appalachian areas were studied during the period 1965–1966 and 1973–1975. The Cascade, Northcoast, Southcoast, and Rio Grande areas were studied between the years 1966 and 1973. In the rural areas, enough time as a participant-observer was spent in each region to ensure that virtually all communes with a public identity within the region were at least enumerated. The one exception to this rule, because of its great size, is the Appalachian region, where only selected counties were thoroughly covered. The criteria of selection for the ten communes within each of the six rural areas were intuitively based upon a broad knowledge of the communes in the areas in an attempt to make them as typical as possible of the range of communes to be found in that region.

The urban phase of the study was begun in five of the six SMSAs in August 1974. In each urban area, prior to the study, an informal census of the communes was undertaken. On the basis of these censuses certain characteristics of communes in each city were determined, such as location within the city, ideology type, population size, presence or absence of children, and year of founding. The ten communes to be studied within each city were not randomly selected from the census list. Instead, an attempt was made to let the sample be as representative of the census as possible with respect to the characteristics just mentioned. In each SMSA, a set of ten communes was selected in such a way as to minimize the differences between the distribution of the characteristics given in the set as compared with the larger census. The sample is thus weighted by location* and by the distribution of key commune characteristics in each city insofar as these are accurately estimated by the census. (Further information on the relationship between the census and the sample of communes in each area may be found in Appendix A.)

The rural-urban distinction is fundamental, but there is also, within the sample, ecological variation within each of these categories. Of the rural communes, the majority (65 percent) occupied working farms. Nine of them lived

---

into the largest room in the house, and, in the style of that time and place, it was almost completely covered with wall-to-wall mattresses. The census taker was invited in and proceeded to interview the only commune member who happened to be home at the time, while I sat and watched. Also, in the style of that time and place, the commune member responded to the interview by inventing a fantasy household based upon what must have been his conception of the typical American household, with himself as the head. What is significant about this incident is not the respondent's deception, but the census taker's complete credulousness. If he saw the obvious signs of communal life all around him, they clearly made no impression because they had no symbolic referent.

*Because ten communes were selected from each city, the probability of a commune's being included from an SMSA with many communes was less than the probability of its being included from an SMSA with fewer communes. For example, using the preliminary census as a measure of commune density within an SMSA, any given commune in Houston was four times as likely to be included in the sample as any given commune in Boston. This is what is meant by the sample's being weighted by location.

in what could only be called wilderness land, and, of these, four communes claimed no more than squatters' rights to the territory. Six of the rural communes were located in villages and were engaged in some form of craft production and trade.

Among the urban communes, almost half were found in the inner-city slums or "transitional neighborhoods." Another third of the urban communes were located within city limits but not in the inner city. Twenty percent of the communes classified as urban were actually located in the suburban areas of the SMSAs. Surburban communes were found in each of the six urban areas, and these were classified as "urban" for the purposes of this study. The great majority (80 percent) of urban communal housing was detached or semidetached single-family housing. Only in New York City did the majority of communes occupy row houses and apartment houses. Among those communes not found in the inner city, neighborhoods were characterized as follows: working class, 31 percent; middle class, 56 percent; upper class, 13 percent.

A majority of the communes selected for study had been in existence for more than one year at the time of initial contact. Several were just getting started, and one, at the other extreme, had already been in existence for twenty-eight years. All but 8 of the 120 groups, however, were founded in the years between 1965 and 1975.

Table 2-4 lists each commune by region, year contacted, year of founding, and year of demise. Where a year of demise is not given, the commune was still in existence in 1978. The names given for each commune are pseudonyms. Where the same name appears more than once in different regions (e.g., Spectra in Atlanta and Spectra in Boston), the communes are part of a larger federation and take their names from that federation. They are still, however, treated in this study as separate communes (see Appendix A).

Effects of Location

Communitarianism emerged in America in the 1960s as a nationwide social movement. But, in its finer details, it was shaped by specific local conditions. Each of the twelve geographical regions drew its supply of members from a somewhat distinct pool. Each placed somewhat distinct constraints of environment and custom upon its communal settlements. Each provided an economic environment that, through both constraint and opportunity, affected the stability of the communes within it.

Rural communes did not, in general, draw their members from the local countryside but largely from cities and suburbs. These migrations began at different times. The Rio Grande communes were largely a product of migrations from California and, to a lesser extent, from the East Coast in 1967 and 1968. The Cascade region communes were a product of similar migrations from California, from the East, and, to some degree, from the Midwest in 1968 and 1969. The Taconic region was populated almost entirely by East Coast communitarians from the large Atlantic seaboard cities, in contrast to the Appalachian cluster which attracted its members from all parts of the nation.

The urban communes got started somewhat later except in New York and San Francisco. Local informants agree that communes did not arrive in any appreciable numbers in Minneapolis until around 1969 or in Atlanta and Houston until 1970 and 1971. The Houston counterculture particularly has suffered from a consciousness of having lagged behind the rest of the nation by several years. (One informant attributed the relative lack of Houstonian success in communal counterculture ventures to the belief that social movements and innovative ideas arrive in Houston only after they have run out of steam elsewhere.)

Although Atlanta also lagged behind the coastal cities by several years, its situation is complicated by the fact that the Southeast was the principal breeding ground of a rudimentary communal movement (1946–1954). Thus, when the counterculture began there was already more of a traditional basis for communitarianism in the southern Appalachian area than in any other part of the country.*

Rural differences became exaggerated as their stereotypical reputations served as magnets, selectively attracting recruits from differing personality stocks. For example, rural communes on the north California coastline could in general be characterized as anarchistic, violent, individualistic, and highly practical. Those in the Rio Grande Valley, by way of contrast, were characterized as spiritual, hierarchical, and matriarchal. Similar self-perpetuating labels came to characterize, within the counterculture, each of the six rural areas in the study.

Each city also displayed unique communal characteristics. Often these conform to the stereotype of the city itself. Atlanta communes, for example, seemed in general to be gracious, relaxed, patriarchal, and relatively stable. Los Angeles communes appeared individualistic, busy, egalitarian, and relatively unstable. A stronger heritage of cooperative values could be observed in Minneapolis than, say, in New York.

One result of membership recruitment from geographically distinct pools is that the personal background characteristics of the members of the communes in our sample show distinct regional differences. These are greatest, of course, for the sixty rural communes as a group as contrasted to the sixty urban communes. For example, urban commune members were six times more likely to have been born in the same state as the one in which the commune was located. Rural commune members tended to be older (30 years as opposed to 25 years mean age). Fifty-nine percent of the urban sample grew up in an urban area as opposed to only 47 percent of the rural sample. Lesser distinctions could be observed among the individual regions. The Boston communes, for example, drew 85 percent of their membership from outside the state of Massachusetts, whereas the

*Minneapolis and St. Paul, drawing on the Minnesota tradition of radical cooperative organization, parallel this situation in some ways.

TABLE 2-4. Years of Duration of Communes in the Sample[1]

	Time 1	Duration[2]		Time 1	Duration[2]
Rural Communes					
North Coast			Cascade Mts.		
Homestead	1967	1966–1970	Liberation	1968	1966–1975
Astar	1969	1968–1969	Snowcap	1969	1967–1973
Ashram	1971	1969–	Goldrush	1968	1968–1969
The Family	1972	1971–1973	Hobbithole	1968	1967–1969
Philosophy	1968	1967–1968	Pillowrock	1969	1968–
Wholewheat	1968	1968–1971	Bringyerown	1970	1970–1973
Waystation	1972	1970–	Holyriver	1971	1948–
Freehaven	1971	1967–1977	El Dorado	1971	1969–
Poictesme	1968	1967–1969	Mantra Flower	1971	1967–
Christian Hotel	1968	1951–	Oldbridge	1968	1968–
South Coast			Taconic		
Riverside	1968	1967–1968	Rockypoint	1969	1967–1969
Sylvan Hills	1966	1965–1967	Headhaven	1965	1965–1968
Flowing Water	1969	1966–	Ecology	1974	1972–1974
Barnyard	1972	1970–1978	Dry Creek	1967	1967–1967
Real Time	1966	1965–1970	Halfway	1965	1950–[a]
Mountainside	1966	1966–	Lemoncake	1971	1969–1971
Wellwisher	1972	1963–1972	Ahimsa	1965	1960–1976[a]
Big Daddy	1971	1971–1973	Dawn	1966	1966–1967
Steep Meadow	1972	1970–1974	Old Farm	1965	1964–
The Temple	1969	1968–1969	Grey Rainbow	1971	1968–1975
Rio Grande			Appalachia		
Zodiac Village	1968	1966–1973	New Beginnings	1965	1937–
Big Dome	1968	1967–1968	Steepacres	1965	1965–
Shady Lady	1968	1966–1974	Eaglenest	1968	1967–1968
Mandala	1968	1967–	Sky Lovers	1972	1971–
Boonesboro	1969	1968–	Vanguard	1969	1967–
Sunflower	1969	1969–1971	Gospeltown	1965	1942–
Gray Eden	1969	1969–1971	Ruskinville	1972	1970–
The Old Fort	1968	1967–1971	Weather Station	1972	1971–1976
Mesa Camp	1968	1968–1975	Avatarlove	1969	1968–
Earth Mother	1968	1967–	Deep Root	1974	1974–1978

Urban Communes

	Time 1	Duration[2]		Time 1	Duration[2]
Atlanta			**Houston**		
RMC Commune	1974	1971–	Hillbrush	1974	1973–
Loch Lomond	1974	1973–	Gable House	1974	1973–1976
Southern Comfort	1974	1974–	Nightingale	1974	1973–
Alabama Avenue	1974	1973–	Belleview	1974	1969–
Love from Above	1974	1972–	Third Eye	1974	1970–
Youth and Truth	1974	1974–1976	Youth and Truth	1974	1974–?
Spectra	1974	1973–1975	Grandesur	1974	1970–1977
Icthus	1974	1974–1975	Clementine	1974	1974–1976
Karp House	1974	1974–	Cove Community	1974	1974–1977
Old Plantation	1974	1974–1975	Metamorfis	1974	1968–
New York			**Twin Cities**		
Brownstone House	1974	1970–1978	Needle's Eye	1974	1973–
Love from Above	1974	1973–1976	Sill's House	1974	1971–1975
United Lotus	1974	1966–	Love from Above	1974	1972–
Nickel Island	1974	1972–1977	The Dove	1974	1972–1976
Beaux Arts	1974	1971–1976	West End	1974	1974–1977
Siddhartha	1974	1973–1975	White Tower	1974	1971–1978
Derek's	1974	1974–1975	Joy of God	1974	1973–
Workers of the World	1974	1973–	Thorn and Thistle	1974	1971–
Youth and Truth	1974	1974–1975	Youth and Truth	1974	1974–?
Roanoke Commune	1974	1972–1977	Elm Tree	1974	1970–1974
Los Angeles			**Boston**		
Nova Vita	1974	1970–	Treetop House	1975	1973–
Red River	1974	1970–1977	Delmonico House	1975	1973–
Small Planet	1974	1971–	Embarcadero	1975	1973–1977
Utopia House	1974	1972–1974	Kingston Kamp	1975	1972–1975
Driftwood	1974	1973–	Zephyra	1975	1974–1976
Liberty House	1974	1969–	The Summit	1975	1972–1975
Love from Above	1974	1974–	Third Eye	1975	1972–
Youth and Truth	1974	1973–1975	Love from Above	1975	1972–
Habakkuk House	1974	1973–1975	Youth and Truth	1975	1974–1975
Workers of the World	1974	1973–1974	Spectra	1975	1972–1977

[1] All names of contemporary communes in the sample are fictitious.
[2] Open-ended dates indicate communes still in existence as of August 1978.
[a] Approximate founding date.

Twin Cities communes drew only 46 percent of their members from outside of the state of Minnesota. In general, however, background differences by region were not great enough to be a persisting area of concern for the study (see Appendix A).

Just as the pool of members was somewhat different in each region, so was the pool of neighbors and neighborhoods. Communes have had to adapt to local environmental constraints. These adaptations have been particularly marked for urban communes, more constrained as they are by population density and physical environment; for example, the adaptation to scarcity of space in New York City, to strict public morality in Atlanta, and to high geographical mobility in Los Angeles. Such adaptations do not affect communal stability, but they do constrain life-style choices within the communes.

New York was the only city in which communal groups seeking a place to live were not able to find ready access to large decaying mansions abandoned by a vanishing urban aristocracy. For the most part, communes, especially those in Manhattan, have had to adapt to apartment living. The most interesting example of this phenomenon occurs in the Spectra Commune in New York.* Spectra rents six apartments in a luxury high-rise building on the East Side of Manhattan. The apartment house has a doorman and strict security precautions. Within the building, therefore, the Spectra members feel free to leave their apartment doors open, and this allows members to circulate freely throughout the "community." Interestingly, the apartments are so similar in decor that it was at times difficult for us to tell one from another. It seems likely that this similarity provides a sense of continuity and community to the communal home, even though it is physically separated into nonadjacent apartments. The property agent has carefully worked out a quota of apartments in the same building that may be rented by Spectra, estimated so that the commune may approach but not exceed the threshold of New York City anonymity. At the time of the study, the Spectrans did not believe that the other tenants in the building were aware of their corporate identity as a commune.

Atlanta was the one city in our sample where moral standards did not condone unmarried men and women living together freely. This has resulted in a kind of adaptation on the part of those Atlanta communes concerned with public opinion; there are nominally separate houses, or sections of the same house, for men and women, but they are actually pretty well integrated into a close communal life. Although field observation has not indicated that such formal separation interferes with communal life, sociometric indicators suggest a greater division of labor and a greater pattern of cliquish interaction between men and women in Atlanta than in the other five cities. But this might also be due to cultural factors.

In Los Angeles, the adaptation to a high rate of geographic mobility has

*Spectra in New York City was not selected as one of the 120 communes in the sample. But it is ideologically similar (see Chapter 5) to the Spectra communes in Atlanta and Boston, which are in the sample.

provided a peculiar institution of intracommunal subletting, a phenomenon that appeared only in this city of all those studied. This is a transaction which occurs when a commune member going away for a period of time sublets his or her place in the communal household to an outside person. This person is then subject to only minimal screening procedures before being accepted by the house. Such subletting, while it exists in other cities, is much less straight-forward and entails far more active scrutiny by the other communes members.

Finally, and perhaps most significantly, communes exist within regional or urban economies. No commune in our sample was completely self-sufficient economically. All were dependent upon markets to buy and sell or at least to barter. Urban communes, in addition, were dependent upon local economies for employment.

Regional economy seemed to have a slight but measurable effect upon communal stability. Houston is an interesting case because it was booming during the test year of 1974–1975 while all the other cities were suffering economic recession. On virtually all economic indicators, Houston was experiencing economic expansion, while other cities were contracting. Houston was also the only one of the six cities studied in which no commune disbanded during the test year.

The Houston Chamber of Commerce estimated that Houston was growing by immigration alone at the rate of one thousand people per week (*U. S. News and World Report,* 1975). The economic prosperity of the Houston area may be one factor involved in the extraordinarily low degree of societal alienation experienced by Houston communitarians as opposed to those in other cities. For example, in response to the question from the Srole Anomia Scale, "In spite of what some people say, the lot of the average person is getting worse, not better," 71 percent of the commune population of Twin Cities agreed, whereas only 28 percent of those in Houston agreed. The comparable figures for the commune population as a whole were 55 percent and, for a NORC sample of the American population as a whole, 61 percent. To another such question from the Harris Alienation Scale, "The rich get richer and the poor get poorer," 91 percent of those in Minneapolis but only 59 percent of those in Houston agreed.

The relationship of the prosperity of the surrounding area to communal stability is reversed for rural and urban areas. In rural areas, outlying poverty is associated with communal stability. Appalachia (the poorest region) has the lowest rate of disintegration. South Coast (the wealthiest area, and the one with the lowest unemployment) has the highest rate of disintegration. For urban groups, the opposite is true. Houston, the city with the lowest unemployment, had no disintegrating communes during the test year. Los Angeles, New York, and Boston, the cities with the highest unemployment, had three disintegrations each. The other two cities were intermediate on both employment and rate of commune disintegration.

The likely reason for this reversal becomes clear if we compare the dependency of rural and urban communitarians on outside jobs. Whereas 46 percent of the urban sample was employed in regular full-time jobs, only 4 percent of the rural sample was so employed. The austere self-sufficiency of rural communitarianism will be perceived as less of a relative deprivation to the members to the extent that the surrounding territory is also impoverished, whereas the lack of dependence on jobs prevents this regional poverty from harming the commune economically. Urban communes, however, are frequently dependent on members' salaries and wages from jobs and thus are highly vulnerable to a fluctuating job market.

Conclusions

In this chapter, we have explored some of the historical, cultural, demographic, and ecological background of the specific communitarian experiments that will be the object of our investigations for the remainder of this book. We have established the fact that there was a distinct social movement in America, beginning in 1965 and disappearing about ten years later that resulted in the establishment of thousands of rural and urban communes in all parts of the United States. We saw that the ending of the communitarian social movement did not mean that communes themselves disappeared. On the contrary, they became more numerous than ever, but as a manifestation of an alternative lifestyle, rather than a social movement.

The evidence presented in this chapter leads us to conclude that, despite a number of important idiosyncracies, the communitarian movement of the period 1965–1975 is best seen not as a unique historical phenomenon but as a part of the recurrent tradition of utopian communitarianism which has repeatedly flourished in the interstices of Western civilization over the last two millenia. It is now time that we open the door and take a look at the communes and the commune members themselves.

Come along in then, little girl!
Or else stay out!
But in the open door she stands,
And bites her lip and twists her hands,
And stares upon me trouble-eyed:
"Mother," she says, "I can't decide.
I can't decide!"

Edna St. Vincent Millay

CHAPTER 3

Joiners, Stayers, and Leavers

Who are the people who have chosen to direct their energies to communitarian experiments? David Plath has defined them in terms of their world views (1971, pp. xii ff):

> Taking a cue from Max Weber's studies of the great religions, we might pose the problem in this way: What circumstances inspire men to choose utopian rather than other conceivable forms of world rejection? . . .
>
> In contrast to, say, the hermit or the migrant, the utopian rejects his world by seeking to transform it. His rejection is wedded to a demand for domestic action, for he does not believe—like the chiliast—that a new life will transpire by divine machination or by the working out of automatic dialectics of history.

There is a certain truth in this, but more needs to be said. Communitarian recruits are driven by personal needs at least as much as by ideal purposes. The need to belong, the need for family, the need for communion, and, most important, as we shall see, the need for preference crystallization all contribute to the attraction of the individual to communal living. Moreover, lack of preference crystallization is reflected in a sense of uncertainty and indecisiveness, among commune members, that characterizes not only their acts of joining, but their acts of staying, and of leaving as well.

This chapter has been organized around the following questions: (1) What kinds of people join communes? (2) How does one go about joining a commune? (3) How is a person's behavior affected by living communally? (4) What factors influence the decision to quit living communally? (5) What happens to former communitarians after they stop living communally?

Because of the wide-ranging nature of these concerns, it may be useful to summarize the findings at the beginning. We shall see that there is great diversity in the communitarian population. Members come from all parts of the country, from every social and economic level, and they range in age from 15 to 78. Nevertheless, certain patterns emerge. Many communitarians are young, white, middle children from intact middle-class homes. Most are alienated from themselves and confused. A minority, however, are utterly convinced that they know how they (and others) should live. Virtually all share the need to reduce the world (especially the world of choice) to a manageable size. Less than half join for predominantly ideological reasons, but, among those who do, a substantial number radiate the power and inspiration (to varying degrees) of charismatic vision. We find that, by nineteenth-century standards, admission to a commune is very easy to achieve. The actual patterns of recruitment and admission depend to a great extent upon the organization of charismatic authority or the lack of it.

Individual behavior changes in a variety of ways in the course of communal living. The most important of these changes has to do with the diffusion of affection. The inability, in communes, to focus love upon a single specific other (with the possible exception of the charismatic leader) makes it difficult for marriages to survive in communal settings.

This conflict between dyadic love and communal stability is seen to be the principal structural contradiction of communal organization. Being loved is found to be the surest way to bond people to the commune, but the diffusion of love (either sexual or nonsexual) toward the limiting case of all-inclusiveness is, at the same time, the surest way to drive people out. It is further seen that the maintenance of some degree of psychic distance of the self from the commune is helpful in preventing membership attrition.

We find that about half the commune members leave per year. Communes vary considerably from one another in annual attrition rate, but this important topic of investigation is not treated until Chapter 4. In this chapter, the focus is on individual leavers. Many of these went on to join other communes. Those that chose to return to noncommunal life appeared to find it easy to reenter conventional life situations. The self-esteem of the leavers increased more than the self-esteem of the stayers. Alienation from American society decreased more for the leavers than for the stayers. Whatever else their function, then, it can be argued that communes can serve to aid in the transition from traditional youth to traditional adult roles for those who wish such a transition. Communes can sometimes be places in which people on their way to dropping out can temporarily intermingle with people on their way back in from social roles more deviant than communitarianism.

Having summarized our major findings let us turn to a systematic investigation of communitarianism as an individual-level phenomenon. The careers of the members of the 120 communes in our sample now take center stage. But not merely their communal careers. Childhood, adolescence, and precommunal adulthood round out the picture, and, for leavers, the first year of postcommunal life is also examined.

First we must define the population to be studied. Communal populations fluctuate rapidly. Therefore, an arbitrary day during the first month of field work was selected for each commune, and its population was defined as all adults living there on that day. Adults were designated as all persons 15 years of age or older. "Living there" was defined to mean physically present (or recognized as present but away on a trip of not more than one month's duration) but not obviously a transient or short-term visitor. Admittedly, in many communes, this distinction is a cloudy one. Children are never, in this book, considered as part of the population under investigation, but are discussed separately.*

In this manner, 2,999 communitarians were counted as a baseline population, an average of 25 members per commune. The rural communes, however, were much larger than the urban. The mean population of the rural groups in the study was 39, of the urban only 11. The rural groups ranged in size from 5 to 320, the urban groups from 4† to 68.

Systematic background, behavioral, and attitudinal data were collected from the members of the urban communes only. Of the 668 urban commune members, 82 percent (545) responded to the basic questionnaire. Slightly more than half of these also participated in in-depth interviews. Although no systematic attempt was made to collect individual-level data in the rural communes, 8 percent (195) of the rural communitarians were interviewed and asked about themselves in a manner that permits comparison with the urban sample.

In this and the following chapter, individual-level analysis has been largely confined to the urban communitarian. This group has been treated as if it were a sample drawn from the population of all urban communitarians, with specific

---

*This is not because children don't play an important role in communal life but because the focus of this study is on intentionality, and most children are not present in communes by their own choice. Even where children are present by choice, it is generally not so much that they have expressed a preference for communal living *per se* but that they have expressed a preference for living with that parent who happens to live communally.

† The operational definition of commune used required a minimum of five adults. But, in two cases, the population fell to four during the time interval between selection of the commune sample and enumeration of the population.

commune designation treated as a variable property of the individual (see Appendix A).* The 195 rural communitarians for whom comparable data were available obviously do not comprise any sort of sample. But ethnographic comparisons failed to come up with any significant way in which this rural 8 percent differed significantly from the 92 percent not interviewed. Therefore, the mean values of basic background indicators have been used as crude estimators for comparison with urban means. But very little further analysis of individual-level rural data was attempted.

Who Lives in Communes?

Commune members are a distinctive but not widely deviant population. Table 3-1 lists selected background characteristics compared with various national samples. We can see from the table that commune members tend to be younger than the national average; that married people, Protestants, and blacks, are underrepresented; that college graduates and Jews are overrepresented; and that commune members tend to come from intact families to a higher degree than the nation as a whole.†

The profiles of rural and of urban communitarians are similar, for the most part. Rural commune members are older than the urban, more of them have been married, and more of them have had children. Aside from these differences, their major distinction from one another is occupational. Rural communitarians may take paying jobs from time to time but they generally do not have occupational careers outside the commune. Many urban communitarians do have such careers. Moreover, although the table does not show it, the kind of paid or unpaid work done by rural communitarians is very different from the kind of work done by commune members in the cities. The jobs undertaken by the former tend to require more physical effort and less formal training, even though the educational profiles of the two subpopulations are quite similar.

Table 3-2 introduces a way of categorizing communes and commune members according to their ideological type that will not be discussed in detail until Chapter 5. At this point, it is only necessary to know that we group the communes in our sample into eight ideological categories — four oriented toward the alteration or expansion of consciousness and four oriented toward direct action. The first set includes the Eastern religious, the psychological, the cooperative, and the countercultural communes. The second includes the Christian, the rehabilitational, the family oriented, and the political communes.

*This convention should pose no problems of interpretation provided that it is remembered that there is, strictly speaking, no *sample* of communitarians and that what we are studying instead is the entire membership *population* (minus refusers) of a *sample* of communes.

† In most respects, our communitarian sample is demographically similar to that reported by other commune researchers (see, for example, Levine, 1972). It is distinctive, however, in two respects: the relatively low proportion of middle-class members (discussed subsequently) and the high proportion with college degrees.

TABLE 3-1. Comparison Commune Population with United States as a Whole

Background Characteristic At Time of First Wave of Study	Commune Population			Comparison Populations	
	Rural (N = 195)	Urban (N = 545)	NORC (1974) (N = 1,481)	U.S. Census	Samples of American youth[1]
Median Age (over age 15 only)	30	25	42	37 (1976)[a]	23 (1974)
Percentage single, never married	66%	72%	12%	43% of those in age group 18–29 (1974)	49% (1974)
Education: Percentage with college diploma	48	50	14	24 (1974 est.)	[27][b]
Employment: Percentage not in full-time remunerative occupations (regardless of whether seeking)	96	54	57	—	—
Percentage with service, farm, or blue collar occupations	—	27	49	51 (1974)	58 (1974)
Percentage whose father's occupation is service, farm, or blue collar	—	28	71	—	—
Percentage who grew up with both parents in the home	90	90	76	—	79 (1974)
Percentage Male	45	54	45	49 (1975)	100 (1974)
Percentage who have had one or more children	29	20	78	—	[24]
Middle-class self-definition	—	48	46	—	—
Religious background: Protestant	47	44	66	—	63 (1974)
Catholic	28	26	28	—	20 (1974)
Jewish	15	19	3	—	3 (1974)
Other, mixed	10	11	3	—	14 (1974)
Percentage black	<1	<1	12	11 (1974)	[8][b]

[1] Entries in brackets are from Wuthnow (1976, p. 159) subsample aged 16 to 30 (N = 565). All other entries are from Bachman (1970) and Bachman et al (1978).
[a] Calculated on population over age 14.
[b] Taken from full sample.

TABLE 3–2. Selected Personal Attributes by Ideological Type[1]

	Entire Urban Commune Population	Highest	Lowest	Statistical Significance[2]
Ascribed Attributes				
Median Age	25	Family 32	Eastern 24	*
Sex: % Male	54%	Eastern 62%	Christian 41%	n.s.
Father's Occupation: % service, blue collar, and farm	28	Christian 32	Psychological 18	n.s.
"Broken Home": % lived with both own parents while growing up	90	Family 94	Psychological 84	n.s.
Religious Background: % Protestant	44	Christian 73	Political 30	**
Achieved Attributes				
% Middle Class Self-Definition	48%	Psychological 70%	Counter Culture 18%	**
Marital Status: % single and never married	72	Eastern 82	Family 34	**

Have Children:				
% yes	20	Family 51	Eastern 15	**
Education:				
% college degree	50	Family 74	Eastern 33	**
Employed:				
% employed full or part time	67	Family 86	Psychological 56	n.s.
Occupation:				
% service and blue collar	26	Eastern 45	Family 7	**

[1] Rehabilitation communes have been excluded from this analysis. See Chap. 5 and Appendix A for explanation.

[2] n.s. means F or Chi-square statistic is not significant at p = .01.

  * = significant at p = .01.

  ** = significant at p = .001

As Table 3-2 indicates, these ideological types seem to differentially select their members according to achieved attributes but not according to ascribed attributes. In other words, among those characteristics of individuals over which the individuals themselves have no control (e.g., age, sex, stability of family of origin), few significant differences exist among the eight ideological categories. But, among those characteristics that reflect individual choice (e.g., having children, a particular kind of job, or a college degree), significant differences do exist. Family, psychological, and Christian communes tend to be composed of individuals with relatively high rates of achievement in these areas, whereas Eastern religious, cooperative, and countercultural groups tend to be composed of people with relatively low rates. These distinctions will be taken up in greater detail in Chapter 5.

Ethnicity

The differential affinity of various ethnic groups for communitarianism was noticed as far back as 1875 by Charles Nordhoff, one of the first scholars to write about American communitarianism. Nordhoff (1875, p. 177) said:

> In origin, the Icarians are French; the Shakers and Perfectionists Americans; the others are Germans; and these outnumber all the American communists. In fact, the Germans make better communists than any other people *unless the Chinese should someday turn their attention to communistic attempts.* What I have seen of these people in California and the Sandwich Islands leads me to believe that they are well calculated for communistic experiments. [emphasis added]

Although such differential ethnic affinities no doubt exist, the only two for which the current data provide evidence are those of blacks (underrepresentation) and Jews (overrepresentation).

Nonwhites are rarely found in the American commune movement.* More than three-quarters of the communes in the study were 100 percent white. Of those that were not, only 13 percent had at least one black member.† In the remainder, the nonwhites were of Oriental or Hispanic origin.‡

There is no evidence that this is a result of racial prejudice on the part of white commune members. Although such prejudice is undoubtedly present in some communes, the commune population as a whole was uniformly liberal in expressed racial attitudes. Many spontaneously remarked that they would prefer to have more racial integration. Some communes deliberately tried to recruit

---

*This has been reported in many studies. See, for example, Glock and Bellah (1976, pp. 22, 39). Jonestown, however, was a major exception to this rule.

†If the communes in this study had selected their members randomly from the American population, the expected proportion of communes with at least one black member would have been 78 percent.

‡To investigate the possibility of Hispanic underrepresentation, Hispanics were arbitrarily included in the questions about "nonwhites."

black applicants (usually in vain), whereas others waived customary admission procedures when presented with an opportunity to integrate racially. Although failure to integrate remained an embarrassment for many communes, the overwhelming obstacle was simply lack of interest on the part of nonwhites.*

This has not always been the case throughout history. Sponsored "black utopias" (Pease, 1963) existed in America after the Civil War, and the Father Divine movement of the 1930s (Kephart, 1976) was organized along communal lines at a time when white interest in communes was at a low point. More recently, in the late 1960s, the Black Panthers experimented briefly and unsatisfactorily with communal organization in Houston and in a number of other cities. On the other hand, even so large and cosmopolitan a communitarian federation as the Bruderhof has never been able to recruit a single black member, and mass religious cults, for example, the Krishnas, are hard put to maintain a sufficient level of black representation to achieve their organizational goal of racially mixed proselytizing street groups. By way of negative evidence, it is probably significant that communitarian organization has played only a modest part in black separatist movements.

Black culture in America is often so different from white culture that the absence of blacks in the movement is a matter worth speculating about in the search for the cultural etiology of communitarianism. For what it is worth, those few blacks in the communitarian sample often appeared to be among the most cynical and marginal members of their communes. Blacks in predominantly white communes often seemed uninterested in consensus, cool to the joys of communion, and immune to the charms of white charismatic leaders. Although just as alienated from the larger society as the white members were, black communitarians were perhaps less confused about what they wanted.

If it is true that the utility of communes lies largely in their ability to crystallize preference orderings and narrow fields of choice for members, this might explain their lack of felt relevance to most blacks. This study was conducted during that period of time in which American blacks were, for the first time, organizing an effective national political power base. Historically, this is an activity that has rarely coincided with interest in communitarianism.

The high frequency with which Jews are represented is the opposite side of the coin. Jews are characteristically joiners (NORC, 1974) and are disproportionately well represented in almost all contemporary social movements (Glock et al., 1976, passim). Piazza (1976; pp. 253ff) has shown that, at least among Berkeley undergraduates, Jews are much more likely than Catholics or Protestants to express the desire to live communally. Their interest in communitarianism appears to be, according to Piazza, negatively correlated with their degree of identification with traditional Jewish life. Goren (1970) and Sklare (1971) have documented the historical importance of the idea of community in

---

*Although a major effort was made to assure that the sample of communes chosen would be ethnically representative of the commune population, we cannot, of course, totally exclude the possibility that absence of blacks in our sample may be due to sampling bias.

American Jewish life. Among Zionists, the reputation of the kibbutzim has given communitarianism a good reputation without counterpart among any other ethnic collectivity. The decade 1965 to 1975 witnessed the breakup (under the strains of geographic mobility) of many of the close-knit extended families that had survived since the great waves of Jewish immigration a half century earlier, and left a hunger for some functional equivalent. The quest for family, the quest for community, and the quest simply to belong combine to give Jews, especially secularized Jews, a high propensity for communal living.

It is interesting to contrast the kind of alienation from American society experienced by young blacks in the late 1960s with the kind of alienation experienced by young Jews. Both were among the angriest and most restive of the ethnic groups in the national population. But, whereas blacks were increasingly discontent with their exclusion from significant roles within the society, Jews had access to these roles but were coming increasingly to question their meaningfulness. Lewis Feuer (1962) has criticized the sociological use of the concept of alienation because it possesses the confusing property of being applicable at one and the same time to the frustration of the disenfranchised and to the anguish of the elite. But it is precisely this property that gives the concept its sociological value: it enables us to tie together the very different ways in which different strata and different subcultures within the society respond to a general crisis of institutional legitimacy.

Religion and Politics

There is no one particular ideological type of commune to which non-whites appear particularly drawn. There is, however, one aspect of ascribed background in which the eight ideological clusters introduced earlier differ significantly among themselves. The eight ideological clusters show significant and interesting differences in the mixes of their members' religious backgrounds (Table 3-2 and Figure 3-1).

A preponderance of Jews is to be found in the consciousness-oriented communes, particularly the Eastern religious and psychological groups. Protestants, on the other hand, tend to be concentrated in action-oriented communes. Catholics seem to be disproportionately drawn to communes with Christian or political ideologies. These observations do not reflect any overall explanation for why people select themselves into various ideological categories. However, they do suggest strongly that ideological choice of commune is potentially understandable in part in terms of the person's history of the evolution of identity. Ideological orientations in childhood predispose one to specific ideological sensitivities in later life.

Another background characteristic closely associated with ideology (but not showing, as pronounced differentiation by commune ideological type) is family political loyalty. Our commune sample comes from homes that are 46 percent

FIGURE 3-1.   Religious Backgrounds of Families of Origin

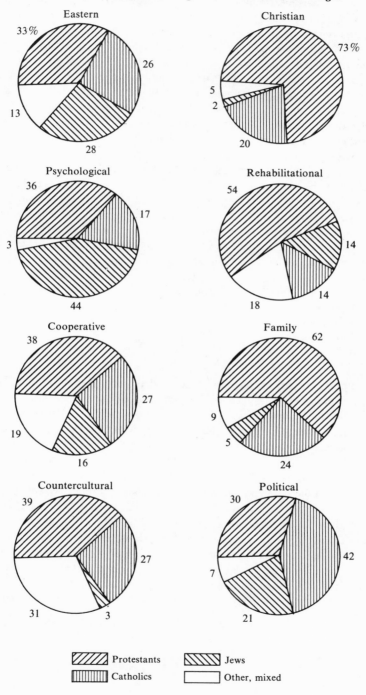

Eastern

Christian

Psychological

Rehabilitational

Cooperative

Family

Countercultural

Political

Protestants   Jews

Catholics   Other, mixed

Democrat, 31 percent Republican, and 23 percent independent, apolitical, or mixed in allegiance. Except for relative abundance of Democratic backgrounds among the members of the political communes, the ideological types do not differ among themselves on this attribute nor are they significantly different from the national population.

However, in examining the urban commune members' current political orientation, we find a pronounced shift to the left. According to retrospective accounts in the summer of 1974, only 14 percent of those who voted in the 1972 election* voted for Richard Nixon. Almost all these were members of the Christian communes. Virtually all the remaining 86 percent cast their votes for George McGovern rather than for any of the minority candidates. In interpreting these findings, it must be remembered that the recollections were made during the height of the Watergate scandal, when many people who voted Republican two years earlier may have been reluctant to admit it.

Of course, many of the communitarians who voted for George McGovern in 1972 would have been happier supporting a major candidate still further to the left. But almost 80 percent of the membership claimed that no organized political party or movement represented their views and beliefs. Of the remaining 20 percent, only 1 percent claimed allegiance to the Republican Party, 7 percent to the Democratic Party, and 12 percent to a variety of liberal-to-radical movements including the yippies, the provos, the feminists, the Socialist Workers' Party, and Common Cause.

Social Class

Communes are not exclusively a middle-class phenomenon. Popular imagination has it that commune members are rather like hippies and campus radicals— the disaffected children of the middle and upper-middle classes. Earlier studies of communal living have contributed to this belief by stating without proof that participants are almost exclusively of middle-class origin. However, at least in terms of education, occupation, and father's occupation, a significant minority of commune members would have to be classified as non-middle class.

Using the usual demographic indicators (Tables 3-1 and 3-3), we can see that commune members are drawn from all strata of society. Forty-eight percent reported their family of origin as middle class, as opposed to 46 percent of the national (NORC) sample for the same year. Half had no college diploma. Six percent had not graduated from high school. Fifty-four percent were unemployed when interviewed.† The median income was reported as $370 per adult per month in the urban communes. Very few in the rural group had cash incomes. Although a relatively high percentage (Table 3-3) of those who were

---

*A surprisingly high 62 percent of all those eligible to vote claimed that they did vote.
†Only about half of these, however, were actively seeking employment.

TABLE 3-3. Occupations of Urban Respondents and Their Fathers

A. Classifications and Prestige

	Professional	Managerial	Sales/Clerical	Service	Farm/Blue Collar	Mean Occupational Prestige ISCO Scale[1]
Fathers (N = 512)[2]	32%	12%	27%	4%	24%	51.0
Male respondents (N = 170)	42	8	11	7	33	44.5
Female respondents (N = 141)	57	2	28	8	4	50.1

B. Specific Occupations Engaged in by 2 Percent or More of Male and Female Respondents and Their Fathers

Fathers		Male Respondents		Female Respondents	
Managers	12%	Social workers	12%	Teachers and teachers' aides	16%
Salesmen	10	Managers	10	Secretaries	10
Engineers	7	Teachers and teachers' aides	7	Social workers	8
Military	5	Carpenters	5	Clerks	6
Lawyers	3	Laborers: Semi- or unskilled	3	Nurses	5
Physicians	2	Social scientists	2	Waitresses	3
Professors	2	Gardeners	2	Professors	2
Truck drivers	2				
Farmers	2				
Laborers: Semi- or unskilled	2				
Accountants	2				

[1] Standard International Occupational Prestige Scale (Trieman, 1977).
[2] Includes all fathers of commune members responding whether or not they themselves hold jobs. No significant differences appear in the subsample of fathers whose children were employed.

working held jobs classified as "professional,"* one-third of the men were blue-collar workers and more than a third of the women were in sales, clerical, or service work.

A similar pattern of occupations can be seen for the fathers of the respondents. The respondents do not come overwhelmingly from middle-class backgrounds. About 28 percent of the commune members had fathers in service, farm, or blue-collar jobs. In general, the female respondents and, to a lesser extent, the male respondents tended to be concentrated in a narrower range of occupations than their fathers. Eighty-five percent of the female respondents were in either professional or sales and clerical occupations. Seventy-five percent of all the male respondents were either professionals or blue-collar workers.

Perhaps the clearest picture of the heterogeneity of the commune population with respect to class can be obtained by looking at the specific occupations held by commune members and their fathers.† There were about as many children of truck drivers, farmers, and laborers in communes as there were children of lawyers, physicians, and professors. As Berger (1972) has also noted, military children have been disproportionately represented in communal life.

Among the respondents themselves, males were modally found as social workers, females as teachers. Carpentry and gardening were popular jobs among the men, as was social science research. Among the 60 percent of the employed women who were not teachers, social workers, secretaries or clerks, the only job categories that describe at least 2 percent of the sample were nurse, waitress, and college professor.

It should not be imagined that this job heterogeneity is attributable to the fact that, for example, some communes are composed of the children of doctors and lawyers whereas others are composed of the children of blue-collar workers. On the contrary, the variance of occupational prestige of fathers is not much greater among the communes than it is within them. Although there are in the sample a number of groups whose members all have middle-class fathers or all have working-class fathers, the majority of communes have members with fathers representing the whole range of social strata.

There are reasons for the persistence of the notion that communes are exclusively a middle-class phenomenon. One is that communes composed largely or entirely of middle-class people have, in general, been far more accessible to research than those with a working- or welfare-class membership. (This is an example of the distortions that have plagued this field of investigation because of reliance upon small, unrepresentative samples.) Another is that in communes with a mixture of working-class and middle-class members, the middle-class

---

*The "professional" classification may be misleading. Breaking this down for our population, we find the bulk of these "professionals" to be social workers, teachers, and teaching assistants of various sorts. Among the commune members, there are relatively few doctors, lawyers, engineers, and the like.

†Not enough of the mothers of the commune members worked steadily at paying jobs to allow the use of mother's occupation as a valid indicator of status.

members have generally been spokesmen for the communes, or at least have been more willing to play this role. Most studies of American communes have been based on short visits and interviews with whichever members happened to be most available. Returning from the field with tape cassettes that recounted mostly middle-class family histories, many researchers drew the inaccurate inference that middle-class backgrounds predominated among the uninterviewed as well.

It would be more correct to view commune members as marginal to the class system as a whole. In terms of dress, occupation, demeanor, and informal organizational affiliations, communitarians tend to be neither middle class, working class, nor *lumpenproletariat.* They are distinctive for the ways in which they pick and choose for themselves stylistic and behavioral elements of each.

If we define class in terms of consumption rather than production and think of the working class in America as those people who are concerned with obtaining the primary needs for survival and the middle class as those people who have successfully attained the basics and are now concerned with achieving secondary goals, only then may we say that communitarians pursue middle-class goals from the perspective of middle-class problems. Communitarians have satisfied their primary wants to a great extent and are engaged primarily in the satisfaction of secondary desires.

Stage in Life Cycle

Communitarianism is not exclusively a phenomenon of youth. About one-sixth of the urban commune members and half of the rural were over the age of 30 at first contact. The oldest participant was in her late seventies, and a scattering in their fifties, sixties, and early seventies was found in both the rural and the urban groups. Nevertheless, communal living is generally associated with that loosely defined, postadolescent stage of the life cycle known as "youth."

Perhaps a major proximate cause of the decision to join a commune is simply stage in life cycle. Communes are most popular during the period between 20 and 30 years of age. Eisenstadt (1971, p. xiv) has argued that, "To some extent, youth is always defined as a period of 'role moratorium'—that is, a period in which one may assume various roles without definitely choosing any." This is an important clue to a reason for joining communes: not youth per se, of course, but the youthful need for a moratorium prior to the fatefulness of adult role choices.

We saw in Chapter 2 that the decade under investigation was one in which, economically speaking, there was a glut of youth in the United States. A comparatively affluent society was ready to give a generation of highly trained and expectant young people consumer roles to play with no questions asked, but it lacked enough producer roles to go around. It is interesting to note, in this respect, that the dominant response to this situation, at least for communitarians, was not the expression of outrage, of the absurd, or of resignation, but, rather, an oppressive sense of nothingness. Statements by commune interviewees about their lives immediately prior to joining indicate a widespread sense of "the Void." Respondents told stories of crises of anxiety, most often related not to achievement but to identity. What both frightened them and fascinated them, generally, was not loss of status but loss of self. Life seemed not so much hopeless as hopelessly convoluted. What was needed perhaps was someone or something to cut through the tangle and define a meaningful new order. Meanwhile, it was hard not to just drift. All this is expressed in some typical examples of respondents' descriptions of their lives just prior to joining:

> I was very much satisfied but I knew it wasn't a permanent state, was aware of the fact that it was temporary. Now I feel at home. There is no place I'd rather be.

> I was dissatisfied with my life-style. I felt stagnant and knew I'd be happier in a commune . . .

> I felt good about life in general, but sensed that something was missing. I had the feeling that I should be doing more.

> I had no goals except in the good old tradition of going to school. I had no real ideas about what I was going to be doing. Felt ready to do anything if anything came up.

> I was really satisfied but I went totally crazy after I separated from my old man, until I found a job.

> Something was lacking. What was important in life was not being confronted.

> Life was comfortable but flat. Extremely bored, it was obvious that something was missing.

> There was something lacking in life. I was a loner, related to few people, kept distances. My major crisis was the void in my life.

> I was feeling like I had to make a lot of changes. Feeling confident about the direction of these changes but feeling unconfident about the process [of change].

Paradoxically, it would seem that young communitarians, far from being designers of rigid utopian programs, are people who don't know what they want. Through the collective process they seek criteria by which to rank for themselves those ambitions that go beyond biological imperatives, but that perhaps have been insufficiently programmed into their training, culture, and background. They are reminiscent in this sense of Koznyshev in Tolstoy's *Anna Karenina*, whose abstract idealism stemmed not from conviction but from the lack of "the impulse which drives a man to choose some one out of all the innumerable paths of life and to care for that one only."

Family of Origin

The typical communitarian grew up in a close-knit nuclear family with two parents and at least one sibling. This finding was unexpected. Early research on the hippie movement (Pittel, 1968) had revealed that a very large proportion of Haight-Ashbury hippies came from home environments that were broken through death, divorce, or separation. This led to the hypothesis that certain deficiencies in the hippies' socialization process, due to their having been reared in broken homes, were responsible for what were considered at the time to be the deviant qualities of the counterculture, particularly the use of drugs. It was predicted that communitarians would also, even more so, be found to be compensating by their life-style for the psychological deficits of broken homes. However, 90 percent of the sample communitarians were found to come from intact families as compared with only 76 percent in the population as a whole.* Moreover, both sociometric and verbal portraits that communitarians sketched of their early home environments most often suggested networks of affection and mutual involvement (although liberally mixed with a certain amount of conflict). Only rarely was isolation, atomization, or schism suggested.†

It is clear that communitarianism does not flourish among those with traumatic experiences in early life but rather among those who come from tight-knit nuclear families. Disillusionment, alienation, and subsequent radical rebellion come as a result of life experiences encountered later in the developmental process. Retrospective evidence of familial conflict is found, if at all, in adolescence rather than early childhood. Communitarianism seems to require a personality constellation that, in Erik Erikson's terms (1970, p. 17), combines an extraordinary degree of trust (acquired in the infant stage of development) with a poorly articulated identity (deficiency of the adolescent stage):

> I will emphasize here the infant's *mutuality* of responses with the *maternal person* . . . which assures that *hope* becomes the fundamental quality of all growth. All this combines to form *an unusually strong first developmental position.* . . . The group style generally subsumed under the term Hippiedom is . . . a totalization of the first developmental position. In the midst of our technocratic world young men and women encourage each other to live like the proverbial lilies in the field, *with trusting love as their dominant demand and display.* [emphasis added]

*The NORC national survey for the same year (1974). Another control group whose mean age is identical to that of the commune sample, the *Youth in Transition* sample (Bachman, 1970), had 79 percent in intact homes. Even when controlling for race and other relevant background characteristics, the communitarian proportion remains quite high.

†Monsour and Stone (1974) have reported very similar findings in a study of American youth who dropped out of straight society into what they hoped would prove to be a tropical utopian paradise—the island of Maui, Hawaii. The great majority of them came from intact two-parent middle-class homes and felt accepting of and accepted by their parents.

Erikson argues that an important segment of contemporary radical youth is characterized by high trust. Typical ideological and autobiographical statements of commune members bear this out:

> [Joining the commune] was like a birthday of my soul. I'd been reborn. I had no relationship to what went on before. I didn't have to search any more. I had found it. Not having to search any more takes a lot out of the trips you are into, and having found the Truth put you automatically at ease.

> I knew I could do whatever I wanted to do within the limits of these 450 acres. I felt like it would only be another step to try to create more and more communities like this one. And then, as people grew strong and as conscious- ness spread (through writing, and talking, and by example), to go on to try and liberate the cities. It seemed to me that, once you had some thing and some people to fight for, you'd be much more inclined to fight and to win. I couldn't imagine how anyone would *not* want to live this way. It was so very much better than any way of life I had known before. It was even better than any I had ever dreamed of, because my dreams were always unreal and one-sided, but here we experienced real conflicts, and we knew the satis- factions of working through them, and getting to the other side of them, and growing from them.

> We found out that, if you told no one to leave, the land (the vibes) selected the people who lived on it. We also found out that in this supportive, *no-rules* environment, hostilities could find little breeding ground. Interpersonal relations could grow and flourish as naturally as the seasons, without the need of programs, counseling, or other would-be substitutes for openheartedness.

Another familial characteristic of commune members is at least some degree of sibling interaction. Fewer than 1 percent of the respondents reported being an only child, as compared with 5–6 percent in comparative national samples.* The commune members had, on the average, fewer siblings than these national samples, although it is impossible to say to what extent this is due to intervening factors such as urbanicity or socioeconomic status.

Birth-order effects in the expected direction did not occur. Stanley Schachter's (1959) theory of birth order and affiliative needs predicts that low rank in the birth order will be positively associated with the need to affiliate to reduce anxiety. Schachter has shown, using laboratory experiments, both that first-born and early-born subjects tend to be more anxious and that they affiliate more frequently at any given level of anxiety than do those with a later birth order.†

---

*NORC, 1974; *Youth in Transition* (Bachman, 1970).

†More recent replications and elaborations of this theory have yielded mixed and inconclu- sive results. Dember (1964) was able to replicate Schachter's finding that first-borns have a higher need for affiliation than later-borns, using projective tests. He ignored, however, the factor of anxiety, which is crucial to Schachter's formulation. Weller (1964), on the other hand, was not able to produce greater cohesiveness among first-borns than among later-borns when he threatened a sample of female college students with electric shocks. Masling (1965) found no relationship between birth order and preference for rooming with others among college freshmen. However, Smart (1965) found significantly more

It is not early-borns but middle children who are found in communes in disproportionately high numbers. Of all the respondents in three-sibling families, slightly over half (rather than the expected one-third) were middle children. This pattern was repeated for respondents from larger families as well. Does the vantage point of middleness (in the thick of things, so to speak) give a child the kind of outlook and temperament that provide a differential advantage to the communitarian? Psychological research on birth order suggests this possibility. Weiner and Elkind (1972, p. 90) have reported:

> A middle child, unless he has special abilities or characteristics or in some other way qualifies as his mother's or father's favorite, is particularly *likely to feel unequal to the competition,* both in his own family and in the academic and social circles of his peer group. . . . On the other hand, it is not unusual for middle children, who have had *front line experience placating opposing interpersonal forces* in both age directions, *to become easygoing and likable people.* [emphasis added]

Our test of the birth-order hypothesis has revealed two ways in which communal affiliation is different from affiliation in the small group laboratory. Laboratory-induced affiliation has been shown to vary strongly and inversely with birth order (eldest siblings having the greatest need to affiliate), whereas communal affiliation has a very different pattern of correlation with birth order. But, whereas laboratory-induced affiliation is independent of number of siblings, communal affiliation has a weak inverse relationship to number of siblings, as long as there is at least one sibling.‡

It thus seems reasonable to infer that the propensity to join a commune has an origin different from that of the general urge to affiliate. The short-term affiliation measured in the laboratory is largely an unconscious mechanism for coping with anxiety. The long-term affiliation of the commune member, we are arguing, is often rather a conscious mechanism for coping with alienation.

Alienation

To what extent can commune members be considered alienated from society and self and driven by their alienation into communitarian experiments? As Table 3-4 indicates, commune members as a whole are not especially alienated from society by conventional measures of political and economic powerlessness

---

social group memberships among first-born as opposed to later-born males (but not females). When de Lint (1966) reexamined Smart's data, he showed that the possibility that the two variables were merely spuriously correlated through their joint correlation with social class standing had not been considered. This battle continues to rage. For a good review essay, see Adams (1974).

‡Only children and children from very large families are both somewhat underrepresented in the commune population. It is impossible to say, however, to what extent this is a spurious result of other peculiarities of the sample.

and normlessness.* However, when we shift our attention away from these widely used dimensions of alienation and towards the dimensions of meaninglessness and value isolation instead, we do begin to see an effect of alienation on communitarianism.

These dimensions are not as easy to measure. In the immediate precommunal period of the joiners' lives, we have noted a tendency toward meaninglessness, drift, and life-style experimentation. Communal living is rarely seen as an opportunity to engage in deviant behavior; far more often, as we shall see, it represents a retreat from the chaotic aftereffects of heavy experimentation with drug use, sexual behavior, political radicalism, and religious seeking. Such experimentation generally leads to a widening of cognitive horizons. For every choice that arises in life, the individual comes to be aware of a great many feasible and attractive action alternatives. Each of these action alternatives, moreover, may seem morally justifiable in terms of some viable system of ultimate meanings. Precommunal alienation is frequently expressed in the inability to determine one's preferences, and thus to make decisions, under such cognitively kaleidoscopic conditions.

Evidence from a number of sources leads to the conviction that this type of alienation is endemic in both rural and urban communes. One source of such evidence is the retrospective history of respondents' precommunal lives.[†] Such alienation makes collective action difficult even in the presence of a high degree of ideological convergence. In its most extreme form, as we shall see in Chapter 5, it can lead to the ideological call for the elimination of categorical thinking itself.

As we noted in Chapter 2, during the decade of our research, young persons were faced with a multiplicity of incompatible ideologies or cultural themes. The counterculture emphasized many values and goals that were completely contradictory to traditional cultural patterns. The countercultural values themselves, however, were very far from being integrated into a single consistent ideology. Yankelovich, the primary collector and analyst of large-scale survey data on representative samples of young people in this decade, has divided a segment of American youth into two categories of approximately equal size: the nonpolitical (hippie) and the political (new left). Havighurst, using Yankelovich's typology, says (1975, p. 124):

*There is some evidence that, even as measured by the conventional scales, the alienation of commune members increases as one expands in concentric circles from the commune itself. On the dimension of powerlessness, crude alienation scores increased from 8 percent, to 27 percent, to 41 percent as the commune, the city in which the commune was located, and the U.S.A., successively, were treated as objects of investigation. For normlessness, the rates went from 22 percent, to 22 percent, to 45 percent. For social isolation, they went from 4 percent, to 17 percent, to 67 percent.

†See Table 5-2 and associated discussion for further evidence at the level of individual attitudes.

TABLE 3-4. Alienation Scales[1]

A. Measures of Anomie (Srole)

Item	NORC Sample 1974 Only	% Agree Urban Communes		% Change
		1974	1975	
Nowadays, a person has to live pretty much for today and let tomorrow take care of itself	44%	59%	62%	+3%
The lot of the average man is getting worse, not better	61	55	62	+7
It's hardly fair to bring a child into the world with the way things look for the future	37	21	17	−4
Most public officials (people in public office) are not really interested in the problems of the average man	66	67	66	−1

B. Harris Poll Alienation Questions

	Harris		Communes	
	6/74	9/74	8/74	8/75
The rich get richer and the poor get poorer	79%	77%	57%	78%
People running country don't care what happens to you	63	48	54	67
What you think doesn't count much any more	60	54	15	16
You feel left out of things going on around you	32	32	16	17
Most people with power try to take advantage of people like yourself	60	56	51	65

[1] Commune N = 398 in 1974; 180 in 1975.

The counter culture contains two sub-groups who agree on some things and disagree on some things. Keniston calls these the cultural and political wings, an important distinction. . . . To put it over-simply, the cultural wing . . . are the hippies, while the political wing . . . are the new left.

This notion of two distinct wings within the counterculture is quite common in analyses of youth in the 1960s and is certainly supported by survey data. However, our evidence in looking at communitarians tends to dispute the validity of dividing countercultural individuals into these two groups. Communitarians show a rapid movement between the two wings. The countercultural communitarians indicate a previous history of participation in political-type activities and vice versa. The problem seems to be the cross-sectional survey methodology, which at any given time might find approximately half of its subsample classified as political while the actual turnover or movement between the two groups may be continual and quite high. The normal assumptions of response stability do not necessarily hold for a population characterized by protean identity shifts and ideological confusion.

An important traditional measure of alienation from self is estrangement from work (Seeman, 1972). In both their behavior and their attitudes, communitarians seem to be significantly alienated from the capitalist work ethic and from participation in the labor force. Almost none of the rural commune members and fewer than half of the urban ones that we interviewed were steadily employed at full-time paying jobs and even fewer wanted to be. Although many commune members worked very hard at subsistence and ideological tasks as well as at tasks that earned income, there was widespread personal and ideological resistance to measuring self-worth in terms of occupational achievement.

In fact, nowhere have the attitudes of commune members been more diametrically opposed to those of the general American population than with respect to the work ethic (see Table 3-5).

When asked to agree or disagree with the statement that "hard work will always pay off," only 16 percent of the commune members (aged 15–25) agreed as opposed to 74 percent of a representative sample of American youth queried at about the same time.* Because agreement with this item is known to be strongly associated with college education,† the extent of agreement was calculated separately for those with college degrees and for those who had no exposure to college. However, among those with no college, only 19 percent agreed with the statement, whereas the proportion dropped to 12 percent among those who had completed college.

In most communes there were one or a few members who did not appear alienated at all. Many such communes may be thought of as composed of charismatic minorities and alienated majorities. The distinction is not caste rigid, of course. Quite the contrary, the boundaries are often so fluid that individuals may be hard to classify. Unless a single powerful charismatic leader deliberately seeks to monopolize the trait, charisma may be shared in any given commune. Nevertheless, the distinction is an important one. The interactions between these two statuses will turn out to explain much of the dynamics of communal living.

*The national survey was performed in May 1974, three months prior to the first wave of commune interviewing. *Current Opinion* 3 (June 1975): 6. The age range of the national sample was 14 to 25 years of age. The age range of the commune members included in this tabulation was 15 to 25.

†Studies by Yankelovich et al. (1974) indicate that in 1969, 56 percent of college youths agreed with the statement whereas 79 percent of noncollege youths agreed. In 1971, the proportion of college youths' agreeing with this statement had fallen to 39 percent.

TABLE 3-5. Work Ethic

| | "Hard Work Will Always Pay Off" (% Agree) | | |
	1969	1971	1974
All youth, 14–25	NA	NA	74%
College	56%	39%	NA
Noncollege	79	NA	NA
Commune youth, 15–25	–	–	17
College	–	–	12
Noncollege	–	–	19

NA – Not available.

A minority of charismatic leaders must somehow find a way to motivate a majority of alienated people if the typical commune is to work. Because of the peculiar nature of communal alienation, self must be invested into the collectivity for this to occur. (See a further discussion of this point in Chapters 6, 7, and 8.)

Becoming a Commune Member

So far we have merely described a population of individuals. But joining a commune is a social process and cannot be viewed solely as the acquisition of a status to be correlated with other statuses. On the contrary, as we shall see in later chapters, the process of joining a commune often alters the very identities of both the joiner and the commune being joined. Let us therefore turn our attention away from the question of who joins and toward the question of how they join, in terms both of their motivations and their opportunities.

Reasons for Joining

The social forces that cause some people to self-select as participants in communal experiments may or may not be consciously known to or acknowledged by the joiners themselves. However, the reasons given by joiners for their decision to join are important in themselves, as indicators of the distribution of consciously articulated motivational factors, regardless of how accurately these reasons portray the causes of the decision. Table 3-6 lists the most commonly given reasons for the decision to join a commune. Major differences appear along the urban-rural and the religious-secular dimensions.* Except for the rural-religious communes, the proportion of members giving primacy to non-ideological reasons is quite high. In the urban-secular groups, seven out of every

*Although the rural tabulation is based upon an unrepresentative sample and the rural-religious subsample, in particular, is built from a very small number of cases, the gross patterns seem to fit ethnographic observations. The urban sample is based on the responses only of those participating in the longer interviews.

eight of the respondents gave as their first-mentioned response a nonideological reason for joining. Many of these, however, mentioned ideological reasons among their second responses. In both urban and rural religious communes, ideological reasons are considered primary by a majority of the members. A large proportion of those in rural secular groups also find them important.

These findings tend to corroborate the argument that communitarian organization is based upon the attempts by the charismatic to mobilize the alienated. This task is never fully completed. In many instances it is a losing battle. The following excerpt from an interview with a would-be charismatic leader surveying the wreck of his (urban-secular) communal dream illustrates this:

> Right from the beginning it wasn't that well planned, or it was planned but people dropped out. We put ads in the paper in July, and we had at least 30 people come in that we talked to. We were trying to get together with a house that could be like a family. We couldn't even get it together on food, work around the house, or on much of anything.

Q. Did people care about these things?

> I don't know if they cared. . . . I wound up paying all the operating costs. People did not respond to what was happening so that for a long time it was like the house was empty. When people did start responding they were *not the particular type of people that I had envisioned.*

Q. How did you find people to move in? How did you find them?

> I ran ads—it was an advertising campaign. What it came down to was people were more attracted by the fact that it was cheap rent than anything else.

Q. How did you decide who could live here?

> How do you raise your criteria? We sat down and talked. If you have any sensitivity at all it's like you can tell when somebody is bullshitting you.

The charismatics, of course, represent only a small proportion of those whose reasons for joining are ideological. In many communes, as we shall see in later chapters, there were no charismatic leaders at all. But the general pattern of a small group that cared very much and a larger group with less, little, or no commitment was repeated with striking regularity. Even the religious groups that achieved the closest approximations to ideological unanimity were always fighting battles against backsliding.

Those with ideological reasons for joining can be further subdivided into those who perceived the commune as a means to some external ideological end and those whose ideologies focused on the commune as an end in itself. An example of the former is the following:

> Living this way provides a means of serving each other and combining our resources to organize and strengthen propagation of (our movement's beliefs and practices).

TABLE 3-6. Reported Reasons for Joining Communal Household (First-named reason only)

Type of Reason	Urban			Rural		
	Religious	Secular	All Urban	Religious	Secular	All Rural
Ideological	54%	13%	30%	83%	36%	44%
To achieve goals already held			(N = 64)			(N = 95)
Conversion to goals of group						
Transfer, member of larger community						
Relational	6	15	11	10	22	24
To join individual friend			(N = 24)			(N = 39)
To join group of friends						
To join lover or family member						
Personal	29	37	34	0	32	24
Loneliness			(N = 72)			(N = 53)
To improve interpersonal skills						
To experience new lifestyles						
Convenience	11	35	25	7	10	10
Economic advantages			(N = 55)			(N = 19)
Desired location						
Childcare arrangements						
Total	100%	100%	100%	100%	100%	100%
	(N = 87)	(N = 128)	(N = 215)	(N = 30)	(N = 165)	(N = 195)

Such people tend to be more tolerant of communal shortcomings than the charismatic leader just quoted. On the other hand, those who see the commune as an end in itself may often be prepared to put more of their personal energy into the group. The following is an example:

> I perceived the bankruptcy of the two living options available in the U.S.A. (alone or with a mate). I am committed to developing a third alternative.

For balance, a commune will do well to have representatives of both these types among those who have joined for ideological reasons.

Personal reasons for joining communes represent the modal response in urban-secular groups and are a close second in the rural-secular groups. Such reasons vary widely. Some join communes to open themselves up to new experiences, but many more do it to achieve a respite from a life that has become overly filled with undigested experiences.

Whereas many join communes as a moratorium and a respite, both from the future need to assume responsible and permanent roles and from the past chaos of excessive experimentation with alternate life-styles, for a minority, communal living is truly a way of shaking up a stale and dormant life. This type of motivation is particularly prevalent in the early years of a communitarian movement and also in the early stages of its arrival in a new territory.

A knowledgeable informant, in on the beginning of the arrival of communitarianism in Houston, told a story of the formation of one of the first counter-cultural communes in Houston. This was at a time when the counterculture in Houston was small enough so that most of its active adherents could meet together simultaneously, but well after the peak of the movement in such places as San Francisco, Boston, and New York:

> Everyone announced we are fucked up by society and we want to change ourselves and support each other in reaching this goal. No one else had been involved in politics except for me and a black woman who had been an officer in the Black Panthers, but we both had since given up politics. A commune was started, but it lasted only three months. However, it did what we had announced it would do—change how we live to a great extent. Several women became lesbians and both married couples got divorced. Everyone split up. People tried suicide with no successes. I personally felt that I could not get rid of chauvinism and male supremacy as long as I was straight, as long as there were walls between me and other men and other women. I became active in the gay movement, and it freaked out the people in the house.

More often, the commune is perceived as a sanctuary or place of healing or transition from one stage of life to another. In this, we have already seen, lies a large measure of its appeal to youth. Older people, adjusting to the trauma of marital failure, also make use of communes in this personal way:

When my wife and I decided to separate (with our pastor's concurrence), I tried living on my own for a while but soon realized that I needed people around for support and to talk to if I was ever going to grow and work through problems. I presented that to my pastor and the community elders and they asked me if I would like to try living in a communal household. It has been a real blessing.

In another context, a women expressed similar sentiments from a somewhat different prespective:

I wanted to avoid the divorced-woman-and-two-kids syndrome—in a small apartment getting on each other's nerves.

At times, when personal reasons are not quite so self-involved, it may be difficult to distinguish personal from ideological motivations. The following respondent expresses, out of his own need, a sentiment not very far removed from an ideological critique of his entire society:

It's similar to a village community. It certainly gives the individual say-so that he or she doesn't have if living alone. Oddly enough, you are having a voice that counts in a minisociety. When there is no such possibility in society as a whole, you create your own society.

Note that this person expresses an idea similar to that quoted earlier from Erikson. The individual gains an enhanced sense of identity, paradoxically, by giving up his lone identity to the collective.

A third set of reasons given for joining communes may be called relational. Bennett Berger stresses the importance of friendship networks for the recruitment of new members to the commune. Berger's notion is one of an almost accidential affiliation among those who are diffusely seeking alternative styles of life (1973, p. 7):

There is one other source of recruitment that deserves special mention. There is a great deal of mobility—simple movement from place to place—in the hip world; and much of this mobility takes the form of hitchhiking, much of the time with no particular destination in mind. Those who pick up and those who are picked up often strike up quick friendships that lead to an invitation to spend the night. Often the form that this takes is for a communard with a vehicle to pick up a woman, with or without her baby. He takes her home, where she becomes his old lady. He may leave again a few weeks later, leaving her with the commune as a "member" with an ambiguous status as "his" old lady—although he may not return or return with another woman.

More often, perhaps, the relational motive is quite intentional and only one degree removed from the ideological. Often a conversion process does not work equally strongly or with equal speed for both partners to a marriage. In such instances, if the marriage is to survive, one of the pair must be prepared to make compromises:

My husband was very into the idea. I thought it would be a good experience for me—even if I didn't like it. I love it! I didn't think I could feel this way about sharing and living with other people.

Relational reasons for joining are not commonly reported except in rural-secular communes (the type that Berger studied), where more than one in five falls into this category. However, there is some reason to suspect that cognitive dissonance obliterates relational reasons in favor of ideological ones more often than is the case with other categories. Only ideological reasons were cited more than relational among the secondary responses to the question about reasons for joining.

Finally we come to reasons of convenience pure and simple. Minorities, ranging from 35 percent among the urban-secular communitarians to 7 percent among the rural-religious communitarians, fall into this category. The following is a typical example:

The location was convenient; the house was beautiful; the people were O.K.; we got along without too many hassles. Also, I didn't want to go back to my parents, and I didn't want to live alone or with one person. Also, it's cheap.

Informal observations of successive cohorts of communes from the middle 1960s to the middle 1970s indicate that convenience factors have continually increased in their importance as reasons for joining as communes have ceased to be perceived as threatening by the larger society. The idealistic, pioneering impulse has been partially displaced by a perception of communes themselves as institutions provided to the individual by society, to be used, in the words of one commune member, for "fun, excitement, economy, sex, and to process my karma faster by using group energy."

The Admission Process

Let us turn now to the perspective of the commune faced with an applicant for admission. Two separate but related issues define the situation from the commune's point of view. First, what are the norms (treated here as obstacles that the commune places in the way of applicants)? Second, by what decision-making process are these norms brought to bear on specific individuals who apply for admission?

Communes may be distinguished by the number and kinds of obstacles by which they limit new membership. Historically, these have always ranged from the most severe to the most minimal. Saint Benedict, writing in the sixth century A.D., advised the utmost caution in the admission process (Doyle, 1948, p. 79):

When anyone is newly come for the reformation of his life, let him not be granted an easy entrance; but, as the Apostle says, "Test the spirits to see whether they are from God." If the newcomer, therefore, perseveres in his knocking, and if it is seen after four or five days that he bears patiently the harsh treatment offered him and the difficulty of admission, and that he persists in his petition, then let entrance be granted him, and let him stay in the guest house for a few days.

But this monastic formula has rarely been applied among communes. As Infield and Dichter have remarked, "A survey of known practices of selection shows the absence of sound and tested methods. The utopian communities, the religious as well as the secular, were hardly aware of the problem at all" (1943, pp. 10ff).

The 120 communes in our sample exhibit a wide variety of membership procedures. They range from the absolutely open communes, into which anyone may come and nobody can be asked to leave, to the absolutely closed groups, which start with fixed memberships and are unwilling to consider the idea of new admissions even to replace leavers. When the communes in the sample are grouped according to restrictiveness of admission (Table 3-7), the obstacles placed in the way of membership are found to lie on a unidimensional scale.* For any commune, the presence of any given obstacle always implies the presence of all obstacles of lesser severity.

In Chapter 4 we will see that admission severity as measured by this index is highly correlated with communal stability. The harder it is to get in, the harder it is eventually to get out.

As can be seen from the table, urban communes tend to be clustered in admission categories of medium severity, whereas rural groups tend to be bipolarly distributed in either easy or severe categories. Nineteen percent of the rural groups were completely open: anyone could come and live there without restriction. Although the policy of open admission created certain organizational problems, it did not destroy these groups in the way the open admission policy of New Harmony destroyed that Owenite experiment in 1827.

---

*The admission categories listed in the table were found to describe a perfect Guttman scale. It should be noted that this is an empirical finding not an *a priori* condition of measurement. Each obstacle to membership was found to imply that each obstacle higher on this list was also enforced. Thus, for example, every commune that required new members to exhibit certain objective traits (e.g., steady employment, ability to play a musical instrument) also required that room be available for a new member, that the communal group believe itself to be ready to assimilate new members. All those groups that required a period of personal acquaintanceship with the prospective new member also required all of the above. Note that the first category on the list indicates that there are no obstacles to admission and that the last category indicates that the obstacles to admission are infinitely great.

TABLE 3-7. Admission Requirements

Type of Admission Requirement	Urban		Rural	
	Number	% of Total	Number	% of Total
Anyone may join any time	0	0%	11	19%
Group readiness required	0	0	11	19
Room available required	2	3	6	10
Objective trait(s) required[1]	9	15	5	8
Acquaintanceship required	29	48	6	10
Trial membership required	13	22	16	26
Novitiate readiness required	6	10	5	8
Group absolutely closed, even to replace those who leave	1	2	0	0
Total	60	100%	60	100%

[1] This is the first category on the list in which the commune gives itself the option to choose among various candidates rather than simply deciding whether or not it is appropriate to admit a new member. This represents a critical point of transition between communal openness and communal selectivity.

Only one group in the sample was completely closed. Most fell in between, requiring some degree of personal contact with the applicant before the decision to accept or reject him or her as a member could be made. A high proportion did not require trial membership.

Communes may be further distinguished by the decision-making process used to apply their admission norms. The groups in our sample fall into five major categories, whose frequency distribution is given in Table 3-8: (1) *charismatic communes with absentee charismatic leaders*—decisions about admission tended to be made on the basis of non-rational criteria and transcendent forces; (2) *charismatic communes with charismatic leaders in residence*—decisions were made according to criteria defined and interpreted by the charismatic leaders; (3) *routinized charismatic communes*—admission decisions were made by a leader according to specific constitutional rules; (4) *consensual communes without charismatic leaders*—decisions were made by the group as a whole; (5) *anarchistic communes*—individual decisions were made on the basis of resolution of conflicting forces (i.e., in the terms used by a commune itself, according to the natural flow of events).

Charismatic Communes with Absentee Charismatic Leaders. These were, in most cases, transcendent communes with a very high saliency to the ideology and a very high degree of consensus. They relied upon metaphysical or teleological arguments in making decisions, and they proselytized vigorously to recruit new members on a vast scale. Few rules governed admission. Above all, the members wished to avoid having to make decisions. The mystical "presence" of their absent guru allowed them to do just that. A member of Love from Above gave an example of this perspective:

TABLE 3-8. Frequency Distribution of Charismatic Categories Among Rural and Urban Communes

Decision-Making Category	Rural		Urban		Total	
	Number	% of Total	Number	% of Total	Number	% of Total
Absentee charismatic leadership	5	8%	25	42%	30	25%
Resident charismatic leadership	16	27	6	10	22	18
Routinized charismatic communes	3	5	[a]	—	3	3
Consensual communes without charismatic leaders	19	32	24	40	43	36
Anarchistic communes without charismatic leaders	17	28	5	8	22	18
Total	60	100%	60	100%	120	100%

[a]Three urban communes classified in the absentee charismatic category were showing signs of moving toward routinization. One of the earliest such signs is a shift in the way admissions are handled. Therefore these three communes are discussed in this section along with the three truly routinized rural communes.

There are actually no decisions to be made. Everything is perfectly clear at all times. It is only if you are coming from a place of confusion that you see that there is confusion and you see that there is some decision that has to be made. But actually it is always perfectly clear, and when you are meditating you are in that space of clarity. Then you see the clarity and that there is no decision to be made. The decision has already been made.

Another person gave the following example:

Once we had a lot of people who wanted to move in. We only had room for two people, and so we just had this house meeting, and *we couldn't decide anything. We couldn't decide like how you choose—you can't choose* (laughter). I forgot how it happened, but you know it ended up it was Ann and Olivia. Olivia, I think the main reason Olivia—well, *I don't know how the decision was made, but it was made. I mean it was clear; it was right.*

Decision making based upon mysterious criteria is often justified in terms of the communal ideology:

In our situation it's the energy that we are individually and collectively aware of. It's something that we are all in tune with and we can feel, whether it's satisfying to each of us. If it is satisfying we go for it, and if it isn't we reject it.

Communes with Charismatic Leaders in Residence. In communes of this type, the specific process by which a person becomes recognized as a member is clearer:

We would definitely pray and make a serious consideration before we took on a new member. ... We would pray about it until everybody received a word from the Lord. We would pray as a group. God speaks to you in a group. He speaks in the form of a prophecy or a vision, and then each of you share what God has given you. Then if there is no unity you have to go back and seek God as to why there is no unity. Either someone is not hearing the Lord or there is some other problem that is creating the fact that it is not coming through with uniformity because God doesn't contradict Himself, and (our leader) has the final authority. It's hard to explain what that means, but it means that God puts certain people in the position of authority, and we as Christians are expected to submit to them as we do unto God. The same thing occurs with expulsion.

Routinized Charismatic Communes. In the third type of commune, we generally find a heavy emphasis on selection, socialization, and orthodoxy. Attention is given to making certain that the individual adheres to the communal ideology. Often, too, in this type of commune we find a requirement that is surprisingly absent in most of the communes in our sample (see Kanter,

1972, by way of contrast). This is the requirement that the individual make sacrifices of possessions or certain desired activities to gain membership. Vows of commitment tend to be associated with the routinized charismatic communes, whereas such vows are not required in either of the types of active charismatic communes. In answer to the question of whether a vow was necessary for a person to gain admission to the group, one member of a charismatic commune in the process of routinization said:

> First you must desire to move in. Then you must feel clear about moving in. Then you must get permission from the local director to be considered, and then I guess you would talk to [our guru] and he would see where your heart is and maybe explain to you things that you didn't understand about what it means to live here. . . . Then if you still wanted to move in and if [our guru] was clear that you were suitable and would fit into the harmonious situation that we have here, you would be allowed to move in on a trial basis.

Consensual Noncharismatic Communes. Decision making is more rational in this fourth type of commune than in any of the charismatic groups. These communes are characterized by low input and low output. They do not proselytize and rarely expel. Recruitment often takes place through network links with friends or former members.

Admission decisions are made by the group consensually. This means that a person with one "no" vote would not be admitted. The following is an example of the way this kind of process works in a consensual commune in Atlanta:

> Bringing new people in has been kind of a separate thing. It's been mostly boyfriends and girlfriends that have come to move in. . . . There have been a few other people and the first time we had somebody move in we had them on a sort of probation for some period of time. We didn't have a system or anything. He didn't come to meetings at the beginning, and he didn't do childcare at the beginning because we wanted to see what kind of relationship he would have with the kids first, and then when it really seemed right and when he really seemed ready to make a long-term commitment, well, that was it.

Anarchistic Communes. There is little to say about this type because there is no formal procedure. People come and stay at will. The fittest survive. The process of being accepted may be all the more convoluted for this very reason. But, in terms of formal procedures, this is the easiest of the communes to join. This type, of course, is coterminous with the admission severity category referred to as "open."

But it is not only in open communes that finding a place is easy. It is important to recognize that commune membership in general is not difficult to achieve for those who wish it. Highly restrictive and difficult initation periods and trial memberships are relatively uncommon among contemporary communes, as compared with Rosabeth Kanter's (1972) nineteenth-century sample. Both urban and rural communes of all vintages have been characterized by relative non-exclusivity and by turnover rates averaging in the neighborhood of 50 percent per year. Although, in the early years of the movement, commune membership was sometimes sought in vain, by 1967 in the seedbed areas (i.e., New York, Boston, San Francisco, New Mexico), by 1970 almost everywhere else, and by 1972 even in such places as Houston, communes were in such plentiful supply that almost anyone could find a home in one.

Behavioral Effects of Communal Living

Popular belief has equated communal living with rebellion, expressed in defiant religious, psychological, political, sexual, and cultural patterns of behavior. However, although personal rebelliousness can be a source of motivation for joining a commune, it is by no means a major one. Measurements of the rate of performance of a number of activities associated with rebellion before and after living communally (see Table 3-9) indicate that, for most, these rates decline after joining. The collective rebellion implicit in a communitarian experiment often makes individual rebellion seem both superfluous and obstructive.

Of the twenty-one experiences listed in Table 3-9, nineteen of them diminished after joining a commune. Only meditation and celibacy showed an increase in numbers of participants after joining. Sharp decreases can be noted for all items having to do with police arrests and participation in riots and demonstrations. Perhaps these can be explained by the changing times. The sexual items also show significant decreases, however, and these are less easy to explain in this way. Overall, a picture emerges of the substitution of experimentation in the inner life for participation in various outward acts of social rebellion. These results are found to hold not only for the religious communes but for political and other secular groups as well.

Findings such as these are based upon retrospective evidence and are measured for time periods that vary with each individual. However, it has also been possible to observe individual behavior directly both at the beginning and at the end of a test year. For selected behaviors, we can measure the changes that have occurred during a year of communal living. Drug use, sexual behavior, and cooperative working relationships were selected as three examples of behavior that might plausibly be affected by a year of living communally.

TABLE 3-9. Diversity of Members' Social Experiences Before and After Joining Commune[1]

Characteristic	Before	After	Never	Total
Abstinence from certain foods	55.4%	53.3%	28.6%	542
Male	54.1	51.7	29.9	298
Female	56.9	55.9	27.0	244
Group psychotherapy	23.8	17.3	66.6	542
Male	26.5	18.8	62.4	298
Female	20.5	15.6	71.7	244
Individual psychotherapy	29.2	12.6	64.9	542
Male	27.2	9.4	67.4	298
Female	31.5	16.4	61.9	244
Consciousness raising group	39.9	36.4	46.1	542
Male	38.9	38.6	46.0	298
Female	41.0	33.6	46.3	244
Encounter or sensitivity training	41.0	24.9	47.6	542
Male	42.3	23.2	48.3	298
Female	39.3	27.0	46.7	244
Sex with more than one person at a time	23.6	14.0	68.3	542
Male	23.4	13.7	68.8	298
Female	23.7	14.3	67.6	244
Homosexuality	13.1	9.4	82.3	542
Male	14.7	8.4	81.9	298
Female	11.1	10.6	82.8	244
De facto or legal open marriage	15.7	6.6	81.7	542
Male	15.5	6.1	81.9	298
Female	16.0	7.0	81.6	244
Group marriage	2.2	0.9	96.9	542
Male	3.0	1.0	96.0	298
Female	1.2	0.8	98.0	244
Participation in riots	22.0	3.0	76.7	541
Male	25.3	3.4	73.1	297
Female	18.0	2.4	81.1	244
Participation in anti-war demonstrations	56.6	8.5	42.3	542
Male	57.7	6.7	41.3	298
Female	55.3	10.6	43.4	244
Participation in civil rights demonstrations	33.2	6.1	64.6	542
Male	32.5	5.7	65.8	298
Female	34.0	6.6	63.1	244
Arrested by police	29.5	4.2	68.6	542
Male	38.0	5.7	59.7	298
Female	19.2	2.4	79.5	244

TABLE 3–9. Diversity of Members' Social Experiences Before and After Joining Commune[1] (continued)

Characteristic	Before	After	Never	Total
Vegetarianism	42.3%	35.8%	48.0%	542
Male	41.6	34.2	49.7	298
Female	43.0	37.7	45.9	244
Falling in love	84.0	48.5	12.4	542
Male	84.9	47.3	11.1	298
Female	82.8	50.0	13.9	244
Meditation	47.1	50.1	38.6	541
Male	45.7	50.0	39.9	298
Female	49.0	50.2	37.0	243
Yoga	39.9	34.3	50.2	542
Male	38.2	34.2	51.3	298
Female	41.8	34.4	48.8	244
Public or group nudity	40.4	31.6	48.3	542
Male	43.9	32.2	44.0	298
Female	35.3	30.8	53.7	244
Celibacy	23.3	30.8	60.5	542
Male	22.8	32.8	59.7	298
Female	23.8	29.6	61.5	244
Had a close scrape with death	41.0	11.4	55.9	542
Male	47.7	14.1	48.3	298
Female	32.7	8.1	65.2	244
Has visited a foreign country (including Canada and Mexico)	62.9	27.5	30.5	541
Male	64.3	27.2	29.0	297
Female	61.1	27.9	32.4	244

[1] The row percentages will not total 100% because some respondents in each case reported the activity both before and after joining a commune.

Patterns of Drug Use

The use of consciousness-altering drugs was commonplace in the decade 1965–1975 among those countercultural elements of society from which the communitarian movement evolved. Whatever else the use of drugs may have signified, it was also a form of personal rebellion against the established mores of that period. By examining drug use behavior, we can test the hypothesis that communal living dampens individual rebelliousness.

By no means have all communes had favorable policies toward drug use. As Table 3-10 indicates, one-third of the urban communes and one-sixth of the rural communes outlawed marijuana. Among the rural groups this taboo was likely to be enforced only within the commune grounds and was often adopted as an expediency in relationship to the local police. Among the urban groups that outlawed drugs, most forbade their members to take them at any time, whether on or off the commune property. Urban communal taboos on drugs were more likely to be a part of the group's ideology than a matter of expediency. Little change was observed in communal policy toward marijuana during the test year. Almost all the communes in both the rural and the urban sample stayed in the same category listed in Table 3-10A. This indicates that the changes in drug use patterns observed during the year of study were not attributable to policy changes on the part of the commune involved.

Table 3-10B indicates the change in the relative use of various types of drugs in rural communes from the first wave of the study to the second wave. Note that only stayers (i.e., those present in both waves) were included in this tabulation. Some interesting changes can be noted.

The most popular drugs in the first wave were marijuana, tobacco, and alcohol, in that order. At the time of the second wave, tobacco had replaced marijuana as the most popular drug, marijuana had fallen to second place, and alcohol had held its third-place position, being used by slightly under one-third of all the members observed in both waves. The biggest decreases observed were for psychedelics (LSD, mescaline, psilocybin) and marijuana. The greatest increases were for heavy drugs—barbiturates and heroin. However, two cautionary points should be made here. One is the great difficulty that relatively untrained field observers had in distinguishing barbiturates from amphetamines in their observation during both waves and particularly in the first wave. The second is that the number of people involved in the use of barbiturates and/or heroin was so small and the observational methods so crude that the increase might very well be attributable to nothing more than heightened sensitivity. The same, of course, might be said for the switch from marijuana to tobacco. However, these drugs were used more openly and publicly and were more easily distinguishable by smell, and the switch in emphasis between the two drugs was often mentioned by commune members themselves. It should be noted that these data were obtained by observation in rural communes only over a period of seven years. Because the two waves of the study were spread out over time for the various groups, the possibility that the differences observed can be attributed to an historical trend (*zeitgeist* effect) is somewhat reduced. When the data are recoded by year, rather than by wave, no clear and consistent trends are discernable, except for a slight continuous decline in the use of psychedelics.

TABLE 3-10. Patterns of Drug Use

A. Communal policy on drugs in urban and rural communes

Communal Policy on Marijuana	Rural (N = 60 communes)	Urban (N = 60 communes)
Promoted as part of ideology	15.0%	11.7%
Fully accepted	48.3	33.2
Neutral or mixed reception	15.0	10.0
Discouraged	5.0	11.7
Forbidden within commune	10.0	11.7
Forbidden to members at any time	6.7	21.7
Total	100%	100%

B. Observed use of selected drugs in rural communes[1]

Drug Type	First Wave (N = 230)	Second Wave (N = 230)
Heroin	1.3%	3.0%
Amphetamines	5.2	7.0
Barbituates	—	4.8
Psychedelics	22.1	8.7
Marijuana	54.4	38.7
Tobacco	51.3	59.1
Alcohol	32.6	31.3

C. Reported use of any illegal drugs before and after joining urban commune[2]

Drug Use	Before	After	Never	Total
By sex				
Male	85.9%	42.0%	12.4%	298
Female	79.1	45.9	18.9	244
By city				
Atlanta	80.9	45.0	15.7	89
New York	91.6	34.7	6.9	72
Twin Cities	68.5	47.9	24.7	73
Houston	85.0	31.3	14.9	67
Los Angeles[3]	74.0	26.9	26.0	119
Boston	95.0	68.8	4.1	122
By ideology of commune				
Eastern religion	96.4	16.1	3.6	137
Christian	56.2	8.8	43.9	57
Psychological	95.1	91.4	2.5	81
Rehabilitation	63.2	5.3	36.8	76
Cooperative	90.4	75.0	7.7	52
Family	60.0	60.0	30.0	40
Counter culture	94.8	70.2	5.3	57
Political	83.3	69.0	9.5	42
By year of joining commune				
1969	100.0	83.3	0.0	6
1970	66.7	60.0	13.3	15
1971	69.2	34.6	23.1	26
1972	81.7	47.0	14.3	49
1973	78.4	40.2	20.1	139
1974	86.5	42.9	13.2	296

[1] Each percentage represents the proportion of all members who used any drugs publicly during a week of observation, among members present in both waves only. Selection in first wave from various years 1965–1971, for second wave from 1966–1972.

[2] The row percentages will not total 100% because some respondents reported use of drugs both before and after joining a commune.

[3] There is reason to suspect that the Los Angeles commune members substantially under reported use of illegal drugs both before and after joining due to concerns about unfavorable publicity.

In Table 3-10C, we note that the use of illegal drugs dropped by almost 50 percent in that almost half the 1974 members who reported using drugs before joining claimed to have stopped. Undoubtedly, this finding reflects a certain amount of underreporting for reasons of communal security. There are also opportunity factors that are partially controlled for by examining the various cohorts of joiners. However, the possibility of a self-selection effect cannot be eliminated. In a number of autobiographical statements made by urban commune members, the desire to retreat from a perceived psychological over-dependence on non-addictive drugs was stated or hinted at among the circumstances leading up to joining.

The before-and-after measure used in part C of this table is, however, tricky to interpret with confidence. This can be seen most easily in the case of members who had just joined the commune. Obviously the opportunity to use drugs after joining would be at a minimum for such people. On the other hand, those who have been members of the commune for many years have had ample opportunity to experiment with drugs after joining but may have been too young prior to joining or may have joined before drugs came into fashion in their city. Because drug use is often a regular practice, these differential-opportunity effects are not so great as they would be for certain other sporadic activities. Nevertheless, in an attempt to separate out differential opportunity, the year in which the person joined the commune was controlled for. It can be seen from the table that in every cohort the amount of drug use declined after membership, although this decline was greatest for those who joined after 1970.

It is interesting to note that, although the measurement techniques used in Tables 3-10B and 10C suffer from certain shortcomings, they represent two radically different kinds of measurements used on two different populations that nevertheless yield the same basic result: use of illegal drugs tends to decline after membership in a commune is attained. This is the result predicted by the hypothesis that communes diminish individual rebelliousness in favor of collective ideological rebellion.

Those communes with the most totalitarian ideologies—Eastern, Christian, and rehabilitational—experienced the greatest degree of decline in drug use, a result also predicted by our hypothesis. Another pattern should be noted in the statistical breakdown of drug use by ideology in Table 3-10C, although its significance will not become clear until we discuss the ideological types at length in Chapter 5. Those communes with ideologies oriented toward the strategy of consciousness display consistently higher amounts of drug use than do their counterparts oriented toward the strategy of direct action (i.e.: Eastern more than Christian among the religious; Psychological more than Rehabilitative among the self-concerned; Cooperative more than Family among the group-concerned; and Countercultural more than Political among those concerned with society).

Sexual Behavior

In one way or another, sex is a problem for all communes. The various methods by which communes have attempted to regulate sexual attractions and energies—ranging from prescribed celibacy to prescribed group marriage—are discussed in Chapter 8. Here we are concerned simply with changes in sexual behavior as a function of time.

Communal living is hard on marriages. Of the 102 legally married couples in rural and urban communes who were followed over the test year, 47 percent were no longer living communally by the year's end. This is not in itself remarkable, as the membership turnover rate for couples is not significantly different from that for single people (as we shall see in Chapter 4). However, of the 54 couples who stuck it out for the full year, a majority (57 percent) were divorced or separated at the end of the year.*

Rural communes would appear to be harder on marriage than urban communes. The odds were almost three to one against a rural commune marriage's remaining intact for a year. The odds were two to one in favor of an urban marriage's remaining intact for a year (still very low compared to the odds of about fifty to one of an average American marriage remaining intact for the year).

Before attempting to explain the high general rate of dissolution and the large rural-urban difference, two not completely obvious points must be made clear. The first is that, among the hidden agendas behind the more socially acceptable reasons people give for joining communes, an important one is the attempt to save or end a marriage that is in trouble. The other point is that, from the perspective of personal privacy, rural and urban communes inhabit quite different kinds of ecological spaces. Although there is far less square footage per person in the urban commune, there is far less anonymity in the rural. As isolated, more or less self-sufficient communities, the rural communes are often like small villages where everyone knows everyone else's business. Urban communitarians are able to make use of the protective cover of the city if they wish to have private lives.

Now one of the popular conceptions of communes is that they are situations of expanded sexual opportunity. Unlike many other popular conceptions, this happens to be true. It is particularly relevant to our discussion of dissolved marriages. Twenty-six of the thirty-one marriages that did not survive the test year foundered in part because of extramarital sexual involvements, real or imagined.

Even the securely married often confessed in interviews that they found communitarian sexual opportunity a trial. For the great majority of the marriages that were shaky to begin with, the strain was usually even greater. Because joining a rural commune, as we have seen, generally requires more intentionality than joining an urban commune, it is possible that this may be reflected in the greater degree of desperation found in rural as opposed to urban communal

---

*We heard informally that several of the couples whose marriages are listed as dissolved at the end of the test year were later reconciled, however.

marriages. If this is true, it would help to explain a part of the greater instability observed in the rural marriages.

But a greater, or at least a more immediate cause of difference has to do with the ecology of privacy. Love affairs in rural communes were more obtrusive, harder to hide, harder to ignore. Where these stemmed from experiments in nonpossessive relationships, the physical implications of nonpossessiveness were harder for the aggrieved party to overlook. Where they stemmed from old-fashioned cheating in communes that were supposed to be monogamous, the love affairs were usually discovered faster in the rural communes. For example, our urban field workers reported a number of cases in which covert sexual triangles lasted for a year or more with the wife or husband apparently knowing nothing of the extramarital relationship. This never happened in our rural researches. Thus the rate at which troubled marriages reached the breaking point was considerably greater in rural communes than in urban, even though the ultimate fate of such marriages in both types of commune may have been pretty much the same.

Something about a commune does not love a dyad. Observers from Noyes and Nordhoff in the nineteenth century to Berger, Kanter, and Bennett in the present day have commented on the strain between marital commitment and communal commitment. The amount of ideological attention communes give to sex is further testimony to the importance of this issue.

So far we have been talking just about marriage, but the number of (self-reported) informal sexual relationships between unmarried stayers also diminished sharply during the test year. About a fifth of those reporting membership in an informal sexual dyad* at the beginning of the test year were no longer so reporting at the end of the year. The number of those dyads that were not sexually active at the beginning of the year but reported sexual activity at the end was negligible by comparison. This finding is particularly interesting because, as trust developed over the year, respondents became more willing to talk about their private lives with fieldworkers. Therefore, in the absence of a systematic effect, we should have expected a net *increase* in the number of reported informal sexual dyads.

It might seem at first that these findings contradict the statement made earlier that communes are situations of increased sexual opportunity. But, so far, we have been discussing only stayer dyads (i.e., couples both of whose members remained in the commune for the entire test year). The majority of new sexual dyads formed during the year were composed of one stayer and one

---

*As with all sociometric measures used in this book, this is based on data from the urban communes only. Because of the reluctance of many people to discuss their sex lives, a "weak and relaxed" definition (see Appendix A) of relationship was used. By this definition, a dyad was considered to be sexually active if *either or both* of the parties claimed to be *sometimes or regularly* sleeping with the other. It is very likely that even this measure undercounted the number of informal liaisons.

recent joiner. In a process reminiscent of the way in which freshmen become prime dating candidates in small residential colleges, new commune members often become, for a brief period, the object of widespread sexual attention.

It is not only old member/new member pairings that allow a prevailing sense of heightened sexual opportunity to coexist with diminishing sexual interest among couples who have lived together communally for a while. The charismatic nature of communal life provokes in many communes a generalized cathexis. Every possible dyad becomes emotionally charged (although not necessarily sexually active) and (perhaps for this very reason) no particular dyad can retain an exclusive fascination for very long. This important process has implications not only for couples but for the stability of the commune itself. We therefore give it detailed attention in Chapter 4.

In communes with residential charismatic leaders, the person of the leader is often the junction of the various generalized sexual desires. In four communes in the sample, having sex with the charismatic leader was a legitimate and prestigious step in the path to enlightenment. However, in nine other groups (seven of which were strictly celibate by rule), major or minor scandals linking charismatic leaders sexually with various of their followers occurred during the test year, and others occurred at the time but were not discovered until later.

A final point about sexual behavior needs to be made. Although sexuality is an important force in communal life, and although joining a commune appears to lead, willy-nilly, to a sense of increased sexual opportunity, the actual amount of sex and sexual experimentation occurring in most communes is fairly low. As we have already seen in Table 3-9, homosexual and multisexual involvements tend to decline slightly after joining a commune. According to self-reports, 42 percent of urban communitarians, in the 54 communes where such data were available, were not involved sexually with any of the other commune members at the beginning of the test year. Of those who were, 71 percent were mono-gamous, 22 percent were informally bigamous, and only 7 percent were involved in serious sexual relationships with three or more fellow members at the same time. Although these data undoubtedly suffer seriously from underreporting, they surely indicate (even if the true rates are double or triple those reported) that communal sexual activity, except in the rare group marriage commune, is much more exclusive than it is all-inclusive.

Cooperative Work

All communes seek to modify the prevailing patterns of economic production, distribution, and/or consumption; and, in doing so, all communes espouse some form of the cooperative ideal. As with our discussions of drugs and sex, we defer to Part II of this book a discussion of the successes and failures of cooperative ideologies, being concerned here only with cooperative behavior.

An ambivalence concerning work is well expressed in a poem by Kahlil Gibran that has become part of the credo of many communes:

Work is love made visible. And if you cannot work with love but only with distaste, it is better that you should leave your work and sit at the gate of the temple and take alms of those who work with joy.

This quote is often used to legitimize the reluctance of many communes to impose regular work responsibilities on themselves and others.

The kinds of data that can be used to examine changes in the work patterns of commune members are different from those used to look at changing drug and sex patterns. Although sociometric reports on the extent to which the individuals in a commune claim to spend time working with one another exist for both the beginning and the end of the test year in the urban communes, they do not adequately measure cooperation. These data alone show small net increases in both the degree of connectedness and the degree of knit in these graphs, thus suggesting that cooperation modestly increased over a year of communal living.

Ethnographic observations, however, reveal a much more complex pattern of events. For one thing, it is clear to anyone who has spent any time in communes that the spirit of cooperation as manifested in common work is accompanied by a palpable emotional experience. The problem is that this experience has little to do with whether people are physically working together on a common task or off separately doing individual chores. Another complicating factor is that, unlike drug use and sexual behavior (which are largely functions of the individual's career in the commune), working patterns are very much a function of the stage of the entire commune within its own lifespan. New communes are given to alternating bursts of heroic cooperative labor and introspective lethargy. Old communes will often have reached an equilibrium between communal and individual endeavors and responsibilities.

Whatever the triumphs of American communitarianism, they have certainly not mounted a threat to the capitalist system. French and French, who studied the commune movement from a strictly economic point of view, had the following generally negative evaluation (1975, p. 89):

Only in the rarest cases did communes really come to terms with their environments, forming units that could survive without a steady flow of gifts from outside. Stranger still, all too seldom did communards fully come to terms with one another, massive propaganda to the contrary notwithstanding. Many more communes went under because the dishes never got washed than were ever forced out of town by hostile neighbors or zoning boards. As the 1960s ended, the suspicion grew that the counterculture was ultimately far more concerned with escaping the old world than building a new one.

Findings from our own sample of 120 communes tend to corroborate this judgment. By comparison with the work projects of the kibbutzim, the Shakers, or the Bruderhof, those undertaken by contemporary communes were generally (with a few notable exceptions) primitive in scope. A great majority (approximately three quarters) of the major projects started or being planned at the beginning of the test year for completion in that year were not completed by the end. It should be noted that many of these projects were completed later, reflecting perhaps nothing more than relaxed communitarian attitudes toward deadlines. Many others, however, were no longer even considered communal goals by the year's end, indicating the unstable focus of communal attention under conditions of rapid membership turnover and rapid changes in personal interests among the staying members.

The conditions of communal enterprise are such that it is necessary to plan major undertakings enthusiastically rather than rationally. As in all complex collectivities, there is always much more in need of being done in a commune that can possibly be accomplished with available resources. It is therefore necessary to establish priorities. But we have already spoken of the great reluctance of commune members to adjudicate differences of opinion in legislative assembly. This is nowhere more tellingly illustrated than in the process of economic decision making. In both rural and urban communes, the pattern is similar. Projects are born out of the enthusiasm and conviction of one or two individuals and are sustained only as long as their originators can mobilize collective interest in their behalf.

None of this applies to communes in which there are charismatic leaders in the full flowering of their authority. A charismatic leader, at the height of his power, is able to get a commune to accomplish more than could ever be attempted under similar conditions by the most efficient or wage-based firms. Many of the exceptionally wealthy communes throughout history owe their economic success to this factor. One of the wealthiest, the Harmony society of the nineteenth century, attributed its success to the charismatic leader George Rapp. Nordhoff says of Rapp (1875, pp. 91ff):

> The young people were very fond of him. "He was a man before whom no evil could stand." "When I met him in the street, if I had a bad thought in my head, it flew away." He was constantly in the fields or in the factories, cheering, encouraging, or advising the people. "He knew everything—how to do it, what was the best way." "Ah, he was a man! He told us what to do, and how to be good." In his spare moments he studied botany, geology, astronomy, mechanics. "He was never idle, not even a quarter of an hour." He believed much in work; thought hard field-work a good cure for spiritual as well as bodily diseases. . . . He was "a good man, with true, honest eyes."

Similar phenomena were found among the communes in our sample. In one rural commune, the charismatic leader motivated a work team of ten hippie men without prior training in construction to build cabins at the astonishing rate of one a day, using poor equipment and often battling terrible weather conditions. The grueling pace of this work was not resented by the members but rather considered to be a valuable spiritual discipline. Of course, attitudes and achievements of this kind are commonplace in the Israeli kibbutzim, but they have been rare in the American commune movement.

The only problem with this sort of enterprise is that when routinization sets in or the charismatic leader gets in trouble (as they often do), the work grinds to a halt. Older and more experienced communes, like the Hutterians and the Bruderhof, have learned to insulate their charismatic hierarchies from their workaday administrative hierarchies so that the periodic tremors that seem inevitably to accompany charismatic leadership need not disturb the economic life of the community. But few of the charismatic communes in our sample have as yet become so differentiated.

We have been speaking about the undertaking of major enterprises, but what about everyday cooperation? Every commune must accomplish a certain amount of daily work in order to survive. In particular, how does communal living affect behavior with respect to household chores and cooperative child rearing? In neither case is there a clear trend. In some communes, rigidly rotating job assignment schemes at the beginning of the year gave way to naturally complementary work roles by the end of the year. In other groups, movement occurred in the opposite direction: spontaneity and naturalness gave rise to feelings of exploitation and thus to the formal assignment of rotating work responsibilities. Similarly, with respect to children, familiarity among sets of parents sometimes gave rise to trust and increased willingness to surrender parental authority to the group. But, in other situations, disputes with other parents about discipline and anxieties of the children brought about by rapid membership turnover have led to nuclear family withdrawal from cooperative child rearing. In still other instances, of course, the problem has been quite the reverse: natural parents have foisted off responsibility for children onto the unwilling commune.

In summary, it may be said that a measurable degree of cooperation does not appear to be learned or developed in a year's time. Although the indicators used to measure this were crude, the failure to discover even net trends in the direction of cooperation seems to suggest that finer instruments would not have revealed more. From the experience of many multigenerational communes, we know that young children can be socialized to cooperative dispositions. But it is a sad commentary on the state of knowledge in this field that we still do not know whether even long-term exposure to communal living creates a greater disposition toward cooperation on the part of adults. The results of this study suggest that, in the absence of a charismatic leader, communal cooperation, at least in the short run, is sporadic and dependent upon the stage of the commune in its own lifespan and the prevailing degree of communal stability.

Communion and Individuality

Drug use, sexuality, and work are obviously only a few of the many areas of behavior influenced by communal living. They serve adequately, however, to delineate a characteristic pattern of short-term individual change. The myth of ego transcendence overstates the extent of this pattern although it correctly marks the direction of the change. Collective rebellion replaces individual rebellion; diffuse sexuality (for many) replaces specific sexuality; enthusiastic and contagious decision making replaces calculating and deliberative decision making. These very general trends underlie and support a wide spectrum of personality changes ranging from major alterations in states of consciousness (ego loss) to simple reductions in the felt need to rank individual preferences ordinally and make choices.

The problem of choice proliferation is thus not solved but circumvented by living communally. Only to a small degree do commune members use the reduced scale of their intentionally small social worlds to experiment with decision making in the search for personal authenticity. To a much greater degree, the intersection of all members' preference sets gives rise to a highly delimited, and thus manageable, range of choices. This intersection is experienced as group unity or communion and may itself be the source of gratification and renewed commitment. However, in most instances, individual preference sets are not really modified but merely reordered. The resulting communion rests upon shifting layers of potentially divergent individual preferences. As we shall see in Chapter 4, in the absence of some force strong enough to keep these divergent tendencies in check, communion is necessarily highly unstable.

Distinguishing Stayers from Leavers

The instability of communal households provides a rare and valuable opportunity to examine the sources of group membership disintegration and decay. Time intervals as short as one or two years are sufficient for ample observation of these processes both at the group and at the individual level. As Table 3-11 indicates, 80 percent of the initial sixty urban communes survived the test year, and 63 percent were still in existence* after two years. At the individual level, 49 percent of the members whose communes survived the test year were still living in these communes at the end of the test year. Within the two-year subsample, the proportion of stayers dropped to 32 percent. Although group-level and individual-level instability are obviously closely related phenomena, we find it convenient to discuss them separately. Accordingly, turnover rates and communal disintegrations will be treated in Chapter 4, and only the problem of within-commune variance in the propensity to leave will be examined in this chapter.

The reasons given by commune members for leaving may be classified as pushes or pulls. Pulls emanate from outside the commune and thus are not subject to individual-level prediction; that is, the conditions of the study did not permit estimation of the likelihood that any given individual would be

---

*In this study a commune was considered to be intact at the end of the test year if there was no particular point in time at which its membership disintegrated or its formal organization was disbanded. (See Appendix A for a more detailed definition.) But small sequential changes in membership during the course of the year could (and in one case

TABLE 3-11. Urban Commune Membership Turnover in One-Year and Two-Year Panels

	Panel A One Year, Two Waves (1974 –1975)	Panel B Two Years, Three Waves (1974–1976)
Number of communes at start	60 communes	60 communes
Surviving communes	48 communes (80%)	38 communes (63%)
Surviving communes for which complete membership turnover data sets were obtained	46 communes (77%)	24 communes (40%)
Total membership at start	668 people (60 communes)	668 people (60 communes)
Membership at start (first wave) of surviving communes with complete data sets	562 people (46 communes)	292 people (24 communes)
Number of stayers	284 people (46 communes)	93 people (24 communes)
Percentage of members staying until end of panel	51%	32%

tempted by opportunities in the outside world. This is less of a problem in estimating rates of turnover. Except perhaps in dealing with intercity differences, it can be assumed that the proportion of pulls experienced by any given commune will be fairly constant and that endogenous characteristics of the commune will determine the extent to which such pulls are resisted. For individuals, however, the potential intrusion of "pull" factors represents a major disturbance in attempting to predict who will leave and who will stay within any specific commune.

Predictive Discrimination

The conditions under which people leave communes resemble, in one respect, the conditions under which molecules evaporate from a liquid. By observing the membership of a commune, it is possible to make fairly accurate predictions as to the proportion that will leave in a given future time period but it is much more difficult to predict which specific members will leave. Moreover,

---

actually did) result in 100 percent turnover by the end of the year in a nondisintegrating commune.

as with molecules of water boiling in a pot, the probability that a person will leave appears to be a function of the current circumstances of the person and the commune, not of their past histories.

Given our knowledge at the end of the test year of who stayed and who left, what combination of information available at the beginning of the test year would have best enabled us to predict these outcomes?* Table 3-12 summarizes the results of attempts to discriminate between stayers and leavers.† A modest improvement over chance is achieved when all communes are included in the analysis and discriminative ability increases a bit more when we restrict the sample to exclude from consideration communes with very high membership turnover. All of the independent variables in the table are measured in units of deviation from their communal means rather than in raw units, in order to focus exclusively on intra-commune discrimination between stayers and leavers.

The most powerful single predictor of leaving is defined at the relational level of analysis: the amount of love received from fellow commune members.‡ Except for age in the more stable communes, individual attributes are of no help in predicting propensity to leave: the distribution of sex, education, income, marital and parental status, years of communal membership, and so on are virtually identical among leavers and stayers. Attitudinal measures, particularly alienation and trust, do better but are still weaker predictors than relational measures such as loving.

Looking first at the full sample of urban communes, we see that the number of times that a person is mentioned by fellow commune members as an object of love is strongly and *inversely* related to probability of leaving. Next in importance come alienation, as measured by the Harris Alienation Scale (see Appendix B) and the number of people in the commune over whom one claims to have power (again, both inversely related to leaving). Finally, the more agreement there is with the statement, "The people in this commune are my

---

*To a limited extent, its predictive efficacy is then validated by making predictions from the state of the same variables at time two to leaver-stayer status at time three. But by this time, the end of the second year, the sample has degenerated too far to allow rigorous evaluations.

†The N's on which the analysis in Table 3-12 is based are small because members of disintegrating communes and "transferers" have been excluded. Transferers are defined as follows: Recall that we have defined a commune as a single communal household even in cases in which several such households are linked in a larger federation. A subclass of leavers was identified made up of people who had actually transferred to another such commune (not necessarily one in the sample). These "transferers" tend to resemble stayers more than they do other kinds of leavers. Therefore, they have been excluded from the analysis on the grounds that their status has more to do with a sociologically imposed boundary definition than with the process of leaving.

‡For a fuller discussion of this and other relational measures, see Chapter 4 and Appendix A.

TABLE 3-12. Discriminant Analysis: Leavers versus Stayers

Variable (Z-score)[1]	Mean Score Higher for		Absolute Value of Standardized Discriminant Function Coefficients (rank order of importance in parentheses)		
	Leavers	Stayers	All Communes	Communes with 70% or Fewer Leavers	Communes with 60% or Fewer Leavers
Love choices received: Number of times mentioned as a person who is loved by another commune member		X	.82 (1)	.76 (1)	.65 (2)
Alienation: as measured by Harris Alienation Scale		X	.48 (2)	.33 (5)	.33 (4)
Number of persons that one claims to dominate in the hierarchy of sociometric power choices		X	.43 (3)	not significant	not significant
Agreement with the statement: "The people in this commune are my true family"	X		.40 (4)	.70 (2)	.69 (1)
An index of communal trust[2]	X		not significant	.50 (3)	.29 (6)
An index of urban trust[2]		X	not significant	.40 (4)	.27 (7)
An index of communitarianism[3]		X	not significant	.21 (6)	not significant
Agreement with the statement: "There is a distance between me and the other commune members"		X	not significant	.20 (7)	.34 (3)
Age		X	not significant	not significant	.32 (5)
			$N = 136$ (stay = 81; leave = 55) 66% correctly classified	$N = 119$ (stay = 78; leave = 41) 71% correctly classified	$N = 95$ (stay = 67; leave = 28) 77% correctly classified

[1] Each person's score on each variable is measured in units of deviation from the person's commune mean for that variable.
[2] Based on Trust in People Scale (see Appendix B).
[3] Based on a composite of attitude items (see Appendix B).

true family," the greater the likelihood of leaving at some time during the following year.

When we restrict our analysis to those communes in which fewer than 70 percent of the first-wave members left by the end of the test year, the model now requires not four but seven predictors to achieve the same proportional reduction of error. Sociometric power does not discriminate once we remove the most unstable groups, but the other three full-sample predictors are still present, and *loving* retains its paramount position. Trust also enters the equation at this point in a perplexing manner. Stayers had greater trust in the general population of their city than did leavers; but leavers had greater trust in the specific members of the commune. Finally, stayers scored higher in positive orientation toward communitarianism as a social movement and agreed more with the statement, "There is often a distance between me and the other commune members."

Restricting the sample still further by excluding all communes with membership turnover greater than 60 percent yields an increase in predictive power. Disagreement with the statement, "The people in this commune are my true family," being named frequently as an object of love, and agreement with the statement, "There is a distance between me and the other commune members," are the three major predictors of propensity to stay in the commune. By this time, 77 percent of the sample are correctly classified, but the modal category, stayers, includes 71 percent of the cases.

Taking as baseline the rate of error achieved by classifying everyone in the modal category, we can reduce by 15 percent in all communes and 21 percent in the stable communes the error in predicting who is going to leave and who is going to stay. It remains to be asked, however, what theoretical sense can be made of the pattern of variables that statistically discriminate between leavers and stayers.

The Relative Deprivation of Love

The extent to which individuals are bound together in a group has generally been referred to as cohesiveness, and cohesiveness has been equated with the strength of positive affective bonds. The finding that love acts like a glue to hold people to the commune should not then be surprising. What is surprising is not that, within any given commune, leavers receive less love than stayers but, in the sample as a whole, that the mean love received by leavers is greater than for stayers.

Findings such as these strongly suggest the presence of a compositional effect. In fact, we find the specific effect known as "the relative deprivation effect," (Davis, 1961, p. 20), to be operating.* Looking more closely at the commune data on loving and leaving, we find the identical situation: the probability of staying is greater for the loved than for the unloved, but the probability of staying decreases for both categories as the overall saturation of love in the group increases.

Commune members appear to be most content being loved in contexts in which there is not much love to go around. They seem to be well content to do without much love if the other people in their commune are not getting much either. At the other extreme, those least content and most likely to leave are people who receive little love in communes in which love is abundantly distributed.

Further explanation of the loving-leaving association will obviously require more information on what commune members mean when they speak of love. This quest is undertaken in Chapter 4. Here, however, one additional point should be noted. We spoke earlier, in discussing the instability of marriage relations in communes, of the generalization of cathexis in communal life. Specific emotional attachments become diffused and generalized in communes, except perhaps in the presence of a charismatic leader (who serves to respecify them in his own person). A less cynical alternative explanation of the phenomenon at hand, then, is that love tends to bind at the individual level but that the diffusion of love creates group-level instability that affects the individual not directly but indirectly. Still a third explanation reverses the causal assumptions: love is "produced" by a group in proportion to its felt instability, and this love is lavished most fully on those who have made the greatest commitment to staying. Let us leave these matters to be dealt with more fully in the next chapter.

Commitment, Trust, and Disillusionment

The most obvious approach to the problem of predicting propensity to stay or leave is simply to ask people their intentions. The following three measures of commitment were used:

a. Which of the following best describes your future plans with respect to this commune?

I would like to live my entire life as a member of this group and have my children carry it on after me.

I expect to live here a good long time.

*Recall that, in the classical relative deprivation situation (Stouffer et al., 1949), satisfaction is greater for the promoted than for the nonpromoted but that it decreases for both groups as a function of the proportion promoted in the group.

I may leave tomorrow but, as long as I'm here, I try to act as if I were going to be here forever.

I'm not really sure of my plans right now.

I don't expect to be here very long.

I can hardly wait to be able to leave.

other (specify)

b. Which of the following best describes yourself with respect to this commune?

one of the more active members of this commune

just an average member

somewhat less involved than most right now

rather marginal to this commune

there are no such distinctions among members of this group

other (specify)

c. If you were offered $10,000 in cash by an anonymous donor to leave this commune, and never again live communally in this house or with any of these same people (spouse, children, relatives excepted) would you:

definitely accept the offer

have to think about it

definitely reject the offer

prefer not to answer

In none of the three cases was there a significant difference between leavers and stayers, and in the last of the three measures, the leavers registered higher commitment than the stayers. In other words, there was no consistent relationship between stated commitment to the commune at the beginning of the test year and presence in the commune at the end of the year.

That future intentions do not correlate with later actions is well known within sociology, particularly in studies of community satisfaction and residential mobility. This finding, therefore, should not surprise us. It is, however, ironic that even the members of what have been called "intentional" communities cannot seem to match intention with choice of action, even on so basic a matter as the decision to stay or leave.

The relation of communal trust to propensity to leave is both more subtle and more revealing of underlying social psychological mechanisms. Communal trust is lower for stayers than for leavers; stayers agree more often than leavers with the statement, "There is often a distance between me and the other commune members," and leavers agree more than stayers with the statement, "The members of this commune are my true family." All these indicators point in the same direction, and all throw additional light on the finding that the propensity to leave increases as the communal network structure becomes saturated with love.

A fundamental truth about all communal structures is revealed here: they tend to reduce interpersonal distances beyond the humanly tolerable. Whereas the desire for scaled-down community, in which people can relate openly and authentically to each other, is a powerful motivating force in the act of joining, the problem becomes reversed in the act of staying; the need is to retain certain minimum distancing mechanisms without destroying the sense of communion. Among those leavers with exceptionally high trust in their commune, we find, in fact, a profound sense of disillusionment when the group fails to live up to their idealistic expectations. This contrasts sharply with the more realistic expectations of what needs the commune can and cannot fulfill, which characterize many members of the longer lasting and more stable groups.

Leaving as a Function of Time

The probability of leaving a commune remains fairly constant over time. This is true regardless of whether the passage of time is measured from the member's date of birth (age) or from the date of joining the commune (seniority). Age does discriminate between leavers and stayers. But, upon closer examination, the rate of leaving is remarkably constant until age 35, when it begins to drop sharply (see Figure 3-2).

Even the apparent membership stabilization beginning at age 35 is probably an artifact of the research design rather than of a real change. If the research had gone on for several more years, we probably would have discovered, in addition to leavers and stayers, a small third category of "long-term stayers." The fact that our sample includes communes at various stages of duration assures that such long-term stayers, if they exist, will be disproportionately represented among the oldest members. There were not enough older members in total, however, to test this possibility by partitioning them into their various seniority cohorts.

Perhaps the distinction between stayers and long-term stayers can be made more vivid in terms of a classification scheme that developed out of the early years of field work. Drawing analogies between the commune and the university, we identified the following membership types:

1. *The Freshman:* Naïvely idealistic; utopian; high investor in both self and collectivity; lacks experience and expertise but makes up for it by his or her enthusiasm, particularly for learning and trying new things.
2. *The Sophomore:* Bored and cynical in reaction to his or her previous freshman enthusiasm; low investor in both self and collectivity; discouraged; realizes that one's inner problems do not automatically disappear in response to a change in environment.
3. *The Junior:* Worldly wise; realizes that there are ways to live comfortably within the system; pursues "independent studies"; low investor in the collectivity, high investor in self.

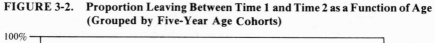

FIGURE 3-2.   Proportion Leaving Between Time 1 and Time 2 as a Function of Age
(Grouped by Five-Year Age Cohorts)

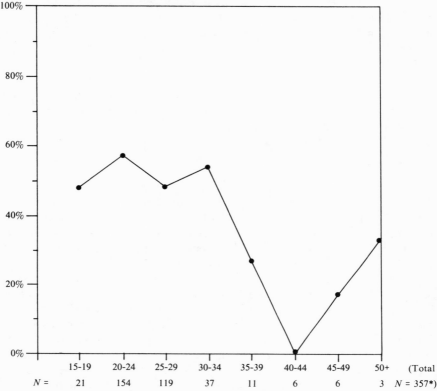

*Those for whom age and leaver-stayer status were both available as data.

4. *The Senior:* Moderately enthusiastic; a rebirth of commitment, now but-
tressed by realism: you get back only what you put in; concerned with
the future of the commune often because of increasing age, desire for a
family, and so on; balanced investment in both self and collectivity.
5. *The Graduate Student:* Has had previous (usually unsuccessful) commune
experience; has been through the whole cycle before; has learned from
past mistakes and now knows exactly how to avoid future failures, if only
the other members would listen to him.
6. *The Professor:* One of the minority who are really into it as a lifetime
commitment; tends to seek out his own kind for close relationships; his
relationships with those in other categories are often superficial and transitive; attempts to embody and enforce, so far as possible, the commune's
institutionalized goals; often considered a nuisance by the other members.

Although the educational analogy is accurate only as a broad caricature, it does provide some useful insights. In particular, the professor/student dichotomy helps to remind us that only a minority of the commune members (not always the most idealistic) is really in it for keeps.

Seniority does not discriminate between leavers and stayers at all. In terms of the analogy just given, the "drop-out rate" in each class is the same as the proportion of seniors who "graduate." This is precisely what a thermodynamic model would lead us to expect. Leaving or staying is dependent upon current pushes and pulls, not upon past history of commune membership.

But what about precommunal personal histories? Are there factors that distinguish leavers from stayers in the early lives of the individuals themselves? A hypothesis may be formulated as follows:

> To the extent that an individual's personal background is characterized by stability, both in family of origin and in life career, the individual will have a high probability of being a stayer. Those individuals who experiment quite a bit with alternative life-styles before joining and whose family of origin is characterized as unstable will have a very high probability of leaving.

According to this interpretation, the earlier a person leaves home and the sooner he or she joins a commune, the greater the likelihood of his or her leaving. Examination of the age at leaving home and at time of joining for leavers and stayers shows no support for this hypothesis. Neither does loss of one or both parents or frequent residential mobility as a child contribute to an explanation.

Another way of looking at this question is to ask whether the precommune life-style volatility of a person is positively associated with the propensity to leave the commune. Although this interpretation probably gets somewhat closer to what is actually going on, the data provide no strong evidence to support it. Interview data give the impression that people whose precommunal lives have been characterized by long-term commitments are more likely to be long-term stayers. But there is no association at all between prior divorce or separation and propensity to leave, or between failures to complete high school or college and propensity to leave. With respect to number of previous communal memberships, there is no association among those who have been members of fewer than four prior groups, but, among the handful of people in the sample who have been members of four or more communes prior to the current one, the probability of leaving during the test year jumps appreciably.

Any discussion of communal membership instability should include the phenomenon of serial communitarianism. As has already been noted, many commune members are or have been members of more than one commune. Several have been members of over a dozen.* Hicks's study (1971) of Banner

---

*As the women quoted in a paper by Kanter (1974, p. 19) said, "Of course communes work. I'm in my fifth."

Community, B. Berger's study (1973) of communes in California, and the current study all testify to the high proportion of commune members who join more than one. In addition, an extraordinarily high proportion of the ex-members (85 percent) reported that they expected to be living communally in ten years' time. Devotion may often be stronger to the commune movement on the whole than to the particular commune in which they happen to be living at a particular time.

Becoming an Ex-Commune Member

In a majority of instances, the transition from communal to postcommunal life is a transition to noncommunal life. However, for some, as we have seen, communal living is a lifelong commitment. Some will probably never leave the commune that we found them in, and others may continue to move from one to another for the rest of their lives.

For some, the act of leaving was as painful as divorce. For others, it was not much more traumatic than changing dorm floors at school or bunks at camp. In none of those interviewed as ex-members, however, was there evidence of the readjustment trauma that characterized, for example, the early postcommunal lives of Bruderhof apostates (Zablocki, 1971, Ch. 6). Despite the sincerity of their convictions and the intensity of their communal experiences, most of the participants studied seemed to drift as easily out of communal life as they had earlier drifted easily into it.*

We were able to contact about half the first-year leaver cohort and interview them briefly by phone or mail about one year after the act of leaving. For this part of the study, the population of leavers was restricted to those whose communes were still in existence at time two. Three topics were covered in these interviews: (1) reasons for leaving the commune, (2) extent to which leaving was voluntary or coerced, and (3) attitudes and life-style of postcommunal life.

Reasons for Leaving

An examination of the reasons given for leaving (Table 3-13)† corroborates our earlier finding that the key factor is to be found in the network of relation-

---

*It should be noted that there is a high probability of sampling bias in the selection of the ex-member respondents. The most traumatized ex-members may have been under seclusion or psychiatric care and would be unlikely to have been encouraged to participate further in the study.

†It should be noted that our analysis of reasons for leaving is based upon a somewhat different sample than was used in our analysis of leaver-stayer distinctions (Table 3-12). Leaver-stayer distinctions were based upon first-wave data collected from the full cohort. Only about half the leavers were contacted for the postcommunal interview, and fewer than half of these responded to the questionnaire, and the portion of the sample contacted was heavily biased against the footloose and fancy free. Furthermore, people transferring from one commune to another were included in the reason analysis (Table 3-13) but were excluded from the leaver-stayer analysis.

TABLE 3-13. Reasons Given by Ex-Members for Leaving Their Communes (Coded three different ways)

A. Type of Reason	B. Sources of Reason	C. Reasons: Direction of Influence
Ideological reasons 54%	Commune-related reasons 47%	Pushes from within the commune 43%
Personal conscience 27%	Communal relationships 44%	Pressured to leave 95%
Disillusionment with ideology 33	Communal ideology/ organization 27	Expelled 5
Desire new experiences 27	Commune's power structure 8	100%
Personal inadequacy 13	Commune's financial condition 4	(N = 43)
100%	Communitarian movement 17	
(N = 48)	100%	
	(N = 48)	
Relational reasons 46%		Pulls from outside the commune 42%
Commune unpleasant 29%		Outside attractions 60%
Relationships with members 39	Personal and related reasons 38%	Transfer to other branch 40
Personal relationship with leaver or nonmember 32	Unhappiness 21%	100%
100%	Spouse, children 34	(N = 42)
(N = 41)	Family of origin 5	
	Occupational, educational changes 21	Defunct commune 15%
	New outside relationships 5	(N = 15)
	New other outside activities 14	
	100%	
	(N = 38)	
	Other sources (N = 15) 15%	
(N = 89) 100%	(N = 101) 100%	(N = 100) 100%

137

ships among the commune members. Although, when reasons for leaving are grouped by type, the majority are ideological, almost all the rest (almost half) can be categorized as relational. Moreover, when we group reasons by type or direction of influence instead of by source, the largest subcategory within each of the two main categories has to do with relationships within the commune. In sharp contrast, family of origin and new outside relationships are each listed by only two of the respondents.

The propensity to leave is a function of both pulls from the outside world and pushes from within the commune, as well as personal dispositions. Although 49 percent of the reasons for leaving given by ex-members emphasized pulls over pushes, this should not dissuade us from attempting to explain membership turnover by factors endogenous to the communes themselves. It must be remembered that we are using the observable distinction between leaving and staying not so much for its own sake as for the purpose of getting at the unobservable strength of the communal bond. When a commune ex-member lists an opportunity in the outside world (e.g., marriage, career, education) as a reason for leaving, it would be erroneous to presume that similar opportunities were not available to others who chose to stay. It seems more reasonable to assume that attractive opportunities to leave are part of the centrifugal force that all communes must overcome if they are to survive. This is not meant to negate the importance of exogenous factors but rather to suggest that communes offer an unusual opportunity, in the modern urban world, for explanations based upon endogenous grounds alone, and thus for the understanding of whole communal systems.

The Special Case of Expulsion

Most departures from communal life are voluntary. Although a commune may bring many subtle or not so subtle pressures to bear upon an unpopular member, in only 2 percent of the cases (see Table 3-13) were matters forced to the extremity of formal expulsion proceedings. Many communes are uneasy about the implicit sovereignty claimed in the power to expel. About one-quarter of the rural communes specifically deny themselves the right ever to expel anyone under any circumstances. Some groups state vaguely that circumstances might arise that would warrant an expulsion but insist that they won't know until an actual case comes up whether or not the commune would really ever go so far as to cast out a member.

Communes with charismatic leaders seem to have more ability to cope with expulsion situations without recourse to rules. The charismatic leader can make specific and unambiguous rulings. He can decree that affection be withdrawn from a person until the pressure to leave voluntarily makes actual expulsion unnecessary. A commune of this type in Atlanta had a member who said:

Someone who lived here was creating a lot of strife. . . . We had to pray for this person and pray for the situation. . . . In relating to this person these things kept cropping up so we were cautioned [by the leader] just not to relate to this person.

Most communes have difficulty dealing with expulsion even when formal rules apply. This seems to be primarily because of the unwillingness or inability of many members to express strongly negative feelings about another person. The following is cited as an example from a consensual commune in Minneapolis:

Most . . . were in opposition to them, but not very many people were able to deal with it openly. At any rate, there were some really bad feelings. Finally these two people left, and there were still some very bad feelings. These people had some shares, and there is a whole legal issue now as to how they will divest themselves of their shares in the corporation. . . . It's a really messy situation.

Expulsion in anarchistic communes is in some ways the most interesting. In some anarchistic communes it is truly the case that no one can be asked to leave for any reason. A member of an anarchistic commune in Minneapolis, however, stated the following:

Expulsion? Yes, it's fairly common. It occurs through social pressure. People express that they don't like someone and eventually, probably, that person moves out.

Another example from Los Angeles, however, indicates the extreme difficulty that sometimes can occur in using this technique in an anarchistic commune:

I have expressed that I want Joe to move out. Tom has expressed it, Karen has expressed it. I don't know how long he can tread water. How long does he think he can stay where he is not wanted?

Curiously, in many anarchistic communes we found an outcast: often a person with what would probably be diagnosed as a severe psychological character disorder. For example, in one rural commune there was a man who was an alcoholic, a bully, and a thief. He was older than most of the other members and had nothing in common with them in terms of social or educational background. He had no interest in or understanding of the commune's countercultural ideology. He freely admitted that he was there only for the free ride and frequently mocked the other members' idealism. Everyone was a little afraid of him; he was always abusive and could get violent when drunk. But in his physically debilitated state he was no match in a fight with any of the other men, several of whom would beat him up from time to time. Neither was he treated much better than he treated the others. He was often mocked, even by the children, and was frequently the victim of cruel practical jokes. He was often asked to leave, without much conviction.

One could speculate, with Simmel and with such utopian writers as Paul Goodman and R. D. Laing, that such an individual performs a positive function for his commune, serving both as a scapegoat and as a way of releasing communal tensions. By his unwillingness to obey the norms of the group, the outcast provides a way in which these norms can be defined and made concrete to the other commune members. By his refusal to leave, no matter how cruelly he is reviled, he reminds the members of a fundamental difference between community and association. Under other circumstances, as we shall see, the charismatic leader can also play this role.

Postcommunal Life

We have seen that it is difficult to make inferences about future plans on the basis of the expressed attitudes of commune members. In fact the two subpopulations, leavers and stayers, showed remarkable similarity in their attitudes at time 1. An examination of the attitudinal changes of the two subpopulations between time 1 and time 2, however, revealed some interesting patterns.

Table 3-14 shows the degree of change in selected attitudes of leavers and stayers. (The leavers, of course, were interviewed the second time outside of a communal setting.) The differences between the two populations is striking. During the test year, the self-esteem of the stayers decreased or stayed the same on seven of the eight items of the Rosenberg self-esteem scale. The self-esteem of the leavers, on the other hand, increased on seven of the eight items.

These opposite directions of change are all the more intriguing when we note that the first-wave scores of the two populations were in all cases almost identical. Although the counterhypothesis that the commune somehow predisposes the leavers toward higher self-esteem cannot be dismissed, we can say that, if any such effect occurred, it must have happened between the first-wave interview and the time when the leaver left. It is thus more plausible to infer that the differences noted are a result rather than a cause of leaving.

Clinical arguments have been made for the existence of a high correlation between communal self-investment and societal self-investment. In England, the assumption is an important basis for the mental health program of the highly influential Tavistock group. Jones (1953, p. 156) was a pioneer in the gathering of clinical data in support of this assumption:

> Our findings appear to justify the conclusion that it is possible to change social attitudes in relatively desocialized patients with severe character disorders, provided they are treated together in a therapeutic community. Our results show that six months after leaving hospital, two-thirds of the

patients followed up had made a fair adjustment or better, and one-third were rated poor or very poor adjustments . . .; just over one-half had worked the full time since leaving hospital. We believe (but cannot prove) that the results described could not have been achieved by individual psychotherapy and hospitalization alone.

W. Bion and R. D. Laing have continued to work out the clinical implications of the assumed relationship between community and alienation in England. What light does the commune data throw on this issue? Table 3-14 shows that the alienation of leavers decreased on all five measures during the test year. The alienation of stayers had no definite pattern of change. The combined greater self-esteem and lower alienation of leavers one year after the first test would tend to support the theory that communal living can help to prepare one for postcommunal life. The alternative hypothesis, that communal living dampened the naturally higher self-esteem of the leaver group and artificially increased the alienation, is less plausible.

Finally, we look at attitudes about communitarianism. Here we see a possible short-term history effect. Attitudes of both leavers and stayers grew more negative over the year of study. However, the leavers start out more positively disposed toward communal living than the stayers. One year later, after the leavers are no longer living communally, they are still more positively disposed toward communitarianism than the stayers. Again we see that positive attitudes may promote high expectations and therefore bring about greater disillusionment.

Although one year is not enough time to assess the effects of communal living on post-communal life, some preliminary conclusions can be drawn. Table 3-15 indicates that leavers return to life-styles that are, at least superficially, normal. Only 5 percent of the leavers interviewed at time 2 were neither employed nor going to school. Almost half of them reported a financial situation that had improved since leaving the commune, whereas only 17 percent said that their financial situation had gotten worse.

It is interesting to note that almost a third of the ex-member respondents report that they were currently living in another commune. The strong, continuing positive disposition toward communitarianism again indicates that communitarianism as a life-style may be more viable than specific communes as organizations.

Conclusions

In this chapter, we have looked at the flow of individuals into and out of communes. This flow is both rapid and fairly unrestricted. It's easy to get in and, for most, it's easy to leave. The memberships of many communes can be decomposed into alienated majorities and charismatic minorities. Although

TABLE 3-14. Changes during One Year on Measures of Self-esteem, Alienation, and Communitarianism: Panel of Stayers Compared with Panel of Those Who Left during Test Year

Item	Stayers			Leavers		
	Time 1 (in commune)	Time 2 (in commune)	Change	Time 1 (in commune)	Time 2 (postcommune)	Change
Self-esteem						
I can do things as well as most people (+)	1.7	2.0	−0.3	1.7	1.5	+ 0.2
I feel left out of things around me (−)	4.3	4.1	−0.2	4.2	4.4	+ 0.2
I take a positive attitude toward myself (+)	1.7	1.9	−0.2	1.8	1.4	+ 0.4
I feel I don't have much to be proud of (−)	4.2	4.2	−	4.3	4.8	+ 0.5
At times I think I am no good at all (−)	3.8	4.0	+ 0.2	3.7	3.4	−0.3
I have worth, on an equal basis with others (+)	1.4	1.7	−0.3	1.5	1.2	+ 0.3
I have a number of good qualities (+)	1.4	1.6	−0.2	1.5	1.3	+ 0.2
What I think doesn't count very much (−)	4.2	4.2	−	4.1	4.4	+ 0.3
Alienation						
Unfair to bring child into world today (+)	3.7	4.2	−0.5	3.9	4.0	−0.1
No guidelines in relationships between man and wife (+)	3.4	3.2	+ 0.2	3.1	3.4	−0.3

Reform in system better than revolution (−)	3.0	3.0	–	3.0	2.5	−0.5
People running country don't care about me (+)	2.4	2.4	–	2.6	2.8	−0.2
People with power want to take advantage of us (+)	2.8	2.6	+0.2	2.5	2.9	−0.4
Communitarianism						
Communitarianism will solve many problems (+)	3.2	3.3	−0.1	2.5	2.6	−0.1
After experiencing communal life would be unhappy elsewhere (+)	3.2	3.4	−0.2	3.0	3.3	−0.3
Healthier for child to grow up in commune than an isolated nuclear family (+)	2.3	2.7	−0.4	2.2	2.4	−0.2
Good chance I'll live communally in ten years (+)	2.4	2.5	−0.1	2.3	2.3	–
Commune life a means to goals not an end in itself (−)	1.7	2.2	+0.5	1.9	1.8	−0.1
Commune people are less practical than those living noncommunally (−)	4.4	4.5	+0.1	4.3	4.2	−0.1
I'd like to create a communitarian world (+)	3.0	3.2	−0.2	2.6	2.8	−0.2

TABLE 3-15. Postcommunal Life Situations of Leavers

	Number	% of Total
Current employment status		
Neither employed nor attending school	4	5%
Attending school full time	40	38
Employed part time	16	12
Employed full time	73	55
	133	100%
Current financial situation		
Much better	22	21%
Slightly better	27	26
About the same	38	36
Somewhat worse	14	13
Quite worse	4	4
	105	100%
Currently live with		
Alone	16	12%
Commune	43	31
Parents	15	11
Legal spouse	16	12
Lover	23	17
Roommates	17	13
Children	2	2
Institution	2	2
	134	100%

some of the communes lack charismatic leaders, this attribute, generally rare in modern society, is remarkably abundant in communal settings.

The paradoxical aspect to all of this reliance on charismatic authority is that, as Rigby (1974, p. 12) has pointed out, the communitarian mentality requires that the world be perceived nonfatalistically, as a place where individual decision making responsibility matters:

> They have realized that, although it may appear that man in society has little choice but to follow the social demands made of him in his various roles, in fact man does have a choice so far as he can step outside his social roles, the taken for granted routines of society.

Yet it seems to be the very number of choices available to the individual that makes the exercise of the decision making faculty so difficult for the average commune member. Commune members may be characterized as having a high degree of faith in the belief that choice can make a difference in the outcome of events, combined with an inability to make decisions. In later chapters, we will treat this inability as an important form of alienation, and shall argue that charisma is best understood as a relational property functioning to overcome this alienation, and that communitarian organization is specifically conducive to the emergence of charisma.

The importance of dyadic love in determining communal stability has begun, in this chapter, to develop as a parallel theme. We will continue to see evidence, in subsequent chapters, of the importance of the dyadic love relationship. Here it has functioned as a predictor of whether an individual will stay or leave. We have discovered an intriguing reverse order compositional effect whereby love is negatively associated with leaving at the individual level but positively associated with leaving at the aggregate level. It is to the further examination of stability at the aggregate (commune) level that we now turn our attention.

The theoretical importance of love is thus seen to be in the sociostructural patterns which are developed to keep it from disrupting existing social arrangements.

William J. Goode

CHAPTER 4

Dyadic Love and Communal Instability

Communes are typically but not intrinsically unstable.* A great many of them begin life full of hope and enthusiasm, only to perish before being able to celebrate a first birthday. Some, however, like the Shakers and the Harmony Society, have endured for a century or even longer. The Hutterians, to cite an extreme example, are today still strongly committed to communal living after practicing it, punctuated only by occasional lapses into private enterprise, for 450 years. The Hutterian rate of membership turnover has been only about 0.0006 per year (Hostetler, 1974a, p. 273). The sixty urban communes in our sample, by way of contrast, have experienced a cumulative annual turnover rate of 0.49 per year, with individual commune rates varying from 0.0 to 1.0. Evidently, there is a great deal of variance in communal stability to be accounted for.†

---

*The term instability refers in this chapter to a dual concept. The term is used to denote either a high probability of disintegration or a high membership turnover.

†Annual turnover data were available only for the urban communes in this study. Disintegration data were available for the full sample of rural and urban communes. The cumulative turnover rate cited in the text includes not only leavers but also all members of disintegrated communes. This represents a somewhat different perspective from the one

There is, as we shall see, a strong and complex relationship between dyadic love and communal instability. Love is at once the bond and the bane of communal life. We have seen in Chapter 3 that the number of sociometric choices that a person receives as a love object is the best single available predictor of the likelihood that the person will stay on as a member. But this predictor works only as long as we are comparing the staying likelihoods of two members of the same commune. When we attempt to make comparisons among communes, and when we shift from a concern with individuals to a concern with aggregate turnover rates, we find the effect of love reversed. The more sociometric love relations existing at any time in a commune as a whole, the more likely it is that the commune will disintegrate or, if the commune should survive, the higher its annual membership turnover is likely to be.

To make matters still more complicated, this very strong association between dyadic love and communal instability is almost completely suppressed by the physical presence, in the commune, of a charismatic leader. Only under direct daily charismatic influence, among the communes in our sample, is it possible for very high densities of dyadic love relationships to coexist with very low membership turnover rates. Charismatic leaders themselves, on the other hand, are just as likely to leave their communes in any given year as ordinary members. The three-way relationship among the variables—instability, love, and charisma— is obviously a convoluted one. Before attempting to untangle it, let us describe more precisely the phenomena to be accounted for.

Variation in Communal Stability

Some confusion will be avoided if we distinguish at once between long-term and short-term instability. Most studies of commune instability have focused on the long term. For example, Kanter (1972), to enhance historical validity, deliberately undersampled communes with less than three years' total duration and oversampled those that had endured for twenty-five years or longer. The current study, in direct contrast, is concerned with studying the short term. The communes in our sample had had a mean duration of only 2.4 years at point of first contact. Although the communes in our sample ranged in age from newly born to twenty-eight years of existence, the focus of attention in this chapter is largely on communal stability in the first few years of life. Ninety-three percent of the 120 communes in this sample had been in existence for less than five years when first contacted.

Studies of long- and short-term stability are, of course, theoretically complementary. Students of long-term stability have discovered that institutions make the difference. Those communes that have evolved institutions of communal survival will survive the longest. These·may be institutionalized commit-

---

taken in Chapter 3 where, with the focus on the individual, a distinction was made between "leavers" and members of defunct communes.

ment mechanisms (Kanter, 1972), or institutions regulating religious and sexual practice (Noyes, 1870), or institutions of multicommunal federation (Zablocki, 1972a). But institution building takes time. The current study, by focusing largely on the preinstitutional period of commune development, is able to search for those more elementary forms of stabilizing structure that precede the development of more complex institutionalized forms.

Life Expectancy of Communes

To examine the question of life expectancy, we should ideally have a sample of communes followed from birth. We are not able to do this because the communes in our sample varied in age at time of first contact. We can, however, divide our sample into cohorts on the basis of how long they had already endured by the time they were first contacted. In this manner, we identify a zero-year cohort made up of the twenty-nine communes that had been in existence less than half a year, a one-year cohort made up of the thirty-nine communes that had been in existence between half a year and one-and-a-half years, and so on. We can then look at disintegration rates of each of the cohorts separately.

The zero-year cohort is the most important from the point of view of estimating life expectancy. With all other cohorts we have no way of directly determining the number of disintegrations that took place before initial contact was made. Figure 4-1 shows the proportion of each cohort surviving over a period of four years from time of first contact for each of the four cohorts.

Examination of the zero-year cohort graph seems at first to suggest that communal disintegration is a half-life phenomenon. Half the communes in the cohort had disintegrated in little over two years, and almost half those remaining were gone by the end of the following two-year period (i.e., after four years). However, for commune disintegration to be a half-life phenomenon, each commune would have to have the same probability of disintegrating during any given period of time, and this probability would have to remain constant over time. That this is not so is clearly seen by examining the disintegration graphs for the one-, two-, and three-year cohorts. Each succeeding cohort shows progressively more stability (with two minor crossovers). This would not be the case if the communes had disintegration probabilities that were homogeneous and independent of past history.

What seems more likely is that communes are heterogeneous in their disintegration probabilities, either starting that way or becoming that way over time, probably both. The disintegration rate is most rapid in the beginning of a commune's life and thereafter tapers off for those communes that survive. Among those communes in the sample that were first observed eight or more years ago, the disintegration rate tapers off quite a bit after the fourth year of survival. This suggests that the fact that the cohort halves after each of the first

FIGURE 4-1. Survival of Communes over Time by Cohort

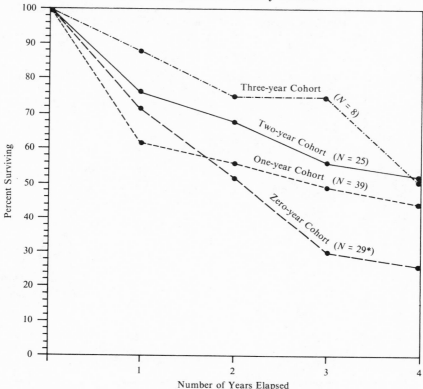

*After two years the zero-year cohort is reduced to $N = 27$ when two communes in the cohort are lost track of.

two two-year intervals is a coincidence and that we should not expect the cohort necessarily to halve again in the third two-year interval.

In Figure 4-2, we use the zero-year cohort's observed disintegration rate to estimate what initial size group of communes would have been needed to give rise to the other cohorts. Recalculating disintegration rates in terms of these estimated cohort sizes, we find that all four cohorts behave fairly similarly. No sharp deviation from the tendency to halve at two-year intervals during the first four years of life can be observed.

All in all, 59 percent of the 118* communes that were followed had disintegrated by 1978. Although the remaining communes will undoubtedly continue to produce disintegrations, there is a great likelihood that at least a few of those communes remaining will still be in existence beyond the turn of

*Two of the 29 communes in the zero-year cohort were lost sight of after two years.

FIGURE 4-2. Hypothetical Survival of Commune Cohorts over Time Using Zero-year Survival Rates to Estimate Original Sizes of Cohorts

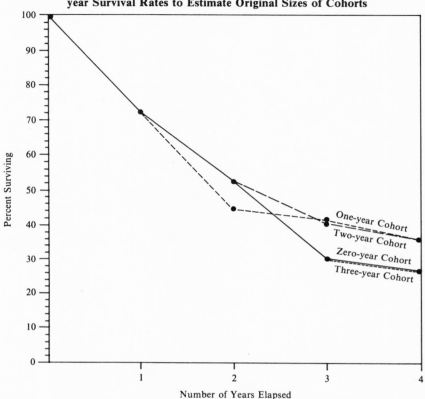

the century. But which specific ones will survive is impossible to predict based upon the data of this study. We might guess, based upon previous research on long-term stability, that religious communes with strict admission requirements, strong commitment mechanisms, controls on sexuality, and forged links of federation with other communes will be likely candidates.

Figure 4-3 seems to give evidence of a fascinating development just beginning to emerge. With respect to religion, we can begin to see, even in this short-term study, evidence of its differential advantage coming to the fore. Figure 4-3 shows the disintegration graph of the zero-year cohort divided into religious and secular subsets of communes. It is interesting to note that, for the first two years of communal life, religious communes disintegrate at an even faster rate than secular communes. It is only after two years that the curves cross over and that secular groups begin to disintegrate faster. Can it be that the greater emotional excitation present in religious communes, although excellent fuel for

FIGURE 4-3.   Religious versus Secular Survival Rates in the Zero-year Cohort

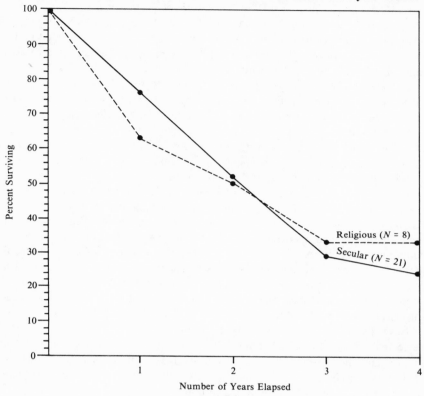

building long-term commitment mechanisms, is actually a net disadvantage to the commune until the emotional excitation of spiritual pursuits is actually channelled into these institutions?

Reasons for Disintegrating

Disintegration is a concrete event. A commune that has existed in space and time ceases to exist. Most of the time (among the 70 disintegrations that took place among our sample of 120 communes), it was not difficult to observe the event and the circumstances under which it took place. Often the commune itself would publish an announcement of its own demise advancing its own reasons for the occurrence. Often there would be a funeral or farewell dinner or some other ritual to mark the passing. Sometimes there would be a violent explosion. But at other times there would be only a gradual melting away of structure and purpose accompanied by no consensus as to the actual time of death. In a few instances, what passed for a sociologically defined disintegration* was not defined as such by the commune participants.

Despite these difficulties, it was possible to locate each of the seventy disintegrations that occurred at least to the year if not always to the exact month. In each case, enough consensus existed to assign the commune to a category denoting principal reason for disintegrating.

A frequency distribution of these reason categories is given for rural and for urban communes in Table 4-1. The table does not reflect the frequent occurrence of multiple-reason breakups; neither does it reflect the considerable confusion and uncertainty with which members of disintegrating communes often perceived the event. Nevertheless, it gives a fairly good approximation of the relative frequency with which commune members assigned various categories of explanation to the collapse of their communes.

Reasons, of course, should never be mistaken for causes. Our table represents the distribution of subjective explanations of commune members. These may not have any direct relation to underlying objective causes. Frequently, commune members will mention insurmountable group crises as reasons. But all communes face crises. The underlying issue is rather one of determining the factors that give some communes the will and the resources for surmounting crises when they occur. Loss of interest or saliency is another reason frequently cited. Here, again, it might be more to the point to know what factors caused this withdrawal of attention from the collectivity.

Nevertheless, the indirect relationship of reasons to causes should not be neglected. Subjective dispositions have objective consequences in any community and most especially in an intentional community. What the members of a disintegrating commune believe went wrong tells us, at the very least, how the underlying causes of decay impinged upon the members' consciousness.

Table 4-1 tells us that commune members tend to share a key assumption of this book—that important communal events (such as disintegrations) are usually generated from within. More than three quarters of the communes believed that the primary reasons for their disintegration derived from within the commune itself. Rural communes, facing harsher environmental conditions, were more willing to see the problem as stemming from outside forces.

Relational reasons were cited more than any other kind. Among relational reasons, although sex accounts for a fair share, by far the most salient relational dimension is that of power and authority. Fully 25 percent of all the communes that disbanded offered explanations having something to do with the exercise of power. Sometimes the power of the leader over the followers was faulted. At other times the more diffuse power of males over females, founders over newcomers, or the less committed over the more committed was cited.

An example of the last of these occurred in a rural commune that had existed for four years with very few restrictions on who might join. The commune had

---

*The definition of communal disintegration used is discussed in Appendix A.

TABLE 4-1. Reasons for Disintegration of Commune

Type of Reason	Rural	Urban	Total	
			Number	% of Total
External generators				
Legal, official	4	1	5	7%
Public opinion/action	4	0	4	6
Severity of environment (including disasters, e.g., fire)	2	1	3	4
Policy decisions of sponsor organization	1	3	4	6
			16	23%
Internal generators				
Health and safety	2	1	3	4
Economic failure	0	1	1	1
Ideological				
Schism, dispute	3	3	6	9
Loss of saliency	4	7	11	16
Relational				
Power, influence, dispute between leader and followers	12	5	17	25
Sexual	4	4	8	11
Personal loss of interest	2	6	8	11
			54	77%
Total			70	100%

initially attracted a group of highly skilled and idealistic craftsmen who had built an extensive and impressive physical plant in what was rather forbidding country. As the commune became more capable of supporting people in a certain degree of comfort, it began to attract members who were both less skilled and less idealistic. The original members had foreseen this result and agreed that it should be allowed to happen. The original members did not foresee (nor could they comprehend when it happened) that rather than the newcomers being uplifted and inspired by the example of the originals, the very presence of uncommitted people seemed to sap the commitment of the originals and interfere with their ability to function as a community. In every aspect of communal life, from housekeeping and dishwashing to cutting fire-wood and preparing for winter, the commune seemed naturally to find a level of activity at the lowest common denominator. After belated efforts by the originals to get their authority to be accepted as legitimate ended in failure, the commune broke up amid widespread guilt, depression, and mutual blame.

It is interesting to note that only one of the seventy communes for which we observed disintegrations attributed the event primarily to economic failure. After relationships, the second greatest bugaboo of communal survival would appear to be ideological problems. Among those grouped in the ideological category, almost twice as many attributed the demise to a loss of ideological saliency as attributed it to a concrete ideological schism or dispute. This may be a result of a classification problem, however. The categories in this table are somewhat arbitrary. Recall that each group was arbitrarily assigned to one and only one category. Frequently, groups breaking up after ideological schisms would see these as resulting from the inequitable or unfair distribution of power in the community. In such cases the power problem was usually judged to be more basic and the group was assigned to a relational category. Other researchers, less concerned with relationships, might well have classified some of these as primarily ideological breakups.

Membership Turnover as a Form of Instability

Thus far we have been speaking of instability as if it were synonymous with disintegration. But communes are both formal organizations and aggregates of individual people. Accordingly, instability can be manifested either as organizational disruption or as loss of members. Let us refer to the organizational disruption aspect as *disintegration* and the loss of members aspect as *turnover*.*

The relationship between disintegration and turnover is not a simple one. Both are measures of instability, but each measures a quite different aspect of instability. Neither does turnover always portend disintegration. Five communes in the sample experienced annual turnover rates of over 50 percent per year for three consecutive years without ever threatening to disintegrate. At the other extreme, five communes in the sample disintegrated after a year of zero membership turnover.

Membership turnover can serve any of the following three functions: (1) It may sometimes be a prelude to disintegration. (2) It may be a long-term functional alternative to disintegration among communes that cannot sustain a committed membership. (3) It may be a sorting device for building long-term stability. There is no difficulty in treating turnover as a manifestation of instability in each of the first two instances. In the third instance, we must bear in mind that what is rightly being defined as instability in the short run may be part of a program for building long-term stability.

Two additional points about the function of communal turnover should be made. One is that, in rural subsistence communes, a certain degree of membership turnover can be an important economic asset. This is because new members generally bring with them more wealth than they take away when they leave. The higher the membership turnover, the greater the development of the commune's capital. The second point is that, in certain mystical charismatic communes, high membership turnover may be something of an ideological asset. In preaching the message of nonattachment along with the message of love, it can often be quite instructive for a guru to have a steady stream of leavers and a steady stream of new joiners available as cases in point. Several times

---

*Turnover at time t is defined as that proportion of the membership of a commune at time $t-1$ who are no longer members at time t (Price, 1977, p. 17).

per week (sometimes even per day) the disciple must learn how to unflinchingly renounce old comrades while unflinchingly reaching out to new ones. In some communes, we find that the membership turnover is very high precisely because the communal organization is focused entirely on the ideological goals and not at all on communal relationships. Individuals in such communes are replaceable parts. They come and go, but during the period of their membership they maintain total commitment to the relatively unchanging ideology. As long as a steady stream of new applicants is available, such communes can continue to survive.

High membership turnover is not necessarily a sign of coming doom, and, on the contrary, it can sometimes serve positive functions for the commune's survival. Nevertheless, it is quite definitely a manifestation of communal instability. The reason is that all communes, even those with authoritarian charismatic leaders, thrive on consensus, and membership turnover continually rends the fabric of consensus and forces it to be woven anew. This is why the event of a person's leaving a commune (no matter how good a riddance) is always a shock and the event of a new person's coming is always disorienting. The commune may survive and even reap economic or ideological benefits. But, for the real work of the commune, which is collective decision making, turnover is always a setback.

Commune membership turnover is high but not extraordinarily high compared with that of other organizations. Price (1977, pp. 50ff.) brings together turnover data for a large number of occupations and business and professional organizations. Commune members would place on the high end of Price's turnover continuum, but not at the highest point. Hospital nurses and factory workers both turnover a bit faster then commune members. University professors, civil servants, and prison wardens, at the other extreme, turnover quite a bit more slowly. However, it should be noted that Price's data are presented in terms of crude separation rates (which count comings and goings during the middle of the year), whereas our data are presented in terms of what Price calls instability rates (which look only at beginning- and end-year rosters). Instability rates tend to be lower than crude separation rates, so that, if comparable data were available, communes might well capture the highest turnover spot.

Predictors of Communal Instability

We saw in Chapter 3 that professed statements of commitment at time 1 were not good predictors of time 2 membership turnover,* but that a relational measure, density of dyadic love bonds, tended to be a good predictor; the higher the

---

*By instability at time 2, of course, we mean membership turnover or disintegration that has taken place between time 1 and time 2. Recall that time 1 refers to the month of first contact that was August 1974 for all urban communes (except those in Boston, for which it was February 1975). In all cases, time 2 was one year after time 1, measured to the nearest month. Time 3 is one year after that, and so on. Time zero always refers to the month in which the commune was founded.

density of loving, the greater the membership turnover. This intriguing and counter intuitive finding raises a number of questions. To what extent does the strong association between love and turnover hold up when other predictors are controlled for? What are the other predictors and to what extent are they also measures of the relationship network? How much of the variance in membership turnover actually can be explained? To what extent do the same variables that explain turnover variance also distinguish between communes that disintegrate and communes that survive the test year?

A series of multiple regression equations, presented in Table 4-2, were computed in order to answer these questions. The overall regression model focussed on four kinds of variable: relational, organizational, ideological, and aggregated individual, all measured at time 1. Regressed upon these was turnover, the dependent variable measured at time 2. On the basis of preliminary analysis, aggregated individual variables were eliminated from consideration. No aggregated attribute or attitude except mean age showed any appreciable zero-order or first-order association with turnover, and the association of mean age with turnover disappeared when relational variables were controlled for.

The sociometric density of mutual loving bonds appears in the equations as the variable "dyadic cathexis." The reason for this designation will be made clear later in the chapter. Dyadic cathexis is by far the most powerful single predictor of turnover. It alone explains 38 percent of the variance in turnover, over 60 percent of all the variance which can be explained by our model.

In our earlier (Chapter 3) discussion of communitarian sexual behavior, we suggested that communes, by diffusing emotional charge over all possible dyads, may prevent any one dyad from maintaining a constantly high emotional charge. Does this also help to explain the relationship of love to turnover? Is so, we should expect to find an inverse relationship between turnover and the proportion of dyads in a commune that acknowledges a special relationship between the two individuals in the dyad. This variable is included in the equations under the designation, "dyadic partiality." (See Appendix A for a discussion of how this variable was measured.) When dyadic partiality and a measure of negative emotional cathexis were entered (equation 2) an additional 10 percent of the variance in membership turnover was accounted for, virtually all of it by dyadic partiality. Although dyadic partiality was not as powerful a predictor of turnover as dyadic cathexis, it did predict in the expected direction; the more partiality shown, the less the turnover.

Rationality in the decision-making process was the only significant organizational correlate of turnover: the more rational the process, as measured crudely by fieldworker observation, the greater the membership turnover. Here we see one of the primary distinctions, alluded to by Weber, between association and community. In an association, it is likely that the reverse finding would be true: the more rational, the less turnover. But communes are not primarily associations; they thrive on investment of self not of resources. Rational decision-making procedures make it difficult to avoid situations in which some define themselves as relative losers on any issue on which there is difference of opinion. Nonrational decision procedures are better capable of leading to a sense of general will prevailing (Zablocki, 1971, ch. 4), and thus are more able to keep the question of continuing personal commitment separated from the evaluation of personal benefit.

The last variable to be considered in the model is decomposed into a set of dichotomous variables that distinguish among the eight ideological types discussed in Chapter 5. The political/non-political distinction is the only one that made a net contribution to our ability to predict turnover. Political communes have a lower rate of membership turnover than can be explained simply by their relational patterns and by their patterns of decision making. As far as can be determined by examining turnover in subsequent years, this finding seems to be more of a sampling artifact than an enduring property of political communes. The addition of the two non-relational variables, rationality and political ideology, to regression equation 4, increased to 63 percent the proportion of variance in membership turnover explained.

How do these predictors of turnover fare in predicting disintegration? Knowledge of the rationality of decision making of a commune does not help us to predict the likelihood that it will disintegrate. In other words, although greater rationality may suggest weakness in the hold of the commune over its participants, it does not vary with weakness in the viability of the commune as a corporate actor. Dyadic cathexis (love density) and dyadic partiality, on the other hand, correlate with disintegration propensity in the same direction that they correlate with turnover rate.

The various ideological types differ among one another in disintegration rate more than they do in turnover rate. Recall that only the political type stood out in the turnover model as having a lower rate of turnover than the others. But, with respect to disintegration, psychological communes stand out as having unusually high likelihoods of folding (89 percent were defunct within four years), and rehabilitation communes stand out as being particularly durable (25 percent defunct after four years). Among the groups concerned with large-scale social change, the religious communes show fewer disintegrations than the political and countercultural communes, but this, as we saw earlier in the chapter, is a difference that emerges only after the first two years. In general, it may be said that communes with ideologies emphasizing individualism show a greater tendency to disintegrate, but not a higher rate of turnover, than those whose ideologies emphasize discipline.

Nonpredictors of Commune Stability

A number of additional factors were initially hypothesized as predictors of communal stability that turned out to have little or no short-run predictive power. For example, there was almost no association between ideological homogeneity and turnover or likelihood of disintegrating (for turnover, $r = .02$).

TABLE 4-2. Urban Commune Population Turnover Regressed on Time 1 Predictors[1]

a. Regression equations

Predictor Variables	Equation 1 B	Equation 1 β	Equation 2 B	Equation 2 β	Equation 3 B	Equation 3 β	Equation 4 B	Equation 4 β	Equation 5 B	Equation 5 β
Relational Variables:										
Dyadic cathexis	.83	.63	.67	.51	.60	.46	.53	.40		
Dyadic partiality			−1.53	−.41	−1.29	−.34	−.88	−.26		
Negative cathexis			a		a		a			
Organizational Variables:										
Rationality in collective decision making					.08	.35	.09	.42	.11	.50
Severity of admission process					a		a		a	
Level of charismatic authority					a		a		.05	.36
Ideological Variables:										
Ideological homogeneity							a			
Political/non-political (dummy variable)							−.22	−.23		
Constant term	.15		.24		.09		.05		.24	
(adjusted) R^2		.38		.48		.55		.63		.32

[1] $N = 37$. Analysis excludes twenty urban communes with missing data and the three charismatic deviant cases discussed in the text.

[a] Unstandardized regression coefficient was less than twice its standard error. Variable was excluded from the equation for final computation of βs and R^2.

TABLE 4-2. *(continued)*

b. Zero-Order Correlation Matrix ($N = 37$)

	Population Turnover	Dyadic Cathexis	Dyadic Partiality	Negative Cathexis	Rationality in Decisions	Severity in Admission	Charismatic Authority Level	Ideological Intensity	Political Non-Political
Population turnover	1.0								
Dyadic cathexis	.63	1.0							
Dyadic partiality	-.53	-.35	1.0						
Negative cathexis	-.11	-.15	.42	1.0					
Rationality in decisions	.50	.22	-.14	.26	1.0				
Severity in admission	-.12	-.11	.08	-.05	-.10	1.0			
Charismatic authority level	.31	.41	-.55	-.50	-.05	.18	1.0		
Ideological homogeneity	-.02	-.18	.07	.10	-.13	.05	.32	1.0	
Political/non-political	-.30	-.21	.28	.11	.21	-.04	-.39	.03	1.0

This is at first surprising because ideological homogeneity has had a strong impact on communes in the long run and an impact on other types of normative organizations as well. The low predictive power of ideological homogeneity reinforces our argument that, in the preinstitutional years of communal life, normative factors are second in importance to relational factors.

Among the organizational variables, admission restrictiveness (discussed in Chapter 3) and level of charismatic authority (to be discussed in Chapter 6) are two whose zero-order associations with population turnover largely disappear when controlling for relational variables. The causal ordering of the relational variables, the organizational variables, and population turnover has not yet been made clear. However, the working assumption has been that relational measures are in some sense primary. As Equation 5 of Table 4-2 indicates, an association of admission restrictiveness with population turnover cannot be demonstrated, even when only other organizational variables are controlled for.

It may be surprising to note the positive correlation between charismatic level and population turnover. It is not yet possible to say whether this is due to the role of charisma as a direct cause of turnover or to the indirect role of relational configurations as a cause (or as an effect) of charismatic level. Observational evidence suggests that charismatic leaders are profligate sowers of communes and do not hesitate, at times, to disband a particular commune that is not working to start again with more promising material. We held an interview once with a bewildered and chagrined charismatic leader sitting with his wife in an abandoned house on an abandoned farm, the entire membership having left after a violent and complex dispute. There was no doubt in the leader's mind, however, that he had been right and that all the rest of them had been wrong, and he was already planning another try.

In addition to the above variables, whose theoretical association had been assumed, an exploratory analysis of a great many other commune level variables was undertaken to discover possible additional correlates of instability. We found in an earlier work (Zablocki, 1972) that the existence of federated intercommunal bonds was important for long-term communitarian stability. Among the Hutterians and the Bruderhof, for example, reasons for this are often seen. When any given commune in the federation loses perspective on the nature of its own problems or crises (as they frequently seem to do), a relatively uninvolved member of a federally linked commune can step in with authority and restore order. But no such relationship was found among the communes in our sample. What seems instead to happen during the early years of communitarian federations is that the more committed members of the stronger communes frequently transfer within the federation to weaker communes where their leadership skills are needed. There is a tendency for federations to spread their leadership material too thin.* Eventually, in many cases, these strong members are not able to salvage the weaker communes that they transfer into. Meanwhile, their absence tends to reduce the survival chances of the strong communes that they have transfered out of. However, such people generally stay loyal to the federation and are not lost to it even after repeated breakups. Over a long enough period of time, they give the federation an edge in producing at least one long-lived commune out of all of this talent and experience. Therefore, we might say that the existence of a federation works to ensure the survival of the federation, not of any particular commune within it.

Of all the aggregated individual-level variables (education, occupational prestige, sex ratio, etc.), only age showed a significant zero-order correlation with turnover. Turnover decreased with increasing mean age of a commune's members ($r = -.22$). It is interesting to note that it is biological age, not seniority (time spent in commune), that correlated with turnover. The association, however, was far from linear. The correlation came mainly from a cluster of highly unstable young groups and a cluster of highly stable older groups. Age did not add to the overall R^2 beyond what had already been explained by the relational variables.

Size of commune is a very weak predictor of membership turnover. The larger communes have a slightly greater rate of turnover than do the smaller ones. This is consistent with findings in other organizations. Price (1977, p. 89) reports that evidence on the general relationship between size and turnover in organizations is contradictory. Some investigators have reported a positive correlation, some a negative, and some no correlation between the two variables. Such a relationship, when it is found, is usually weak.

Much of the evidence discussed in this chapter has indicated the importance of relational variables in determining communal stability. A strong negative association with love, a strong positive one with dyadic partiality, and a weak positive one with negative emotional feelings have been demonstrated. It therefore seems to make sense to ask what other relational variables are associated with stability. But no other such associations were found. Instability was not found to be correlated with the average amount of time that commune members spend with one another, with the extent that they work together, with the structure of their power hierarchies, or with the frequency or saliency of their relationships with people outside the commune. Lack of direct association of stability with power is particularly surprising in light of the importance that power had as a factor in the conscious reasons that people gave for commune disintegration. However, the indirect way in which power plays a part in determining communal stability will be discussed later in this chapter, when we discuss the role of charisma.

*This, by the way, has happened in the Bruderhof as well (Zablocki, 1971, pp. 103ff.).

Many other background, behavioral, and attitudinal variables were also tested for possible association with communal stability. However, no further clues as to the determinants of instability emerged from this exploratory analysis. In particular, as examples, we might mention that commune instability was not demonstrated to be a function of mean self-esteem of members, of their expressed alienation from social institutions or from the commune itself, or of any aspect of the communal economy, from sharing of property to rotating of household chores.

Network Patterns of Dyadic Love

A perennial theme in Western literature has been the corrosive effect of stable social structures upon dyadic love. Our data have suggested that we can also reverse this perspective and investigate the corrosive effect of love upon stable social structures. We have found that the greater the sociometric density of love choices within a commune, the greater will be that commune's instability. This effect is both surprising and intriguing enough to warrant further elaboration.

Cathexis as a Sociological Concept

Sociology lacks a conceptual framework for talking about the collective manifestation of positive (or negative) affect. Cohesiveness is the term most often used to describe the strength of affectual bonds in a group, but in this context it is plainly inadequate. To use it would force us into the position of having to defend such absurd propositions as, "The more cohesive the commune, the less likely it is that it will cohere." The very concept of cohesiveness assumes what should be tested, that dyadic bonds aggregate to group bonds. In this sense, its general utility as a sociological concept is open to doubt.

We turned to the field of psychoanalysis to find more appropriate imagery for thinking about the measurement of affect in a collectivity and framing hypotheses concerning the correlation of affection with instability. Freudian theory (Rickman, 1957, p. 180) has used the term "cathexis" (c.f., Parsons et al. 1953) to denote a relationship involving emotional excitement:

> "Cathexis," from the Greek [verb] "I occupy." Any attempt at a short definition or description is likely to be misleading, but speaking very loosely, we may say that "cathexis" is used on the analogy of an electric charge, and that it means the concentration or accumulation of mental energy in some particular channel. Thus, when we speak of the existence in someone of a libidinal cathexis of an object, or, more shortly, of an object-cathexis, we mean that his libidinal energy is directed towards, or rather infused into, the idea (Vorstellung) of some object in the outer world.

The use of this relational term is easily extended to characterize networks of individuals. Imposing this psychoanalytic concept upon the imagery of networks of social relationships, the cathexis of a commune or any relationally involuted group can be thought of as the proportion of network paths that serve as conduits for highly charged emotional interchanges. Cathexis may thus be operationalized as affect density. In any given group of population N, there will be $N(N - 1)/2$ possible connections linking any one person in the group with any other. Let us operationally define cathexis as the proportion of these bonds characterized by a relationship of affect. In practice, when we use the word "cathexis" in this book, we will mean positive cathexis, the density of reciprocated loving choices. When we mean to refer to negatively-charged bonds, we will use the term "negative cathexis."

The Love Density (Cathexis) Effect

In Chapter 3, we briefly alluded to the high correlation between cathexis and turnover and labeled it a relative deprivation effect. From an individual perspective, this seems reasonable. We know that it is the least loved members of the most densely cathected communes who are most likely to leave. If it were only turnover that correlated with cathexis, we might be tempted to leave the matter at that. However, the association of cathexis also with (often bitter) communal disintegrations, and a tendency that we will discuss shortly for communes to maintain relatively constant cathexis levels as specific members come and go, lead us to seek further for a more sociological explanation of the love density effect.*

So far, all that we know about the love density effect comes from a statistical analysis. Let us now take a closer look at the shape of the relationship itself.

Figure 4-4 presents the scatter diagram of cathexis plotted against $1 - T$ (where T is the turnover rate). Each dot represents a commune. From the diagram, we see that the relationship is fairly linear throughout the entire domain of cathexis. In other words, turnover varies with cathexis not only in general, but also, more specifically, within the low, the medium, and the high ranges of cathexis.

Furthermore, looking at the lower right-hand portion of the diagram, three deviant cases (circled) can be seen. There is something distinctive about these three deviant cases. It turns out that, in the urban commune sample, there were just six communes with charismatic leaders in continuous daily residence.† Of these six charismatic leaders, one (perhaps the shrewdest) refused us permission to gather any data pertaining to relationships, although all other research instru-

---

*Another problem with the simple explanation of the phenomenon as a relative deprivation effect is that it fails to account for the very high levels of turnover in communes in which the love density approaches 100 percent.

†Many others, of course, had charismatic leaders who lived in the commune only some of the time or who governed from a distance.

FIGURE 4-4.   Scattergram of Cathexis by Membership Stability

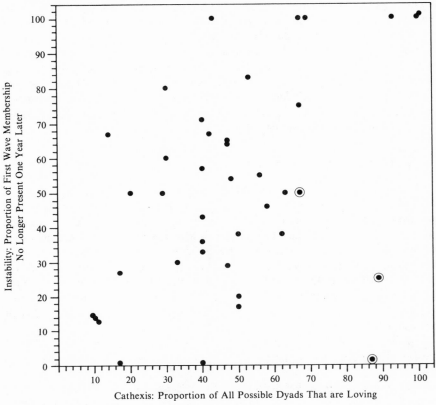

ments were permitted. Two of the others presided over communes that disintegrated within the first year. The remaining three were the leaders of precisely those circled deviant cases. Thus, we must qualify our formulation of the love density effect by asserting that it seems to hold only for those communes without charismatic leaders in continuous residence.

In Figure 4-5, we look at the love density effect from a different perspective. The urban communes are divided into five categories—cold, cool, warm, hot, and smoldering—based upon the proportion of all dyadic relationships in each commune that are loving. A strong montonic relationship between dyadic cathexis and both disintegration and turnover can readily be seen. The disintegration rate increases from 0.00 in the two least cathected categories to 0.60 in the highest category.

It would be plausible to speculate that the observed relationship between cathexis and membership turnover is a spurious effect of commune duration.

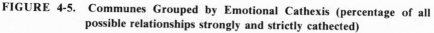

FIGURE 4-5. **Communes Grouped by Emotional Cathexis (percentage of all possible relationships strongly and strictly cathected)**

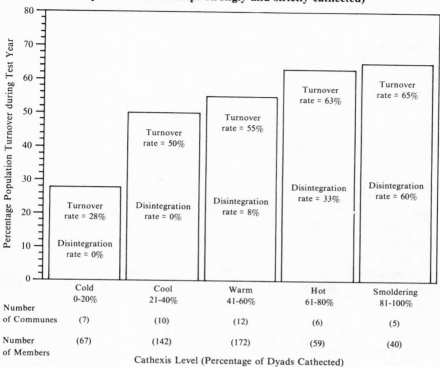

This speculation could take the following approach: It could be argued that new communes are more likely to be highly cathected and are also more likely to have high rates of turnover. Table 4-3 indicates that this is not the case. The table indicates that in the five-year spread during which almost all the urban communes in the sample were founded, neither cathexis nor turnover diminish with time.

Perhaps the most astounding aspect of Table 4-3 is the finding that the mean cathexis level for successive cohorts of communes remains virtually constant across the five cohorts examined, although we know that disintegration propensity steadily drops as a function of cohort age. This is interesting because it is evidence that points in the same direction as the finding that communes with resident charismatic leaders were able to tolerate high cathexis and still keep turnover low. Both charismatic leadership and accumulated duration can increase commune stability, but, however they may achieve this, they do not do it by reducing cathexis. This fits with what we know about historical communes such as the Harmonists, Shakers, Oneidans, and Bruderhof. Their success was due to the channelling of cathexis, not its reduction or elimination.

TABLE 4-3. Communal Disintegration Rate, Population Turnover, and Emotional Cathexis as Functions of the Year Commune Was Founded

Cohort	Year Founded	% of Communes Disintegrated (1974-1975)	Mean Cathexis[a]	Mean % of Stayers[a]	N^1
Year 4	1970	17%	52%	50%	(6)
Year 3	1971	17	43	62	(6)
Year 2	1972	27	52	45	(11)
Year 1	1973	17	46	50	(18)
Year 0	1974	27	55	51	(15)

[a]Calculated on subset of communes for which data were available (c.f. Table 4-2).   Total N = 56

^1N = number of communes founded 1970 or later, regardless of whether completed data sets were available.

Finally, let us look at effects of cathexis level change in the test year. From our observations of this 1975 data, cathexis is not a rapidly changing variable within any given commune. For the thirty-three urban communes for which relational data were available at the first two points in time, the zero-order correlation between cathexis at time 1 and cathexis at time 2 was r = 0.66. The average change over the year was fourteen percentage points in either direction.

But, when cathexis does change, it changes, more often than not, in a direction consistent with its assumed ability to predict third-wave stability. One-half of all the communes* that increased or remained the same in cathexis level from time 1 to time 2 were either disbanded by time 3 or experienced very high membership turnover (75 percent or more) during the year preceding time 3. By way of contrast, only 15 percent of those communes whose cathexis level dropped between time 1 and time 2 were unstable by these criteria at time 3.

It seems reasonable to conclude then that level of cathexis is a structural property of communes as well as being an aggregate property of networks of dyadic relationships. We might speculate that communes develop role structures that sustain constant levels of cathexis regardless of who are the occupants of these roles. If this is true then perhaps it is role structure stability that is the causally intervening variable between cathexis and commune instability.

Is sociometric love density a valid measure of what we have been calling cathexis? Let us leave aside for a bit the fundamental validity question: What do

---

*Overall N = 20. Both the quantity and the quality of data deteriorate by time 3. The validity of these measures is therefore somewhat lower than the validity of measures involving only time 1 and time 2 data.

respondents mean by the word love? Even if we grant that asking people whom they love is a valid way of finding out about love relationships, it still must be understood that what we have is a measure of density, not of intensity. If X, Y, and Z are involved in a love relation, we have no way of telling which link is strongest or who loves whom more. It is encouraging that we have been able to get good results using such a crude measure. But future research along these lines should attempt to measure love intensity as well and thus, perhaps, achieve even clearer results.

One might also question the appropriateness of the unit of analysis. After all, if a dyadic measure of love helps us to predict instability, might not a triadic or still higher-level measure predict even more? Cognitive balance theory (Heider, 1958; Newcomb, 1961) provides reason to believe such investigation might prove fruitful. Bradley (1979) has, in connection with another problem, analyzed the triadic configurations of love in these communes. His results show no evidence of an association between triad patterns (i.e., frequencies of occurrences compared with expected random frequencies) and either of our measures of stability. If triadic measures do not help to predict stability, it would seem reasonable to assume, in groups this small and connected, that measures defined on still higher-level subgraphs will do no better.

Communion and Cathexis

The primacy of sentiments in human relationships has been identified by Schmalenbach (1961) as the principal means by which communion as a fundamental form of human association can be distinguished from community:

> Often feelings are construed as the basis of community relations, because they are erroneously thought to be deeper or nearer the unconscious than rational thought. . . . Now, it is precisely in this context that the fundamental differences between community and communion may be established. The reality and basis of community do not consist in feelings. . . . The essence of community is association constituted in the unconscious. Community, as an organic and natural coalescence, precedes emotional recognition of it by its members.
>
> In the case of human communion, this is radically different. Emotional experiences are the very stuff of the relationship.

According to this perspective, communions evolve into communities to the extent that variable emotional investments are absorbed into invariant unconscious dispositions. There is also evidence, however (Zablocki, 1971; Turner, 1969), that collectivities can, under certain conditions, oscillate between states of communion and states of community.

Schmalenbach (1961, p. 337) speaks of communion as an intrinsically unstable form of human association and of community as an intrinsically stable form. Let us assume that the distribution of communes in a given year on a continuum from no membership turnover to complete membership turnover is isomorphic to the distribution of these same communes on a continuum from ideal-typical community to ideal-typical communion. Schmalenbach's formulation then provides us with an alternative explanation of the effect of cathexis on intercommunal variation in stability:

> Only where periodic excitement calms down once more—perhaps even dies out—and is then replaced by a kind of coalescence between emotion and unconscious disposition, can one speak of community. It is for this reason that, in the case of younger religions, the meetings of similarly excited persons are more likely to lead to communion than to community.

If Schmalenbach is correct, and if cathexis level may be taken as an indicator of where a commune stands on the communion-community continuum, then we can explain the love density effect in terms of the intrinsic stability of two different types of social structures. As Schmalenbach goes on to argue in the remainder of his essay, the communion form is intrinsically unstable and will decay over time into either community or association. In the true community, emotional display will be threatening rather than solidarity building. It will threaten the status quo by giving the individual too much autonomy. In the association, emotional relationships become contracts that can be made or broken at the pleasure of the participants. In neither case will cathexis, if it has not been absorbed into unconscious disposition, promote the solidarity of the group.

Some evidence of the communion expressing function of cathexis may be seen in the tenacity of the love relation in communes. Once formed, few loving bonds are broken except by one or both of the parties' leaving. Table 4-4 indicates the stability of choice in the love relation as compared with seven other types of emotional and behavioral relationship bonds, as a function of time. The table suggests that loving alone, of all these relationships, is an absorbing bond. New dyadic loving bonds may be formed over a year's time, but few are dissolved.

Although the proportion of all possible dyads that are loving is high, it is important to note that in no commune is there failure to discriminate between those who are always loved, those who are sometimes loved, and those who are not loved. Although we should not dismiss the very likely possibility that ideological imperatives have an effect on cathexis level, in almost no cases does ideology totally destroy the capacity for individual discrimination. We find that cathexis level varies between 10 percent and 100 percent.

We have discovered a convenient and intriguing "social thermometer" with which to diagnose communal instability. We can measure the degree of emotional cathexis in any commune and then predict what proportion of its membership will still be present one year later and whether the commune itself will

TABLE 4-4. Loving as Compared with Seven Other Kinds of Relationships in Terms of the Proportion of Old Bonds Broken and the Proportion of New Bonds Created Between the Two Waves

Relationship[1]	Broken Bonds[2]	Created Bonds[3]	Net Change in Number of Bonds
Loving	.03 (7/254)	.20 (11/55)	+ 4
Working together	.13 (21/156)	.23 (17/74)	− 4
Sleeping together	.32 (14/44)	.06 (18/319)	+ 4
Improving	.15 (40/263)	.36 (25/75)	−15
Sexual attraction	.32 (18/57)	.06 (18/316)	0
Power	.21 (22/103)	.14 (36/266)	+14
Hateful	.67 (24/36)	.02 (6/327)	−18
Exciting	.15 (22/143)	.11 (13/115)	− 9
$N^4 = 101$	$\sum_i N_i (N-1)_i = 380$		

[1] All relational bonds are treated here in their asymmetrical form (i.e., X chooses Y, regardless of whether Y reciprocates).

[2] A bond is considered broken if it existed at time 1 but no longer existed at time 2.

[3] A bond is considered created if it did not exist, or even "sometimes" exist, at time 1, but has come into existence at time 2.

[4] Only those commune members are included in the analysis for which valid measures of all eight relationship loadings, in both waves of the study, were obtained.

still exist. By predicting population turnover rates and disintegration probabilities directly proportional to the proportion of cathected dyads, we will be right considerably more often than would be predicted by chance.

But we must now face the validity problem that we postponed earlier. What do we mean by loving? Or more to the point, what do communitarians mean when they say that they love somebody? Is communal love spiritual, sexual, fraternal, merely a reflection of ideological conformity, or all or none of the above? And does the meaning of communal love influence the workings of the love density effect?

The Subjective Meaning of Dyadic Love

In ordinary usage, love has many meanings, and these meanings are often a source of confusion among those who use the word. In communes, the situation is further complicated by the fact that love frequently has an ideological as well as a personal meaning.* The kinds of difficulties to which confusion of the two meanings can lead are well illustrated by a quotation from a study (Katz, 1971, p. 147) that describes the attempts of a female commune member:

---

*The widespread alienation of commune members from productive work as a source of meaning in life seems to impel them to exaggerated efforts to find this meaning in love.

... to be honest about her feelings toward Christopher by whom she was visibily repulsed and who she was disgusted by the thought of having touch her, and to whom she had kept saying, "I don't think I am ready to relate to you, Christopher." These words were said with such a tremor of despair and brokenness that Christopher had not known at all what to make of them, especially as she also had said, "I love you, remember that. I really do." *Love* being the absolute minimum which one extends toward any other in the commune, as *courtesy* is in lower associations of society.

Erik Erikson (1970, p. 20) has presented an interesting clinical observation of this attempt to universalize, or "totalize" in his terms, the love relationship in what he calls "utopian group formation":

> In adolescence, a favourable ratio of the basic strengths and the basic estrangements established during the pre-adolescent stages must be renewed within a viable psychosocial identity. ... Under special conditions, however, either the estrangements or the strengths are *totalized* at the expense of their counterparts. Thus in *pathological states* basic mistrust may seem to have totally submerged basic trust, shame and doubt to have obliterated autonomy —and so on. Utopian group formations, in contrast, attempt to forestall the dangers of regression and to assure joint progression by forceful attempts to deny all estrangements ... such group retrogressions originate in the incapacity or the refusal to conclude the stage of identity on the terms offered by the adult world.

It is interesting to note that the dysfunction of high cathexis levels is perceived by Erikson to stem not from potential role conflict but from the ideological denial of the reality of negative feelings in favor of a point of view in which all interpersonal feelings were positive ones. The small but independent contribution that negative cathexis made to our ability to predict turnover gives a bit of support to this argument. Communes that were able to express negative emotions in dyadic relationships had slightly greater stability than did those that could not.

The demand for universalism in love can lead to an agapeic quasi-intimacy that is not based upon personal traits of the "loved" one. This kind of love can lead to confusion when the members of a commune differ in the significance they attach to the loving relationship. For some, the agapeic, quasi-intimate network of love relationships is perceived as a justification for avoiding direct engagement with other individuals and is seen as allowing a kind of extended family relationship without the tight and constricting role obligations that characterize real families. For others, however, the love network justifies a total surrender of personal autonomy to the all embracing and all nurturing community.

Avoidance of direct emotional engagement with fellow members is justified by some commune members in terms of an ideology that has evolved out of a larger-scale trend in American society against all forms of psychological dependency. The credo "we should not be dependent upon one another, and should no longer have to take responsibility for *all* of any one other person's needs" may at times become interpreted as, "we don't have to be responsive to *any* of another person's needs." The search for *open* relationships, which is not simply restricted to the sexual realm, slides into the search for *interchangeable* relationships.

Another distinctive and somewhat paradoxical element in the communitarian concept of love is the presumed ideological transitivity of the relationship: A loves B and B loves C ideally implies that A should love C even if A and C have never met. The implications of this relationship network are vividly expressed in a novel that has been popular among communitarians—Robert Heinlein's *Stranger in a Strange Land*. The term "water brother," used by Heinlein to describe intimate relationships, became in many communes, a term to describe the nature of relationships. Significantly, the tribe composed of water brothers is not thought of as a closed network. Various members of the tribe have water brothers in other tribes and in the noncommunal world. Thus, in one sense, the tribe is the group of anywhere from five to several hundred or so people who are living together in a communal setting. But, in another sense, the entire counterculture is the tribe. Traveling communitarians expected, and often received, kinship-type hospitality during their travels, which is at least partially explained by the shared notion that, through some linkage, they were probably already water brothers. In still another sense, the entire world is a tribe. This affiliation might not yet be fully realized in actuality; but, it is still an important latent goal. It is important to understand that, when countercultural communitarians speak of universal love, this is conceived of as an ultimately all-embracing network of dyadic relationships. It is not an absolute unity, imposed from above, as in the more traditional Christian model of a loving community of believers.

In this way, some contemporary communitarians are both similar to and different from the early Christians. Love is universal, but it finds its expression in pair relationships. This pairwise love is supposed to be able to serve as the building block for the development of a structure of universal love. In fact, however, the multiplication of loving bonds is just what we have defined here as cathexis, and cathexis, as we have seen, is *inversely* correlated with communal stability, ideological hopes notwithstanding.

Other observers of contemporary communes have commented on the quasi-intimate nature of communal loving relationships. French and French (1975, p. 85) have observed:

> To guard against intimacy demands constant attention. Gradually we began to see a brittleness in the ways group members dealt with one another. . . . Compassion was felt to be condescending. . . . Ideological confrontation was valued: "That's a male chauvinist thing to say"; "How can you have such a reactionary attitude?" . . . Someone wrote a note in The Group's weekly newsletter advising: "You sniveling, back-stabbing shitheads [his fellow members] I hope you curl up and die." Others laughed, pleased at his directness. It had to do again with preserving mobility. Compassion would have

led to involvement, involvement to commitment, and commitment to chains on tomorrow.

Kanter (1975, pp. 17ff.) has speculated as to the emergence of a fragile love as an enduring new form:

> High turnover and easy replacement are indicators of the fragility of urban communes. Relationships are often tentative and easily broken. . . . A key to understanding communal households as public families is the fact that the group can continue even when specific members leave, that the group is defined by the *place* it occupies, and not by the people who occupy it.

We have observed that communal love is at times ideological, at times ambivalent, and at times fragile. In some communes love is defined as a fraternal feeling, in other communes it takes on primarily sexual connotations. In Table 4-5, we compare the conditional probabilities of sexual feelings being present in a dyad given the presence of love with the conditional probabilities of fraternal feelings being present given the presence of love. The table illustrates that, to a great extent, these are mutually exclusive alternatives. The specific patterns of defining love as either fraternal or sexual, however, vary quite a bit from commune to commune. In the following pages (Figures 4-6A to 4-6E), we shall take a look at some network diagrams illustrating the overlap among sexual, loving, and fraternal feelings in communes selected by level of cathexis.

The sociograms are to be read in the following way: three examples of each cathexis category are presented in each figure. Each commune is represented by a band of three sociograms, reading across the page. The basic graph, labeled "Loving," occupies the central position on the page and also determines the relative positions of the nodes for all three graphs. Distancing is arbitrary. A line between any two nodes indicates that both of them have reported that the relationship is always characterized by the given attribute. A darkened line in the sexual or fraternal graph indicates that the relationship has also been designated as loving. Thus, for example, the set of graphs that constitute Figure 4-6B3 indicates that there are three loving relationships (1-8-7, 3-5, and 6-9). Two of them (8-7, 6-9) are also sexual, and there are no other sexual relationships. There are also two relationships characterized as brotherly or sisterly (fraternal), but there are no relationships that are both loving and fraternal. To the limited extent to which we can generalize from these data, therefore, we can characterize this commune as more erotic than fraternal in its love.

As we have already seen from Table 4-4, there is a marked tendency for any given commune to experience its love as either sexual or fraternal, but not both. The sociograms also indicate some degree of complementarity between the two functions. Perhaps most important, we also note a tendency to move from a sexual orientation to a fraternal orientation as cathexis increases.

In the lowest cathexis category (Figure 4-6A), the sociograms suggest that communal stability is associated with a communal suppression of love, except

TABLE 4–5. Conditional Probabilities of Multiplex Relationships
Involving Love

Commune List	Probability of Sexual/Given Loving	Probability of Fraternal/Given Loving
Atlanta		
Southern Comfort	.67	.00
Karp House	.60	.30
Loch Lomond	.53	.33
Alabama Avenue	.15	.20
Old Plantation	.17	.33
RMC Community	.26	.52
Love from Above	.00	.57
Youth & Truth	.10	.85
Icthus	.00	.83
New York		
Brownstone House	.75	.38
Beaux Arts	.33	.17
Youth & Truth	.00	.25
United Lotus	.00	.44
Los Angeles		
The Coop	1.00	.00
Liberty House	.47	.21
Utopia	.52	.34
Habakkuk	.04	.85
Houston		
Capitol Avenue	1.00	.00
Cove Community	.83	.17
Hillbrush House	.40	.40
Gable House	.00	.33
Third Eye	.17	.64
Grandesur	.13	.88
Metamorfis	.00	.89
Twin Cities		
Sills House	1.00	.00
Thorn & Thistle	.57	.21
White Tower	.15	.39
Needle's Eye	.00	.50
Love from Above	.04	.61
The Dove	.02	.63
Youth & Truth	.13	.81
Joy of God	.04	.80
Boston		
The Summit	.54	.00
Treetop House	.50	.00
Embarcadero	.40	.00
Delmonico House	.25	.08
Third Eye	.06	.01
Love from Above	.02	.02
Youth & Truth	.00	.04
Spectra	.55	.00

FIGURE 4-6. Comparison of Loving Sociograms with Those Expressing Sexual or Fraternal Feelings[1]

A. Cold for Groups with 20% or Fewer Cathected Relationships

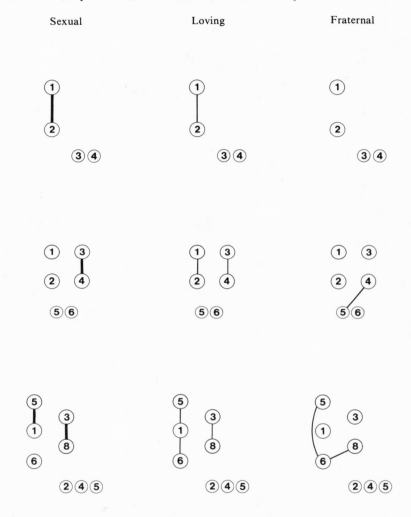

[1]Darkened lines denote that the relationship is also "loving."

for monogamous marital bonds. However, in the almost as stable second and third cathexis categories (Figures 4-6B and 4-6C), the sexual network diagrams are often highly intermeshed.

In the most highly cathected group (Figure 4-6E), reported sexual feeling disappears almost completely, even between monogamous pairs. Loving is

B. Cool for Groups with 21-40% Cathected Relationships

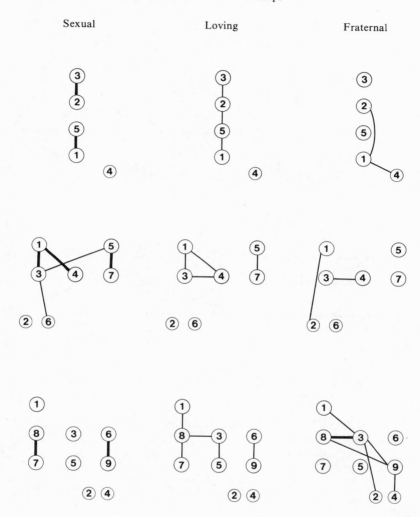

Sexual   Loving   Fraternal

interpreted either in a brotherly or sisterly sense exclusively or, as in the last case, as neither sexual nor fraternal. We must rely on field reports for evidence that fraternal love in the highly cathected groups can be as intense and volatile as the erotic love of some of the other groups. In general, it is interpreted by the participants as a powerful and consuming sentiment—even as powerful as its erotic counterpart.

C. Warm for Groups with 41-60% Cathected Relationships

Sexual   Loving   Fraternal

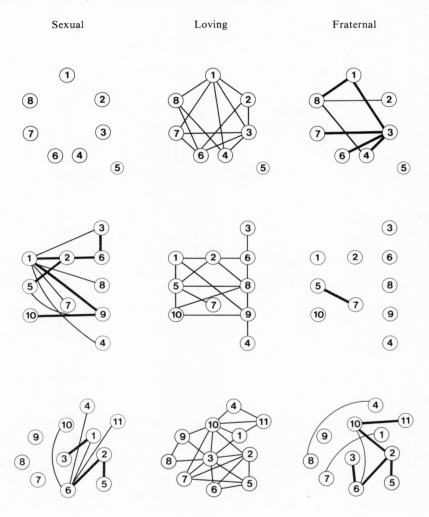

Generalization of the Love Density Effect

The love density effect is interesting because it is counterintuitive. We very well might have guessed that the amount of love in a commune would be directly associated with stability; instead we find that there is an inverse association. It is reasonable, therefore, to ask whether this effect is peculiar to the communes that we have studied or if it is a more general phenomenon.

D. Hot for Groups with 61-80% Cathected Relationships

Sexual   Loving   Fraternal

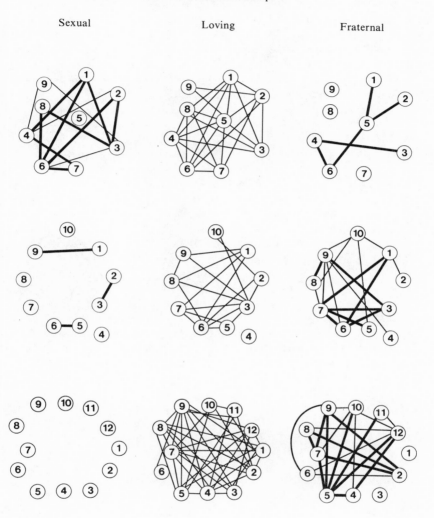

The extensive literature on cohesiveness would lead us to believe that the proposition, love density equals group stability, is well established. In fact, there is no evidence for this except in the very special circumstance of men in combat situations (Janowitz, 1959). Etzioni (1975, p. 280) has demonstrated that there is no necessary association between group cohesiveness in the workplace and either compliance to company norms or absenteeism.

But Etzioni seems to imply that this is because cohesiveness breeds commit-

E. Smoldering for Groups with 80% or More Cathected Relationships

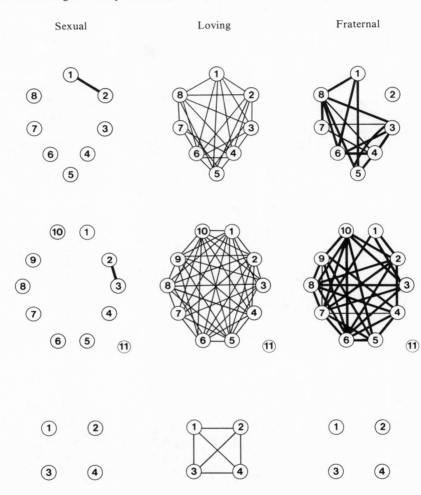

ment only to the group's own norms, which may be different from those of the company. We are going still further and arguing that (in a purely voluntary group) the group's own norm of survival not only can, but generally will, become alien to the members in their roles as network participants.

There has been a good deal of implicit recognition of the love density effect in the literature on communes. That eccentric unsung forefather of social

psychology, Charles Fourier (Manuel, 1962), recognized its theoretical importance and made it the foundation of his utopian system through his "law of
passionate attraction." Fourieristic communitarian planning rested upon the
premise that social and physical proximities among the members of a community had to be constantly and harmoniously varied for the collectivity to
survive. His elaborate and impractical plans for making what Gerald Suttles
(1972) has called "distancing mechanisms," the organizing principle of his
communes, were never really tried in the American phalansteries. But the fact
that he attached so much importance to these mechanisms and that his approach
to community so obviously struck a chord with many Americans in the 1830s
and 1840s can be taken as evidence that there was a widespread perception that
dyadic love was a major enemy of intentional community.

Much attention has been given to the avoidance of dyadic intimacy among
the nineteenth-century utopian communities. The Shakers, for example, not
only prescribed celibacy, but also took great pains to reduce to a minimum the
ordinary dyadic intimacies of everyday life (Nordhoff, 1875, p. 177):

> Brethren and sisters may not unnecessarily touch each other. If a brother
> shakes hand with an unbelieving woman, or a sister with an unbelieving man,
> they shall make known the same to the elders before they attend worship.
> Such salutes are admissible, for the sake of civility or custom, if the world
> party first present the hand—never without. All visiting of the world's people,
> even their own relations, is forbidden, unless there exist a prospect of making
> converts, or of gathering some one into the fold.

John Humphrey Noyes, of course, both as charismatic leader of his own
Oneida community and in his analysis of the successes and failures of the communes of his day (Noyes, 1870), made something of a fetish out of the avoidance of what he called "special attachments." It has often been assumed that the
function of the group marriage practices of Oneida was to avoid *exclusive* dyadic
loves. But perhaps a latent function may well have been the routinization of
sexual intimacy to the point where it made only minimal contribution to the
aggregate intensity of all dyadic loves.

The love density effect has been noted outside of communes as well. Forsyth
and Kolenda (1966) observe strong internal sanctions, in ballet companies,
against the formation of friendships. They conclude that the dancers perceive
the formation of friendship groups to be incompatible with their highly valued
corporate activity. It would seem that the common thread then is the high
value that the participants themselves place upon the agenda of the corporate
actor. When this is valued highly enough, the group itself may seek to minimize
cathexis as a way of maximizing stability.

There is no evidence that the love density effect works at all in the great
majority of small group situations. It seems to operate most clearly in the kinds
of groups James Coleman (1972, p. 2) has called "transcendent corporate
actors." Such groups are defined as those in which each individual member

identifies so fully with the goals of the collectivity that he acts "as an intrinsic part of the corporate actor, and receives his benefits directly as part of that actor." This process is the same thing that we have been calling investment of self.

An interesting analog to the love density effect in nontranscendent collectivities is provided by Granovetter's (1973) theory of the strength of weak ties. Granovetter argues that, within large sparsely connected social networks, weak dyadic ties make a more important contribution to social integration than strong dyadic ties because of their greater likelihood of bridging otherwise disconnected subnetworks. Again we encounter the apparent paradox that strong ties weaken the social structure to the extent that they are relied upon exclusively in dyadic interaction.

Although these two theories (love density and strength of weak ties) come to a similar conclusion, there is not much overlap in the posited causal mechanisms leading to this conclusion. In the first instance, connectivity is no problem at all, but maintaining social distance and emotional stability of bonds is very much a problem. In the second, individuals are well insulated from those to whom they are tied and the problem is one of maintaining connecting links that permeate the entire collectivity.

However, both theories lead to similar conclusions about the role of relationships in social structure. Both lead us to perceive that too much relatedness can be as harmful for social structure as too little. We should therefore be led to expect curvilinear associations between measures of relational intensity and measures of structural stability.* In a quite different way, this is the result also pointed to in the work of Nadel (1957) and White et al. (1976) stressing avoidance behavior as the key to role structure. In general, we may expect the intricacy and stability of most any kind of structure to be at a maximum when relationships among components are of an intermediate intensity.

Cathexis in the Presence of Charisma

A striking aspect of the love density effect is its failure to work in communes with resident charismatic leaders. As we saw in Figure 4-4, the three such communes for which data were available deviated sharply from the linear clustering that characterized most of the rest. Although the number of cases involved is small, the pattern is so clear and so intriguing that it deserves further investigation.

One of the charismatic communes that was able to combine high cathexis with low membership turnover was a fundamentalist Christian group organized as a patriarchal extended family. The commune stressed obedience and clear lines of authority. The wife of the leader, although clearly subordinate to her

---

*The reason that we are able to fit our findings to a linear model is that the entire communitarian phenomenon is located within the extremely intense range along the continuum of relational intensity.

husband, functioned as a communal mother figure and had quite a bit of power in her own sphere of activities. The other commune members occupied big and little brother and sister roles with respect to one another, exercising very limited but still well-defined authority where appropriate. Status in this hierarchy was dependent upon age, seniority within the commune, and strength of faith as discerned by the charismatic leader.

The charismatic leader in this commune had the ability to channel the high degree of cathexis into nondestructive areas. He seemed to do this by using the available positive feeling evoked by the cathexis to continually force the group to transcend its own limits as a corporate actor. For example, for some time, the group had been tormented by the discrepancy between its ideological belief in complete economic sharing and the fear of its members of relinquishing all private property. In between the time 1 and the time 2 visit, the commune finally took the big step and adopted total economic communism. The shared joy accompanying this achievement may well have prevented the very high density of loving relationships in the commune from creating instability.

A second commune (not religious) dealt with its cathexis in a very different way. This group was composed almost entirely of married couples and formerly married single people. The commune was explicitly organized as an extended family. The leader used multiple sexual relationships* among the members as a channel for the heavy love density of the commune. This commune never quite became an explicit group marriage, and tension between the monogamous and the nonmonogamous continued throughout the year. But the excitement of new intimacies and potential intimacies absorbed whatever cathexis might otherwise have damaged group stability.

This was not nearly as satisfactory a long-term solution as that chosen by the first commune. These were people of fairly conservative temperaments. Once the novelty of successfully breaking a sexual taboo had worn down, these liaisons were no longer able to counteract the destabilizing effects of high cathexis. The increase in generalized physical intimacy among the commune members may well have even aggravated the problem. Although these after effects did not take place during the test year, they happened soon afterward. Turnover increased from zero to .45 by time 3 (August 1976). Among the leavers, during this year, was the charismatic leader himself. By time 4, one year later, the commune was defunct.

The third of our deviant cases was again a religious commune. In this commune, cathexis was almost palpable. The members of this commune were so tuned in to the moods and expressions of their charismatic leader, and through the leader tuned in to each other, that they seemed at times to the observer to blend into one another's personalities.

---

*It should be noted for later reference that, insofar as our records are complete, it would appear that each female who became involved in the multiple sexual network became involved initially by having an (at first covert) affair with the charismatic leader and each male by his wife's having such an affair.

The charismatic leader of this commune developed no plan for coping with this high cathexis. On the contrary, the leader was forced to take almost the entire destabilizing burden of this cathexis upon himself. Although the membership turnover was far less in this commune than in the others of similar cathexis level, one of the leavers making up the turnover cohort was the charismatic leader himself under conditions that were far from either voluntary or cordial. The use of the charismatic leader as a scapegoat has often been observed in communal groups. In the Bruderhof (Zablocki, 1971), for example, it was raised practically to an art form. This act of *lèse majesté* seems to serve as the moral and functional equivalent of more generalized group instability.

These three groups, very different in their coping mechanisms, all have in common the use of a sense of personal renewal (Turner, 1969). The high density of dyadic love is tolerable because the love relations themselves are experienced as renewed, by successfully meeting an ideological challenge in the first group, by sexual expression in the second group, and by killing and eating the father, so to speak, in the third group. One might perhaps say that, under these conditions of renewal, the dyadic relations themselves become charismatic.

The cases that we have described tell only half the story. Having learned that it is possible to suppress the effect that love density has upon group stability, it is reasonable to ask why noncharismatic groups and groups governed by absentee charismatic leaders do not also avail themselves of these opportunities. This question brings us closer to the need for a structural explanation, for which we need to inquire more closely as to how charisma operates in communes.

The Correlates of Charisma

The communitarian charismatic leaders in our sample do not all come from the same mold. Most of them are male (92 percent), and most of them are older than the commune mean age (88 percent). But they do not differ insofar as can be determined from the full sample of commune members in other background characteristics. Those for whom we have data tend to have very high self-esteem and to be significantly less alienated from both the commune and the larger society than the average commune member. They occupy positions at the top of the informal as well as formal sociometric power hierarchies. Some are recipients of many love choices but some are not.

There is evidence of an association in the communitarian's mind of charismatic leader with patriarch. A factor analysis was performed on fifteen characteristics that commune members were asked to apply to their fellow members where applicable. The fifteen traits load onto four factors, which we have identified as good father, bad father, strong woman, and submissive person.*

*The strong woman is associated with loving, interest in children, supportive, dependent,

The good father is associated primarily with the following characteristics: charismatic, intuitive, strong, supportive, influential, decisive and loving. The bad father is associated with dominant, decisive, and narcissistic and negatively associated with loving and supportive. It is interesting to note the association of decisiveness with the bad father figure in the light of our hypotheses about charisma. If charisma operates upon the group by modifying the preferences of its members so that they can achieve consensus, the followers have a moral obligation to be moldable (i.e., indecisive). If consensus is to be achieved, only the charismatic leader has the legitimate right to be a decisive person. In fact, the loading of decisiveness on the good father (charismatic) factor is lower than on the bad father factor. The trait is there but perhaps less salient. The bad father, by being decisive without being charismatic, offends the moral order of the group.

Further justification for associating charisma with the father role in communes is the substantial effect of charismatic leadership on the perception of the commune members that the commune is their true family. Seventy-six percent of the members of resident charismatic communes agreed with this statement; 52 percent of the members of communes with absentee charismatic leaders agreed; and only 18 percent of those in communes without charismatic leaders agreed. Note that the loyalty that the charismatic leader engenders is to the group, not just to himself. Sometimes, as with the scapegoat described earlier, it is directed to the group instead of to himself.

The mystique surrounding charismatic leaders often prevents us from effectively observing their true functions. Although this is less true in communes than in other kinds of social movement organizations, it is still a problem. One way of getting a peek at the essential charismatic role behind the charismatic pomp is to look at an interesting attempt by a noncharismatic group to legislate the functional equivalent of charisma.

Rosabeth Kanter (1972, p. 27) describes an interesting attempt by a contemporary commune to develop a role that is functionally equivalent to a portion of the charismatic role. This commune, Walden Two, is one that would be characterized as having no charismatic leader and low charismatic potential (see Chapter 6):

> Typical forms of communication are written opinion surveys, notes on bulletin boards, or news-of-the-day broadcasts over the commune radio. The whole group meets together rarely. *At one time, complaints about other people were taken to a third person known as the generalized bastard, so that direct confrontation was avoided.* [emphasis added]

An important function of the charismatic leader is to allow an alternative pathway for indirect communication and interaction among participants so that

---

sexy, and intuitive. The submissive is associated with being passive and holy and negatively associated with dominant and decisive. See Sprague (1978) for a fuller discussion of these factors and their correlates.

they can avoid, if need be, the highly cathected direct pathway. Of course, the charismatic leader is able to draw upon his vast reserves of prestige to get away with doing this without being seen as a generalized bastard. When his prestige account is overdrawn, the charismatic leader runs the risk of becoming a scapegoat.

The generalized bastard role was one that indicated a great deal of insight and ingenuity on the part of the Walden Two members. But it didn't work. Prestige of the kind needed to serve as such a conduit cannot be bureaucratically created. This is one of the reasons that noncharismatic groups are not successful at avoiding the destabilizing effects of cathexis.

Charisma and Power

Another important distinction between charismatic and noncharismatic communes has to do with their organization of interpersonal power and the relationship between power and love. Recall that earlier in this chapter we indicated that, in the minds of the commune members, power disputes ranked first as a category of reasons for communal disintegration. But, when we examined the statistical correlates, we found that it was not power relations but love relations that seemed to be associated with disintegration.

An important key to resolving this discrepancy, and also to explaining the charismatic suppression of the cathexis effect, lies in the interrelationship of the spheres of love and of power in charismatic as opposed to noncharismatic communes. There is some social psychological evidence that the entire domain of personal attribution may be largely organized around two dimensions: love-hate and dominance-submission (D'Andrade, 1965). If this is so, it is plausible that the interrelationship between these two dimensions will largely determine the organization of participants' role-attributive relationships with one another.

It is important to note that there are power structures in charismatic communes. The absence of formal offices of superordination and formal chains of command has led to a misconception. From Weber on down, an erroneous assumption has been accepted as fact—that the followers of a charismatic leader were necessarily linked to one another in relations of fraternal equality.

Precisely the opposite is the case in communes. A charismatic leader defines a power structure among his followers that is, in some ways, less ambiguous and more sharply articulated than is that of a commune without a charismatic leader. This will be discussed in Chapter 7. The charismatic situation produces consensus with respect to rank and authority. Therefore, power differentiation within the group does not have to be reinforced by the imposition of formal status positions and role expectations. In other words, externally observable ranks and positions may often be a sign not of well-articulated but of poorly articulated status hierarchies. A charismatic leader does not need such externally observable signs because he has imposed a shared consciousness of the *de facto* hierarchy upon the minds of all his followers. Community—particularly charismatic community—gives rise to an infrastructure of hierarchy beneath a façade of egalitarianism.

Moreover, in charismatic communes, the network of power is more interwoven with the network of love. In Chapter 6 we shall examine the conditional probabilities of love given power in charismatic and noncharismatic communes and shall see that these conditional probabilities are quite a bit higher in the communes with charismatic leaders. In other words, it is more likely that a power relation will also be a love relation in charismatic communes. This is true from the subordinate's as well as the superordinate's point of view. Because, as we shall see in Chapter 7, all communes generate well-defined and behaviorally salient power hierarchies among their members, the question of whether love can flow across power lines is obviously important.

Power as a subjective reason for, and love as an objective correlate of, communal instability can now be brought together. It seems reasonable to surmise that love, by engendering interpersonal vulnerability, makes power relations potentially destructive for communes. But charismatic leadership, by linking the exercise of power to the commitment of love, removes much of this threat. It provides an exemplary prototype (i.e., the relationship between the charismatic leader and each of his followers) in which subordination is just as rewarding as dominance and personal vulnerability is the conduit for love. By creating such a prototype, the charismatic leader allows dyadic relationships to find their natural place in the dominance hierarchy without power conflicting with love or people using their power to exploit the love of others. Of course, as happened in one of our earlier examples, if the charismatic leader himself begins to use his power to exploit the love of his followers, the system may well break down.

Conclusions

In this chapter, we have shown that a relatively small number of variables, measured at time 1, is able to account for almost two-thirds of the variance in commune population turnover rates, as measured at time 2. The most important of these predictor variables was seen to be dyadic cathexis, a measure of the density of reciprocated loving relationships within a commune network. The direction of the relationship is surprising; the more love, the greater the turnover. However, the pattern of association continued to hold up when we looked at time 3 turnover as a function of dyadic cathexis change between time 1 and time 2. Cathexis was seen to have a similar effect upon commune disintegrations. Whether the love of the commune members for one another was experienced as sexual, fraternal, or both, or neither appeared to make no difference. But a deviant case analysis of three intensely charismatic communes strongly suggested that the association between dyadic love and communal instability may be completely suppressed in the presence of charisma.

Our analysis thus far has led us from an investigation of the alienated state of meaninglessness as a cause of the need for charismatic community, to the corrosive effects of emotional cathexis upon communal stability as a function of time, to the countervailing ability of charismatic authority to maintain stable community under these otherwise untenable conditions. We have come as far as we can under the self-imposed constraint that we leave the subjective values of specific communes out of consideration and treat the commune as an objective entity. While this simplifying assumption has expedited the analysis in the first four chapters, the time has now come to abandon it and go on to consider ideological differences among the communes themselves.

PART **II**

Ideological Aspirations
and Achievements

In Part I, we saw evidence that communes tend to be short-lived and unstable forms of social organization. However, stability is not always a reliable indicator of success. One of the most successful communes of the nineteenth century, Brook Farm, managed to last only a few years and was plagued with very high membership turnover. One of the most long-lived and stable communes of the nineteenth century, the Harmony Society, lingered on for many years after the utopian spark had died. It is necessary to look at the achievements of communes independently from their rates of survival.

It is time to go beyond the analysis of observed events and attempt to understand the entities we are studying on their own terms. This does not mean that we are going to try to evaluate them. There will be no effort to divide communes into the successful and the unsuccessful or to rank them on an ideological success index. It seems to make more sense to try to identify the major obstacles to communitarian success and the strategies for overcoming these obstacles.

Chapter 5 is largely descriptive. We discuss first how communitarians in general are ideologically distinctive and then go on to develop a typology of communitarian ideological orientations. The following three chapters are each organized around one of the major obstacles to communitarian success: the problem of autonomy, the problem of inequality, and the problem of vulnerability. In each instance we see failure of the commune manifested largely in the inability to gain or maintain consensus and to achieve some form of charismatic intervention as the main technique for regaining consensus. The charismatic interventions, of course, create problems of their own. Throughout this part of the book, particularly in Chapters 6, 7, and 8, we develop the rudiments of a theory of alienation and charisma as reciprocal concepts and attempt to use it as a tool for explaining the discrepancy between ideological aspirations and achievements.

In the United States there is no end which human will despairs of attaining through the combined power of individuals united in a society.

Alexis de Tocqueville

CHAPTER 5

The Varieties of
Communitarian Ideology
by
Benjamin Zablocki
and
Angela Aidala

That communes have always differed from one another enormously in ideology cannot be doubted. It is a fact reflected not only in the data now at hand but also in the extent to which the sociology of communes has been dominated by analyses based upon ideological taxonomies.* The religious/nonreligious dimension, for example, has provided a constant theme in this literature from the time of Noyes and Nordhoff to the present.

We shall also find it necessary to develop a typology of ideological orientations. However, let us first ask a logically prior question: What components of ideology remain constant across all communal types? In other words, what are the elements of the most general communitarian ideology?

---

*For a basic review, see Richardson (1976). Here are a few examples of typologies that have been used in recent comparative studies or reports: self-actualizing, mutual support, activist, practical, therapeutic, religious (Rigby, 1974); creedal, noncreedal (Berger, 1971); service, retreatist (Kanter, 1972); erotic, hip, mystical, political (Roberts, 1971); commune, intentional community (Houriet, 1971).

The General Communitarian Ideology

The contemporary commune movement, like its historical counterparts, is far from being a monolithic social movement. Communitarianism is a diffuse social response within which utopian as well as practical values and goals have been molded into a wide range of sometimes coherent structures. But a high degree of differentiation does not necessarily imply an empty core. All communitarians, for example, share an idiosyncratic response to the problems of social integration into family and community. What, then, are the uniformities amid the ideological differences?

Like so many sociological concepts, "ideology" has meant different things to different investigators. Some define it narrowly as a system of beliefs and concepts about the political order; others consider ideologies, by definition, to be composed of false or distorted ideas.* For research on communes, a broad, nonevaluative definition seems more appropriate. Let us operationally define ideology as:

> A system of ideas held in common by members of a collectivity, with the following properties: it is an integrated pattern of beliefs and concepts including, but not limited to attitudinal beliefs, core values, social goals, and behavioral norms; it describes and interprets phenomena both empirically and normatively; it serves to focus and simplify action choices facing members of the collectivity; it stands in opposition to alternative ideological perspectives within the same society.

We shall concentrate, in this section, on two important aspects of ideology, the construction of meaning and the definition of goals. Because the ideologies of communal groups are so varied, our search for the rudiments of a general communitarian ideology must undertake comparative analysis of the measurable components of ideological systems. No ideology, of course, is merely the sum of its measurable components. However, the strategy of this section of this chapter will be to confine analysis to data produced by standardized instruments. This is so because we are searching for uniformities, not distinctions. Within the confines of this study, such standardized data are available only for the urban communes and only for beliefs, attitudes, values, and goals measured at the individual level. Later in this chapter, we shall shade in some of the subtler commonalities not captured in this analysis.

Three types of evidence will be considered, two at the individual level and one at the group level. At the individual level, we will be concerned, first, with *distinctiveness* (the extent to which communitarians as a class are ideologically different from other Americans) and, second, with *homogeneity* (the extent to which communitarians are ideologically alike). Finally, at the group level, we

---

*For discussions of the development of the concept of ideology, see Lichtheim (1965; pp. 164–195) and Birnbaum (1962). On the question of whether ideology necessarily implies distortion, see Geertz (1964).

will be concerned with *communal similarity* (the extent to which individual ideological heterogeneity is attributable to variation *within* the communes rather than to variation *among* the communes).

It should be noted that almost all the data to be examined here were gathered from individual commune members, not from observation of group processes. As such, the data are subject not only to insider biases but also, possibly, to fallacies of aggregation. Although there has been, in general, an attempt to cross-validate findings from members' responses, ex-members' recollections, and field-workers' observations, the reader should be aware that the arguments of this section rest heavily on the first of these sources.

Construction of Meaning

All communitarians look to their ideologies to help them impart meaning to the world.* For analytic purposes, we can distinguish two separate dimensions upon which this reality construction† activity is performed: the cognitive and the evaluative, although commune members themselves do not generally make such distinction in their meaning construction activities. Let us first discuss observed differences and similarities in the cognitive beliefs and attitudes of commune members and then go on to discuss how they rank order their values.

Beliefs and Attitudes. A questionnaire that included agree/disagree statements concerning social and political issues and beliefs about and attitudes toward the major institutions of American society was administered to the urban commune members.‡ These attitude data are presented in Appendix B. The responses of a small (N = 26) noncommunal control group made up of Columbia and Barnard College students are also presented in Appendix B for purposes of comparison.

The commune members were more skeptical about the value of university education, and the college students were more skeptical about religion and, more generally, "anything that tries to tell me the right way to live." Commune members were more likely to affirm the validity of living in the present and letting tomorrow take care of itself and of not feeling bound by constraints of

---

*This would appear to be particularly a characteristic not only of communitarians, but of any youth oriented social movement. As Erikson (1970, p. 15) has said:

> The cognitive facts established by Piaget make it plausible enough that youth thinks ideologically, that is, with a combination of an egocentric, narcissistic orientation determined to adapt the world to itself and a devotion to idealistic and altruistic schemes and codes, whether or not their feasibility can be proven or disproven with adult logic.

†Cf. Berger and Luckmann (1966). It is interesting to note in this context that one commune in New Mexico in the 1960s named itself The Reality Construction Company.

‡Usable attitude data were actually collected from 398 individuals (60 percent of the sample) in 57 of the communes (95 percent). No significant differences in background were discovered between respondents and nonrespondents. Not all of the items were designed specifically to ascertain beliefs. Some reflected opinions or personal preferences (see Appendix B).

TABLE 5-1. Proportion Neither Agreeing nor Disagreeing with Questions Concerning Selected Institutional Areas

Institutional Area	% Nonchoice
Attitudes toward present communal living situation	10%
Attitudes toward oneself	12
Attitudes toward human nature	14
Attitudes toward the university and education	19
Attitudes toward religion and religious issues	21
Attitudes toward marriage and family	21
Attitudes toward work and career	23
Attitudes toward politics and political issues	24
Attitudes toward respondent's city	24
Attitudes toward communitarianism as a social movement	25

heredity and environment. However, the college students were more likely to agree that it is good to live in a fantasy world occasionally. But items that did not discriminate between college students and commune members predominated over those that did by a ratio of about ten to one.

However, when we look at the proportion of neutral, don't know, and no response for each item, the situation is markedly different. It is not so much the choices that they make but their lack of capacity and/or willingness to choose that distinguishes our commune members from the college control group. Moreover, as Table 5-1 indicates, this lack of choice specificity is not distributed evenly over all beliefs but is associated primarily with certain institutional areas. In general the further from home the questions get, the larger the proportion of nonchoice.

In examining the commune members' responses for signs of consensus, a strong and a weak criterion were used (see Table 5-2). To meet the strong criterion, the modal response had to include at least 90 percent of the individual respondents (i.e., 90 percent had to either agree or disagree with the statement); and at the aggregate level, all the communes had to line up in the same direction, that is, with their means tilting in a positive (agree) or negative (disagree) direction. An item could meet the weak criterion if only 75 percent of the respondents fell in the modal category and if either all or all but one of the groups (98 percent) lined up in the same direction.

Of the ninety-nine attitudinal items tested, only one met the strong criterion: "Raising children is important work." Ninety-two percent of all commune members agreed with this statement. However, only 57 percent of the respondents expressed a personal perference for having children themselves, and only 53 percent agreed that it is healthier for children to grow up in communal rather than nuclear households. Because there is much dissensus on these last items,

TABLE 5-2. Attitudinal Consensus among Commune Members

	Respondents	Communes
Strong Criterion: 90% of individuals in modal category and 100% communal means in modal category		
Raising children is important work (agree)	92%	All
Weak Criterion: 75% of individuals in modal category and 98% of communal means in modal category		
Disagree that no one in this commune cares what happens to me	88	All
Disagree that there is a distance between me and other commune members	84	All
Disagree that it is hard to get my opinion to count for anything in this commune	82	All but one
Disagree that letting others influence your opinions is a sign of weakness	82	All
Disagree that every able-bodied male should serve in the military	81	All
Disagree that, in recent years, blacks have gotten more than they deserve	77	All
A good teacher is one who makes you wonder about your way of looking at things (agree)	76	All
Disagree that I feel left out of things around me	75	All
Disagree that the golden rule is impractical in today's world	75	All

we cannot consider attitudes toward children the kernel of any general communitarian ideology.

Dropping to the weak criterion, the first point to be noticed is a negative one. With the exception of a shared negativism toward the military, there is no consensus among commune members in beliefs about any of the major social institutions. No statement concerning world or national politics, the economy, education, or religion was able to strike a common chord in even three quarters of the commune sample. Getting closer to home, with questions about work and career, marriage, the city in which the commune was located, and communitarianism itself as a social movement, yielded no different results. As a whole, commune members seem neither alienated from nor positively disposed toward the major social institutions.

It is only when commune members are asked about their beliefs regarding their own communes or regarding themselves that consensus emerges. These beliefs tend, in Bennett Berger's (1972) phrase, "to be rather self-congratulatory" (see Table 5-2). Within the limited circumference of the commune, a person apparently can feel connected, powerful, and cared for.

In the light of our previous discussions concerning a special kind of communitarian alienation, two items that meet the weak criterion are worth noting. Commune members tend to agree that a good teacher is one who makes you wonder about your way of looking at things, and they tend to disagree that letting others influence your opinions is a sign of weakness. Although this is not real evidence, one might speculate that these two items are indicators of charismatic susceptibility—the felt desire to be told what to believe and what to want.

We must conclude that communitarians are not particularly distinctive in their beliefs and attitudes and that, in most areas, they are almost maximally heterogeneous. The major area of distinctiveness is to be found in the extraordinarily high proportions of those who cannot or will not answer questions about their attitudes. A composite image emerges of an aggregate of people who are confused about the world and their relation to it, open to and eager for authoritative leading, and content (at least temporarily) to have contracted the boundaries of saliency to the self and the communal household.

Values. To examine the values of commune members, a well-known and widely used ranking instrument (Rokeach, 1973) was used. Each commune member was shown two lists of phrases, the first identifying values such as freedom, equality, and wisdom, which are generally considered *ends* in themselves, and the second identifying values such as ambition, honesty, and politeness, which are generally considered *means* to other ends. The respondents were asked to rank order each list separately in terms of the personal importance they attached to each value.* The value lists and median ranks are displayed in Table 5-3.

While the values of a collectivity are not simply the aggregation of individual value orientations, collective values, like all components of ideology, are socially created and maintained and thus do not have existence entirely separate from the personal values of individual group members. Aidala (1979) found a high

---

*All data on the value rankings of commune members were obtained from follow-up studies carried out in 1976 and 1977. Although the communal households were the same as in the earlier study the membership often was not. In some cases, the findings presented in this section would therefore have been different had the instrument been administered at the same time that the rest of the study was being carried out. Despite Rokeach's claim to the general applicability of this instrument, on the basis of pretesting, we found it necessary to make two alterations. There were consistent criticisms that "justice" was not included in the list of terminal values. This seemed to be an important concern for many commune members, so it was added. On the original list the instrumental value, "ambitious" was parenthetically defined as "aspiring, hard-working." The pretest population objected to the confounding of what they saw as two very different values. The final list therefore included both "ambitious" (striving, aspiring) and "hard-working" (diligent, industrious). Thus caution should be exercised when comparisons are being made with noncommunal populations that were given the original instrument.

TABLE 5–3. Value Lists and Median Ranks[1]

Value	Rank	Median Rank	Standard Deviation	Range High	Low
	Instrumental Values				
Loving	1	2.6	3.6	1	16
Honest	2	3.3	3.7	1	18
Responsible	3	6.5	3.5	1	18
Helpful	4	7.5	4.1	1	18
Courageous	5	7.6	4.8	1	19
Forgiving	6	7.8	4.3	1	17
Capable	7	8.3	4.2	1	19
Broadminded	8	8.6	5.3	1	19
Cheerful	9	9.1	4.6	1	19
Imaginative	10	9.7	5.1	1	19
Independent	11	10.2	5.4	1	19
Hard-working	12	10.5	4.3	1	19
Self-controlled	13	11.0	5.5	1	19
Intellectual	14	12.7	5.1	1	19
Logical	15	13.9	4.1	1	19
Clean	16	14.1	3.8	2	19
Polite	17	15.8	3.6	3	19
Ambitious	18	16.2	4.6	1	19
Obedient	19	16.8	5.8	1	19
	Terminal Values				
Inner harmony	1	3.3	4.3	1	18
Wisdom	2	4.3	3.9	1	19
Mature love	3	5.4	4.0	1	19
True friendship	4	6.7	4.3	1	19
Self-respect	5	6.9	4.1	1	17
Happiness	6	7.2	4.5	1	19
Freedom	7	7.9	4.2	1	18
Equality	8	8.1	4.5	1	19
Peace	9	8.3	4.7	1	18
Exciting life	10	10.3	4.6	1	19
Accomplishment	11	10.6	4.7	1	19
Beauty	12	11.0	4.0	2	19
Family security	13	12.1	4.2	1	18
Justice	14	12.4	4.9	1	19
Comfortable life	15	14.6	4.0	2	19
Pleasure	16	15.3	4.3	2	19
Social recognition	17	15.6	3.7	1	19
Salvation	18	16.0	7.6	1	19
National security	19	17.8	3.5	2	19

[1] $N = 174$

correlation between independently determined group values and the individual value rankings of the group members. The value rankings of commune members reveal certain distinctive patterns. In direct contrast to a national sample of ordinary Americans,* commune members rank *inner harmony* and *mature love* quite high and *family security* and *national security* very low. Commune members also tend to assign high ranks to *honest* and *loving* and low ranks to cognitive values (e.g., *logical, intellectual*), but in these matters they are in agreement with the general American sample.

It is interesting to note that, as Table 5-4 shows, the overall value profile of communitarians is most like those of hippies, students, and certain academics and most unlike those of disenfranchised collectivities—blacks, the poor, and the elderly. This supports the hypothesis advanced in earlier chapters that the alienation of commune members from their society is fundamentally different from the chronic deprivation that Marx and the Marxians have associated with the isolated, exploited, and powerless; and that it perhaps is better understood in terms of the structurally induced overexposure to choice alternatives that Sartre has called *la nausée* and that we have identified as another form of alienation. In Chapter 6, this issue will be taken up again in an attempt to reunite these two concepts of alienation.

The argument has been put forth in previous chapters that communitarianism is a cultural response to cognitive and choice overload: it will occur when people find themselves overwhelmed by competing belief systems, value systems, and action alternatives. If this argument is correct, it should follow that the communal sample is heterogeneous in its values. This is what, with two exceptions, we do find. Whereas the median values of communitarians exhibit a distinctive profile, there is little evidence of value consensus. The mean of the standard deviations for value rankings is about one quarter of the entire range. Variance is high both among and within communes. Almost three quarters of all the values ranked (27/38) show up among the most highly valued in at least one commune in the sample, and almost all of them display the full range of rankings from top to bottom.

The commune sample is nearly unanimous in its high regard for only one value: *loving*. Half the respondents rank *loving* as their first or second most important instrumental value, and 90 percent place it in the top half of their lists. In light of the findings of Chapter 4, it is understandable that, although *mature love* as a terminal value is also ranked fairly high, overall communal unanimity is to be found only in the list that treats love as a transaction or a process rather than as an end state. Truly, it can be said that love is the common coin of the entire communitarian movement.

The other exception to the heterogeneity pattern is a negative one. More than half the commune members assign the value *national security* to one of the two

---

*National Opinion Research Center, 1971, reported by Rokeach (1974). Note that it is impossible to specify the extent to which the three-year gap between the two studies is responsible for the differences observed. However, more recent as yet unpublished surveys of American youth by Yankelovich et al. provide some evidence that young people in general, in the late 1970s have come somewhat closer in their value profiles to communitarians in the mid 1970s.

TABLE 5-4. Index of Value Similarity to Commune Members*

+ 8	Hippies[1]	Similar to Commune Members
+ 6	U.S. College Students[2] More than 16 years Formal Education[3] Professors of Art[4]	
+ 5	College Degree[5] Social Science Professors[9] Physical Science Professors[10] Business Professors[6] Jews[14]	
+ 4	20–29 Year Olds[11] 17 year olds[16] $15,000 Income or Above[8] Catholic Priests[7] Prison Inmates (males)[18] Service Station Dealers[17]	
+ 3	American Population (NORC 1971)[19] 30–39 Year Olds[13] Completed High School[12] American Catholics[14]	
+ 2	50–59 Year Olds[15] Police[20]	
+ 1	Black Americans[21]	Very Different from Commune Members
0	Poor (income less than $2000)[22]	
− 1	Old People (over 70 years old)[23]	

*A score of +12 indicates that the given population agreed completely with the commune population in the three highest ranking and three lowest ranking values in both the instrumental and terminal list. A score of 0 indicates no overlap in the lists. A score of −12 indicates that every value which the given population ranks among the top three is ranked by the commune members among the bottom three and vice versa.

[1] $N = 78$ Tested in 1968. Reported in Rokeach (1973) p. 141.
[2] $N = 298$ Tested in 1968. Reported in Rokeach (1973) pp. 145–146.
[3] $N = 61$ NORC 1968. Reported in Rokeach (1973) pp. 64–65.
[4] $N = 22$ Tested in 1969. Reported in Rokeach (1973) pp. 145–146.
[5] $N = 90$ NORC 1968. Reported in Rokeach (1973) pp. 64–65.
[6] $N = 38$ Tested in 1969. Reported in Rokeach (1973) pp. 145–146.
[7] $N = 80$ Tested in 1966. Hague (1968).
[8] $N = 95$ NORC 1968. Reported in Rokeach (1973) pp. 60–61.
[9] $N = 50$ Tested in 1969. Reported in Rokeach (1973) pp. 145–146.
[10] $N = 51$ Tested in 1969. Reported in Rokeach (1973) pp. 145–146.
[11] $N = 267$ NORC 1968. Reported in Rokeach (1973) pp. 76–77.
[12] $N = 426$ NORC 1968. Reported in Rokeach (1973) pp. 64–65.
[13] $N = 298$ NORC 1968. Reported in Rokeach (1973) pp. 76–77.
[14] $N = 28$ Tested in 1968. Rokeach (1969).
[15] $N = 236$ NORC 1968. Reported in Rokeach (1973) pp. 76–77.
[16] $N = 193$ Tested in 1969. Beech and Schoeppe (1970).
[17] $N = 235$ n.d. Reported in Rokeach (1973) pp. 157–158.
[18] $N = 363$ Tested in 1971. Cochrane (1971).
[19] $N = 1205$ NORC 1971. Reported in Rokeach (1974) p. 230.
[20] $N = 153$ Tested in 1969. Rokeach, Miller and Snyder (1971).
[21] $N = 213$ NORC 1971. Reported in Rokeach (1974) p. 230.
[22] $N = 139$ NORC 1968. Reported in Rokeach (1973) pp. 60–61.
[23] $N = 169$ NORC 1968. Reported in Rokeach (1973) pp. 76–77.

lowest rankings, and over 90 percent of them place it in the bottom half of their lists. This negative consensus, while extreme when compared with the opinions of the general American population, is not very different from that to be found in other youth subcultures in the mid-1970s. Therefore it is impossible to determine how much of this negativity toward national security is a specific historical reaction to the Vietnam defeat and how much represents an intrinsic communitarian withdrawal from larger social responsibilities. In either case, it can fairly be taken as an indicator of pervasive alienation from the state, if not from the society, among commune members.

We must conclude that, as measured along the value dimension, there is little in the way of a general communitarian ideology. However, certain value characteristics do stand out as important. Again, we see evidence, from a new source, of the central importance of love in communal organizations. We also see evidence of a shared alienation, but one quite different from that of society's underclasses. Even the very lack of value consensus, both within and among communes, may be evidence of the kind of alienation that shapes communal ideologies. In only three communes did all the members agree on their highest-ranked value (inner harmony, salvation, and loving, respectively), and all these were religious households under tight charismatic leadership.

It is remarkable that the members of any given ideological commune should agree neither in their primary value orientations nor in their preference orderings among sets of values. But, if the evidence of earlier chapters is a guide, it is precisely this lack of common ideological mooring that makes the communitarian mode of organization attractive to people who have the will to be ideological out of season.

The Definition of Goals

Let us turn now from the discussion of the way communes construct meaning to a discussion of the way they define goals. Communitarians are different from most Americans in that they are actively pursuing shared utopian goals. In response to some dissatisfaction in their precommunal lives, they have joined with like-minded others to create alternatives. However, as will become evident in Chapter 6, it is one thing to seek shared goals and quite another thing to find them. To examine the goals of communes and their members, a variety of open- and closed-ended questions were asked, most of them devised specifically for this study. Individuals were asked about personal as well as communal goals. In about a quarter of the cases, published charters, manifestos, position papers, or advertisements were available and also examined.

With respect to the specific goals of communitarians, the only consistent pattern was maximal heterogeneity. Table 5-5 shows responses to questions expressing various social and personal goals. The table also includes "nonchoice" responses.

With respect to political change, about one-third favored working gradually

TABLE 5-5. Goals of Communes and Communitarians: Degree of Consensus

	Proportion of Individuals Who			Proportion of Communes Exhibiting More Agreement than Disagreement[1]
	Agree	Disagree	Can't or Won't Decide	
A solution to many of our society's current problems is to build communitarianism into a widespread social and political movement.	38%	33%	31%	49%
I would like to help bring about a world in which most people live in communes or intentional communities	39	29	32	54
I am convinced that working slowly for reform within the system is preferable to working for a revolution.	35	32	33	49
This country would be better off if religion had a greater influence in daily life.	48	32	20	56
I would rather be married than single.	32	34	34	39
There are so many interesting things to do in the world, I can't see how people narrow themselves to a single lifelong occupation.	47	32	21	53
I am sure that I would rather have children than not have children.	57	18	25	79
I have very definite, established goals in life that I intend to pursue at all costs.	59	32	9	56
For myself, communal living is not an end in itself but a means of achieving certain goals.	73	12	15	88

[1]$N = 57$

199

for reform, one-third favored revolution, and one-third couldn't or wouldn't decide. At the aggregate level, half the communes registered a net tilt toward working for political reform, whereas the other half favored the revolutionary response. This pattern is repeated with respect to communitarianism as a social movement, religious revival, and other social goals.

Even with respect to personal goals, the trichotomous pattern (substantial numbers favoring, opposing, and undecided) is found. For example, one-third of the sample expressed a preference for being married, one-third prefered being single, and one-third couldn't or wouldn't decide. The greatest consensus in personal goals is associated with the desire to have children. But even here only 57 percent of the respondents and 79 percent of the communes prefered children to no children.

This pattern persisted when commune members were asked to describe their commune's goals in their own words. Specific goals of communal groups vary widely. It was possible to delineate twenty-seven types of goal constellations, discussed later in this chapter.

Communal goals or members' descriptions were also coded into expressions of various themes (such as friendship and consensual community). Even here, no category of communal goal was mentioned by more than a bare majority of the respondents (see Table 5-6). Although intracommunal consensus was quite a bit higher on goals than on values, there was only one commune in which 100 percent of the members completely agreed about group goals.

Consensus itself is the most prominent goal among communitarians. During historical periods (such as the present) characterized by ideological proliferation and the multiplication of meaning systems, to find a group of people with whom one can agree about fundamental values and goals can, as we have seen earlier, become an end in itself. Because most of the communes under investigation were not more than two or three years old at the time these baseline data were gathered, the fact that few of them had achieved any significant degree of measurable consensus should not be taken as evidence of hypocrisy in their claims to be seeking it.

However, consensual community is only one modality of a more general set of goal orientations that can fairly lay claim to being a component of the general communitarian ideology. As footnote 2 of Table 5-6 indicates, relational goals were mentioned by fully 76 percent of the respondents. Consensual community, friendship, interpersonal relationships, and family can be seen as four aspects of a new form of social organization that communitarians are struggling to articulate and to create. Cutting across all their differences, there is a widespread common concern for the creation of a form of social organization, a vaguely defined "community," that may be located on a scale of intimacy somewhere between the neighborhood and the nuclear family.*

---

*But it is not the case that intensity of intimacy is midway. Rather, the dimensions diverge, partaking of the closeness of the family but the commitment of the neighborhood.

**TABLE 5-6.   Any Mention of Various Type Communal Goals
Among Urban Commune Members[1,2]**

1.	Consensual community (live with likeminded others, puts shared beliefs into practice)	55%[a]
2.	Extracommunal (change society, provide a service, be a model for the rest of the world)	38
3.	Friendship (live with prior friends, find group of people who care about each other, avoid loneliness)	31
4.	Utilitarian (live economically, easy sex, make housekeeping easier, further commune-related business venture)	25
5.	Interpersonal relations (learn to cooperate and share, develop ability to communicate, attain personal growth through interaction	25
6.	Family (create a new family form, achieve family-like feelings among members, share parenting)	12
7.	Other	4
8.	None	5

[1] $N = 239$.

[2] 76% of the respondents mentioned one or more forms of relational goals (1) or (3) or (5) or (6).

[a] Note that percentages add to more than 100% because multiple responses are possible.

In Chapter 4 it was demonstrated that relationship patterns rather than personal attributes or dispositions explain communal stability and account for its variation. Now we see evidence that interpersonal relationships are critical not only for the objective but also for the subjective understanding of communes. Although individual communes vary from the most selfishly hedonistic to the most selflessly ascetic, they share in common the fact that the commune itself is never seen wholly as a means to these selfish or selfless goals but becomes, in full or in part, the end in itself.

It would seem that our analysis thus far has brought us to the not so startling conclusion that communitarians are homogeneous and distinctive primarily in pursuing the goal of creating communal households. But forming a communal household has to do not only with common location but also with a particular type of relationship among members. As John Bennett (1975, p. 20) puts it, "The commune tries to redress the bonds between the family and the institutions, to bring love back into the relations of humans by bringing back *gemeinschaft* functions and roles."

Bennett, however, as well as other researchers (Kanter, 1972; Berger, 1974), sees contemporary communes as not simply striving for *gemeinschaft* but quite specifically striving for familial relations, motivated by discontent with traditional family forms. It is argued that communes are alike in their pursuit of some kind of extended or alternative family.

A cursory look at the evidence presented in Table 5-6 would lead us to reject this hypothesis out of hand. Only 10 percent of the respondents specifically mentioned family goals. Yet the fact that a communal group's principal ideological goals are other than family oriented does not negate the possibility that desire for familial-type relationships are secondary or perhaps latent goals. In response to open-ended questions about their individual goals and reasons for joining their communes, members mentioned family themes more often (18 percent) than in the statements of group goals. Furthermore, at least half the membership in 62 percent of the communes agreed that members should strive to create a family feeling among all members; and fifty-nine percent of our sample agreed with the statement, "I feel that the people in the commune are my true family." Although responses varied by type of commune, in all communes at least 30 percent agreed.

It is difficult to thread through the issue of alternative family building. In the first place, there are communes that are expressly family oriented and that perceive alternative family building as an end in itself. More often, communes are spawned by larger religious, social, or political movements.

In the decade 1965–1975 we witnessed the inception of many such movements, having in common major dissatisfactions with contemporary society. But their programs stressed the importance of what type of person to be and how to relate to others, as well as how to change society. The nature of these movements leads to a focus on family life—the "right" family form is seen as important in achieving larger goals—yet family issues may not be salient to respondents; questions about goals tend to be answered in terms of principal or ultimate ideological goals.

Another complicating factor in our analysis is that comparable data about goals are not available for the rural groups, in which there is reason to believe that alternative family building is of greater importance than it is among the urban communitarians.

Some researchers have inferred a goal of seeking alternative family from the fact that communitarians have obviously chosen an alternative to the nuclear family life-style. The communitarians do show much uncertainty about the family as an institution. Also, commune members are far less likely to be married than other Americans. However, this difference is reduced or reversed when we compare communitarians with a sample matched for age and educational background.* Given the current data, it is impossible to discern whether an individual's participation in communal groups is motivated more by rejection of the nuclear family household or more by rejection of the life-style choice of living alone or with a roommate.

In summation, no final answer is possible to the question of whether commune members are alike in seeking a new form of the family. We can say that

*In one Bay Area survey ages 16–30 (Wuthnow, 1976a, p. 159), 87 percent were single and never married, which compares with the urban commune population of 72 percent single and never married.

communes and commune members are united in their rejection of the nuclear family as usual, but not in their commitment to goals explicitly concerned with the creation of alternative family forms.

Regarding goals, then, we must conclude that there is little along this dimension in the way of a general communitarian ideology. However, communitarian goals do share at least one important characteristic: the desire for *gemeinschaft* as an end in itself. The intimacy of relations sought by commune members may or may not reflect a desire for a new family form.

The strategies and norms of organization by which communes attempt to implement their goals demonstrate even more heterogeneity than the goals themselves. Aidala (1979) has, through a content analysis of field notes, taped instruments, and open-ended responses to questions in interview schedules, identified 323 specific organizational norms. In no case was a specific norm found in even as many as one quarter of the communes. In many cases the exact opposite of one group's norms were found in another group. The sample includes communes that are highly egalitarian and others whose populations are completely stratified; anarchistic communes and authoritarian communes; communal groups striving for the eradication of traditional sex roles and households striving to intensify sex-role distinctions; celibate communes and groups exhorting promiscuity; communes dedicated to collective child rearing and communes from which children are barred; communes that pool all wealth and property and communes founded to facilitate individual accumulation of wealth; —and so on.

It is only at an abstract level of general normative themes that any general communitarian ideological unity emerges. Norms of some sort governing admission and expulsion, interpersonal relations, autonomy, inequality, and interpersonal vulnerability were found in every commune. Admission and expulsion norms were discussed in Chapter 3. Interpersonal relations norms were dealt with specifically in Chapter 4. The normative theme areas of autonomy, inequality, and interpersonal vulnerability will be discussed in Chapters 6, 7, and 8 respectively.

Summary

The characteristics of ideology that we have been discussing were formally measured only among the urban half of the commune sample and have been reported only for the first wave of the study. However, we can, without loss of generality, extend most of our findings to refer to the rural communes as well and to all the communes in subsequent years. Although individual communes changed, no net ideological trends were observed.

What, then, are these common denominator characteristics that we have defined as the general communitarian ideology? Love, *gemeinschaft,* and preference uncertainty are the three major headings under which such characteristics can be grouped. However, it should be noted that each of these involves a fundamental contradiction. Love, as we have seen, is the universally esteemed common coin of communal transactions. However, as was demonstrated in Chapter 4, love is also the primary correlate of decay in communal systems. The more love in circulation, presumably the more pleased most commune members would be. Yet we have seen in Chapter 4 that love is correlated with instability of the commune as an organization.

Gemeinschaft tends to be valued for its own sake and to be manifested along a continuum from family to community. Yet family and community are often each other's worst enemies—each jealously competing for the full allegiance of the individual.

Finally, preference uncertainty is the experiential problem that moves people to cast their utopian dreams in communitarian molds. Yet communitarian organization, with its consensual decision making, rituals of communion, and charismatic leadership patterns, tends to act to overcome preference uncertainty and thus undermine the commune's very reason for being.

It is safe to conclude, therefore, that the distinctly communitarian aspects of the ideologies of communes are not only rather minimal, but also fairly unstable. Whatever fullness and richness that communal ideologies possess lies in their specific, not in their general, traits. It is to a discussion of these specific traits that we now turn.

An Eightfold Classification of Communes

Let us attempt to group communes into a number of relatively homogeneous types. The two dimensions that we find most fruitful for distinguishing among communal ideologies are *strategic philosophy* and *locus of attention* (c.f.: Stinchcombe, 1968, pp. 237-248).

The strategic philosophies that dominated communitarian thinking in the 1960s and 1970s may be labelled the strategy of *consciousness* (or non-action) and the strategy of *direct action*. Advocates of the former sought change through the evolution of consciousness and generally saw social action as useless or counterproductive. Advocates of the latter held to the belief that the way to change things was through directly applied human effort. This distinction has often been remarked upon in discussing the differences between the hippie movement and the New Left of the 1960s, but this is only one of several relevant distinctions that can be made among ideological orientations on this basis.

Four loci of attention have dominated the concerns of communitarians: the spiritual world, the individual person, the commune itself, and the secular society. Each of these loci of attention is associated with a pair of communitarian types: one based on the strategy of consciousness and the other on the strategy of direct action. Table 5-7 indicates the eight major types of communitarian ideologies that result, along with the empirical labels that best describe the occupants of each category.

The purpose of introducing a classification scheme at this point is not to

TABLE 5-7. Eight Types of Commune Ideologies

Locus of Attention	Strategic Philosophy		
	Consciousness	Direct Action	
Spiritual World[1]	Eastern	Christian	Religious Communes
Individual Self	Psychological	Rehabilitational	
Primary Group Community	Cooperative	Alternative family	Secular Communes
Secular Society	Countercultural	Political	

[1] The spiritual world as seen by religious communes includes not only the unseen and holy but also the mundane society invested with sacred meaning.

impose a unique taxonomy upon the subject matter. Although other schemes might have been equally justified, the choice of a single classification scheme is necessary to avoid drowning in the wealth of ideological diversity evinced by the 120 communal groups in our sample. Which taxonomy is ultimately best is a question in which we have no interest.

Although religious systems as diverse as Judaism, Sufism, and Druidism inspired communes in America in the period 1965–1975, the great majority of spiritually focused communal experiments during this period derived their beliefs either from Eastern Hindu and Buddhist traditions or from the Western traditions of Christianity. Although each of these religious traditions has components of a consciousness orientation as well as components of an orientation toward action, it is nevertheless fair to say that the former predominates in the Eastern ideologies and the latter in the Christian.

The most significant differences among the eight ideological groups, both in membership composition and social structure, are to be found not between the consciousness-oriented and action-oriented communes but between the spiritual pair of types and the six secular types. Our research substantiates the long-standing claim that the religious/secular distinction is important in the analysis of communal groups.

Among the secular communes, those whose members are primarily concerned with self-actualization have what we have called *psychological* ideologies, emphasizing the importance of creating a communal environment in which consciousness can expand and personality thrive. They see psychological change as a spontaneously liberating process fostered by the relational environment and by collectively supported exercises and abstinences. *Rehabilitational* communes, on the other hand, are action oriented and see the purpose of the communal group mainly as providing the opportunity for doing repair work on an essentially damaged self. Whereas members of the psychological communes tend to value communes as places in which the individual can thrive, members of the rehabilitational communes see them as necessary crutches for weak egos. Often, but not always, the members of rehabilitational communes look forward to the possibility of reconstructing their egos to such degree that they can return to ordinary society.*

We can also identify a pair of ideological perspectives focused on achieving change only (or predominantly) at the level of primary group community. In the *cooperative* category are communes whose major goal is the creation of a collective living situation that functions smoothly. Members believe that people are or can learn to be potentially cooperative enough to live together harmoniously with a minimum of planning and structure. In constrast, members of *alternative family* communes deliberately seek to create a new form of living group modeled after some real or mythical image of the extended family. Their ideologies call for complex and stable organizational structures as necessary to achieve these goals. Cooperative and alternative-family communes, because their ideological goals are essentially private, have attracted much less publicity than their spiritual, psychological, and society-focused counterparts. But communes of this level have always formed a substantial part of the American communitarian population, and, in recent years, as communes seeking to change society have dwindled, the numbers of community-focused communes have continued to increase.

The secular pair of ideological orientations focused upon the accomplishment of change at the societal level we have designated *countercultural* and *political.* The popular distinction between hippies and the New Left will serve as an approximation of the distinctions between these two types. However, these terms cover only parts of the phenomena in question. Not all counterculturalists were hippies (as the term has come to be used), nor were all political communitarians members of the New Left coalition.

The sample of 120 communes studied in this book is composed of representatives of these eight ideological types roughly in proportion to their representation within the universe of American communes during this period (see discussion of sampling in Appendix A). Table 5-8 indicates the numbers and proportions of sampled communes in each of the ideological categories.† As can

---

*For this reason, and also for methodological reasons discussed in Appendix A, the rehabilitational groups are marginal to our definition of commune. They are therefore sometimes excluded from the analyses in this book.

†Typologies are neat but reality is messy. A decision was made to assign every commune in the sample to one and only one ideological category. Although such a classification rule

be seen, religious communes account for almost a third of the entire sample. This is roughly accurate, but only because we have defined the unit of analysis in such a way that, within a religious organization with hundreds of communes scattered among every major American city, for example, each communal household has been counted as a single unit. If commune federations rather than communal households had been defined as the units of analysis, the proportion of religious groups would have been considerably lower.

Some Descriptions of Communal Ideologies

Each of the eight types found in our sample can be divided into three or four subvariants (see Table 5-9). The proliferation of ideological alternatives characteristic of communitarian epochs is clearly manifested within the contemporary communes. Neither would it be necessary to stop with eight types and twenty-seven subvariants; enough ideological variation remains within many of the subvariants to justify further subdivision.. Be that as it may, we shall treat each of the subvariants as a reasonably homogeneous specification.

In the following pages we will present three brief portraits of representative communal groups for each of the eight major ideological categories. Diversity within ideological categories is illustrated by selecting these vignettes from different subvariants. For example, the three descriptions of Eastern religious communes are drawn from the Buddhist, the Hindu, and the homegrown subvariants, respectively. Considered together, each set of three vignettes will provide a general ideological sketch of the uniformities and variations within each of the eight ideological classifications.

Eastern Religious Communes

Although Americans have been interested in the religions of Asia for over 150 years, the decade 1965–1975 witnessed a "turning East" (Cox, 1977) of unprecedented magnitude. China, India, Tibet, Japan, Indonesia, Iran and Iraq are only some of the countries that exported religion to America. Communes with Eastern religious ideologies can be distinguished from one another according to the religious tradition upon which they draw for their inspiration. Although the roots of these ideologies can be traced to ancient traditions, these traditions have been modified, sometimes in major ways, by innovative charismatic gurus. The subtypes are Buddhist, Hindu, Sikh, and homegrown. This last is a residual category denoting communes that have built their own unique religions out of modules borrowed from various Eastern religions, astrology, native American religions, and other sources.

---

is convenient for the taxonomist, it inevitably increases error in the assignment of the marginal cases. Ten of the communes in the sample fell closely between two of the ideological categories. At least thirty others, while clearly belonging to one of the categories, exhibited elements of another of the categories.

TABLE 5-8. Frequency Distribution of Communal Ideological Orientations

	Rural		Urban		Total	
	Number	% of Total	Number	% of Total	Number	% of Total
Religious						
1. Eastern (India, Japan, Tibet)	7	12%	15	25%	22	18%
2. Christian	7	12%	8	13%	15	13%
	14	24%	23	38%	37	31%
Secular						
3. Psychological (personal growth, therapy, self-actualization)	4	6	5	9	9	8
4. Rehabilitational	1	2	3	5	4	3
5. Cooperative	8	13	8	13	16	13
6. Alternative family	6	10	5	9	11	9
7. Countercultural	21	35	8	13	29	24
8. Political	6	10	8	13	14	12
	46	76%	37	62%	83	69%
Total	60	100%	60	100%	120	100%

TABLE 5-9. Ideological Categories and Their Subvariants

Categories	Consciousness Oriented	Action Oriented
A. Religious (37)		

1. Spiritual locus (37)	Eastern religions (22)
	  Hindu (14)
	  Sikh (2)
	  Buddhist (3)
	  Homegrown (3)
		Christian (15)
		  Sectarian withdrawal (3)
		  Charismatic renewal (6)
		  Evangelical youth (3)
		  Social gospel (3)

B. Secular (83)		

2. Individual locus (13)	Psychological (9)
	  Mystical (3)
	  Gestalt (3)
	  Psychosexual (3)
		Rehabilitational (4)

3. Community locus (27)	Cooperative (16)
	  Cooperative enterprises (5)
	  Cooperative households (5)
	  Devolved utopias (4)
	  Crashpads (2)
		Alternative family (11)
		  Patriarchal (2)
		  Matriarchal (2)
		  Fraternal (6)
		  Group marriage (1)

4. Society locus (43)	Countercultural (29)
	  Cultural demonstration projects (7)
	  Hippie farms or houses (10)
	  Tribal settlements (5)
	  Utopian reservations (7)
		Political (14)
		  Socialist (4)
		  Anarchist (7)
		  Social-democrat (3)

Mandala (Buddhist) Founded 1967; adult pop. = 25 (14 men, 11 women, 5 children); adult age range = 15–53 years.

Mandala is an isolated mountain-top commune devoted to a religious practice that is a mixture of Mahayana Buddhist and other Eastern spiritual traditions. At the time of the study* almost all the members were repentant users of psychedelic drugs. The commune was organized on the basis of a shared sense that the use of drugs was a false path toward spiritual development. All the members had agreed to forsake drugs in pursuit of higher consciousness and, in particular, to fulfill the demands of the Bodisatva vow: "The ways of the dharma are numberless; I vow to experience them all. Sentient beings are numberless; I vow to save them all." The Mandalan Bodisatvas were thus dedicated simultaneously to the pursuit of personal transcendence and to working in the world to help those less advanced in consciousness than themselves.

At Mandala, as in all Eastern spiritual communes, the major ideological problem was the residual autonomy of individual members: each individual ego was to become conscious of its illusory nature and thus was to be subsumed into the collective ego. At a meeting every morning, everyone accounted for how all of his or her time was to be spent. Each person was responsible for fulfilling the contract specified by this morning report and, furthermore, was subject to criticism and pressure from the group if what he or she was intending to do with the day did not seem to meet communal needs.

The Mandalans attempted to govern themselves by consensus, all individuals being bound by decisions made by the group. In addition, individuals were bound by several communal rules built into the charter of the community that could not be changed: absolute prohibition of coffee, alcohol, and drugs; vegetarian limitations on diet; and severe limitations on the access of the commune to visitors.

In its attempt to discover the right path toward spiritual enlightenment, Mandala had placed itself loosely under the care of an absentee guru who served not as an authority but as a source of advice and guidance. Real day-to-day authority over the life of the commune rested in the hands of a young, energetic charismatic leader who was one of the commune's founders. Directly under him in authority were his wife and several other commune founders.

Under them were those members who had made a long-term commitment to the life. The lowest tier in the hierarchy was for new members or those still tentative in their commitment. This was justified by the belief that, although all people are progressing along the same spiritual path, no two people have come exactly the same distance. In particular spheres of life, this hierarchy might vary according to degree of concern and expertise, but always some stratification was accepted.

Sex-role differentiation was encouraged by the religious ideology. Women

*Unless otherwise stated, all statements in these vignettes refer to the communes as they were during the first month of contact, during the first wave of field work.

were not considered inferior to men but were considered to have different natures. The sexes were encouraged to be in tune with their true natures and thus focus only on appropriate concerns. This led to a *de facto* exclusion of women from certain technical executive decisions regarding the communal economy, but women did participate fully in long-range policy decisions. The community was vaguely opposed to sexuality and considered celibacy a preferable, although not a required, mode of sexual relationship.

It was agreed that a spiritually inspired philosophy of child rearing should be an important part of the communal ideology, so as to spare future generations the struggle common to adult members of the present generation to overcome wrong patterns of socialization. However, no consensus on communal child-rearing policy had in fact developed, and children remained subject to the unconstrained authority of their parents in all matters.

Love from Above/Youth & Truth (Hindu) Founded 1971; pop. = 13 (10 men, 3 women, no children); age range = 21–28 years.

Love from Above represented the largest subgroup within the Eastern religious classification, which was composed of communes whose ideology is Hindu in inspiration. The Love from Above movement was a national federation of urban religious communes dedicated to the practice of a neovedantic philosophy as expounded by a highly charismatic guru. Within this movement there were two types of communal households, to accommodate differences in degree of commitment to the spiritual practice. Love from Above communes were for those who had made a full, lifetime commitment to the commune and had accepted a lifetime of discipleship to the guru. Youth & Truth communes were for followers of the guru who were not yet ready to make such total commitments.

The Love from Above philosophy specified that, through initiation, meditation, and submission to the guru, one could transcend the cycle of death and rebirth and reach nirvana through reunion with the Creator in an experience of eternal bliss. However, the guru emphasized that the direct, immediate experience of bliss was not dependent on an understanding of the theology. Most members ignored the theology in practice. Unlike many religions that teach that a blissful experience of oneness with the universe will occur only after years of patient devotion and practice, Love from Above offered such experiences during the first initiation sessions and thereafter with relative ease as long as the worldly ego did not get in the way.

Formally receiving bliss, a ceremony that took place in the initiation session, was a transforming experience. Bliss became central to the devotee's existence from that point. It was claimed that the experience itself was addictive and reattainable through specific meditational practices that were pursued with zeal. Bliss is energy. Love from Above households buzzed with smiling, hyperactive members who boasted that they now needed much less sleep and rest than before.

"Everything bliss touches becomes perfect." This is meant quite literally: finances improve, gardens flourish, personal disabilities disappear, rocky marriages mend. In a more abstract sense, the perfecting quality of bliss works through a changing awareness of cause and effect. For a person with bliss, both large and small events in the world are seen in a different light, seen as arranged for one's benefit, as signs of various sorts. For example, a financial venture that ended in disaster was seen as a sign of God's benign intervention because managing a business would have taken time away from meditation.

Discipline was emphasized in Love from Above. Beyond renunciation of worldly pleasures and private property, bliss required nurturance through constant meditation. Members followed a set schedule of daily activities that was organized around periods of collective and individual meditation, as well as daily attendance at catechism. In these latter sessions, members shared tales of how bliss had transformed their lives and reported instances in which lapses in the disciplined life of meditation had led to "clouding" of bliss and other ill consequences for the devotee.

Unlike Buddhist communes, those in the Hindu category emphasized the absolute necessity of a direct, personal relationship between disciple and guru. Love from Above members believed that bliss was not simply revealed by the guru but was absolutely dependent upon a continuing relation with him. This was the basis of the lifetime vow of submission to him. Members of a Love from Above commune submitted totally to the guru in mundane as well as spiritual matters. An elaborate national hierarchy descending from him monitored the daily lives of all members. Each household in the federation was in direct daily contact with national headquarters via a Telex system. The household leader, acting as the guru's representative, had absolute authority over the commune. Members did not participate in decisions affecting the communal group such as admission or finances. The local leader had control over individual members' personal lives as well. Prospective members were assured that the decision to move into a Love from Above commune would be the last real decision they would ever have to make in their lives.

Despite the hierarchical organization, equality was a key theme in Love from Above ideology. Members believed that there were no distinctions among humans—not even between believers and nonbelievers. There was no notion of a spiritual hierarchy wherein some seekers had progressed to higher levels than others. There was only the distinction between the guru and all others. Some followers believed the guru to be a reincarnation of Christ or God.

Philosophy (homegrown) Founded 1967; adult pop. = 26 (10 men, 16 women, 11 children); adult age range = 15-51 years.

Philosophy was a rural commune founded at the height of the hippie movement in northern California by one individual who attempted to develop a communal following for a very elaborate ideological perspective formulated by him from esoteric sources. This ideology stressed a rather difficult astrological and mystical discipline seen as necessary to understand the complex spiritual forces that were determining the historical and cultural developments of the time.

In its prophetic myth, the commune foresaw the imminent advent of an Aquarian age in which all economic, political, and social institutions would be transformed. But this cosmic revolution would be governed by the laws of karma and could not, therefore, be guided or pushed. In fact, a kind of karmic backlash was the inevitable result of any attempt to tamper with the laws of change. The commune, therefore, was anarchistic, believing that nothing good could come from the use of force or authority but that the time was ripe for a revolution of consciousness so that people could find within themselves the maturity and responsibility necessary for ushering in a revolutionary society.

Despite its adherence to anarchism, Philosophy evolved into a complex hierarchical commune. In fact, authority was divided between two competing and nonoverlapping hierarchies—the spiritual and the secular. Position in the spiritual hierarchy was dependent upon knowledge and revealed understanding. These concerns tended to draw the individual into the role of teacher and away from the world of common work. Position in the secular hierarchy was dependent largely on length of membership and concern with the mundane (i.e., farming, building, cooking, cleaning, and maintenance). The leaders in the spiritual hierarchy believed that the secular sphere would function automatically if only proper attention were given to the laws of spiritual harmony. Ignored by the spiritual hierarchy, the leaders of the secular hierarchy became increasingly estranged from it, as survival became an overriding goal in itself. With the legitimacy of their positions continually challenged both by brahmanism from above and anarchism from below, the attainment of such survival became ever more elusive.

The community equated character structure with karma and saw disciplined expansion of consciousness as the only escape from socialized patterns of human relationships. The community was permissive in its attitudes toward sexual and parental relationships. The ideology completely failed to reconcile the call for discipline necessary for ascending the spiritual hierarchy with the call for freedom necessary for avoiding karmic backlash. For example, parents were expected to guide their children toward spiritual enlightenment. But, at the same time, parents were not to interfere with the working out of children's karma by disciplining them in any way. Mothers, especially, found these contradictory demands of the ideology completely frustrating.

Philosophy community had a short-lived and chaotic existence. As in a number of other anarchistic communes, the leader wound up being exploited by commune members who were not selected very carefully and who had only a very superficial interest in the community's ideals and ideology.

Christian Communes

The Christian communes do not divide neatly into subcategories based upon ancient religious distinctions, as do the Eastern groups. Instead, it has been found convenient to subdivide them according to the goals toward which they are oriented. Those classified as *evangelical* communes are perhaps the most familiar. These are simply households composed of people who support one another in their joint efforts to achieve their own and others' salvation.

Examples will be given of each of the other three subtypes: *charismatic movement* communes, *sectarian withdrawal* communes, and *social gospel* communes. The first of these is composed of groups concerned with revivalist movement building, primarily through the collection, acquisition, and use of pentecostal gifts or powers (known as *charisms*). The second is concerned with maintaining piety, purity or fundamentalism in belief. The last is concerned with furthering Christian justice or righteousness through social action.

Curiously, no examples were found of Christian communes oriented toward impending millenia. Religious community as a way of life suited for the final days before the end of the world, a view prevalent among Christian communes from the sixteenth to the nineteenth centuries, is eclipsed in our own generally apocalyptical time. Even the evangelical groups appear to be more concerned with the revival aspect of their work than with evangelism as a prophetic prerequisite for the Second Coming. It is interesting to speculate that perhaps future-oriented religious seekers have been differentially recruited to the Eastern religions, whereas seekers oriented to the past have gravitated to Christian groups. Unfortunately, the data of this study do not permit testing of this hypothesis.

Alabama Avenue (charismatic movement) Founded 1973; pop. = 6 (2 men, 4 women, no children); age range = 22–36 years.

The Christian charismatic movement surfaced in America in the 1960s and is still growing. By the fall of 1976, an estimated three million Americans had participated to some degree in this movement, only a small fraction of whom, however, participated to the extent of living communally (Briggs, 1977). The movement has affected both the Catholic and the Protestant churches with its insistence on the importance of direct personal experience of Christ and with the argument that "the main goal of pastoral efforts in the Church today [is] to build communities which make it possible for a person to live a Christian life" (Clark, 1972, p. 11).

Charismatic Christianity has been a perennial blossom of American religious culture since the seventeenth century. The latest version of the movement has begot hundreds of rural and urban communes in every part of the country. Alabama Avenue was typical of these. A small group of born-again Christians, following the lead of a charismatic pastor, attempting to keep one foot inside the church while revitalizing it from without, moved into the slums of Atlanta and asked the Lord to tell them what to do next.

An attitude of waiting upon the Holy Spirit permeated every aspect of Alabama Avenue's ideology. Members could not describe their group's goals beyond the intention to do whatever God wanted to glorify Him, "but we don't know what it will be yet." The commune collectively sought the Lord's counsel for even such minor decisions as a member's purchase of a new coat.

The autonomy of individual personality was not valued at Alabama Avenue. On the contrary, it was seen as an obstacle to the personal emptiness needed for the emergence of Christ's personality within oneself. It was felt that this emptiness could be cultivated through the sharing of emotional lives as well as material goods. This led to an initial focus on developing deep relationships among members of the commune. At times these relationships became so intense that the personalities of some seemed to melt into those of others. This was particularly striking in the case of the charismatic leader (male) and his chief lieutenant (female). The two were seldom observed together without the female follower's positioning herself in such a way that she could observe his every expression. She mirrored his expressions and gestures, seemingly oblivious to her mimicry.

Spiritual egalitarianism was recognized in potential ("Christ may choose to speak through the least of us"). In practice, a hierarchy of authority developed about the criterion of closeness to God. In Alabama Avenue, as in many charismatic groups, a single leader was recognized as possessing this quality to a supernal degree. Individualism was condemned as contrary to the goal of surrender to Christ's will. Authority was legitimate to the extent that the authority holder had surrendered his or her own ego to Christ more totally than had the followers. Thus legitimated, however, the authority of the leader was vast. Submission to local authority was seen as good training for submission to Christ. All decisions about the communal household were made by the leader. His authority reached deep into the personal lives of all members as well, including decisions on such matters as employment, use of free time, relations with parents, whether to marry, and so on.

Spiritual rebirth was seen as a prerequisite for complete submission to the will of the Lord. At Alabama Avenue, spiritual rebirth was perceived not as a sudden ecstatic experience but as a gradual and painful process. Sexuality, while not regarded as evil per se, was seen as a possible obstacle to rebirth. The ability to sustain a relationship with a member of the opposite sex in a true Christian spirit was perceived as a fundamental indicator of transcending character structure (i.e., Original Sin). For some, this seemed to require a vow of lifelong celibacy; for others, a vow of premarital chastity followed by Christian marriage.

Although the ideology of Christian charismatic communes mitigates against sexual expression, these groups often seem, to the observer, to be highly charged with diffuse collective sexuality. Alabama Avenue, with its young male leader and its predominantly female followers, radiated an ambience of sublimated sexual interaction. Eventually, the commune almost disintegrated in an out-burst of sexual scandal involving jealousies and recriminations that have per-sisted down to the time of this writing.

Christian Ranch (withdrawal sect) Founded 1951; adult pop. = 72 (31 men, 41 women, 48 children); adult age range = 15–68 years.

Christian Ranch was an old-fashioned fundamentalist Christian community very much like a Hutterian bruderhof in some of its external trappings. It was founded in 1951 by a charismatic leader who led a group of serious Christian seekers away from the established churches toward the development of an isolated rural sectarian community. The community practiced farming and operated a variety of roadside businesses. Its members lived austerely and kept nonbusiness contacts with the outside world to a minimum.

The primary goal of this commune was to overcome pride and to submit fully to the will of the in-dwelling Holy Spirit. More dour than the Anabaptist sects of similar intent, the Christian Ranchers did not regard the outward mani-festation of joy as a sign of submission. The average member appeared meek, fearful, guilty, and preoccupied with the struggle against sin. The women seemed like Simone Weil dolls. Sex-role relationships and age-role relationships were treated as valuable opportunities for exercising the capacity for obedience. Everyone in the commune, including the highest executive officers, was under continual scrutiny for the slightest signs of pride.

A spiritual executive committee strictly governed the community on the basis of its interpretation of biblical and church law. At Christian Ranch great emphasis was placed upon developing a willingness to accept authority unques-tioningly. Authority was legitimated largely on the basis of seniority and piety. Unlike the Alabama Avenue commune, Christian Ranch did not require of its leader personal evidence of charismatic gifts.

This orientation toward authority must be understood in terms of the com-mune's history. The original leader used his charismatic powers to draw his followers safely away from the temptations of the world. However, this leader also distrusted charisma as a reliable basis for authority. He therefore deliber-ately groomed no successor and, furthermore, took steps to hasten the process of charismatic routinization by gradually delegating more and more of his own authority to committees of relatively uninspired elders.

The supreme value of obedience was also reflected in the commune's child-rearing philosophy. Children were raised strictly with the intention of "breaking the spirit" and inculcating the proper Christian submissiveness and willingness to subordinate individual ego to the collectivity. All members were expected to marry young and have large families. The commune's own children were looked upon as the major pool of potential recruits.

Work roles were gender segregated, both in the small business enterprises that provided economic support for the group and in the internal organization of the commune itself. Women were allowed to attend decision-making meetings but were not expected to take central roles, and women had only a minor involvement in the group's missionary activities.

Karp House (social gospel) Founded 1974; adult pop. = 5 (2 men, 3 women, 2 children); adult age range = 22–32 years.

Karp House was a small Christian urban commune oriented toward the regeneration of Christian family life and community service. The nucleus of the commune was a single Christian nuclear family. The other members were all single adults who shared the same Christian philosophy. Almost all members had a history of involvement with activist Christian organizations since their high school or college days. Several had jobs in church-funded social-service agencies. They deliberately located their communal house in a predominantly black, lower-class neighborhood to better enable them to put into practice their liberal integrationist values.

The ideology of the community was deliberately vague. It provided room for each individual to work out his or her own set of specific goals. Members worked together toward the central goal of providing a positive living situation in which they could work out their lives as Christians. Members held in common a belief in Christ and Christianity, along with a desire to help others and to have open, loving, and deep personal relationships with one another. They did not, however, believe that it was necessary to undergo the specific spiritual experience of being born again to live an exemplary Christian life.

Family life was an important value to the members of Karp House. The commune members all shared an interest in child-rearing and a belief that early childhood experiences are crucial in determining the later spiritual life of the adult, and a sense that proper Christian child rearing is very difficult or impossible in the isolated nuclear family. Single people provided help in raising the children of the central nuclear family and in turn received the benefits of inclusion in a close Christian family structure. There was a strong emphasis on age relationships. The relationship of elder to younger was seen as a fundamental basis of true Christian family relationships and one difficult to achieve outside of intentional community.

Authority was emphasized in the ideology of Karp House. The lessening of authority and clear leadership in various spheres of life was thought to be at the root of many contemporary social ills. To members of Karp House it was wrong to think that there could be meaningful collective life without clear lines of authority. Their model was, of course, the patriarchal family, and they relied upon biblical sources for justification of the essential rightness of this form. Family life, with its traditional internal authority structure, was seen as necessary to integrate individuals into larger communities.

Yet this emphasis on authority coexisted with a concern for equality, based on the traditional Christian emphasis upon the equality of all persons in the eyes of God. This was the underpinning of the members' dedication to working for the elimination of social and political inequalities. It was also a source of difficulty. Members of Karp House attempted to juggle their commitment to both patriarchal authority and equality in the operation of the communal household. For example, the acceptance of patriarchal authority at home was at times difficult to integrate with dedication to women's liberation issues and activities on the part of several of the women in the group, including the leader's wife. The primacy placed upon the sanctity of the nuclear unit and the father's right to decide what is best for his family often came into conflict with other members' desires to have equal say in decisions affecting the commune as a whole.

These contradictions were difficult to resolve for persons sincerely dedicated to living out their values and scorning the hypocrisy they saw as permeating the lives of less intentional Christians. Value impasses resulted in an ideology that remained vague in most areas. Another consequence was that only less forceful and dynamic personalities tended to remain comfortable in the nonnuclear roles.

Psychological Communes

No communes of Freudians, Jungians, or Sullivanians were found in the sample although many such are known to exist in American cities. Neither were the behaviorist ideas of B. F. Skinner the theoretical force behind any of our 120 communal ideologies, although there are many rural Walden Two communities. The ideological progenitors of the communes in the category labeled psychological were instead such figures as G. I. Gurdjieff, Fritz Perls, and Wilhelm Reich.

The psychological communes are divided, somewhat arbitrarily, into three subtypes: the mystical (drawing on religious imagery to express psychological concepts); the gestalt (organized along the lines of encounter groups); and the psychosexual (devoted to exploring sexuality as the key to community).

Spectra (mystical) Founded 1970; adult pop. = 67 (34 men, 33 women, 12 children); adult age range = 22–35 years.

The Spectra households were urban communes, part of a larger Spectra movement with historic roots in California's personal growth movement. In 1974, there were Spectra households in most large American cities. The communal ideology revolved around a training program developed by a reclusive charismatic leader. The training program was a potpourri of several hundred exercises showing the influence of Fritz Perls, Suzuki Roshi, Gurdjieff and Ouspensky, Wilhelm Reich, Maharishi Mahash Yoga, Ida P. Rolfe, and many others. Despite its heavy mystical component, Spectra attempted to present itself not as a religion but as a scientific system. Its aims were to increase the vitality and mental clarity of members and to eliminate negative emotional states. The movement ideology claimed to require neither guru nor belief to produce results. In this it aligned itself with Gurdjieff's fourth way, with gnosticism, and with the Sufi tradition. Prospective members were told that Spectra could be looked at as a spiritual discipline, as a group psychological process, as a social utopia, or as all three at once.

The ideology specified that individual egos could and should be subsumed within the collective consciousness as a result of the Spectra method and communal experience. However, unlike Eastern religious groups in which ego transcendence is valued for the purposes of submission to the collective, in Spectra, individuals attempted to achieve "a more elastic energized body, a clearer mind, and more expressive emotions" as an end in itself. Ego loss is the term used to describe this more direct experience of living, especially when it led to heightened spiritual awareness as well.

The Gurdjieffian influence upon Spectran ideology was most dramatically shown in a strenuous pursuit of the outrageous. It takes both skill and practice to do rapid sequential imitations of Adolf Hitler, Groucho Marx, and Lucille Ball in a single sentence, while ostensibly pursuing a serious argument. But this was a skill that many Spectrans were good at (without the use of drugs) and were able to use with devastating effect in assaults upon the conceptualizing mind.

Spectrans relished the destruction of traditions, particularly when sex was involved. Nudity and sexual display were encouraged to enhance body awareness and destroy ego defenses. An individual, naked and stroking his or her genitals, might stroll nonchalantly through a busy common room to make a phone call or watch the news on television. Spectrans were expected, for similar reasons, to be open to multiple simultaneous sexual experiences. Enduring couple relationships were discouraged but not forbidden.

The Spectran norms of sexuality reflected a more general philosophy of hedonism in the service of egolessness. The pursuit of worldly pleasures of all kinds was justified by the contention that (often) the shortest path to transcendence is wallowing. However, wallowing was seen as spiritually beneficial only to the extent that it raised consciousness by destroying old moral response sets. New commune members coming from morally restrictive environments might be encouraged to wallow, whereas those from more permissive environments might instead be guided toward asceticism.

A desire for personal freedom led to a minimum of organizational structure within Spectran households and to norms of decision making through consensus. The households were, however, loosely organized into a federation. A central hierarchy was looked to for spiritual and practical guidance. The original charismatic leader still directed the movement, although mainly through his written teachings rather than through direct personal influence. He felt that all of humanity was ready to advance to higher levels of consciousness without any leaders as such and attempted to avoid an active guru role.

In the daily life of the commune, reciprocity was emphasized both in practical matters such as household chores and in pursuing psychic development. A member would be severely criticized for failing to be totally open to another's approaching him or her to work through problem or to be a partner in any of the joint exercises. Although equality and reciprocity were emphasized, there was a hierarchy within the Spectra movement that reflected different levels of training attained. It was observed that those attaining the higher levels were treated with special regard within the communal household especially concerning policy matters. Nonetheless, the commune considered itself a family of equals, and genuine affection and concern for all members was evident.

Mountainside (gestalt) Founded 1966; pop. = 10 (5 men, 5 women, no children); age range = 18–34 years.

Mountainside was a rural commune founded by a group of anarchists who were originally involved in politics and actively working for radical political change. They were converted to the personal growth movement and subsequently channelled their energy into group relations, attempting to found an anarchistic commune based upon Esselen Institute-type psychological principles. The members were not necessarily more anarchistic than were those of some of the other communes we have discussed, but they were more self-consciously anarchistic, more aware of Kropotkin, Tolstoy, Bakunin, Goodman, Bookchin, and other anarchist writers and philosophers. They attempted to a great extent to draw connections between each theoretical anarchistic writing and the anarchies of their own communal life.

At Mountainside, ego was equated with ego defenses, and the goal was thus to become free by transcending ego. People who had fully transcended their egos would become self-realized, no longer constrained by the patterns of culture or childhood socialization. Ultimate faith was placed in spontaneity. A spontaneous act was by definition a good and healthy act. An action that harmed another person could not, by definition, have been truly spontaneous. The Mountainsiders agreed with Wilhelm Reich that ego defenses reside not only in the psyche but in the musculature. Yoga and nude massage were thus important communal rituals. Primal screams and dramatic and violent psychological breakthroughs were highly welcomed events, however disruptive they might be to the workaday routine of the commune.

Sex roles were not pronounced at Mountainside commune, but neither was the elimination of all sex-role distinctions an important part of the ideology. In sexual behavior there was an ideal valuation of group marriage as the highest form of group sexual relationship, and, in fact, the group had a history of transitory experiments in group marriage.

The optimism and enthusiasm of Mountainside commune were contagious and quickly caught up most new members or visitors. Economic and interpersonal problems were tackled by the group in the full faith that every problem has an immediately applicable solution. Schisms and/or high membership turnover provided the safety valves for group tensions that could not be so easily dealt with. The basic tenor of the life-playful, intellectual, sincere—managed to survive these periodic upsets.

Utopia House (psychosexual) Founded 1972; pop. = 9 (6 men, 3 women, no children); age range = 22–38 years.

Utopia House was a hedonistic psychosexual community based upon the philosophy that, whatever you want, the goal of the commune is to help you get more of it. The hedonism of Utopia House was uncomplicated by any spiritual considerations. This Los Angeles commune offered a life based on the pursuit of fun and pleasure and the amassing of possessions.

The Utopian ideology was developed by a former used-car salesman and sexual experimenter who perfected a series of tickling and stroking techniques that led to a heightened sexual experience. He formed an "institute" for teaching these techniques and spreading his hedonistic philosophy, with the goal of launching a worldwide movement that would, in some undefined way, "stay 10% ahead of all other social movements." Most members of Utopia House were teachers for the institute, and the commune's economy was based in part upon fees from seminars in sensuality. Most members wanted their pursuit of pleasure unencumbered by regular employment.

The fundamental rule of Utopia House was "You do what you want to do and you can't do what you don't want to do." Their philosophy was one of antinomian perfectionism. The underlying belief was that everyone is perfect and the goal of life is to strive for ever higher levels of perfection. This implied not worrying about the past or future but living for the present and pursuing the one common goal: pleasure. Utopia House members sought gratification on every level possible, whether it be indulgence in food, drugs, alcohol, sex, or just a total generalized feeling of pleasure. Everyone who lived in Utopia House tacked a "want list" to his or her door. This was a public declaration of personal desires. Nothing was considered too outrageous to lust after. Individuals were expected to learn to know what would please them and to be uninhibited in pursuing it.

The commune's critical assumption was that people are socialized to be unable to accept total pleasure. It followed that the major service of the community to the individual was to provide psychotherapeutic group rituals and techniques enabling him or her to overcome the unwillingness or inability to accept a high degree of pleasure. One of these practices, which is familiar to students of nineteenth century communitarianism, involved a role called "taking the hot seat." From this position, all the attention, primarily negative, of the commune was focused on one member. The member talked about his or her dissatisfactions, and other members added more criticisms and tried to find the subconscious motivations that were keeping the hot-seater from realizing his or her goals. Utopia members believed that people themselves impose upon their lives whatever is wrong with them; all one's dissatisfactions are one's own fault. The external world as well as the individual was believed to be perfect—people need only to see the perfection around. With the proper attitude one can take pleasure from anything. In the words of a Utopia member, "Don't say 'Ick' when you see plastic flowers; say, 'What beautiful plastic flowers!'"

Throughout the Utopia House ideology there was a stress upon reciprocity, particularly in the giving and receiving of pleasure. Utopia House sex seminars centered around the idea that couples should give up the notion of simultaneous orgasm but instead should, each in turn, concentrate totally first upon giving pleasure and then upon receiving pleasure. This reciprocity principle was extended to all areas of the commune's day-to-day life. An actual working community is possible only to the extent that people come to experience pleasure in the pleasure of others. Therefore, for example, chores will get done by those who take pleasure in giving others the enjoyment of a clean living situation.

Rehabilitational Communes

As has been indicated, rehabilitational communes represent a marginal classification. The sample includes only four of them, three urban and one rural. They differ from the other communes in that they make a hierarchical distinction between staff and patient, although all attempt to obscure this distinction as much as possible. Rehabilitational communes involve only a limited time commitment. However, it should be recognized that, as in their famous prototype, Synanon, this temporary commitment may grow into a lifelong commitment for some of the members. Indeed, the membership turnover rate for rehabilitational communes is not significantly different from that of other communes.

Halfway Community Founded about 1950; adult pop. = 127 (70 men, 57 women, 16 children); adult age range = 20–67 years.

Halfway Community was a typical rehabilitational community. It served a varying population of several hundred people, most of whom stayed for less than a year. The philosophy of treatment was centered about self-help and mutual help and the beneficient effects of family and small rural community. As with most other rehabilitational communes, Halfway prided itself on being able to provide a home for people who did not fit in anywhere else—either in institutions or in private life.

The staff strove, with remarkable success, to minimize consciousness of professional status in the daily life of the community. Staff worked and played and had some of their meals with patients, but they also kept separate family lives to which patients did not have access except by invitation. The major conflicts in rehabilitational communes (as in communes in general) arise from conflicts between nuclear family and larger community for the time and attention of members.

Halfway Community based its program on a liberal ecumenical Christian ideology. The rural virtues—hard manual work, cooperation, slowness of pace, and simplicity and modesty of short and long-range goals—were reinforced by every aspect of the communal organization. The economy was keyed to agriculture and animal husbandry even when potentially more lucrative business opportunities presented themselves. Small residential cottages and many scattered barns and sheds dispersed the daily life of the community in ways that were ideologically (but not economically) efficient. The commune always had a long waiting list because of its refusal to expand lest it lose touch with the uncomplicated and unambitious tenor of its members' lives.

Cooperative Communes

Some communes are composed simply of people who enjoy living together and believe that a greater degree of cooperation among people is possible in intentional community life than is generally found in natural American communities. The cooperative communes in the current sample are generally practitioners of ideologies with the community itself as locus of attention. Some cooperative communes trail off into the category of collective living situations that we would not consider communes. The critical defining characteristic is that the members espouse some ideological goal (beyond mere convenience) for which collective living is deemed essential, no matter how minimal the ideological intensity.

Cooperative communes may be conveniently divided into four subtypes: cooperative households, cooperative enterprises, crashpad communes, and devolved utopias. Devolved utopias are communes in which the founding was based on some other clear ideological purpose but in which, for a variety of reasons, this larger purpose had faded into the background or evaporated entirely. Yet individual members still desired to maintain the communal living situation. This residual category is not discussed here, but examples are given of each of the other three subtypes.

Old Plantation (cooperative household) Founded 1974; pop. = 6 (4 men, 2 women); age range = 17–33 years.

This was a cooperative household in a large Southern city whose members were dedicated to gracious living. The communal goals as stated were to live an elegant, quiet life and to pursue one's individual goals to the best of one's ability. The pursuit of individual goals was seen to be facilitated by communal living in that it provided material benefits of greater economy and convenience as well as the emotional benefits of living in an atmosphere of affection and mutual concern.

Members were chosen on the basis of compatability and financial responsibility. All the residents had liberal political leanings, but there was no political component to the commune's ideology. Decision making was by majority vote although compromise was valued as a means of accommodating varied individual preferences.

Many of the residents were professionally involved in the social sciences. All shared the belief that open communication and honesty in relationships are necessary for achievement of the compatability and comfort they desired.

The members of the Old Plantation commune respected one another's understanding of and dedication to the norm of self-interested altruism. Equality was valued not so much in income or influence as in intelligence and sensitivity. The members of this commune were sophisticated enough to be aware of such matters as free-rider problems, n-person prisoners dilemmas, and tragedies of the commons. In such mutual awareness, and awareness of one another's awareness, they saw their communal homeostasis. Altruistic behavior toward one another and toward the group was thus never considered its own reward but rather was regarded as an egoistic investment in warding off the war of all against all, at least within the boundaries of one decaying Southern mansion.

The Old Plantationers were able to make a primary virtue of tolerance by making sure that they would generally encounter little to be tolerant about. All the commune members shared similar cultural traits and the expectations of the white Southern middle-class liberal intelligentsia. Control of deviance was made easy and relaxed by the shared expectation that deviant interludes were the exception rather than the rule. Low commitment and the visible availability of alternative life-styles for all the members provided whatever teeth were needed for the system of social control. It was commonly recognized that it was impossible to exploit the system for long because, rather than be exploited or deal with the exploiter, most of the others would sooner just allow the commune to die. Eventually, although the circumstances were a bit more complicated than this suggests, that is just what happened.

New Beginnings (cooperative enterprise) Founded 1937; adult pop. = 44 (21 men, 23 women, 25 children); adult age range = 23–67 years.

New Beginnings was one of the few communes in the sample in existence before 1965. In fact, by the time it was contacted for this study, the commune had more than a quarter of a century of colorful history behind it. The commune was founded in the Appalachians during the Great Depression on the theory that economic self-sufficiency and rural resettlement of the urban unemployed might be one solution to the political problem of business cycles and the related social problem of occupational overspecialization. An important decision was made by the founders of the commune: Although the land would be shared and opportunities for cooperation facilitated in every way, each household unit would ultimately be responsible for providing the means for its own economic support. The commune therefore attracted a population of rugged individualists to whom communism of any kind was anathema. However, the degree of day-to-day cooperation actually achieved in this commune exceeded that of many of the more economically communistic groups in the sample.

New Beginnings was typical of the general class that we have called cooperative communes in that its members' devotion to personal freedom outweighed their allegiance to all other values. This was never true of every member, however, and the communal history bears frequent witness to the frustrated aims of would-be organizers with ambitious utopian programs who came to New Beginnings to mobilize it but left defeated by their inability to convince the others that anything could be as important as personal freedom. This commune has been the ideological graveyard of about a dozen charismatic leaders, some of whom went on to be successful in other communal settings. A few were actually won over by the freedom lovers and stayed to enjoy the minimal ideological satisfactions compatible with extreme individualism.

The norms governing cooperative transactions at New Beginnings can best be characterized as reflecting tolerant expectations of reciprocity. It was not expected that everyone would contribute to the common good in the same way. Similarly, it was recognized that many sorts of activities other than economic ones went into the creation of a rich communal life. Efforts were made to give as much support as possible to artists and to free spirits, provided that these people were at least minimally self-supporting and aware of the need to contribute in some way to the communal life. Because the level of trust among (most of) the commune members was extraordinarily high, a great deal of time could elapse before a favor was reciprocated without arousing strong feelings of unfulfilled obligation. On the other hand, the greatest stigma that could attach to a person was the label of freeloader, and those who had no skills to contribute to the community were shunned.

Despite the emphasis on freedom at New Beginnings, a narrower range of sexual and parental behaviors was tolerated than in many restrictive communes. The prevailing norms countenanced only monogamy and discrete heterosexual experimentation; child-rearing approaches ranged from the mildly strict to the Summerhillian. Strong group pressures, from ridicule, to gossip, to complete social avoidance, were brought to bear on those who deviated from these alternatives. The freedom enjoyed by the members of New Beginnings was thus more like the anarchist freedom from compliance to authority than the more contemporary antinomian freedom from prevailing moral constraints.

Barnyard (crashpad) Founded 1970; adult pop. = 39 (13 men, 26 women, 14 children); adult age range = 15–50 years.

Barnyard was a rural crashpad commune with a very loosely defined hippie ideology. Even among the relatively loose ideological lives of the cooperative communes, crashpads stand out as particularly minimal in their ideological development. Often the agreed-upon ideology of a crashpad could be summed up in the single proposition, the world owes us a living. Although it might be argued that crashpads are not really communes at all, their presence was definitely an aspect of the communitarian movement, and the two crashpads included in the sample had at least nominal ideologies.

Anarchism was a central part of the collective life, although sometimes it was difficult to distinguish between purposive anarchism and simple lack of structure in the community. The community resembled Homestead (discussed below) in its attitude toward the land and land tenure and in its central anarchist credo—that no one should be denied access, no one should be asked to leave for any reason.

Although people considered themselves members of a commune and shared a sense of collective identity, economic communism (except at sporadic intervals) was minimal. Most individuals and family units were simply camping together on a piece of land and devoting a little time to boundary maintenance. Only a very few uninfluential idealists worried about the settling of intra-communal disputes and the solving of public problems, such as sanitation, that should have been the concern of the entire commune.

The reciprocity of Barnyard represented a minimal grudging acceptance of the necessary interdependence of urban hippies in a rural environment. Unlike Old Plantation or New Beginnings, Barnyard had not accumulated sufficient trust among its members to allow favors to remain on account or transactional equilibrium to be reckoned in larger than dyadic circles. This was one of the only two communes in the sample in which even basic food staples were borrowed and returned in precisely measured amounts. Dunning behavior, when debts were not promptly repaid, was not seen as conflicting with professed brotherly love and communal spirit. Rather, it was explained that the injunction to love everyone demanded a healthy degree of skepticism about the morals of anyone in particular.

If pressed as to how communal love did manifest itself at Barnyard, members generally either equated love with freedom or pointed out the undesirable characters who were allowed to "do their thing" at Barnyard unmolested, in the name of freedom.

Barnyard is not classified as a countercultural commune according to our definition because it had no interests in change beyond its own borders. But the members shared the prevailing countercultural philosophy of the times. According to a common version of this philosophy of the new age dawning, it was necessary to nurture as many diverse and freakish manifestations of personality and social relationship as possible because no one could tell where the seeds of the new culture would germinate. Whether this took the form of mere toleration of oddity, as at Barnyard, or of conscious collective experimentation, as in the actual countercultural communes, the goals were the same: cultural revolution.

There were no ideological guidelines for sex roles or behavior. Each individual or family had its own attitude toward childhood and adulthood, although permissiveness seemed to be the modal coping mechanism. In this, as in all other areas of behavior, concern with personal freedom led to the acceptance of as few constraints upon individual action as possible. The majority of the members of Barnyard shared the hippie philosophy concerning the desirability of experiencing altered states of consciousness, and individual and group use of marijuana and psychedelics was common.

Alternative-family Communes

Alternative-family communes believe that the blood-related nuclear family is obsolete. They see communes as prototypes of the family forms of the future. The ideologies of family communes frequently emphasize a concern with character modification, seeing a generalized evil in the narrow role restrictiveness of nuclear family socialization.

Family communes vary as to their image of the correct alternative-family form. These differences are the basis of further subclassifications within this type: patriarchal, matriarchal, fraternal, and group marriage. Fraternal family communes emphasize equality and brotherly-sisterly relations among adult members. They are the most common but the least interesting from an ideological perspective. We will provide examples of the other subtypes.

The White Tower (patriarchal) Founded 1971; adult pop. = 8 (3 men, 5 women, 8 children); adult age range = 15–50 years.

The White Tower was a patriarchal family-oriented urban commune whose overriding goal was to discover the rules of harmonious living in what the members called an extended family. They were concerned with developing a transcendent consciousness for all adults and providing multiple role models for all their children.

White Tower was eclectic in its ideology, with concerns ranging from the countercultural to the spiritual to the psychological to the political. All these were subordinated, however, to the goal of creating and maintaining a complex family in which many adults could function as brothers and sisters to each other and mutually as parents to all the children.

There was much disagreement concerning sexual relations among adult members of White Tower. Cathexis at White Tower always involved strong sexual feelings, but the communal ideology was ambivalent as to the expression of these feelings. Some attempts were made to experiment with multiple relationships such as triads or mutual "swapping," but the recurrent pattern was covert adultery beneath a façade of stable monogamy. On several occasions, the covert sexual relationships were revealed, resulting in schism and reorganization for the commune.

White Tower commune engaged in encounter group and group-psychotherapeutic techniques as a way of achieving *communitas*. Much of the commune members' free time was spent attending workshops and seminars dealing with new psychotherapeutic techniques. Commitment to the commune as an expanded family was thus seen not merely as an ideological duty but as a joy. Little or no distinction was made between fitness for communal living and self-actualization. Failure to be completely committed to the extended family was always perceived as originating in some psychological problem or block in the individual. When such problems went beyond the skills of the community to handle, a professional psychotherapist would sometimes be called in to lead group sessions.

Although the inspiration and enthusiasm for White Tower communal activities originated with and was sustained by the group's male, fatherly, charismatic leader, no sense of hierarchy could be found in the group life. The charismatic leader functioned not as a father to children but as a patriarch to adults or, to switch metaphors, as a coach to an athletic team.

White Tower was egalitarian in principle and attempted to make decisions by consensus, the leader often trying strenuously to stay in the background. An effort was made to incorporate older children into the decision-making process, although there was a wavering policy concerning the membership status and obligations of adolescents.

Members of White Tower came from middle-class professional backgrounds. Individual financial responsibility was stressed, but contributions to the support of the communal household were calculated on a sliding scale. Emphasis was placed on the efficient provision of meals and completion of household chores.

Earth Mother (matriarchal) Founded 1967; adult pop. = 18 (10 men, 8 women, 7 children); adult age range = 18–34 years.

Among alternative-family communes, matriarchy is more honored in theory than in practice. The ideologies of many such groups showed an awareness of the deep-seated and often unconscious associations in Western culture between family per se and patriarchal authority. A countervailing period of matriarchal influence is often perceived as a useful antidote to such associations. Earth Mother was founded at the height of the rural hippie movement in the late 1960s as an experiment in life simplification based on a study of (and deep sympathy with) Pueblo Indian culture. The commune was not originally conceived as an experiment in matriarchy, but, at the time of first field contact, a combination of ideological goals and fortuitous events had erected a hierarchy with a group of forceful young mothers at the apex.

Little resistance was offered by the men to the concentration of power in the hands of the females. The legitimacy of the matriarchy was defended by both sexes on the basis of the seniority, greater commitment, and greater continuity of residence of the women. The men, having fewer responsibilities, were free to spend periods of time away from the commune; the women paid for their authority with heavy day-to-day responsibilities, leading a few among them to question whether they had not, after all, been duped again. There was no question, however, that the women did exercise considerable power. In practice, a group of the most senior women made most decisions. At meetings of the whole, the opinions of women, just because they were women, were automatically accorded more weight and significance.

Other aspects of the Earth Mother ideology were influenced by the desire of the group to "be like Indians." Individualism was acceptable if it was accompanied by strong loyalties to the tribe. Sexuality was permeated with a concern for the fertility of the females and with the production of a healthy and abundant crop of children. Monogamy was the norm, but little faith was placed in the stability of the husband-wife relationship as a basis for family. Mate changes were frequent—the nuclear family being ephemeral, the larger family (i.e., the commune) enduring. Children were considered to be the collective responsibility of the tribe rather than of the biological parents. Liberal permissiveness in emotional development was combined with a strict insistence on assuming work responsibilities at a very early age. The Earth Mother people hoped to raise a generation of children for whom tribal rather than nuclear family upbringing would become the norm.

Earth Mother commune stressed the value of commitment to the collective but also valued personal freedom. The contradiction between these values was a recurrent theme in the communal life. Matriarchy resulted in part from the inability of males to resolve this contradiction. Attempts to justify a hunter-warrior role for the males, which would reconcile their long absences from the communal home with absolute commitment to the communal welfare, were not convincing in terms of the real economic needs of the commune. With no serious enemies and no real need to obtain meat by hunting, prolonged male absences could only be interpreted as romantic quests, eliciting sympathy and support from the women but little status.

The Family (group marriage) Founded 1971; adult pop. = 20 (10 men, 10 women, 5 children); adult age range = 25-40 years.

The ideology of The Family centered around a rather vaguely formulated notion of spiritual, emotional, and sexual liberation to be achieved by a combination of individual and group effort. A small number of people bought some land and proceeded to seek out enough similarly inclined people to produce an economically self-sufficient rural community in which all the adults would participate in a group marriage for the dual purposes of child rearing and sexual fulfillment.

Group marriage raised ideological differences on two points: Should sexual bonds be restricted to heterosexual dyads or extended to homosexual pairs as well? Was group marriage, as conceived of by The Family, compatible with a residual monogamy in which, for example, a particular couple maintained a special relationship with each other while also entering into enduring sexual relationships with other people within the community? No consensus on either of these issues was achieved during the lifespan of The Family.

With regard to children, it was felt that all adults should take equal responsibility for all children, regardless of whether or not they were the parents of these children or had any children of their own. The differences in perception and outlook between those who were parents and those who weren't created difficulties in implementing this strategy. The community was Summerhillian in its child-rearing philosophy.

The community was actively anarchistic in its internal organization but maintained rigid boundaries in its relationships with the outside world. This exclusiveness was a result of the members' sense of themselves as an elite. Most were disillusioned members of earlier communes. They felt themselves to be among the very few with sufficient responsibility and maturity to live out the anarchist creed that each individual had to voluntarily do his or her share.

The Family was concerned with breaking down the traditional designation of some types of work as male and others as female. This goal was taken quite seriously and pursued more rigorously than it was in most of the other communes discussed. The second and most important goal was the fusion of all the members of the community into one single tribe or close-knit extended family in which each person would take unlimited responsibility for each other person.

The Family ideology saw group marriage as the primary mechanism of commitment. Sex with all possible partners was considered to be a physical prerequisite for developing the kind of communal bonds that members desired. Emphasis was placed on psychological encounter group methods, on meditation, and on the erotic power of shared sexual experiences as the mean by which to produce enduring tribal bonds, though collective mescaline or peyote trips were also sometimes used in the quest for a communal consciousness. But psychology, mysticism, and psychedelic drugs were seen primarily as aids to the achievement of maximum sexual receptivity. The community felt that, for extended family to work, some force as powerful as blood relationship must be present to hold the group together. Sex was the only such force of which they were aware.

Countercultural Communes

Countercultural communes arose out of the hippie movement of the middle and late 1960s, and their ideologies reflect the hippie "hang-loose" ethic with its irreverent attitude toward much of conventional society: civil obedience, the accumulation of wealth, the sanctity of marriage and monogamous relationships, traditional religion, and so on (Houriet, 1972). Countercultural communes are organized to reflect this movement's emphasis on the pursuit of intense experience and the development of the tolerance necessary to allow others to "do their own thing."

The subtypes of countercultural communes are cultural demonstration projects, hippie farms or houses, tribal settlements, and utopian reservations. Cultural demonstration projects are communes set up for the explicit purpose of showing a skeptical world the superiority of a given utopian form. Examples will be given of each of the other countercultural subtypes.

Southern Comfort (hippie house) Founded 1974; pop. = 8 (6 men, 2 women, no children); age range = 22–31 years.

Southern Comfort came into existence when several friends who got together regularly to play jug-band music decided to form a commune and moved into a big, old, rundown house by the railroad tracks. Most people in the house were strongly connected to hippie philosophy. They believed in the ultimate value of relaxing and having a good time, that is, having space to drink and smoke grass, take psychedelics, enjoy sex, and play music. There was a strong belief in "hanging loose," letting each person express himself or herself in his or her own way.

Members of Southern Comfort greatly valued personal freedom but not individualism. Their philosophy expressed the anarchistic theme of faith in the good sense and responsibility of individuals and their capacity to sustain meaningful collective life without rules and formal structure. "The only rule is that there are no rules" was the basis of Southern Comfort's constitution. The commune sought to avoid any form of structure or practice that would constrain the behavior of individuals. But each individual was expected to behave in such a manner as to promote the well-being of the whole.

The goal of maximizing individual freedom and self-determination led to attempts to eliminate distinctions among members. A nonjudgmental tolerance of personal differences and idiosyncracies was expected. For example, one especially slovenly member had never cleaned his room from the day he moved in. In time the room began to emit a strong odor and gave the appearance of a disaster area. Although other members found the situation unpleasant, they tolerated it with good humor.

Equality was emphasized: equal space within the communal household, equal money contribution to all expenses, equal participation in decision making. The commune was committed in theory to consensual decision making but believed that group consensus could make itself felt without specifically working to achieve it. The commune relied on a "natural flow" for the resolution of most issues.

As with counterculturalists in general, the ideology of Southern Comfort espoused freedom not as an end in itself but as a prerequisite for an atmosphere of experimentation with new ways of living. The goal of these experiments was the development of new institutional forms to replace corrupt or obsolete ones. Experimentation permeated all realms of life. Politically, members tended to have radical sympathies. Although they did not participate in organized groups, they often supported causes and issues by writing for the underground press or participating in street theater presentations. Economically, the commune attempted to live as simply as possible. Members supported themselves in nonmiddle-class ways, such as by playing music or peddling craft work, although most had college degrees. The ultimate economic goal of the commune was to be self-supporting through its jug band. They valued drug use as a mind-expanding experience that facilitated creativity. They also engaged in shared drug experiences as a means of achieving communion.

This emphasis on freedom and experimentation was especially apparent in the realm of interpersonal relationships. A loving openness and spontaneity were highly valued. Sexual experimentation was also valued, although members were, for the most part, cautious about experimenting with their sexual behavior.

Astar (tribal settlement) Founded 1968; adult pop. = 12 (7 men, 5 women, 2 children); adult age range = 21–25 years.

Astar was founded around a craft cooperative and a small farm. Its aim was to fuse urban cultural values with the ideals of craftsmanship and homesteading characteristic of the rural commune movement in the late 1960s. We call the particular type of which Astar is an example the tribal settlement because it is defined primarily by the people and their relationships and secondarily by the land and property. Although the Astar tribe spent its entire communal life on one farm, other communes of this type have retained their identity while moving among many physical sites, some even spending long periods of time on the road with no fixed dwelling place.

The Astar members were egalitarian in their sexual relationships and tried to eliminate many aspects of the sexual division of labor. The problem of sex roles and male dominance, however, did not occupy a central place in the Astar ideology. With regard to sexual behavior, the ideology maintained that group marriage was a desirable future state, but no movement in this direction was actually taken. The commune was vague as to child-rearing philosophy, and the few children who were present (mostly infants) were raised according to the principles of self-regulation.

Astar was a rather typical representative of the psychedelic movement that swept through northern California in the late 1960s. The members took psychedelic drugs frequently, both individually and as part of group trips, and saw these trips as a central part of the emergence of a new collective consciousness.

Astar was anarchistic in the sense of wanting to avoid authoritarian rules and relationships as much as possible. The business organization of the commune, however, was complex enough to make this difficult. Those who had seniority tended to gravitate toward positions of authority simply because they knew more of what was necessary to make the farm work. In an attempt to find a creative response to this dilemma, the Astar commune developed a paradoxical form of dictatorship in the service of anarchism. According to this policy, each person in the commune, male or female, was required to take dictatorial control and responsibility for the entire operation of the commune for a one-week period. It was felt that, once the commune had gone through two or three rounds with everyone taking a turn at dictator, the members would be sufficiently imbued with a sense of the needs of the entire operation to be able to return to the desirable condition of an anarchistic commune, based on each person's taking responsibility for his or her own share.

Homestead (utopian reservation) Founded 1966; adult pop. = 38 (29 men, 9 women, 10 children); adult age range = 15–48 years.

In contrast to tribal settlements, utopian reservations are best thought of as large countercultural communes deriving their identity primarily from a particular piece of land and less so from the people occupying that land at any given time. A great many such communes were founded during the 1960s. Homestead is rather a typical example of this genre. An idealistic California ranch owner opened his land to all comers in the name of communitarianism, and, within days, a commune had formed.

The general ideology of Homestead commune was total and absolute anarchism, particularly with regard to land tenure. The basic rule was that access to the land should be denied to no one and that no one could be asked to leave for any reason.* The free-land rule has determined all other aspects of the commune's ideology. Homesteader ideology specified that restricted land tenure is the basis of all or most of the world's evils and that, by setting an example of free land and anarchistic community organization on this land, the Homesteaders would contribute to a gradual political revolution.

---

*The free-land policy was a principle that Lou Gottlieb first enunciated at his famous Morningstar Ranch and that many other rural communes have since emulated. Yet this was not the norm for all countercultural communes and quite rare among stable urban groups—hippie crashpads notwithstanding.

The Homesteaders practiced meditation and yoga and some degree of nature worship but took none of these very seriously. The alteration of consciousness that was the underpinning of their philosophy was to be accomplished on the larger cultural scene. The Homestead commune saw itself as a forerunner of a vast movement that was transforming the existing culture of that time. This existing culture was perceived as based upon power relationships, which in turn derived from land tenure. With power nullified by free land, love would come to be the new basis of a new culture.

There was a very strong feeling of getting out of the way of something that was happening rather than actively practicing a discipline to make something happen. It was felt that the chaos and insanity that were very often the rule at Homestead, because of the absolute anarchism that was practiced, were beneficial in blowing people's minds and breaking down barriers so that the new culture could emerge. It was correctly assumed that most people would not be able to tolerate such chaos for any length of time. Anarchist chaos, pushed to its extreme, would dialectically generate a new countercultural order.

Homesteaders never developed a consistent attitude toward sexual behavior, their actual practices being colored by the social fact of the relative shortage of women. As in all other aspects of behavior, the absolute anarchism of the community influenced ideas with respect to sexual behavior. Possessiveness in monogamous relationships was frowned upon.

Political Communes

Most political communes are striving either to achieve a more anarchistic society or to bring about socialism in America. A cross-cutting distinction has to do with revolutionary activity. Not all political communes are engaged in activities aimed at the eventual overthrow of the state; some see the commune simply as a microcosmic laboratory in which ideas for future political change can be worked out and demonstrated to the population at large as being superior.

Political communes can be subdivided into those whose ideologies are essentially socialist, anarchist, and social democratic. Because the commune sample chosen for this book was confined to groups with public identities, revolutionary political communes, which keep themselves and their activities well-hidden secrets, are not represented, although many such groups exist. Most secret groups would be classified as socialist or anarchist except for black nationalist associations, a subtype of political commune not represented in our sample.

Thorn & Thistle (socialist) Founded 1971; pop. = 7 (3 men, 4 women, no children); age range = 22-26 years.

Thorn & Thistle was seen by its members as a support group for people trying to transform the United States into a socialist society. Its life-style was relaxed, and its members were tolerant of tactical and strategic differences of opinion. For example, advocacy of violent overthrow of the government was a majority preference but not a prerequisite for membership. As with a number of other political communes, this one began out of a discussion group in college as part of an alternative education program. Membership in the beginning was drawn, by design, from both working-class and middle-class backgrounds. The members strove constantly to be involved in the affairs of their city and not to withdraw into their own private utopia.

Thorn & Thistle members saw American society as being prerevolutionary and believed that only modest contributions toward the ultimate goal of revolution were possible. Therefore, the commune concentrated on education through projects including radical theater, help to native Indians, and operation of a "movement" printing press. Participation in these projects was not required for membership, and there were some members who did not engage in any political activities. However, it was necessary for all members to "be political," which meant having a leftist perspective concerning the need for political-economic change and some sort of commitment to its achievement.

Thorn & Thistlers took certain modest steps toward the building of a scale-model socialist utopia in their own household. For example, economic contributions fluctuated according to the members' ability to pay and, on occasion, dropped to zero for members engaged in important but nonremunerative political work. However, the commune never considered taking the further step of abolishing private-property distinctions altogether. Commitment, in other words, was serious but pragmatic rather than heroic.

The commune never completely reconciled its political focus with its aim of being an emotional support group for its members. Emotional support was considered necessary to overcome the capitalist-bred character structure. The bourgeois family was a threat against which the commune was often called upon to circle its wagons. Serious attempts were made to avoid sexist and agist practices and to root out sexist and ageist tendencies. Some members saw psychotherapy as an essential tool for this work, but the majority regarded it as a manifestation of capitalist ideological domination that aimed to adjust individuals to a rotten society, taking the edge off their zeal to change it. This issue, more than any other, divided the membership of Thorn & Thistle.

Liberation (anarchist) Founded 1966; adult pop. = 72 (40 men, 32 women, 15 children); adult age range = 17–28 years.

During the early and middle 1960s, the writings of Paul Goodman, Murray Bookchin, and others struck a political chord among a generation of young students whose sentiments were revolutionary but whose minds rejected the available revolutionary programs of the old and new left. Most of these students (later joined by nonstudent hippie dropouts who had developed political consciousness) remained unaware of the centuries-old anarchistic alternative to the socialist variety of radicalism but nevertheless succeeded in reinventing large parts of it for themselves. It was probably Paul Goodman, more than any other political leader of the 1960s, who imbued these people with a sense of ethical responsibility for developing workable formulas for the postrevolutionary society at the same time that they were working to destroy the prerevolutionary society. Communes were seen as the laboratories in which such postrevolutionary schemes would be tested.

Liberation was a rural commune founded with a revolution in mind. Even its location was determined by studying military strategy maps with reference to the problem of supplying urban guerrillas in San Francisco and Berkeley with food and reinforcements. Liberation members envisioned a protracted struggle (somewhat along the lines of the Cuban revolution) with pockets of ineradicable resistance to the authority of the government in areas of the Sierra Nevadas, Sangre de Cristos, and other rugged mountain territories. Liberationists trained themselves in techniques of wilderness survival and mountain guerrilla warfare while attempting to live together in nonelitist, nonsexist, and nonageist harmony.

Attempts to implement the antisexist aspect of their ideology gave the community the greatest trouble. Periodic disputes over the relegation of housework, particularly parenting functions, to the females finally culminated in a splitting of the commune along lines of gender. The males attempted to set up another commune elsewhere, which quickly failed. The females, along with a few of the more sympathetic males, continued to maintain the Liberation context for a number of years. After the male exodus, however, the ideological emphasis swung from guerrilla warfare to building a successful community.

Workers of the World (social democrat) Founded 1973; adult pop. = 9 (6 men, 3 women, 1 child); adult age range = 18–35 years.

Workers of the World was a federation of urban communes organized for the purpose of bringing communitarianism to bear as a weapon in the struggle of disenfranchised workers against management. The organization was not affiliated with any political party, and it did not have a revolutionary creed. The plan of organization was fairly simple. Labor organizers, workers, students, and other idealistic sympathizers would live together in households of ten to twenty adults, breaking down cultural and class barriers among themselves while working as cells in the overall workers' movement.

Workers of the World was egalitarian, but its notions of equality were permeated with larger ideological concerns with justice. It was not merely among commune members but in the world at large that equality was sought. It was felt that, as long as some workers remained unorganized, equality for them could never be achieved. The necessity for a labor struggle justified some degree of organizational hierarchy (in the name of work efficiency) within the commune itself. Also, compensatory justice decreed that workers, having suffered more in the world, should be of somewhat higher status within the commune than middle-class students, although some ambivalence was felt by all on this last point.

The Workers of the World communes derived their household solidarity first from the communal organization and, through it, from a shared identification with oppressed (i.e., unorganized) labor in general. As in some religious communal federations, members were expected not to form primary ties of allegiance to their specific households, but to be free to be transferred as the need arose to any of the organization's communal households. No communion-generating activities or rituals were used, but a charismatic leader was able to provide something of an embodiment of the groups' collective identity.

The members of Workers of the World constantly reminded one another that they were members of labor-organizing cells first and communitarians second. It followed from the shared choice of identifying with the oppressed of the world that the communal life be based upon hard work, discipline, and a semimonastic asceticism in personal habits. Satisfaction was to be taken in the triumphs of the labor movement, not in the interactions of the commune members.

Ideological Myths and Organizational Realities

The goals of an ideological program do not exist in isolation. They are embedded in a general myth that gives them internal validity, and they are expressed through an organizational apparatus that, in addition to facilitating the goals, also limits and constrains them. Let us now turn our attention to the mythic and organizational backgrounds of the ideological programs discussed in the preceding sections.

Eastern Religious

The basic myth of the Eastern communes is that Buddhism (or Vedic religion, Sikhism, etc.) is on the threshold of a renaissance—the latest in a series of periodic renaissances—this time in the United States. This flowering will be fostered by gurus working with avant garde communitarian followings. Often, the sense of optimism about the future of Eastern religion in America is accompanied by the sense that the religion is decadent or played out in its Asian homeland and that it is the destiny of Americans to save its precious message from extinction. Often, too, there is a sense of a new age about to dawn.

There are two common denominators of Eastern religious ideology: belief in (and striving toward) a higher state of consciousness and belief in the indispensable role of the guru as mediator between seeker and nirvana. These common denominators largely determine both the goals and the organizational patterns of Eastern communes. The communes are places where ego transcendence is to be achieved through the practice of a sometimes harsh spiritual discipline.

The value profiles of Eastern religious communes reflect these concerns. Inner harmony is highly valued as an end in itself, and being responsible and self-controlled is seen as a means of developing inner harmony. The goals of Eastern religious communes are most likely to express themes of consensual community: to facilitate members' practice of their discipline.

In all cases this discipline is imposed by a spiritual hierarchy. At the apex of this hierarchy is always a guru. Every one of the Eastern communes in our sample (N = 22) pays allegiance to a charismatic guru. In slightly over half of these groups, the guru holds absolute and arbitrary powers. Most of the sample gurus rule not over a commune but over a federation of communes and may rarely set foot in any given communal household in the federation. Although some of the other ideological types occasionally exhibit a federal structure, the Easterns are the only communes in which a majority of the households (77 percent) are organized as branches or cells of larger organizations.

The unquestioned legitimacy of the guru's authority as well as the expectation that his role is to impose a discipline upon his followers has structural consequences. The most striking is the extraordinarily high degree of ideological unity achieved in the Eastern communes. Although there are some noteworthy exceptions, the Eastern groups generally display both a preoccupation with ideological matters and a perceived unanimity of belief unmatched in other communes.* A corollary is the sense of collective separateness from the world felt by the members of Eastern groups. More than is true of any other cluster, they are found to wear distinctive clothing or otherwise visibly mark themselves as different. Certainly more than the Christian groups, they have the sense of being islands of alien belief in a sea of noncomprehension.

The daily life of the Eastern commune is structured to weaken individual autonomy and to promote the collective identity. More often than is true in any of the other clusters, the members eat most or all their meals together, and they are least likely to occupy private bedrooms. Eastern groups hold far more frequent formal meetings (an average of seventeen a month) than any of the other ideological clusters.

In most instances, these mechanisms worked. In two-thirds of the Eastern communes studied, a strong sense of communion was palpable to us as outside observers. Interestingly, the same could be said for two-thirds each of the Christian and the rehabilitational communes, the two other clusters that stress disciplined subordination of the individual to the collective. Less often could this be said of any of the other clusters.

The members of Eastern religious communes have higher levels of self-esteem and trust in fellow commune members than do the members of any of the other

---

*On the interesting question of whether this perceived unanimity was genuine or illusory, see Aidala (1979).

ideological groups. They also exhibit by far the lowest degree of tolerance of ambiguity. The ideological manifestation of all these dispositions is the collective insistence that everything is perfect, along with the somewhat paradoxical insistence that everything must be constantly kept under tight control. Eastern commune members exhibit, to an extreme degree, a pattern which exists among commune members in general and which was discussed in Chapter 3: the tendency to combine, in psychodevelopmental terms, a successful resolution of the Eriksonian trust crisis, in early infancy, along with a disturbance of the passage of some later developmental stage.

The Eastern was the only cluster in which just about every member reported precommunal drug use. Involvement in drugs was largely given up after membership in favor of seeking higher levels of consciousness through a regimen characterized by meditation, strict attention to diet, and celibacy or tantric control of sexual intercourse.

Christian

The basic myth of the Christian communes is that the churches have strayed from the truest and earliest form of Christianity and that the Holy Spirit is calling upon believers to be sources of renewal and ecumenicism within the churches or without. All Christian communes are concerned with refurbishing the traditional Christian values of love, honesty, forgiveness and the pursuit of personal salvation through Christ. Rather than subscribing to the future orientation found among Eastern groups, there is instead a nostalgia for an earlier, better time (sometimes as far back as the first century A.D.). This may help to account for the distinctive stolidness and general conservatism of many of the Christian groups.

There is more variation among the ideologies of the Christian communes in our sample than among the Eastern groups. For the most part, however, they may be characterized as seeking a life of submission to the will of Christ and believing that this can be achieved only through a rebirth in the Spirit, which requires the prior acceptance of Christ's absolute authority. Because Jesus is the ultimate "guru" of the Christian communes, there is less concern with structural hierarchy and more with lateral federation among those Christian communes that do belong to larger organizations. Although most (87 percent) have charismatic leaders, these are more often residents of the specific households that they lead and thus are more immediately accountable to (and replaceable by) the followers than are their Eastern counterparts.

In contrast to communes of the six secular ideological clusters, Christian communes tend to exhibit high degrees of observable communion, ideological unity and saliency, and dedication to transcendent purpose. But they rank somewhat lower than the Eastern groups in all these factors. Only in economic communism, the complete or substantial sharing of all material goods, do they outdo the Eastern communes.

However, if Eastern communitarians appear to be more immersed in their ideologies than the Christians, the latter appear to be far more involved in communitarianism as a larger social movement. Members of Eastern groups largely view communal living as a means rather than an end in itself. The greater action orientation of the Christian groups leads them to value the movement as a potential instrument of social change as well as the specific commune as an instrument of their own personal salvation. In some ways, it might be said that the communitarian movement as a whole plays a role with respect to the Christian groups similar to that which the large national gurucracies play with respect to the Eastern groups.

The conservative bias in Christian ideologies is manifested in several ways. The organization of Christian communal households is based upon the traditional sexual division of labor. Christians score the lowest of any cluster on the Harris Alienation Scale, which measures liberal discontent. Their attitudes toward social and political issues in general bear a distinctly conservative stamp. In terms of experimentation with diverse social experiences such as drugs, unorthodox sexual patterns, psychotherapies, or political demonstrations, they consistently exhibit the lowest or near the lowest rates.

Psychological

The basic myth of the psychological communes is that there is a perfect self hidden within every person. Within a group of like-minded, sympathetic comrades, these perfect selves can blossom. More than is true for any other ideological cluster, psychological communes are composed of people who believe that people are basically good but that society brings out the worst in them. Although more than half the psychological communes in our sample have charismatic leaders, these are more often seen as wise or experienced facilitators of perfection than as bringers of the light into darkness.

The ideological perspective of the members of psychological communes is best summarized as utilitarian. In some ways the most sophisticated of the communitarians, they know what they want and are serious about getting it. More of them (74 percent) come to their present communes with previous communal experience than come to any other type. They spend more time (20 hours a day) physically present in their communal households than do the members of any other cluster, but by far the fewest (15 percent) express the intention of spending a large part of their lives living in their present communal household. For many, the communal experience is thus both intense and transitory. For others, communal living itself is a lifelong commitment, but the desire is present to experience many different types of community.

In many ways the ideologies of psychological groups are similar to those of Eastern religious groups. The value profiles of these groups exhibit the most similarity (+9) of any two subpopulations we have compared (see Table 5-4).

In their attitudes, members of Eastern and psychological groups show a distinctive pattern of withdrawal of concern for larger social and political issues. The goals of both show strong interest in consensual community: living with like-minded others in a fashion that facilitates putting beliefs into practice.

Like the Eastern communitarians, the psychological seek ego transcendence, but what they mean by this term is very different from what the Eastern religions mean by it. Psychological ego transcendence involves a liberation from the rigidities of a personal character structure induced by childhood socialization. It frees the individual to become self-actualizing. It is the antithesis of the self-negating ego transcendence of the Eastern religious devotee.* The psychological commune seeks ego transcendence not through hierarchy and discipline but, rather, through reciprocity and personal freedom. Life is compartmentalized into the intensely communal and the intensely private. More psychological communes (two-thirds) were able to develop and run their own communal business enterprises than any other cluster. But more by far (78 percent) insisted on living in houses that provided separate bedrooms for all. Perhaps this heavily individualistic emphasis accounts in part for the fact that, despite their belief in human perfection, the members are marked by alienation and despair. They tend to feel worthless, cut off, and purposeless more often than do the members of any other ideological cluster.

Members of psychological communes show the highest rates of experimentation, both before and after commune membership, with drugs, therapies, mystical practices, and nontraditional sexual relationships. This seems appropriate for practitioners of ideologies that promote direct and intense personal experience.

Rehabilitational

The basic myth of the rehabilitational communes might be stated as follows: Individually we are weak; collectively we are strong. We can use our collective strength to make us stronger as individuals, so that eventually we will be able to live and be strong without communal support if we wish to. Members show less interest in communitarianism as a social movement than do members of any other cluster.

Psychologically, members of these communes appear to themselves and to others as losers. They have by far the lowest self-esteem of any of the types and also exhibit the lowest rate of trust in outsiders. Prior to joining their communes, these people were often drug addicts, prostitutes, and criminals. They tend to have had little exposure to the common culture of most other communitarians: mysticism, psychotherapy, political radicalism, and sexual experimentation.

---

*We are emphasizing differences rather than similarities here, but many followers of both the Eastern and the psychological paths would recognize a higher convergence.

Cooperative

The basic myth of the cooperative commune is that it is possible for a small group of people to create a collective living situation that functions smoothly with a minimum of rules or structure. Individual lives would be better if only people would cooperate in the production and/or use or resources.

Cooperative communes are the only type to express no great concern for consensual community. The values that an individual cherishes are of less concern than are his or her personality traits (e.g., compatibility, responsibility). Cooperative communes have goals focused on friendship and convenience. Often we find a group with no collective goal other than to facilitate the achievement of members' own individual goals.

Cooperative communes tend not to have interests outside their own boundaries. They also place a higher value on freedom than do any other ideological cluster in our sample. Freedom is seen as an end in itself. Value profiles also show a preference for broad-minded, capable, and independent people over loving ones. This is not surprising as these communes desire compatibility but not necessarily emotional closeness. Intense emotional involvements are often seen as threatening to harmonious group living.

The importance of freedom is reflected in the internal organization of the communes. A cooperative commune is the ideological type in which members retain greatest control over individual resources. Cooperative communes are by far the least likely to pool economic resources, and they have the fewest meetings per month (three a month). Cooperative communes in the sample are more likely than any other type of group not to have even informal leadership positions.

The members of cooperative communes appear to be less idealistic and more pragmatic in attitude than other groups. They appear to have little commitment to communitarianism as a social movement. They score in the midrange on scales measuring alienation, anomie, and faith in people. Members of cooperative communes are near the mean in rate of experience with drugs, therapies, mystical practices, and nontraditional sexual relationships. These overall averages mask wide diversity among individuals. Cooperative communes are often minimal communes placing minimal expectations upon members. This allows for a great diversity among membership, even within a particular group.

Alternative Family

The basic myth of family communes is that the blood-related nuclear family is obsolete and that communes are the prototypes of the familial structure that will eventually replace the nuclear family. The critique rests upon the complaint that individuals are limited by traditional sex and age roles and that expansion of traditional family roles is the key to a revitalized family form.

Alternative-family communes tend to be serious one-shot affairs. More rarely than in any other type do members have prior experience living in other communes or, from the limited evidence available, go on to other communes in the future after leaving the present one. Family communes are isolated entities. Only one in the sample had any formal affiliation with other communes, and none was founded by a prior organization.

Members of alternative-family communes invest quite a bit in their fellow commune members and make sharp distinctions between insiders and outsiders—not, as in the religious groups, on the basis of such qualities as belief or movement participation, but on the basis of quality of personality. The norm of equality in family communes is often an elitist form of collegiality based upon reciprocated assumptions of superiority to outsiders. Family communes very much value, but do not often achieve, a high degree of long-term commitment to the creation of a true extended family. As a result of their desire to include only persons who are capable of dealing with the difficulties of creating a superior family form and to maintain membership stability, more care is given to the admission of new members than we found in any of the other ideological clusters.

The concern with expansion of traditional family roles has definite organizational correlates in family communes. Some form of shared childcare was to be found in all of them; often minding the children was one of the many household tasks to be distributed among all members of the commune. Chore distribution in family communes also tends to reflect a serious attempt to break down the traditional sexual division of labor.

Concern for expansion beyond socialized roles is also reflected in the generally positive inclinations toward the new psychotherapies found in alternative-family communes. Members report high rates of participation both before and after commune membership. Family groups are second only to the psychological in their use of encounter group techniques.

Alternative-family communes are outwardly more stable, more sophisticated, and perhaps more bourgeois than other communes. Their political attitudes are distinctly liberal. Their value profiles are more likely than those of the other ideological clusters to place importance upon cognitive and competence values. They tend to get the highest scores in measures of tolerance of ambiguity and trust of fellow citizens outside the commune. Despite the mystique of group marriage, which is often associated in the popular mind with extended family communes, these people report less experience with that form of sexual organization than do any of the other commune types.

Countercultural

The basic myth of the countercultural communes is that a new utopian age is about to dawn. In this they are similar to the Eastern religious communes. What differentiates them is the lack of a spiritual interpretation of this new age.

These communes are oriented toward large-scale secularly induced social change. They believe that most human problems are traceable to ignorance about the new age and to lack of receptivity to the currents of change. Countercultural communes vary in the degree to which their ideologies are programmatic, from those that simply try to stay out of the way of the new emerging culture to those embarked upon establishing a fully worked-out utopian program. However, all believe that experimentation with new institutional forms is necessary because traditional ones have become obsolete.

Counterculturalists value freedom and independence. They seek to obliterate status distinctions among themselves as a means of maximizing freedom and self-determination. They are similar to cooperative communes in the high value placed on freedom, but, unlike coop groups, they value freedom not as an end in itself but as a necessary prerequisite for producing the new experimentally discovered culture.

The optimism of counterculturalists often leads them to be uncompromisingly idealistic. These communes are the most likely to have arisen from the efforts of their own members acting alone with no prior organizational or associational aids. They are even more likely than the cooperative groups to practice an uncompromising anarchism in decision making and the division of chores, owing to their lesser pragmatism and the greater felt need to serve as demonstration projects for the larger society.

Countercultural communes most closely resemble the political communes in their orientation to the larger society. The attitudes of both types are distinctly left of liberal in comparison with those of the other clusters. Many members of countercultural communes report extensive involvement with political activities before adopting their present orientation to the achievement of social change.

In many ways the counterculturalists appear to be risk takers. They have taken part in fewer demonstrations than their political counterparts, but have engaged in more riots in the streets. They have been arrested more often and report the highest rate of close scrapes with death of any of the groups. Sexually they are also experimenters, with an emphasis on the social significance of experimentation. Before joining their communes they exhibited the highest rates of participation in open marriages and, after joining, the highest rates of group marriage experimentation. Counterculture communes tend to have very loose membership requirements (sometimes none), believing themselves to be capable of dealing with any changes brought on by change in commune personnel.

Political

The basic myth of the political communes is focused on the possibility of a new American revolution. Some see this revolution as imminent, whereas others see it as requiring a long period of preparation. The political communes generally believe it their duty to experiment with models of the new post-revolutionary society even as they work to destroy the old society.

Political communes are more likely than any other type to have extracommunal goals. The value profiles of political communes are the only ones to evince concern with such societal values as equality and justice. This concern is reflected in the internal organization of these communes. Decision making is most often consensual, and some groups are committed anarchists. The economy of political groups usually provides for some form of income redistribution. Always, care is taken to guard against the emergence of differential power or status among members on the basis of wealth or income.

Opposition to oppression and exploitation leads to the common goal in political communes of attempting to break down oppressive and exploitating behaviors among members. The traditional nuclear family is seen by all groups in negative terms as a capitalist institution, and usually an experimental attitude is taken toward sexual behavior and relations. Sexism is seen as an oppressive mode of relating to individuals that is particularly amenable to attack at the communal level. More than any other type, political communes are organized around a rotation system of work distribution. Members are expected to learn to perform any task for which their prior socialization has not prepared them.

Conclusions

In this chapter, we have developed a scheme for classifying communes according to their ideological orientations. The ideologies of communes were seen to have little in common with one another, and, despite the fact that a longing for consensus was one of the few things that they all did seem to have in common, little consensus could be observed within ideological types, within subtypes, or quite often even within communes.

We should not have expected otherwise. As we have shown in Chapter 1, communitarian movements occur in times of sudden increase in complexity of social differentiation, when consensus underlying existing social arrangements begins to show large cracks. It is during such times that the freedom brought about by the condition of ideological pluralism makes the formation of intentional communities seem both possible and desirable. The absence of consensus on values, norms, attitudes, and goals creates a longing among some individuals for participation in a goal-oriented community of common believers while, at the same time, making other more grandiose schemes for bringing about social change appear unfeasible.*

The simultaneous longing for consensus and the elusiveness of consensus appears to be the fundamental contradiction within communitarianism as a social

*For a fuller discussion of norms, values, and ideology in communal groups, see Aidala (1979).

movement and as a way of life. In the following chapter, we shall examine this contradiction in greater detail. We shall see that many commune members come to regard their own autonomy as individuals as a stumbling block to the achievement of their deepest wishes. We shall explore what happens when they turn to charismatic leadership as a way around the obstacle of autonomous personal wills that do not add up to a group will.

One matronly lady to another: "My reducing club is a great
success. We've lost 148 pounds. However, none of it was
mine personally."

Anonymous

CHAPTER   6

The Problem
of Autonomy

All organizations must be concerned with finding a stable balance between the needs of the individual for autonomy and the needs of the group for consensus. In communes this issue is particularly salient, for it is against the nature of most communes to admit that the needs of the individual can ever really be opposed to the needs of the group. Any discussion runs the risk of apparent paradox, as, for example, when communitarians talk of "the discipline of anarchism" or "the freedom that comes only with complete submission." At their most extreme, communitarian ideologies are capable of endorsing the goal of absolute personal freedom as well as the goal of complete immolation of the self, while denying that these aims are in any way contradictory.

Much of the apparent paradox comes from sociology itself. Despite the admonitions to the contrary of its founding fathers,* sociology has usually

---

*Robert Park, for example, addressed this danger explicitly when he argued, "Contrary to the premises of political economy, it is known that people's interests are not always tied to their own physical well-being. The error of the opposite view arises from the psychological approach, which always draws parallels between psychic and physiological processes. Actually, a person's "self-interest" is tied to everything for which he decides to feel responsible, whether it is his children, his possessions, the outcome of his activities, or

247

wound up equating the self with the individual person. Although social and psychological theories have long suggested that a self may be at times less and at times more than a person, research has continued to make the comforting assumption that the boundaries of the self must always be located at the skin.

It will be difficult to make much sense of the material to follow if we insist upon holding to this assumption. However, because self* is not an observable entity, we will be able to offer no direct evidence that the boundaries of the self actually do expand and contract. The indirect evidence will be of two kinds. First, the conception of variable self-boundaries will have to rest in part on the overall plausibility of the model of alienation and charisma that is derived from it. Second, we shall see that the conception helps to throw light on other directly observable phenonomena that are otherwise difficult or impossible to explicate. For example,

that charisma allows highly cathected communes to be stable;

that charismatic communes often come to be perceived as alien to their members and that, in extreme cases, they can turn against their own members and, with their active compliance, torture them or kill them.

that crises of charismatic legitimacy (discussed in Chapter 8) affect members in their cognitive functioning in a manner that is clinically similar to the effect on the individual of various sorts of ego impairment.

In this chapter, we attempt to develop the beginnings of a theory of investment of the self in others. We start with a functional problem faced by most communes—that their ideologies call for a greater degree of consensus than they can achieve through ordinary means. We go on to develop the idea that alienation and charisma are best seen as reciprocal concepts, the one providing the motivation, the other the repository, for the investment of self.

Consensus and Alienation

As we saw in Chapter 5, there is often a considerable gulf between ideological myth and organizational reality. It is not possible to explain this gulf solely in terms of the difficulty of achieving ideological goals. A more fundamental problem is that of transforming latent (ideological) consensus into manifest (organizational) consensus.† Left to themselves, ideological dreams and day-to-day organizational realities soon tend to go their separate ways, and the com-

---

even the destiny of his immortal soul. Furthermore, these "self-interests" are so varied and often so contradictory that the empirical self cannot be said to possess a single self-identity. Instead, the empirical self is always changing, and is never self-consistent. This means that the individual cannot be viewed as a basic unit; both from the above standpoint and in terms of the systems of relationships investigated by sociology, the individual does not constitute a permanent uniformity" (1972, pp. 28 ff.).

*Recall that we have defined self earlier in this book as that entity on behalf of which individual choices are made.

†Here, consensus is defined as a state, not as a process. We make the distinction between the

nune rapidly comes to see its own ideological image as something more and more alien to itself as a collective actor.

Why and how do such groups stay together at all? This question must be addressed as part of the larger problem, as formulated by Olson (1968): when do people find it in their interests to participate in collective action? It is difficult enough for groups in a state of consensus to function as collective actors. Is there then any reason for groups to stick together that lack anything but the flimsiest of consensual skeletons (sometimes nothing more than consensus on the desirability of achieving consensus)? The tenacity with which many communes cling to life, despite high rates of failure and of membership turnover, cannot easily be explained in terms of their members' individual self-interests.

The problem has been around for a long time and has often been treated by making the distinction between associational (rational) and communal (affective) groups (Olson, 1968, p. 6):

> The emphasis here will have something in common with what Max Weber called the "associative group"; he called a group associative if "the orientation of social action with it rests on a rationally motivated agreement." Weber contrasted his "associative group" with the "communal group" which was centered on personal affection, erotic relationships, etc., like the family. . . .

Such a Weberian distinction requires, however, that we tautologically assume (as Olson does) that the basis for communitarian solidarity is nonrational. We prefer to deal with the problem instead by introducing a concept of self-investment (altering the boundaries of the self). The idea that the boundaries of the self can change will allow us to preserve rationality but at the cost of introducing a new perspective that is just as tautological.

Our choice is whether to treat the boundaries of the self as fixed (at the skin) and allow groups to vary in their rationality or to treat rationality as an invariant human condition and allow the boundaries of the self to expand or contract. Either way we are building upon a tautology. In the first instance, any manifestation of behavior that seems to indicate an identification with some entity other than the person as a whole can be defined *ipso facto* as irrational. We will thus never find a situation for which we have to conclude that the boundaries of the self have altered. In the second instance, any manifestation of behavior can be shown to be in the interests of some human entity (either a person, or something less than or more than a whole person). Any behavior can be shown to be rational, therefore, just by postulating an appropriate alteration of self-boundary.

Faced with two tautologies, we choose the one that seems to offer the most fruitful perspective. Let us begin then, on the basis of an assumption that com-

---

state of consensus (a situation in which all are content with and actively supportive of the agreed upon decision) and the process of consensual decision making, which is one, but not the only, means of achieving this state.

munes are better understood as collectivities of rational actors with variable self-boundaries than as collectivities of discrete individuals to which the criteria of rationality in decision making do not apply.

The Quest for Consensus

The most striking empirical regularity about communes of all vintages is that they are unlikely to decide issues of mutual concern by bringing them to a formal (or even an informal) vote. Table 6-1 presents eleven hypothetical situations requiring collective decision making. These were presented to the urban commune members, who were asked to assess how their groups would resolve each situation. It should be noted that it is the least ideological of the situations (deciding what color to paint the walls of a common room) that evoked the most claims that members would decide the issue by voting.

We frequently observed a sense of shame associated with meetings at which votes were taken. It is interesting to note, in this regard, that the hypothetical situation with the second most frequent recourse to voting is the issue of the expulsion of a member. Perhaps some of the tendency of vote-avoiding groups to choose to vote on this issue comes from a feeling that the need to expel temporarily destroys the social contract upon which vote-avoiding consensual mechanisms have been based. It is as if the need to expel a member results in a fall from grace—from communion to mere association. Only after the dissident member is expelled can the commune reconstitute itself as a consensus-seeking entity.

Only a few communes report that they vote on more than one or two of the eleven hypothetical issues. Voting communes are most often representative of the cooperative ideological type, the type associated with minimal ideological intensity. Only a single case of a voting norm was observed for a religious commune—expulsion from the New York chapter of Love From Above was decided by vote. Some communes delegated all decisions, even the most trivial, to a charismatic leader (see Chapter 7 for further discussion).

Vote avoidance does not imply that all communes seek the complete subordination of individuality to the communal will. Although this is done in many of the longer-lasting communitarian experiments (e.g., Kanter, 1972), it does not describe nearly all of the youthful communes in our sample. We find instead a continuum from anarchistic attempts to do without any social constraints on the individual to equally uncompromising attempts to eradicate the last vestiges of independent self. Neither, as we saw in Chapter 3, do all of the individuals within the same commune usually agree on the importance of consensus. Most communes have to contend with at least one or two members who are just along for the ride.

Nevertheless, consensus is the primary aim of all but the least ideological of communes. It is the sorely felt need of the befuddled as well as of the convinced. It is expressed in the unwillingness of some communes to make decisions in the face of even token minority opposition. It is expressed in that the lion's share of time that commune members spend together is always given to the decision-making process. Finally, in some but not all the ideological types, it is also expressed in the unwillingness to allow a person with even trivially divergent views to stay on as a member.

Religious communes are more apt than nonreligious communes to require personal uniformity among their members. This can be observed when interest in religion is cross-tabulated with interest in politics within each of the eight ideological categories. Table 6-2 shows the results of this cross-tabulation for each of the eight ideological types. The most striking thing to be observed from this table is that, although everybody in the religious communes is interested in religion, more than a fifth of the population of the political communes professes no interest in politics. A closer examination of biographical interviews with these deviant cases indicated that these results are indeed accurate, however paradoxical they might at first appear. These deviant cases are evenly spread among the political communes. Their presence in these communes goes a long way toward explaining the historically noted fact that religious communes enjoy a significantly greater longevity than do political communes, even when controlling for elaborateness of creed and intensity of commitment. Religious communes, because of their sacral perspectives, are better able to impose ideological unanimity upon their memberships than are their political counterparts. It is often not the intensity with which their beliefs are held but the failure to build workaday consensus upon their (politically) ideological consensus that is the downfall of political communes.

A further point to note about the cross-tabulation is that, although the Eastern religious communitarians are interested in religion to the exclusion of politics, the Christians are able, to some degree, to sustain both interests simultaneously. This, of course, is a corollary of the action orientation of the latter.*

It is not only among the religious communes that interest in religion outranks interest in politics. In fact, it is only at the society-focused level, among countercultural and political groups, that interest in politics is more widespread than is interest in religion. Among the secular communes, interest in politics consistently declines as the locus of attention contracts from society to community to self.

But consensus is much more than mere uniformity in general areas of interest. Even the groups whose interests are most similar have to work hard—indeed, often seem to work the hardest—to achieve consensus in day-to-day decision

---

*In attempting to understand the psychological ideologies among our sample of communes, it is important to note that interest in religion among this type is almost as high as among the religious groups. This reflects, in part, the mystical orientation of much of contemporary psychological communitarianism. Significantly, it is among the psychological groups, not the Eastern religious groups, that one finds the highest incidence of the practice of yoga; and in the practice of meditation, they run the Eastern religious groups a close second.

TABLE 6-1. Patterns of Communal Decision Making in Response to Hypothetical Situations: Urban Commune Members

Issue		Hypothetical Situation	Proportion Who Say Commune Might Decide by Voting (N = 283)
Discretionary economic purchase:	Minor	There is a new coat which you would like to buy.	0.0%
	Major	There is a new car which you would like to buy.	0.8
Short Absence from Commune		You have some reason for wanting to spend a month in a different city. After the month is over, you want to come back to this commune.	3.4
Marriage (endogamic)		Someone in the commune wants to get married to another commune member. They both want to continue living in the commune as a couple.	4.6
Long Absence from Commune		You have some reason for wanting to spend a year in a different city. After the year is over, you want to come back to this commune.	8.3
Marriage (exogamic)		Someone in the commune wants to get married to someone not living in the commune and bring that person to live in the commune.	11.8
Admission		There is an individual who has been visiting the house for a while and who is being actively considered as a possible new member of the commune.	14.2
Communal Diet		There is a group within the commune that wished to follow a strictly vegetarian diet and another group that wants to eat meat. Both groups want to continue having common meals.	14.2

Law versus Morality	A person has been visiting the commune as a guest of one of the members. Now it is discovered that this person is wanted by the police for the violation of a law which all of the commune members feel to be an unjust law. However, some of the commune members feel that the safety of the entire group should not be jeopardized for the sake of one person, who is not even a member. Others feel that the commune is morally obliged to shelter this person, even at great personal and collective risk.	14.2
Expulsion	Some people have a feeling that there is a particular commune member who should be asked to leave the group.	14.4
Aesthetics	The living room of the house needs to be painted. Some people feel that it should be painted one color, others that it should be painted a different color.	17.6

TABLE 6–2. Interest in Politics by Interest in Religion

		Consciousness				Action		
		Interest in Politics				Interest in Politics		
Spiritual				Eastern				Christian
		+	–			+	–	
Interest in Religion	+	2%	98	100	+	37	60	97
	–	–	–	0	–	3	0	3
		2	98			40	60	
Self				Psycho-logical				Rehabilita-tional
		+	–			+	–	
Interest in Religion	+	15	69	84	+	–	25	25
	–	8	8	16	–	13	62	75
		23	77			13	87	
Community				Coopera-tive				Family
		+	–			+	–	
Interest in Religion	+	11	22	33	+	36	28	64
	–	19	48	67	–	9	27	36
		30	70			45	55	
Society				Counter-cultural				Political
		+	–			+	–	
Interest in Religion	+	26	22	48	+	22	4	26
	–	26	26	52	–	57	17	74
		52	48			79	21	

making. Communes differ by ideological type in the amount of time and attention that they give to the process of achieving consensus. Table 6-3 indicates, for example, the average number of meetings per month held by each of the eight ideological sets of communes. It can be seen from the table that the non-religious, action-oriented communes at each level hold meetings more frequently than do the consciousness-oriented communes at the same level. Eastern religious and rehabilitational communes hold meetings two or three times more

TABLE 6-3. Frequency of Meetings by Ideological Type[1]

	Mean Formal Meetings Per Month	
	Consciousness Oriented	**Action Oriented**
Spiritual	17 (Eastern)	9 (Christian)
Self	10 (Psychological)	12 (Rehabilitational)
Community	3 (Cooperative)	9 (Family)
Society	5 (Countercultural)	6 (Political)

[1]$N = 120$.

frequently than any of the other types. The table does not give a picture of the intensity of these meetings, a factor that serves to increase the gulf between the action-oriented and the consciousness-oriented communes. The meetings of Christian, political, and family-type communes are frequently indistinguishable from encounter groups. There are strong emotional ventings of pent-up emotions as well as discussion of issues. In the consciousness-oriented groups, rituals are often the functional equivalent of such meetings.

Latent and Manifest Consensus

Communes are organized around collective efforts to realize ideological dreams. Such a task would be hard enough, as we have seen, even if all of the members of any given commune were equally committed to the ideology and perceived its implications in exactly the same way. It is not necessarily the case, as some have argued, that ideologies are exercises in self-deception and mutual fraud. But the achievement of ideological consensus, however sincere, is always only the first step toward the attainment of true consensus. In the words of T. S. Eliot:

>Between the idea
>And the reality
>Between the motion
>And the act
>Falls the Shadow

Consensus signifies something both less and more than unanimous agreement of all members on every issue. It signifies something less than this in that any situation that allows the collectivity to act in the name of all, and in which all are comfortable with and supportive of the decision, may be considered to be a situation of consensus. Some may consent with misgivings or in the knowledge that the decision arrived at is merely the best of all available choices. Consensus also signifies something more than unanimity in that it implies that the observed unanimity reflects an underlying unity of perspective and is not simply an accidental convergence of interests. Many communes have been able to achieve unanimity on every issue with apparent ease for quite a long time until the first real crisis ripped away the façade.

Mancur Olson deals with the problem of consensus by restricting his attention simply to a class of groups for which it can be assumed that there is perfect consensus (1968, p. 60). Olson shows that, even under conditions of perfect consensus, collective action is often problematic. But, in the world of hopes and dreams that is communitarianism, we cannot assume the existence of a consensus that will lead to an agreed-upon choice with respect to all action alternatives. In particular we cannot count on ideology alone to serve as the foundation of a consensual structure.

In the discussion that follows, we shall deal with the search for consensus—for analytic convenience—as if it occurred at five distinct levels. The first of these, the search for common meanings, corresponds to both the meanings and the values components of ideology. The second, the search for common goals, directly corresponds to the goals component of ideology. The third, the search for common strategies, is an emergent property of the consensual process. The fourth, the search for common norms, again has a direct analogue in our discussion of ideological norms. The fifth, the comparison of alternatives to the ideology (and the commune) as a whole, is, by definition, meta-ideological. It reflects the degree to which participants remain autonomous from ideological commitments and are capable of stepping back from the whole thing and asking, "Is this worthwhile?"

Meanings. Let us begin with shared meanings. As happened when the proverbial seven blind men approached the elephant, there may sometimes be as many images of the world derived from a given ideological perspective as there are adherents to the ideology. As Peter Berger (1969) has pointed out, all social experience involves the imposition of a meaningful order upon discrete experiences. The creation of meaning basically requires the ability to separate out and evaluate relevant aspects of events. To the extent that there is agreement on what is relevant, we shall say that there is consensus at the level of meanings, regardless of the relative importance that individuals assign to these meanings. To the extent that there is not, the commune will experience its world as *meaningless.*

Goals. The definition of ideology given in Chapter 5 requires, however, that the world be not only observed and understood but also criticized and changed. To do so, the commune members must define their preferences, and these preferences must be ranked. As Black (1958), Arrow (1959), and others have shown, the ability of individuals to rank their preferences transitively does not necessarily translate into the ability of the collectivity to do so. To the extent that there is agreement on what is preferred, we shall say that there is consensus at the level of goals. To the extent that there is not, the commune will be characterized as *aimless.*

Strategies. If a group is able to order its preferences collectively, this still does not guarantee that it can agree upon decisions. Decisions lead to outcomes, and outcomes have consequences that may not affect the various members in the same way. The power to make collective decisions involves the ability to adjudicate the various benefits and costs of the possible outcomes in such a way as to maximize some aggregate utility function. The group need not decide in such a way as to equalize risks and payoffs for all members as long as there is consensus on the way that such risks and payoffs are to be distributed. A group that lacks such consensus may have clearly defined goals but will, be *powerless* to implement them.*

Norms. Communes that agree only about meanings, goals, and strategies will be able to make isolated decisions. But consensus requires also that decisions not be made in isolation but be embedded in a framework of norms governing group, not individual, behavior. Only in this way can individuals predict the likely impact of future decisions upon themselves. To the extent that a group must reestablish consensus with regard to meanings, goals, and strategies each time it is faced with a decision, we shall characterize it as a *normless* group. In the restricted technical sense in which we are using the terms *powerless* and *normless,* they apply only to the consensus seeking activities of the collectivity. Powerless groups experience their consensual difficulty in each specific act of decision making; normless groups experience their consensual difficulty in the more general procedure of establishing and maintaining the rules, guidelines and operating procedures needed for decision making as an ongoing activity.

Comparisons with Alternatives. Finally, we must consider what is, for communes, perhaps the most theoretically germane level of consensus, one that involves the decision making process only indirectly. Membership in a commune is always an implied contractual relationship. Over the long run, a group of this nature can function as a viable collective decision-making entity only if it shares an awareness of the circumstances under which the social contract will be broken. In other words, members of a commune must have and share a sense of the worth of their collective enterprise *vis à vis* other possible life courses. Communes that lack such consensus inevitably run the dual risks of being governed by the tyranny of a leader or the tyranny of the least committed.

---

*It is, of course, critically important to bear in mind that such collective powerlessness is not the same as the powerlessness of an individual to influence the collective actions of his or her group. Each of these types of powerlessness may have a causal effect on the other, but they must always be treated as completely distinct phenomena. The same is also true of normlessness.

In order to estimate rationally a commune's worth, individuals must be able to distinguish between themselves as persons and themselves as commune participants. Groups whose members lack the ability to imagine their lives apart from the collective actor will be characterized as *self-estranged.* These constitute a small but extremely well publicized segment of the commune movement—generally referred to as "the cults."

Alienation as Consensus Lost

Up to now in this book we have made do with fairly conventional definitions of alienation, rooted for the most part in mass society theory (e.g., Seeman, 1972). If these explanations of alienation are correct, however, alienation ought to disappear gradually in the setting of communal life. This was not found. Let us then make use of the communitarian perspective in an attempt to develop a clearer image of this elusive concept.*

Let us begin with the following three postulates about alienation: (1) that it has to do with estrangement *from* something to which one had a prior connection; (2) that it has to do with action and with the individual in his or her role as an actor, not wholly with metaphysical, spiritual, or emotional states; and (3) that it is always a relationship between individual actors and a collective actor of which they are a part, or between an individual actor and himself or herself.

In these terms, we may consider an individual to be alienated from a collectivity when either the collectivity has taken action to which he or she cannot consent or the collectivity is unable, because of disagreement among its members, to take any action at all. An individual will be considered alienated from himself when he finds himself taking actions against which his conscience rebels or when he is unable, because of inner conflicts, to take action at all.

Because collectivities, unlike individuals, can rarely act without the mediation of self-conscious deliberation, our definition of alienation becomes closely tied to the process of collective decision making and hence to consensus. In fact, we can say that an individual will be alienated from a collectivity if and only if he perceives himself to be outside of the prevailing consensus or if objectively that consensus itself has been lost.†

*In doing this, we are following a strategy that Seeman himself has suggested for improving our understanding of alienation (1972, p. 516):

> The simple designs that have led to such a concentration on the intercorrelation of attitudes (or correlations with background factors) will have to be improved. Since it is not likely that the sociologist interested in alienation will find the experimental laboratory very congenial, the improvement must be sought through refinements applicable to data derived from natural situations. Two examples come readily to mind: (a) the use of mathematical procedures . . ., and (b) *the use of quasi-experimental designs in natural settings,* in the way described so effectively by Campbell and Stanley [emphasis added].

†An advantage of this formulation is that it minimizes overlap with related concepts such as despair (Srole), uncertainty (Allardt), impotency (Rotter), and anomie (Durkheim,

Individuals, however, are typically members of many collectivities simultaneously. It is therefore important to specify from what perspective alienation is being determined. Take, for example, individuals who are members of (American) society and also members of a commune. Individuals will be considered alienated from the society* when they are not able to participate in the society's consensual decision-making process. We will speak of the society as being characterized by a high degree of alienation to the extent that it fails to involve its members in such a consensual decision-making process. The individuals' alienation from the larger society may impel them to join a commune in which they can experience consensus. Assume for the sake of argument that they will only join a commune that possesses latent (ideological) consensus. Such a commune will find its members alienated from it to the extent that it lacks the ability to use its latent consensus as a basis for allowing collective real world decisions to be reached. Finally, the individuals may intentionally contribute to the consensus of their commune by allowing themselves to become alienated from themselves. They may, in other words, invest a portion of their autonomy in the commune (or in society or any other collectivity) to help it achieve consensus and overcome their alienation from it. Defined in this admittedly cumbersome way, alienation becomes that most useful kind of sociological variable—defined objectively in terms of the larger social structure but measurable in terms of its effect on individual participants. It has no meaning except insofar as it relates the decision making activities of individuals to the decision making activities of a collectivity.

Alienation is a complex and well-traveled concept, and it may seem quixotic to attempt to impose upon it a single sociological definition, narrowly based upon consensus. But a concept with multiple and potentially divergent definitions is worse than no concept at all. Our only purpose is to identify the variable aspects of alienation for sociological research, not to preclude other philosophic or literary uses of the term. The empirical evidence that consensus is an appropriate basis for a sociological definition of alienation is simply this: lack of consensus (and only lack of consensus) appears to be both a necessary and a sufficient condition for the presence of alienation in the sphere of action. Reviews of the literature in this area (e.g., Schacht, 1971; Israel, 1971; Feuer, 1962) suggest to us that, where consensus is absent, there is always alienation and, where consensus is present, no matter what social problems arise, the situation cannot best be understood as a problem of alienation.

Merton). Particularly critical is the distinction between alienation and anomie, with which it is often confused. Merton defines anomie as "a breakdown in the cultural structure, occuring particularly when there is an acute disjunction between the cultural . . . goals and the socially structured capacities of members of the group to act in accord with them" (1957, p. 162). In contrast (but in parallel) to this definition, we have defined alienation as a breakdown not in the cultural but in the social structure.

*In a particular society, of course, an individual may be alienated from certain societal institutions but not from others (e.g., school and family but not work, economic and political but not religious).

The multilevel approach of the current study offers an opportunity to treat alienation as a sociological variable, rather than our having to remain content with the more usual social-psychological formulations. Much of the evidence for the validity of Seeman's (1972) social-psychological formulation comes from the analysis of standard survey data* (e.g., Nettler, 1957; Simmons, 1966; Neal and Rettig, 1967; Seeman, 1967), data for which there is no alternative but to look at alienation solely as an internalized state of the individual. But there exists another research tradition that looks at alienation not as an individual propensity but as a structural property of individuals in their relationships with specific collectivities (e.g., Blauner, 1964). This latter tradition has been less precise in its definition of the concept but is more appropriate for the multilevel data that we get from communes.

Much of the current confusion surrounding the use of the term can be traced to the fact that its historical usage stems not from one but from three distinct root meanings† (1) alienation as *separation* from that to which one has been joined, (2) alienation as *surrender* of that which has been one's own, and (3) alienation as *seizure* or *expropriation* of that which has been one's own. *(Note that all these meanings hold in common the implication that one can only be estranged from that which has first been familiar, a requirement that has sometimes been unjustifiably relaxed in modern usage.)*

Separation is the most common and probably the most ancient of alienation's three root meetings (Schacht, 1971, p. 11):

> The Latin verb *alienare* can mean "to cause a warm relationship with another to cool; to cause a separation to occur; to make oneself disliked." And *alienato* can refer either to this process or to the resulting condition.

In English, the word in this context has had mainly theological usage at least until the time of Hegel, the major biblical reference being to Paul's *"alienatae a vita Dei"* (Ephesians 4:18). Theologically, the term suggests a separation from the wellspring of life, which is the connection with God. A similar connotation later appears in neo–Freudian psychoanalytic theory (Schacht, 1970, p. 157), in which, for example, Horney argues that:

---

*In the first part of this book, such standard survey items served us well enough. They helped to explain much about the original motivations for joining communes (see Chapter 3). But, when we began to look at patterns of opinion *within* communes (in Chapter 5), we saw that it was less distinctive social-psychological positions and more a generalized choice confusion that characterized commune members. Moreover, when looking at the alienated attitudes toward social institutions that helped explain the initial decision to join, an interesting pattern was observed; over the years, the rate of agreement with these items changed very little, but, each year, anywhere from one-third to one-half of those in the panel that made a choice would shift to the opposite choice.

†A fuller discussion of these root meanings may be found in Schacht (1971). The reader interested in fuller discussion of these issues is referred to Schacht's brilliant treatise which deals with these issues in much greater depth than can be attempted here.

Alienation from the real self involves ceasing to be animated by the energies springing from this "spring" or "source." . . . To be alienated from the real self is to be alienated from the most alive center of ourselves. It is to be cut off from or deprived of access to this source of energy.

Through the root of separation alienation has come to be associated with a *sense of loss.*

Surrender is a meaning of alienation whose usage can be traced to land tenure and property law. In medieval times, such law contained provisions as to when a person had the right to "alien away" a piece of land or a house or other such tangibles. In social contract theory, beginning with Grotius, this usage is extended to refer also to the surrender of sovereign authority over oneself (i.e., over the right to make one's own decisions). Although this meaning of alienation survives today only within legal terminology, its connotational effect upon the common usage of the term has been persistent. In Rousseau, we find an interesting foreshadowing of the notion of alienation and charisma as reciprocal concepts. According to Schacht (1971, p. 19), Rousseau:

> . . . considers such alienation to be "vain and meaningless" unless this authority is transferred to a *community* (rather than an individual), in which all are on an equal footing . . . it is to be unconditional: "Each gives himself to all," and gives himself "without reservation." "It must be understood that *the clauses of the social contract can be reduced, in the last analysis, to one only, to wit, the complete alienation by each associate member to the community of all his rights.* "

In our formulation, it becomes possible now to say that an individual may voluntarily alienate a portion of his or her autonomy to a collectivity to enable it to achieve consensus.

Finally, the third root meaning of alienation, expropriation, will have particular relevance to our later discussion of charismatic communes. There we shall see that alienation itself can be charismatically manipulated in such a way that what began as voluntary self-estrangement may become perpetuated as totalitarian dictatorship.

We can identify five components of alienation, each associated with one of the problematic steps in the consensus-seeking process discussed earlier in this chapter. These five components of alienation are nested in a hierarchical pattern. Because they have to do with difficulties encountered in a process of decision making, it will generally be the case that those difficulties encountered at an earlier stage of the decision-making process will ensure that those hurdles occurring later in the process are also not surmounted.*

---

*The reader will notice parallels to cybernetic hierarchy (Parsons, 1960), which has also been used to treat problems of consensus seeking in small groups (e.g., Hare, 1973). Our formulation derives similar categories but proceeds from a diametrically opposed set of assumptions. Rather than assuming that more abstract levels "control" less abstract ones, we assume that autonomous, originally self-seeking individuals must develop a hierarchy of skills to get their interests to converge with those of others.

At this point, the reader should refer to Table 6-4 in which this choice model of alienation is fully outlined and in which it can be seen that the components are related to each other in the form of a unidimensional scale. The table alludes to aspects of the alienation and charisma model that will not be discussed until later in the chapter or until Chapters 7 and 8. At this point it is necessary to take note only of the first two columns of the table and the last six. Note particularly that we are arguing that the levels of effective decision making correspond exactly to the discriminative tasks involved in developing scales of measurement. Let us discuss the table by rows, beginning at the top.

Meanings (first level of alienation). Let us first operationally define break-down of meaning as the inability to distinguish relevant from irrelevant aspects of the partitions of events (Ferraro, 1973, pp. 296ff.). The ability to distinguish aspects of partitions of stimuli is equivalent to the ability to distinguish the existence of various alternative responses to a particular stimulus. In particular the number of possible ways in which a phenomenon can be partitioned very quickly reaches an astronomical figure. To distinguish from these a small number of those that are relevant to the specific decision-making task and the larger number that are irrelevant is quite obviously the first task of effective decision making.

Breakdown of meaning corresponds to a situation in which no scale of measurement can be imposed upon the various aspects of choice. From the point of view of the individual's response, all these aspects function as a homogeneous mass. To the extent that the decision makers begin to be able to agree on how to distinguish relevant from irrelevant aspects, we may say that they have solved the problem of nominally scaling the elements of their collective preference set; that is, distinguishing between those that are relevant and those that are not relevant.

Goals. The next consensual problem is ordering preferences according to the criteria of more preferred and less preferred. It does not, of course, follow that having succeeded in distinguishing relevant from irrelevant criteria one is going to be able to order possible alternatives remaining in such a manner as is required for a preference ordering. To do this requires the existence of an external value function with which these various alternatives can be connected. To the degree to which there exists a value referent that is unambiguous, the collectivity will be able to order these criteria and make them into preferences. But the existence or nonexistence of unproblematic and single values is precisely what we are talking about when we talk about the existence or nonexistence of goals. We will therefore refer to this level of alienation as aimlessness.

Strategies. A third component of alienation in this model is the breakdown of decision-making procedures, the inability to relate preferences to expected outcomes through the assignment of utilities. Once one has succeeded in both distinguishing aspects and ordering preferences, then the third problem is the ability to assign utilities, in other words, to weigh outcomes according to expectations. The assignment of utilities is comparable metrically to the movement from an ordinal scale to an interval scale as one moves from simply saying that a particular choice is preferred over another to the ability to say that such a choice has a specific cardinal utility as opposed to another choice. We introduce now for the first time the possibility of establishing distances among preferences rather than merely orderings among them.

Just as the distinguishing problem has a meaning reference and the ordering problem has a goal reference, so the assignment of utilities problem has a strategic reference. One is concerned for the first time here with action outcomes. It is not simply a matter, at this point, of what the group internally prefers but, rather, the power of the group to take a particular action. We will therefore refer to this level of alienation as powerlessness.

We must be careful not to make the assumption that because the collectivity is powerless to move toward achievement of its goals, this level of alienation is limited to the behaviorally powerless. As Feuer has pointed out (1962, p. 142):

> The human switch or lever can, however, be as alienated as the human cog. A power-driven Stalin, aware of his own tyrannical power, but caught and haunted by never-ending anxieties, in a domain of paranoid self-aggrandizement, is an alienated man, estranged from the mankind around him and the socialist aspiration which once had partially moved him. The superpotent man is complementary in his alienation to the impotent.

In communes, the powerlessness (in our terms) of the charismatic leader (the person with the most power over other people) may at times be greater than that of any of the other members.

Breakdown of consensus on meanings, goals, and strategies are the three components of alienation regarding a single decision. In addition, the model includes two more complex categories of alienation: breakdown of predictability (normlessness) and breakdown of person-group boundaries (self-estrangement).

Norms. The components refer to the way in which a specific decision is linked to the general decision-making process within the group. We define predictability breakdown as the inability to anticipate the strategies or the responses of members of the collectivity with respect to future decisions. This is the game theoretic component of alienation, and it assumes that the commune has achieved an internal level of scaling with respect to its own preferences but has not achieved an interval level of scaling with respect to the multiple decisions of the group over time as they relate to one another. We will refer to this level of alienation as normlessness.

Again, as is the case with powerlessness, it is important to distinguish the normlessness level of alienation from behavioral normlessness (sometimes called

TABLE 6-4. The Components of Alienation

Alienation Category	Objective Conditions of Social Disorganization	Subjective Sense of Social Alienation
Breakdown of meaning	Dissensus concerning the criteria for distinguishing relevant from irrelevant aspects of partitions of events requiring collective decision	Belief that sufficient consensus concerning these criteria to allow a decision to be made does not exist in the collectivity
(Meaninglessness)		
Breakdown of ability to set group goals	Dissensus over criteria for ordering preferences sufficient to assure transitive social outcomes	Belief that sufficient consensus concerning these criteria to allow a decision to be made does not exist in the collectivity
(Aimlessness)		
Breakdown of strategic decision making procedures	Lack of a sufficient congruence between goals and the subjective probabilities of achieving given outcomes to assure that consensus can be reached on rational strategies of action	Belief that subjective probabilities that members assign to outcomes do not converge sufficiently with goals to allow rational strategic planning
(Powerlessness)		
Breakdown of predictability	Lack of sufficient degree of continuity among various decisions to be made to ensure accountability and enforce contracts or bargains	Belief that sufficient continuity does not exist
(Normlessness)		
Breakdown of boundaries between person and collectivity	Lack of a legitimate constitution specifying the minimum sovereign rights of the individual members and the conditions under which members may withdraw from the collectivity	Belief that such a constitution does not or should not exist or is not enforceable
(Self-estrangement)		
Non-alienation	Ability of the collectivity to make decisions that reflect the interests (moral and ideological as well as utilitarian) of the membership	Belief that the group has such an ability

[1] There is a parallel between these components of alienation and the cognitive aspects of the common neuroses. For example, David Shapiro (1965:45ff) says of the typical obsessive-compulsive: "There is another kind of psychological experience that seems to be . . . discomforting to the obsessive-compulsive . . . I am speaking of the process of decision-making. Among the activities of ordinary life there is probably none for which this style is less suited. No amount of hard work, driven activity, or will power will help in the slightest degree to make a decision. But what distinguishes obsessional people in the face of a decision is not their mixed feelings, but rather the fact that those feelings are always so marvelously and perfectly balanced. In fact, it is easy to observe that just at the moment when an obsessional person seems to be approaching a decision . . . he will discover some ne·

Reflexive Experience of Self Alienation: Cognitive Neurosis[1] (see Chapter 8 for discussion)	Achieved Level Preference Specificity					
	Relevant Aspect	Preference Order	Utility	Contingency	CL_{alt}	Scalability of Preference Orderings
Inability to distinguish relevant from irrelevant aspects of partitions of events (extreme form of inability to distinguish any aspects = psychosis) Paranoia[1]	−	−	−	−	−	None
Intransitivity of preference orderings (individual) Obsessive-Compulsion[1]	+	−	−	−	−	Nominal scaling (relevant versus nonrelevant)
Inability to relate preferences to expected outcomes through the assignment of utilities Hysteria[1]	+	+	−	−	−	Ordinal scaling (Preference ranks)
Inability to anticipate the strategies and or responses of others in the collectivity with respect to decisions Impulsiveness[1]	+	+	+	−	−	Interval scaling of preference sets (Units of utility)
Inability to distinguish interests of self from interests of collectivity (or lack of such distinction) (No CL_{alt}) Submissiveness[1]	+	+	+	+	−	Interval scaling of preference sets over time
Ability to set CL_{alt}: to determine the level of utility beneath which one will no longer remain a member of the collectivity and ability to participate with other members in the rational search for consensus	+	+	+	+	+'	Ratio scaling ($Cl_{alt} = 0$)

item that reestablishes that perfect balance. . . . To a person driven by a sense of pressure and guided by moral directives . . . cut off from his own wants, the act of decision, which, by its nature, pivots around wants and normally brings with it a sense of freedom and free choice, can only be extremely discomforting. . . . When he is confronted by the necessity for a decision . . . the obsessive-compulsive person will typically attempt to reach a solution by invoking some rule, principle, or external requirement. . . . *But* . . . the decision, as much as he shrinks from the fact, comes to a choice, a preference." There is evidence that this parallelism can be extended to all of the neuroses listed above. This evidence will be discussed at greater length in Chapter 8.

anomie). It is not that the collectivity fails to govern people effectively through consensually agreed-upon norms. It is rather that the collectivity itself conducts its business in a normless manner. The decision-making process itself is not sufficiently governed by norms.

Alternatives. Finally, with self-estrangement, we come to the last level of alienation. This is defined as the inability to distinguish interests of self from the interests of the collectivity, and it corresponds to the situation in which the individual has scaled his or her own preferences and the preferences of others at an interval level but has not succeeded in converting these to a ratio scale by determining what may be called a zero point. A zero point in the scaling of preferences corresponds to what Thibaut and Kelly (1959) refer to as a Cl_{alt} comparison level for alternatives, that level of utility beneath which the individual will no longer find it in his or her interest to remain as a member of this collectivity. For a person to be in possession of himself or herself is to have the ability to invest and (most importantly) to withdraw himself/herself from any given collectivity. For our purposes, this is equivalent to having a well-defined Cl_{alt}. A person is self-estranged if he or she does not have a well-defined Cl_{alt}. Self-estrangement is a common element of *all* components of alienation. Persons with a well-defined Cl_{alt} are not alienated, although those without it may be alienated on a deeper level.

At each alienation level, a subjective sense of social alienation consists of a belief that a certain type of social disorganization with respect to decision making has come about in the collectivity. The collectivity is no longer able to function as a decision-making entity under its current decision rule, and it is not able to alter its decision rule. This is the basis of all alienation.*

Self-estrangement poses an alienation dilemma. The individual either makes his or her commitment conditional on the evaluation of alternatives or not. If yes, then the collectivity may find itself in the situation of an Olsonian latent group, bound together by common interests but unable to evoke sufficient investment of individual resources to function as a collective actor. If no, then the collectivity may find itself a cult—the capacity to act collectively being absolute while the independent judgments upon which action is to be based are reduced to zero.

Charisma and the Investment of Self

Communes are organizations requiring the highest degree of commitment while possessing few resources with which to call forth commitment.† In many organizations, commitment is rewarded by rank. But the nominal egalitarianism

---

*Note that, unlike public choice theory, no presumption of a democratic decision rule is made. Alienation is defined with respect to the given decision rule of the collectivity, be it anarchy, democratic vote, or the consensus-seeking process.

†A striking feature of many communes is the way in which they demand 100 percent commitment, 99 percent being completely unsatisfactory. The discontinuously large

of most communal organizations makes this impossible. An organization that cannot *reward* persons as actors must seek to *become* incorporated within those persons as action objects.

Communal commitment thus is often based upon what we will call investment of self. This is a difficult investment to manage. There is no reason to suppose that long-term equilibrium is possible between individual needs and collective goals. Individual needs are always the motivation for investment of self by our postulate of rationality, but such investment may involve the individual in the rejection of some of his or her other needs. This rejection may even be permanent—but it is never easy. The needs themselves do not wither away.

Self and Investment of Self

It would be helpful at this point to review the definitions discussed in the introduction. Let the self be defined as that entity *on behalf of which* choices are made. The individual can identify with larger social entities wholly or in part. We shall refer to certain such identifications as "investments of self." An investment of self into a group shall be considered an assignment to that group (or some agent thereof) of some degree of power to shape the opinions, preferences, and judgments of the given individual.*

An individual invests some portion of his *resources* (e.g., land, knowledge, money, or support) into a group in the hope that the group will then be able and willing to take actions benefiting the individual more than the individual could have been benefited by using these resources in his or her own behalf. Similarly, an individual invests some portion of himself or herself into a group in the hope that the group will then be in a position to use its meaning creating and preference-shaping powers to achieve the consensus necessary for some collective action that will benefit the individual more than the individual could have been benefited by retaining action autonomy. Investment of resources invariably involves risk, which thereby justifies the profits that then accrue. However, investment of self involves much more fearsome risks. It is therefore a less common and much less well-understood investment process. Quite often it requires the ideological or mystical justifications of a charismatic leader, or a situation in which life and death are at stake.

A very useful way of distinguishing among collectivities is in terms of the investments of their participants (see Table 6-5). The (Weberian) association comes now to be defined not as the only type of group governed by rationality but as the collectivity in which members invest of their resources but not of

---

utility attached to the last 1 percent is one of the chief ways of distinguishing between communal and associational commitments.

*Swanson (1978), in his important study of charismatic behavior, follows a similar tack in distinguishing between group *users* and group *agents*. Agents "act from purposes which we experience as our own and, simultaneously, as having existence apart from ourselves... in entities that are like ourselves in that they make choices and have objectives...." (p. 257)

TABLE 6–5. A Typology of Collectivities Based upon the Investments Made by Their Members

		Investment of Resources	
		Yes	No
Investment of Self	Yes	Community (unity)[1]	Crowd (homogeneity)[1]
	No	Association (unanimity)[1]	Assembly (uniformity)[1]

[1] Basis for consensus.

themselves. The crowd, by way of contrast, may be defined as the collectivity in which members invest of themselves but not of their resources. This pattern of investment would account for the volatility and instability of crowds and the efficacy of visible gestures of resource commitment (e.g., in combat) in transforming crowds into communities. The communal group is defined as that type of collectivity in which members invest both self and resources. The assembly then becomes a residual category applying to collectivities whose members happen to converge in time and space but with no investment of any kind being made.

Whether or not to characterize a group as one formed on the basis of investment of self is really a question of degree. Everybody surrenders autonomy to a larger collectivity to some extent. So terrifying to most of us is the thought of not sharing at least a set of key meaningful evaluations with significant others, that the emergence of a new, entirely idiosyncratic world view perspective is often taken as a sign of madness. Most people also, consciously or unconsciously, allow significant others a role in shaping their preferences. We can look at the process of surrender of autonomy as continuing along these lines in an easy progression leading eventually to the complete subordination of the individual will to what is experienced as collective will. However, such a view ignores the fact that, at a certain point (different for every individual), a small quantitative increment in self-investment will be perceived as a sharp and often terrifying qualitative break. Conway and Siegelman (1978) call this "snapping," but that is only one of its possible dramatic manifestations. At its extreme form, it becomes a closed trap. This occurs when the individual surrenders to the collectivity even that ultimate control over the determination of the conditions that might make him or her withdraw from the collectivity. The group then becomes an absolute sovereign.

Charismatic Potential

Alienation, charisma, and investment of self are mutually related. Alienation consists of an inability to participate in collective decisions. Investment of self is an action that can be taken by an individual in an attempt to overcome this collective inability. Charismatic influence can then be looked at as the process whereby the collectivity makes use of the "self" that its members have invested in it, to bring the various opinions, preferences, and judgments into sufficient coherence for collective decision making and action to occur.*

Defined in this way, charismatic influence and charismatic authority become derivative terms. Of primary consideration is the potential existing in a group for the exercise of charismatic influence. Let us call this property *charismatic potential.* Charismatic potential is defined to be a variable property of any group, its magnitude being proportional to the difference between the group's underlying consensus and the group's manifest consensus. The greater the perceived difference, the greater the charismatic potential. Charismatic potential is a necessary but not sufficient condition for the emergence of charismatic authority.

Fifteen of the communes in our sample (12.5 percent) were judged both in a state of charismatic potential and without charismatic leadership at the time of the first wave of field work.† Some of these groups later produced charismatic leaders and others did not. Those that did not were unable to tap into the reservoir of willingness of members to invest self. A member of one such commune described the situation in the following way:

> We have mumbled ever since the fall about wanting to have regular worship services here in the house—but we have never been able to get it together. . . . We've had a lot of trouble around this issue. . . . [Someone says] "Like why don't we do it?" and everybody goes "um, um," and "yeah"; now what to do next? . . . I'll throw out suggestions, but I don't have the wildest idea how I could get people to do them. We don't have any charismatic figure. We don't have anybody. . . . There isn't anyone who can kind of stand up to the others and say, "We're going to do this."

---

*There is nothing, of course, in this definition to preclude the possibility of a nonalienated individual's investing of himself in the collectivity and thus being subject to charismatic influence. In general, however, we should expect to find charismatic influence operating only in collectivities in which there is alienation. We can state, as a hypothesis for future research, the proposition that the probability of charismatic influence emerging in a group is directly proportional to the degree of alienation that that group experiences.

†Of these 15 communes, 10 were urban and, of these 10, relationship data were available for 7.

In Chapter 4, we saw that charismatic communes had a greater tendancy than noncharismatic communes to desexualize love and to make it dependent upon acceptance of one's place in the power hierarchy. The phenomenon of charismatic potential gives us the opportunity to view the transformation from noncharismatic to charismatic at an intermediate state. In Table 6-6, we compare communes in a state of charismatic potential with those already in a state of charismatic authority on the one hand and with noncharismatic communes on the other. In some ways, charismatic potential seems to represent an intermediate state, in others a temporary exaggeration of the relational characteristics of charismatic communes.

With respect to cathexis (the density of loving relationships), and with respect to the correlation between sexual and loving among the dyadic relationships, the table suggests that communes in a state of charismatic potential have moved about half the distance on the average from noncharismatic to charismatic patterns.* With respect to power relationships, the situation is more complex. The power density and the number of people directly dominated by the person at the apex of the power hierarchy are both higher for the communes in a state of charismatic potential than they are for either charismatic or for noncharismatic groups.

We may speculate that the charismatic potential groups are in the process of using their increased cathexis to build a power hierarchy. It may well be that members are trading upon their love to obtain power, although this cannot be demonstrated. But the commune members have not yet invested of themselves fully in this power structure. Thus they need more power linkages per person than do the fully charismatic groups.

Figure 6-1 gives examples of power hierarchies in charismatic and potentially charismatic communes. More will be said about communal power hierarchies in general in Chapter 7. Here it is important only to note the general shape of the graphs. In communes with charismatic potential, there is more emphasis on direct power, and consequently the hierarchies are more squat and more multi-rooted. The investment of self, in one or even a core of leaders, allows power to be exercised in a more indirect manner. The hierarchies become elongated and more members are able to occupy intermediate positions between the leader and other members.

Charisma as Consensus Found

If people were not dreamers, there would be no investment of self and no charisma. The desire to invest oneself in something larger than one's own person emerges because people are capable of imagining themselves in situations that are neither currently real nor derivable from current reality by any conceivable

---

*These changes can be seen, in some ways even more clearly, as functions of the triadic structures of the groups (see Bradley, 1979).

TABLE 6–6. Relationships of Love and Power in Communes
with Charismatic Potential

Relational Measure	Charismatic ($N = 20^a$)	Charismatic Potential ($N = 7^a$)	Non-charismatic ($N = 15^a$)
Loving density	.60	.40	.31
Loving/sexual correlation	.14	.35	.41
Power density	.28	.35	.23
Proportion of members directly dominated by sociometrically defined leader	.50	.55	.47
Conditional probability Power/loving	.19	.20	.18
Loving/power	.56	.37	.25

[a]The analysis for this table is based upon the forty-two urban communes for which complete or virtually complete relational enumerations were available (see Appendix A).

rational combination of resources. Such imaginings, when shared, give rise to ideologies. Unattained ideology produces the tension of charismatic potential. It is interesting to note in this regard that Swanson (1978a), in a very different research setting, obtained similar findings regarding the susceptibility of individuals to charismatic absorption. Swanson found the major correlate of charismatic susceptibility to be the extent to which decisions were made by consensus in groups to which the individual had belonged. For instance, children of families that stressed consensual decision making showed a markedly higher degree of openness to hypnosis, mystical experience, imaginative trance, and the experience of being possessed than children of families that did not.

Charisma is one of the most critical and most misunderstood concepts in sociology. History has distorted our vision by allowing us to view charismatic leaders primarily through the testimony of their followers. The need for these followers to believe that charismatic properties actually stem from magical or supernatural powers of the leader has passed into our own sociological judgment. Here we can see both the value and the necessity of studying actual ongoing communal experiments. They have a distinct advantage over such world-shaking social experiments as the great world religions or revolutionary political movements in that they can be viewed from the outside, objectively, *in toto*.

Our study of communal influence reveals charisma as it really is: not a locus of supernatural traits in a particular individual, but a transactional process occurring with predictable regularity in collectivities searching for consensus. This is not to negate the importance of having an individual who can carry the burden of maintaining the leadership role under such circumstances. But it

FIGURE 6-1.   Selected Examples of Power Hierarchies in Communes Grouped by Charismatic Category

A. Resident Charismatic Communes

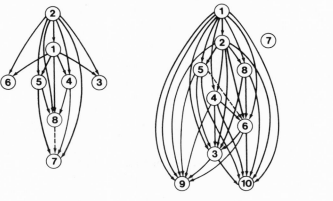

No data: ⑪

B. Absentee Charismatic Communes

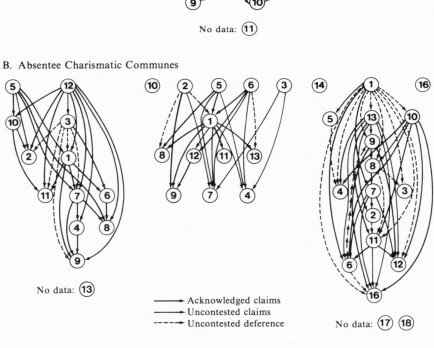

No data: ⑬

⟶ Acknowledged claims
⟶ Uncontested claims
- - -➤ Uncontested deference

No data: ⑰ ⑱

C. Charismatic Potential Communes

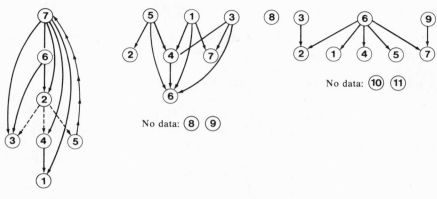

No data: (8) (9)

D. Noncharismatic Communes

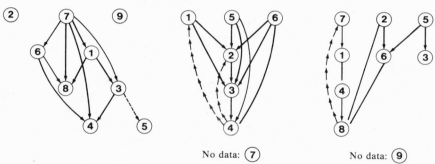

No data: (7)   No data: (9)

is hoped that this investigation will contribute to a demystification of the concept of charisma.*

Alienation from a coherent structure of values makes collective action difficult. Charisma is a collective response to the need for action in the presence of alienation. In the presence of shared articulated values, collectivities are able to mobilize resources to achieve action. Where such value convergence is blocked,

*The argument of this book is in direct opposition, therefore, not only to those who have tried to make charisma a psychological variable, but to those who have tried to identify it with specific historical periods. This latter perspective is well argued by Bensman and Givant (1975, pp. 570ff.): "the concept of charismatic leadership as developed by Weber is of little use to the analysis of modern political and social movements . . . based on the [rational] systematic exploitation of irrationality"

the self must first be invested into the collectivity. Thus the primary function of charisma is to provide structured opportunities for the investment of self. The primary function of the charismatic leader is to provide values that evoke in each follower the desire to invest self and, having invested, to refrain from withdrawing self again. Looking at charisma, sociologists have asked the wrong question. They have looked at the superstructure and asked what are the consequences for legitimacy and stability of the *social fact* that power is exercised based upon these beliefs about a relationship of compliance.

Charisma as a social fact has been wrongly identified with its interpretive and legitimating beliefs. Charisma was held to be real only in the sense that it was perceived as real. This can be understood as a reaction from and an improvement upon the earlier mythologies and the faulty theories of the mass psychologists (Freud, LeBon). But the antithesis has accomplished its task and a time has come for a synthesis. The mana or power that followers experience as flowing from their charismatic leaders cannot be dismissed as existing only at the abstract level of beliefs.

The surrender of autonomy is perceived by many communitarians as an encounter with a very real force. Many commune members interviewed seemed almost desperate to find words to convey what was, to them, the crucial fact about the meaning of their experience. The following remark is typical of many such: "It's something that you feel inside—really deeply inside. . . . You're not thinking or having a feeling about something. You're just knowing something: that this is truth."

Certainly, charismatic authority is and must be based upon a system of shared beliefs, often of a supernatural nature.* But this system of shared beliefs must itself be based upon something. It does not arise simply as a product of cognitive and normative homogeneity, although such homogeneity makes it easier for beliefs about charisma to appear. But all of this ultimately rests on the real altered state of the selves and their merger into the social. The primordially social is here experienced as a will that seems quite unlike the wills of its creators. The invested self is experienced as alien until it is accepted by those who created it:

> Guru has shown us the light of God. Something, which when I first saw it, just caused me to break out into a cold sweat, and it was a really profound experience . . . it's something that's very real. When we experience it, it lifts us totally above feelings, emotions, and things like that to a place like, you might call it a State of Grace. It's really intense and very high.

Commune members were asked to name those whom they thought were charismatic. In general, such ascriptions were not used by the commune mem-

---

*Although see Aidala (1979) for an interesting and careful analysis of the question of the extent to which commune members actually share beliefs compared to the extent to which they think they do.

TABLE 6-7. **Personality Characteristic Correlating Most Highly with "Charismatic" in Each of the Eight Ideological Types**

	Consciousness Oriented	Action Oriented
Spiritual	Influential (Eastern)	Influential (Christian)
Self	Dominant (Psychological)	Influential (Rehabilitational)
Community	Dominant (Cooperative)	Intuitive (Family)
Society	Influential (Countercultural)	Loving (Political)

bers to identify their charismatic leaders. Leaders were mentioned but so were nonleaders. "Charismatics" were identified in those communes objectively defined as noncharismatic as well as in the charismatic ones. Table 6-7 indicates, from a list of fourteen personality attributes, which one was ascribed in a manner most correlated with the ascription of charisma in each of the ideological groups. Overall, the highest correlation ($r = .21$) of "charismatic" was with "influential." But half the ideological types have an attribute that correlates higher with "charismatic." Particularly interesting is the pattern in the narrowly focused, consciousness-oriented communes (cooperative and psychological), in which the leading correlate was "dominant." In general, as we shall see, there was a greater investment of self in the action-oriented than in the consciousness-oriented nonreligious communes. As both focus and action-need decrease, there is less need to interpret charisma as a benign force. In this light it is also possible to explain the high correlation between charisma and loving in the political communes. Here the problem is the reverse. The political groups have the maximum need for charisma because of their wide focus and their action orientation, but they lack the natural religious legitimation for it. They therefore need to interpret charisma as something very good, as do, to a lesser extent, the family communes.

Five Levels of Charisma

One of the advantages of looking at charisma in a communitarian perspective is the opportunity to see the great variety of charismatic situations that exist. Charisma is far from a monolithic phenomenon. In Chapter 7 we shall discuss variations in the organization of charismatic leadership; here we shall look at the levels of autonomy invested in charismatic leaders as they correspond to the levels of alienation discussed earlier.

When we look at the patterns of concentration of authority in communes, a very interesting convergence with our five hypothesized alienation levels can be noted. As Table 6-8A indicates, there are five functional areas in which commune members have been observed to concentrate authority. The interesting thing is that these areas are found to be nested along a unidimensional scale such that any concentration of authority at a given level implies that all earlier concentrations will almost certainly also be made. For example, communes whose members surrender executive authority to one or a few people almost always concentrate policy making and exemplary authority as well. Thus communes can be located on a six-point scale according to their investment of decision-making authority.

In Tables 6-8B and C, charismatic level is cross-tabulated against leadership type and ideology type. It can be seen that the highest levels of charismatic authority tend to be associated with single charismatic leaders and with religious ideologies. The greater willingness of the members of religious communes to accept individual persons as absolute authority figures is probably associated with the greater degree of consensus achieved by religious groups as well as with their greater degree of long-range stability.

Each point on the scale represents a charismatic level. Level 0 is noncharisma ($N = 39$). There is no observable surrender of autonomy in decision making. Of course even these communes observe the larger cultural conventions concerning meanings, which make communication possible. But they do not surrender autonomy, to any appreciable degree, in the act of defining the specific meanings of their shared ideologies.

The unwillingness of the 0-level groups to invest authority in a charismatic leader also implies willingness to tolerate or risk all levels of alienation down to and including meaninglessness. This does not mean that all communes in this category have memberships that are thoroughly alienated. Some may possess a naturally occurring consensus; others may attain consensus without the need to resort to concentration of authority. Many of the communes in this category represent the relatively simple and undemanding ideologies in our sample, making consensus far easier to come by.

Meanings. In level 1 (exemplary) charismatic ($N = 14$) communes, members are chosen to exemplify shared meanings and values only. Exemplary charismatic leaders need not make choices for the group among competing values but only to combine or recombine meanings (Turk, 1971, p. 127) in such a way that some collective values are evident. This is the most elementary charismatic leadership property. It appears as a component of all more complex types. It occurs here in its simple form among those communes that are not willing to tolerate alienation at the level of meaninglessness but are willing to accept aimlessness in cases where the commune as a whole cannot consensually generate its own aims.

At the individual level, the power of many communes to generate shared meanings is demonstrated in the ability that the commune has to serve as a looking glass in which members view their own personalities. Sprague (1978) has investigated the remarkable extent to which commune members tend to view themselves as their fellow members view them. Such consensus, of course, is valuable not only in itself but also in the hold that it gives the commune in enforcing its perspective and applying sanctions.

Goals. Level 2 (policy) charismatic ($N = 19$) communes are those in which the authority is invested not only to define which values are meaningful but also to order preferences among mutually competing values—in other words, to set goals or make policy. Such communes are concerned that the consensus achieved is at least sufficient to ward off aimlessness. They are generally groups that take their ideologies somewhat more seriously. They must be able to make (often ambitious) plans. They do not require of themselves the need to make concrete decisions, however, reserving this to chance confluence of points of view or to the normal interchange of ideas and influence.

The pattern can be seen as a more advanced stage in the evolution of any social movement. As Killian has said (1964, p. 449):

> When the early leaders of a social movement sound their rallying cry, the goals of the movement are usually ill-defined, and the strategy has not been formulated. . . . In this early stage, the values are likely to be negative, in the sense that they constitute a rejection of the existing order rather than a clear-cut vision of a new state of affairs. . . [Later, there is a second stage.] Dissonant viewpoints are suppressed and the charismatic leader begins to define an increasingly specific set of goals.

Riker and Ordeshook relate this problem of consensual potentiality (that they call "coherence") to Arrow's paradox. They discuss the function of charismatically imposed cultural ideals in bringing about "coherence" through the restriction of values (1973, pp. 105ff.):

> In an even broader way, the conventions and ideals of a culture are value-restrictive. Rousseau . . . emphasized that, in practice, the only sure way to have a coherent public policy was to have in the cultural background a great Legislator who imposed a set of ideals. Sparta had Lycurgus, Athens had Solon, Geneva had Calvin—and all these men imposed a set of ideals on their cities. Since the imposed ideals effectively prevented other ideals from being best in any individual ordering, the great Legislator provided, in our terms, for value-restrictedness. Even in larger societies we find similar conventions: North American culture strongly discourages any orderings of states of

TABLE 6-8. Types of Charisma and Leadership

A. Authority Scale

Empirically Observed Concentration of Authority in One or a Few Members	(0) Non-charismatic	(1) Exemplar Charismatic	(2) Policy Charismatic	(3) Executive Charismatic	(4) Normative Charismatic	(5) Absolute Charismatic
With respect to meanings	No	Yes	Yes	Yes	Yes	Yes
With respect to goals	No	No	Yes	Yes	Yes	Yes
With respect to strategies	No	No	No	Yes	Yes	Yes
With respect to norms	No	No	No	No	Yes	Yes
With respect to alternatives	No	No	No	No	No	Yes

Coefficient of reproducibility = 0.93.
Minimum marginal reproducibility = 0.65.

B. Charisma Level by Leadership Type

Leadership Type	Charismatic Level						
	Absolute	Normative	Executive	Policy	Exemplar	None	Total
Routinized	2	1					3
Absentee	12	10	5	2	1		30
Resident	5	8	4	4	1		22
Core group (multiple leaders)				3	5		8
Charismatic potential				4	3	8	15
None			1	6	4	31	42
Total	19	19	10	19	14	39	120

C. Charisma Level by Ideology Type

Ideology Type	Charismatic Level						
	Absolute	Normative	Executive	Policy	Exemplar	None	Total
Eastern	11	9	1	1			22
Christian	6	4		2	2	1	15
Psychological		3	3	2		1	9
Rehabilitative	2	1		1			4
Cooperative				1		15	16
Familial			1	3	2	5	11
Countercultural		2	3	5	8	11	29
Political			2	4	2	6	14
Total	19	19	10	19	14	39	120

society in which a life of religious contemplation is best. Medieval culture, however, encouraged men to put the contemplative life first.

Strategies. Level 3 (executive) charismatic ($N = 10$) communes are organized to make decisions. Self is invested in the formation of opinions, preferences, and strategies, ensuring that consensus can be reached on any specific issue. Level 3 communes refuse, however, to invest of themselves in the charismatic formation of norms. They are willing to tolerate periods of mistrust and lack of overall normative direction. Individuals withhold to themselves the right to make independent judgments concerning the long-term motivations of others. Such groups lack continuity but know that, in a crisis, a decision can always be reached.

Norms. In level 4 (normative) charismatic ($N = 19$) communes, the leader or leaders is given the right not only to make decisions on the part of the group but also to justify these decisions as stemming from an ongoing normative order also defined charismatically. In these communes, charismatic authority is not yet absolute. The normative order that justifies decisions is still seen as one of many possible normative orders rather than as *the* normative order. But the individual no longer retains autonomy in the evaluation of decisions. He accepts the proposition that, if he is not with the commune on each issue, then he is against it. He can no longer say that the group is wrong, only that he himself is out of step with the group and had better leave.

The risky shift phenomenon (Myers and Lamm, 1976; Hong, 1978) is a well-documented example of this type of charismatic compliance. As Hong has shown, the decision-making shift need not be in a risky direction. For example, when the latent normative consensus of the group is cautious, the shift may actually involve the substitution of group decisions that are objectively *less* risky than the original individual decisions. The risky shift is one of the most common observed phenomena among ex-commune members. People who have left communes frequently comment that they cannot identify at all with the decisions that they freely made when they were members.

Comparison of Alternatives. The final and most extreme level of the charismatic commune ($N = 19$), as in Jonestown or Synanon in its later stages, eradicates the last traces of independent judgment on the part of its members.* The

---

*For those readers familiar with contemporary communes, this and the earlier examples are likely to be familiar types. For those who are not, a noncommunitarian example from American history may help to make the concept of charismatic levels clearer. The four-score years prior to the Civil War represent a period in which the problem of achieving consensus over the slavery issue escalated through all of the five levels discussed here. The debate over the Constitution revealed a consensus in that certain values were agreed to as meaningful, including personal liberty, and it was generally agreed that slavery was a bad thing, but there was no consensus that anything ought to be done about it. Many believed that it might disappear by itself. In the early part of the nineteenth century, consensus on a *laissez-faire* policy emerged. The early congressional compromises, especially the Missouri Compromise of 1820, established national preferences and imposed them upon states and candidates for statehood in the form of a decision framework. The later compromises (e.g., the Compromise of 1850) were more concerned with developing a workable normative system that would eventually result in the elimination of the slavery system. The

commune can become more sovereign than the state. The authority of the charismatic leader (in this type there is generally only one) is seen as stemming from a source of unquestionable right. As a member of one such commune put it:

> God puts people into positions of authority and we as Christians are expected to submit to them as unto God. In other words, if Will told me to do something, even though I may not agree with it, I have to trust that God speaks to me through Will . . . if Will's vetoing whatever this thing is that I want to run out and do, there's a reason that God does not want me to do it. . . . God can change your authority if your authority is wrong. . . . God will change Will. I don't try to change Will . . . I submit to him [Will] as the authority, as unto God, knowing that God is ultimately in control.

This final level of charisma is capable of demanding a complete investment of the self. For there to be no private identity left to make decisions has a strong appeal to many people. Recall the commune member mentioned in the previous chapter, who was told that the decision to join the commune would be the last decision he would ever have to make. The charismatic leader's mandate is to attach utilities to preferences at the ratio scale, defining an absolute rather than a relative zero, so that it becomes no longer relevant to compare the communal ideology as a whole with other alternatives. Level 5 charisma can, at its most extreme, bring about a situation of no alienation of the self from the commune but absolute alienation of the self from the person.

This extreme form of charismatic situation is not as rare as one might imagine. There is a pressure toward absolutely selfless devotion to a cause, on the part of both followers and leaders, that makes both go to great lengths to bring about this situation. Killian has defined the martyr as an extreme form of this tendency: "*An important variant of the charismatic leader is the martyr.* By his 'glorious suffering' for the cause he symbolizes full, unreserved commitment and makes lighter by comparison the burden of lesser demands on other followers." (1964, p. 441). But level 5 charisma is quite capable of inducing martyrdom in the followers as well as in the leader.

One of the major functions of the charismatic leader is to channel interpersonal commitment into group commitment. In this context we must distinguish between authoritarian interference into what is generally accepted as being private life and the provision of opportunities for commitment, inducing investment in identity-forming collectivities. Thus the high degree of commitment necessary for investment of self in a charismatic community, because it requires guarantees that the investment level of others will be kept similarly high, demands a degree of involvement of the group in the life of the individual that, by associational standards, would constitute intolerable tyranny.

---

leading figures in these debates— Clay, Calhoun, Webster—were, by the way, typical of the charismatic leader at the fourth level. But it was not until Lincoln's election and the crisis of secession that the issue was raised to one of establishing consensus on Cl_{alt}. The ability of Lincoln to impose this final level of consensus upon the nation is the mark of a charismatic leader of this level.

Commitment and Social Control

Charismatic authority never produces a stable equilibrium. Charismatic leaders, however revered, get old and die. Some may lose interest and go on to other things. Others may get worn out in office or get corrupted by the potentially absolute powers of their position (Zablocki, 1971, ch. 5). Although there seem to be no fixed limits on how long unroutinized charismatic authority can continue unabated or any limits on the number of times it can renew itself, long-lasting communes have generally begun early to make provisions for the eventual routinization of the charismatic authority.

Charisma Routinized as Commitment

Communitarian charisma, as with any other kind, becomes routinized simply as a function of time. Often this takes the form of a shift in membership commitment from the person or persons to be revered to the work to be done. An effective charismatic leader will have, by this time, gradually taken the latent utopian dream and developed it concretely, if not yet in the workaday world, at least in the mind of each participant. But such a shared vision is not by itself adequate. It erodes over time; it is not always equal to the challenge of finding new solutions in crises; it cannot, in the absence of charisma, be successfully conveyed to new recruits. It needs to be bolstered by institutional commitment mechanisms.

Because of the youth of our sample of communes, formal commitment mechanisms do not hold an important place. What we can observe instead is the beginning of the as yet little understood process of transformation of charisma into institutionalized commitment. Most often this transformation involves the intermediate steps of sacralization and tradition building.

Obedience to charismatic authority becomes more automatic to the extent that the authority becomes consensually perceived as sacred. Remember that we are postulating that charismatic compliance is at first deliberate and rational, differing from ordinary rational compliance only in that it involves alteration of the boundaries of self. The sacredness (in the Weberian sense of "that which is specifically unalterable") of the charismatic influence is experienced as internalization. The following reaction of one such commune member is typical of such experience:

> Well, as far as having someone supervise you all the time and telling you what to do, it became more of an independent thing where you just automatically acted because you felt that, not because you were being told what to do.

After a while, if there are no rebellions, schisms, or insurmountable crises, the sacred takes on the additional weight of traditional legitimacy, at which point it can routinely be transmitted even to new members.

TABLE 6-9. Commitment Mechanisms and the Routinization of Charisma

A. Investment of Self

Type of Commitment[1]	Commitment Mechanism[1]	Charismatic Type
Moral	Mortification, transcendence	Exemplary, policy
Cohesion	Renunciation, communion	Executive, normative
Continuance as a commune	Sacrifice	Absolute

B. Investment of Resources

Type of Commitment	Commitment Mechanism	Authority Type
Continuance as an association	Investment	Noncharismatic, "rational" leadership

[1] Kanter, 1972, p. 72ff.

The Commitment Mechanisms

If our theory of charismatic levels is correct and if it is true that commitment represents charisma routinized, we should expect to find commitment mechanisms in communes corresponding to each of our five charismatic levels. In fact we do find a direct correspondence between five of Rosabeth Kanter's (1972) commitment mechanisms and the levels at which self can be charismatically invested. The sixth of Kanter's mechanisms, which she calls simply *investment*, corresponds in our terms to the investment of resources and represents the associational, as opposed to the communal, side of all communitarian ventures (see Table 6-9).

In her now classic work on the subject, Rosabeth Kanter identified six mechanisms of commitment utilized by communes in their quest for survival: mortification, transcendence, renunciation, communion, sacrifice, and investment. Translated into the terms that we have been using, Kanter's central thesis is that use of the commitment mechanisms by the commune leads to an increase in the investment of self by the membership in the commune and thus enhances the commune's survival chances.

In discussing these commitment mechanisms, Kanter divides them into three pairs, each corresponding to a type of commitment. *Mortification* and *transcendence* mechanisms have to do with the type known as moral commitment (or, in our terms, commitment to the viability of the ideology). *Renunciation* and *communion* have to do with cohesion (commitment to the viability of the formal organization). *Sacrifice* and *investment* have to do with what Kanter calls continuance (commitment to the viability of the collectivity itself). Lack of moral commitment corresponds roughly to the meaninglessness and aimlessness dimensions of alienation that we have discussed earlier. Similarly, lack of cohesion has to do with the powerlessness and normlessness dimensions of alienation and lack of continuance to the dimension of self-estrangement. Each pair of commitment mechanisms can be looked at as a set of deliberate attempts to institutionalize erstwhile charismatic methods of inducing the investment of self.

Mortification/Transcendence. This pathway constitutes the direct attempt of the commune to alter preference orderings. Isolation from personal contacts, required public confessions, surveillance, and rigidly structured daily routine are examples of mortification mechanisms. They are the sticks that are used along with the carrots of transcendence to produce preference modifications. It is interesting to note that the examples of transcendence mechanisms given be Kanter (power invested in persons with special magical characteristics) are in many instances similar to the usual sociological descriptions of charisma. In other words, to produce transcendence, an identification with something higher and greater than one's personal self, it is often sufficient simply to have a charismatic leader present, regardless of how he functions in the community.

Renunciation/Communion. This pathway has a different role to play. The task of these mechanisms is not to modify but to delimit and bring into coherence the preferences of the commune members so that decisions can be reached in an orderly and efficient manner. The renunciation of exclusive dyadic sexual relations, of commitments to nuclear families, and of contacts with outside persons, parties, movements, and organizations all help to simplify and homogenize the criteria upon which preferences are ordered and restrict the set of admissible orderings. Singing, dancing, communal dining and working bees, and other collective activities can then foster communion, a kind of mechanical solidarity in which it seems only natural for the preferences of all to be identical. In some communes, these mechanisms operated sporadically, as peak experiences, allowing the commune to reach consensus on isolated decisions in crisis situations. In others, they operated more continually, providing a secure substitute for the executive and normative charismatic functions in collective decision making.

Sacrifice/Investment. This pathway is not concerned directly with building commitment either to the ideology or to the organization. Rather it is concerned with the problem of continuance—the single decision underlying all other decisions that all members of any collectivity (except those which are level 5 charismatic) are constantly making implicitly or explicitly—whether to stay or leave.

There is probably more confusion about the nature of sacrifice than about the nature of any of the other commitment mechanisms. In order to conserve rationality, we define the term somewhat differently than does Kanter. Both sacrifice and *investment* are here defined as having to do with the investment of resources. What Kanter calls *investment* is seen as the rational investment of resources in the hope of some eventual personal profit. *Sacrifice* involves resource investments that do not meet this criterion. For an investment to be termed a *sacrifice,* resources must be invested in a manner that meets the following three criteria: (1) The investment cannot objectively be judged rational from the point of view of the self as a person. (2) The investment can be judged rational from the point of view of some larger version of self. (3) There must be independent evidence that the person has in fact identified with that particular larger version of self.

Both *sacrifice* and *investment* are important for the continuance of the commune over the long run, although, as we saw in Chapter 4, they are eclipsed by relational variables in determining short-run continuance. *Sacrifice* provides the basis for the self-investment activities of the commune. *Investment* provides for its activities as a Weberian association and keeps the commune from degenerating into a mere collective behavior experience or ongoing encounter group. In contemporary communes, the relaxation of the demand for sacrifice often comes after the pioneering work has been accomplished and the opportunity for pursuing personal goals arises. The relaxation of the demand for sacrifice leads to the diminution of commitment to the collectivity (withdrawal of self).

The communes in our sample, unlike those studied by Kanter (1972), are, as we saw in Chapter 4, almost all very young communes. They are largely preinstitutional, expressing their commitment mechanisms through admission procedures (discussed in Chapter 3) and through ritual. It is not feasible to study the consequences of the commitment mechanisms for stability in these communes. However, Gardner (1978) provides an interesting study of thirteen contemporary communes, the scope of which is intermediate between ours and Kanter's. Gardner studied thirteen American communes, all rural and located west of the Continental Divide, founded between 1965 and 1969, and which he visited once in 1970 and again in 1973.

Gardner's data* show that, in the very small oldest cohort, of communes that had been in existence for three or more years at the time of his first wave ($N = 2$ communes), there is a consistent positive association between survival of the commune and each of the five commitment mechanisms† associated with investment of self. In the midaged two-year-old cohort ($N = 4$), these associations are reduced to zero or near zero, two even becoming slightly negative. In the youngest cohort, of one-year-old communes ($N = 6$), the association of each

---

*Gardner's analysis does not distinguish among cohorts and is therefore not directly useful to us. However, his presentation provides the necessary data for the reanalysis that we have reported here. One of his thirteen communes was dropped from the analysis for lack of a comparison group.

†The association of resource investment, Kanter's sixth commitment mechanism, with survival remains about the same, insignificantly positive in all three cohorts.

of the (self-investment) commitment mechanisms with survival is even further reduced, becoming on balance a negative association.

These findings are remarkable because they help to bridge the gap between the early stage of commune life studied in this volume and the mature stage studied by Kanter. Gardner gives us a glimpse of the intermediate period during which the commitment mechanisms are beginning to replace charismatic relational patterns as the bulwarks of commune stability. His data shed additional light on a curious finding that we discussed in Chapter 4: that religious communes are actually less stable than nonreligious communes in the first two years of life, the well known historical pattern of religious communes' greater stability only asserting itself in the third year. Most of Gardner's communes are nonreligious and would be classified countercultural by our definition. However, his demonstration of the increasing importance of commitment mechanisms for survival as communes get older probably is due to the same factors that account for the increasing importance of religion as communes get older. In both instances, ineffectiveness in the early years is a result of premature reliance on symbolic institutional structure before the necessary groundwork of identification and relational ordering has taken place.

Even during the earliest period of communitarian life, however, the charismatic leader cannot take personal responsibility for the entire system of social control, although he or she must remain its ultimate arbiter. In all communes studied, some rudimentary system, at the very least, of rituals and sanctions was practiced. It is in this system that the process of charismatic routinization will begin if it begins at all.

Rituals and Sanctions

When we examine the frequency with which collective rituals are practiced in communal life, it can be seen that, in this respect at least, not much has changed since the nineteenth century. Meditation, prayer, and mutual criticism are still the most common practices, with meditation the only one engaged in by a majority of the communes. Rituals such as drug ingestion and group sex, which have been stereotypically associated with the contemporary commune movement, on the other hand, rank much further down on the list (Table 6-10).

Ritual can work only in a context of charismatic renewal. Turner (1969) argued that a society based on such renewal was in inherent danger owing to the sheer intensity of the communion experience. But communion is dangerous not so much because of its intensity as because the boundaries of the self become permeable during communion, and thus preference orderings can be more easily changed through charismatic influence. We will discuss this important and sometimes fateful matter in more detail in Chapter 8.

Sanctions play a complementary role to rituals in the routinization of charisma. Rituals embody the sacred and symbolic dimensions of the resolution of

TABLE 6–10. Frequency of Commitment-inducing Rituals in Communal Life

Collective Rituals[1]	Proportion of Communes Engaging in the Ritual	
	Urban (N = 60)	Rural (N = 60)
Meditation (63)	27%	79%
Prayer (36)	18	42
Mutual criticism (32)	18	34
Yoga (31)	12	40
Shared silence (30)	17	33
Drug ingestion (23)	13	25
Singing (19)	22	10
Group readings (19)	12	7
Chanting mantras (16)	5	22
Dancing (13)	7	15
Group confession (12)	7	13
Group sex (8)	2	12
Contact with spirits (7)	10	1
Speaking in tongues (6)	3	7

[1] Total engaging is in parentheses.

crises. Sanctions embody the mundane and practical dimensions. Rituals may be viewed as standard operating procedures to regulate the investment of self, sanctions as standard operating procedures to regulate the withdrawal of self from the collectivity.

Sanctions do not play a major role among the social control mechanisms of the communes in our sample (see Table 6-11). Only a minority ever use the threat of expulsion for example. Social control is attained, as might be expected in the early stages, primarily through the flow of influence through the relational network. In the older communes in the sample, however, there is evidence of the greater importance of formal sanctions. Typically, the turning point in a commune's career, with regard to this issue, occurs when consensus is reached that an intolerable member must be expelled. How communes cope with this particular crisis often determines the future path that they will take in the routinization of charisma.

Rituals and sanctions eventually become blended into a coherent system of social control via the commitment mechanisms. In many of the more successful historical communes (e.g., Harmony, Oneida), the system of social control is fully developed during the charismatic stage and is ready to be utilized if and when the charismatic leadership structure dissolves.

Within the period of our study, the commitment mechanisms were not important determinants of commune stability. As we saw in discussing the individual level in Chapter 3, none of the questions tapping sense of commitment to the commune served as good predictors of the likelihood that the person would stay. Moreover, the mean commitment generated by any commune

TABLE 6–11. Communal Methods of Social Control

	% Ever Using the Method (N = 120)
Discussion of the problem by the people involved	88%
Discussion of the problem at a group meeting	76
Mutual criticism	75
Expulsion or the threat of expulsion	44
Removal from a position/office held in the commune	40
Deciding the outcome of the issue by a tribunal of the membership	31
Therapeutic counseling	24
Temporary exile	4
Exclusion from certain communal activities	4
Withdrawal of membership privileges	1

on any of these items does not differentiate between surviving and nonsurviving communes. It is only after about four or five years of a commune's life that such things become important.

Noncharismatic Commitment

The autonomy reducing function of charisma has been emphasized in this chapter, but it should not be thought that all communal commitment is charismatically generated. Many communes exist for long periods of time on spontaneously generated commitment. This is feasible especially in cases where the commune is small, simple, and made up of people who knew each other well prior to living communally. Charisma arises in response to consensus lost, but in some communes consensus is never lost. There is, in addition, a class of noncharismatic communes whose members place much greater emphasis on the shared investment of resources than on the investment of self. Finally, there is a class of communes, of which the Israeli kibbutzim are an example, whose investment of self, although considerable, does not require charismatic underpinning. In this last class of communes, shared danger, a history of shared persecution, and the shared challenge of a pioneering environment provide ample basis for self-investment.*

*An additional factor helping to account for the lack of charismatic potential in the kibbutzim is the strong associational component of these groups fostered by the important role that they play within the Israeli economy. It has often been argued that, in Israel, the land itself, or the people, or the movement are repositories of charisma. But this kind of perspective probably mystifies the concept unnecessarily.

In situations of prosperity and security, however, communes would seem over the long run to have only two viable options for survival. The first involves going through a charismatic stage and beyond to the establishment of a stable system of commitment. In this option, self-investment eventually becomes habitual and is able to happen without any longer needing the charismatic spark. The second option involves the transformation of the commune into an association. Members regain virtually full personal autonomy and the commune becomes a cooperative venture in support of its members' individual self-interests. Many of these latter types last for two or three decades but rarely are they able to produce a second generation.

Conclusions

In this chapter we have explored the implications of the premise that personal autonomy is something that can be assigned to a collectivity, altering the boundaries of the self through the mechanism of identification. This perspective has allowed us both to explain certain anomalies that have persisted regarding the process of charismatic influence and also to explain certain otherwise puzzling empirical regularities about communes, particularly the order in which they surrender various types of individual autonomy over decision making to the group.

The notion of alienation and charisma as reciprocal concepts, both functioning to achieve and maintain consensus in the collective decision-making process, works well for communes. Whether it has any broader applicability, of course, cannot be determined in this book. This or some such formulation is clearly necessary, however, if these widely used concepts are to attain a validity of conception and measurement sufficient for their use in the analysis of social systems.

It seems reasonable to conclude that communes (at least charismatic ones) are not places for autonomous individuals. Members do not act in what is ordinarily thought of as their own self interests because their interests and, indeed, their very selves have become modified as a result of the communitarian experience. But if commune members no longer "look out for number one," is there some alternative mechanism for assuring equity in the distribution of costs and rewards? It is to this question that we turn in the next chapter.

So many of these groups espouse egalitarianism, but find that they need some degree of authority. The most common solution is charisma: the group either begins with a leader with strong, benevolent qualities, or it soon finds one.

John Bennett

CHAPTER 7

The Problem
of Inequality

Is the presence of charisma compatible with the norm of egalitarianism? Part of the legitimating myth of charisma is that it assures equality among the leader's followers. If an individual is going to surrender a portion of his autonomy, he or she will want at the very least to be very sure that an equivalent commitment is required from each of the others. An individual may be prepared to accept the superiority of a single charismatic leader, but it usually will not follow that he or she be prepared to subordinate himself to other of the charismatic leader's followers. However, the fact is that most communes, at least in their early years, value equality but continue to perpetuate hierarchy and privilege. Charismatic authority in communes does not level; it propagates inequality.

This chapter concerns the largely unsuccessful communitarian efforts to suppress, limit, or at least legitimate the emergence of status differentiation into communitarian social structure. The efforts, themselves, involve a kind of juggling act. Through mechanisms for the investment of self in the collectivity and mechanisms for the perpetuation of charismatic authority, attempts are made to support the social order while avoiding hierarchy. But such a goal can be achieved, if at all, only in dynamic equilibrium. Inequalities always emerge

TABLE 7-1.   Mean Number of Recognizable Strata within Commune
by Ideological Type

	Consciousness Oriented	Action Oriented
Spiritual	3.7 (Eastern)	2.6 (Christian)
Self	2.0 (Psychological)	5.3 (Rehabilitational)
Community	1.6 (Cooperative)	1.5 (Family)
Society	1.6 (Countercultural)	1.6 (Political)

and eventually crystallize into stable structures. Rituals can purge these structures at regular intervals, but the guardianship of these rituals then often becomes a new source of inequality.

In most groups, it was informal power distinctions and male/female status distinction that proved most difficult to eradicate. Religious communes attempt to deal with these problems by allowing distinction but maintaining equality in the domain of the sacred alongside inequality in the profane. Rehabilitational communes do the same, using the domains of the healthy and the sick. Charismatic communes of any ideological type sometimes try to accomplish the same thing by distinguishing between the charismatic and the ordinary. But communes with noncharismatic secular ideologies (i.e., those that have only one sphere of valuation) find themselves constantly battling in vain against the encroachments of new sources of stratification.

None of the communes in our sample were fully able to eradicate hierarchical stratification. Among the Eastern religious and rehabilitational groups, there was, to the contrary, a deliberate proliferation of such strata (Table 7-1). Such communes based their social systems upon a strategy of high social mobility among minutely differentiated status positions. Such systems, when continually legitimated, can provide their memberships with a sense of universal upward mobility as a functional equivalent to equality.

Charismatic Authority

Let us begin our investigation by examining, not these highly differentiated communes, but a subgroup of communes that attempt to dispense with leadership and authority altogether. These are the anarchistic communes. They give us the opportunity to observe the entire range of hierarchy formation from 0 to 100 percent. The fact that many communes change quickly and dramatically from absolute anarchism to absolute authoritarianism reflects some of the pressures that are peculiar to communitarian life. The needs to manifest an ideology and to cope with a relational structure potentially charged with love create a different set of problems for communes than those faced by other collectivities.

In the evolution from no authority to total authority, one may observe many paths and as many types of charismatic leaders. What has often been treated as a monolithic phenomenon actually takes on a variety of forms. An understanding of these forms is important both to appreciate the full potential scope of charisma and to avoid confusing it with other related phenomena.

The clearest way to identify the function of authority in communal life is to look at those groups that place themselves in the most uncompromising opposition to authority. If such communes come to need charismatic leaders, it is most likely for reasons intrinsic to the nature of communitarianism itself. It is, therefore, to a discussion of the anarchist commune subsample that we now turn.

From Anarchism to Authoritarianism

Political anarchism is a philosophy that refers to the relationships between the individual and the state. In contradistinction, communitarian anarchism is usually defined in terms of interpersonal relationships. The commune is a primarily non-economic group without an internal locus of sovereignty. The only reliable basis of power is interpersonal.

Some light can be shed on the need for authority structures by examining the development of groups that attempt to dispense with these structures entirely. Twenty-five of the communes in our sample (21 percent), most of them rural, have attempted to govern themselves anarchistically (see Table 7-2). Many have soon discovered that community requires obligation and have experimented with limited authority structures in an attempt to preserve individual freedom while allowing the commune to continue to exist.

In terms of our classification of ideological types, it is only in the secular consciousness-oriented ideological types (countercultural, cooperative, and psychological) that full-blown experiments with anarchistic communitarianism have been found (Table 7-3). Among these, the proportion increases as the locus of communal attention moves outward. Curiously, none of the political communes with anarchist programs were attempting to order their own lives anarchistically at the time of the study. Many of them had in the past, however,

TABLE 7–2. Delegation of Decision-making Responsibility by Rural-Urban Location

Type of Decision-Making Process	Rural		Urban		Total	
	Number	% of Total	Number	% of Total	Number	% of Total
Extracommunal	0	0%	4	7%	4	3%
Monarchial	0	0	11	18	11	9
Exec. committee	7	12	2	3	9	7
Democratic	2	3	5	8	7	6
Consensual deliberate	22	37	27	45	49	41
Consensual casual	7	12	8	14	15	13
Contract anarchistic	11	18	2	3	13	11
Pure anarchism	11	18	1	2	12	10
Total	60	100%	60	100%	120	100%

TABLE 7–3. Anarchist Organization by Ideological Type[1]

% of Communes with Anarchist Pattern of Organization

	Consciousness Oriented	Action Oriented
Spiritual	0% (Eastern, $N = 22$)	0% (Christian, $N = 15$)
Self	33% (Psychological, $N = 9$)	0% (Rehabilitational, $N = 4$)
Community	44% (Cooperative, $N = 16$)	0% (Family, $N = 11$)
Society	55% (Countercultural, $N = 29$)	0% (Political, $N = 14$)

[1] $N = 120$.

and their current avoidance of complete anarchism seemed to be less hypocrisy than a result of taking anarchism very seriously. These groups took anarchism seriously enough to recognize its practical shortcomings in their own communes and to take steps to compromise with these shortcomings or to work out ways of circumventing them.

Freedom is a much more central value in the contemporary anarchistic commune than in the traditional utopian community. Communes cherish the joy of brotherhood but do not focus their lives on it completely. This emphasis on freedom often creates unusual norms of organization. Members come and go as they choose with little or no rancor or guilt. Nobody thinks of asking anybody else to make a permanent commitment to the life. With regard to work, the choice of hours and tasks is strictly voluntary, as is the pooling of money and resources.

Communitarian anarchism has little to do with the classical anarchism of the nineteenth century. It is a naïve anarchism, a *sui generis* response to specific conditions of contemporary society. It can be defined as the belief that the individual is capable of regulating himself in the absence of any external authority and the belief that there is no such thing as good authority, that authority by definition is subversive.

Early hippie communes started out with no restrictions on behavior. Everyone was allowed to do his or her own thing at all times. It was expected that the gentleness, love, and compassion engendered by mystical drug experiences would prove adequate substitutes for the moral and legal constraints that all other societies had found necessary.

The initial experiences were often encouraging and exhilarating. Many of the previously accepted boundary safeguards of our society were declared unnecessary. For some taboos, generally accepted in our society, their reasons for being were not discernible in terms of the immediate negative consequences of breaking them. Pooling all money and sharing one another sexually are examples of such attempts at boundary erasing. After a while, however, the strains inherent in such situations began to reassert themselves. Work slowed down; jealousies arose; people started spending more and more time away from the commune. As the commune movement grew older, it began to give its attention to complex tasks such as starting schools, expanding housing facilities, or developing business enterprises. Increased strain, on the one hand, and more complex tasks, on the other, eventually drove most communes to abandon anarchism in favor of some more restricted alternative.

There can sometimes be an inverse relationship between anarchism and egalitarianism. In Hobbithole, for instance, the desire for anarchism was concentrated among those individuals with greater personal resources, and the antianarchistic or democratic party was popular among those with fewer resources who wanted the communal structure to distribute goods, services, and status equally.

Anarchism can become a means of exploitation. Anarchy without mutual concern favors the tyranny of the strong over the weak and the tyranny of the least committed over the most committed. In one commune the strong and competent males lorded it over the weaker males and the females. Life was not very pleasant without these men around to fix things, eject unwanted visitors, gather food, and score dope. In the early days, and during the occasional recurrent periods of communion, they performed these services freely and graciously. But during times of discord one became aware of the implicit threat that, if things did not go in a way that was pleasing to these members, they might withdraw from active participation in the commune, or even leave.

It is significant that the men in this group were generally anarchists, whereas the women were democrats. The women, especially those with children, were more committed to the commune and less free to leave it. They were more willing to abide by the will of the majority, even if they were opposed to it, as long as some common decisions could be made. The men, freer to leave when things got bad, were less willing to bind themselves in this way. There is a type of Gresham's law that operates in anarchist communes, whereby the less committed gradually drive out the more committed, while the stronger establish power over the weak.

Stages in the Surrender of Autonomy

Most of the communes in our sample began with or rapidly evolved structures of authority. As we saw in Chapter 6, the formal authority structures of the communes in the sample are nested along a unidimensional continuum. This finding is interesting because it suggests an underlying functional dependence relation among the spheres of communal authority (see Table 6-8).

The most common authority positions in communes are those of *exemplars*, individuals who are thought to embody communal values to an unusually high degree. The actions of the exemplars are watched by the other commune members to remind themselves of that fragile consensus with respect to values upon which the commune is based.

Communes that do not recognize a centralized authority in the embodiment of values will not recognize centralized authority for any other sphere of activity. A subset of those communes in which exemplary authority is centralized also centralizes authority over long-term commune policy decisions. A subset of those groups recognize centralized authority in the executive sphere, and so on, down to the smallest subset—those for whom there are no decisions for which authority is not centralized.

Each scale type may be thought of as representing a different level of the social contract. We have looked at the centralization of authority as the sacrifice of autonomy. The order of the scale casts an interesting light on the process of social contract evolution, at least in communes. People are willing to part most easily with moral authority, next with authority over the setting of long-range goals, and next with executive authority. Much harder for them to surrender is their judicial authority; and authority over the personal decision-making process itself is hardest of all to alienate from oneself. There is also, however, an increasing seductiveness, for some, to these levels of autonomy surrender.

Communes do not, in general, require extensive formal organization of authority, however, much as they may choose to centralize it in one or a few hands. The only complex organizational patterns encountered in the commune sample were at the federation level. Within the household itself, one or a few formal offices were almost always sufficient. Even the larger and more complex communes such as the kibbutzim and the Hutterian colonies generally manage to get along with authority structures a good deal less complex than those of villages or business organizations of comparable size.

The Varieties of Charismatic Leadership

Table 7-4 shows the frequency with which urban commune members identify themselves with formal offices. All the open-ended responses to this question were easily identified with only five official functions. Twenty-seven of the twenty-nine people identified by the study as in-resident leaders identified themselves as such. Twenty-two of these self-identified leaders were male (82 percent) and only five were female.

Most commune leaders are charismatic leaders. Only a third of the urban and rural leaders identified could be classified as noncharismatic. These administrative leaders were most often the resident lieutenants of absentee charismatic leaders. Charismatic leadership is not exclusively associated with any particular ideological type within our sample. We find, of course, the greatest proportion of charismatic leaders associated with the religious communes. However, charismatic leaders are also to be found in political, therapeutic, countercultural, family, and rehabilitational groups in the sample.

An important distinction is to be made between absentee charismatic leaders and charismatic leaders in residence. Absentee charismatic leaders do not belong to the communal household itself. Through the act of collective discipleship to an absentee charismatic leader, a commune may be able to achieve a sense of identification with ideological goals beyond the scope of the commune itself. Absentee charismatics thus provide a focus for the overcoming of alienation that resident charismatics might find hard to match. However, problems of maintaining social control arise for the absentee charismatic that the resident charismatic is often able to solve merely by his presence.

Direct contact between each individual and the absentee charismatic leader on certain occasions is extremely inportant. Even communes that are members of federations so large that individuals may no longer actually expect to meet the charismatic leader take pains to keep alive stories of spontaneous visits by the leader to communal households very much like their own and, thus, the possibility that the grace of such a visitation may descend upon themselves. It is common to find an authority structure in which an external charismatic leader shares authority with a resident lieutenant, who derives his authority from the absentee leader and represents him within the household.

Two aspects of communal leadership are particularly deserving of attention. One is the unusually high frequency of charismatic leadership found in communal groups. Second is the high concentration of authority in leaders and the

TABLE 7-4.   Official Positions Held by Commune Members According to Self-reports at Time 1 (urban communes only)

Commune leader	27[a]
Financial secretary	26
House mother	15
Manager of communal business	9
Counselor	4

[a]Not all these could be considered charismatic leaders. In fact, twenty of them were classified as the resident lieutenants of absentee charismatic leaders. Two generally acknowledged charismatic leaders, on the other hand, did not designate themselves as holding any official commune position. Absentee charismatic leaders, of course, by definition, did not respond to the questionnaire.

correspondingly high degree of voluntary compliance among followers in communes that began with anarchistic and/or egalitarian ideologies.

Although it is possible to find charismatic leaders in the political, psychological, and countercultural communes, most communal charismatic leaders are found among the religious. Even political charismatics have a tendency to develop a type of religious influence over time. It may be that charismatic influence is not only correlated with, but also promotes, a high level of emotional cathexis. Such cathexis requires expression, which can be achieved through a shared spiritual experience of ego transcendence, through an increase in interpersonal (and hence often sexual) intimacy among the members, or through a turning of hostility against the charismatic leader and his or her removal from office.

The Special Case of Gurucracy

Our discussion of communitarian charisma would be incomplete without mention of the charismatic leaders who preside not over communal households, but over entire communal movements. These are people, often national celebrities such as the Reverend Moon, for whom investment of self does not require physical proximity. It is interesting, therefore, in light of our theory, to ask in what ways they differ from the charismatic leaders of primary group households. We have already seen one important respect in which they differ—in Chapter 4. Only charismatic leaders in residence suppress the otherwise strong relationship between emotional cathexis and communal instability. They do not, however, seem to differ in the degree of commitment that they evoke or in the ordering in which their followers surrender the various levels of authority to them. It would appear then that the proximity of the charismatic leader affects only the way in which the followers treat each other, not the extent to which they identify with the commune.

There are two perspectives to be examined with regard to the gurucrats. One is their absence from the specific communes that they rule and the organizational implications of this absence in terms of hierarchy, communication, and intercommunal cooperation. The other is the cosmopolitan outlook of the gurucrats, an outlook that quite often views the communal household itself merely as a means to grander ends. Let us look at each of these perspectives in turn.

The authority of the typical charismatic leader is more fully internalized within the commune members in an absentee than in a resident charismatic commune. Before joining the individual has already made a decision to devote his or her life to the charismatic leader and to submit fully to leadership. Therefore, when doubts or questions arise, other members have a basis from which to counsel these recalcitrant members. In all such absentee charismatic communes in our sample, communications did not flow directly to the commune members from the charismatic leader but followed a hierarchical ordering that extended beyond the household.

From a somewhat different perspective, borrowing from Merton (1959), we distinguish between *cosmopolitan* charismatic leaders and *local* charismatic leaders. The former operate at least in potential, on a scale far beyond commune boundaries. Many readers will tend to think of them as the only "real" charismatic leaders. Communal households, to such leaders, are often merely stepping stones to the achievement of greater things, particularly the heading up of large national or even worldwide social movements that may be federations of many hundreds or even thousands of communal households or may even eventually abandon the early communitarian stage of their development in favor of an organizational form more conducive to mass recruitment and conversion. This latter model can be applied to some of the major churches of our time, including, in some respects, the Roman Catholic church.

Killian's description of the charismatic leader is quite applicable to the cosmopolitan variant (1964, p. 441):

> He tends to be bold, even impulsive, given to the dramatic gesture and the stirring appeal to emotions. He is both prophet and agitator. He states the movement's values in absolute terms, often through slogans. ... He simplifies the issues, resolving the ambivalence which potential followers may feel. ... For the confused and dissatisfied, leaders of social movements explain the "real" basis of the struggle and show the way out. For the person who already knows the source of his problems, the leader who professes the same convictions *confirms their validity.* ... *With his confidence in the effectiveness of the solution which he advances, the charismatic leader allays the doubts of his potential followers as to whether anything can be done.* ... As loyalty to the charismatic leader grows, so also does confidence in him and in the movement, for it is characteristic of him that he is beyond ordinary criticism. [emphasis added]

The local charismatic is a different species in a number of important respects. It is not surprising that this variant of the charismatic leader should have been neglected in classical treatments and historical accounts. He or she is not one to shake history through the founding of a large movement based upon a mass following. It would be a mistake, however, to dismiss local charismatics as potential cosmopolitan charismatics that were not able to make it. Charismatic potential is a variable, and lesser concentrations of it are not necessarily the less analytically significant.

There are certain problems that arise for communes only when the charismatic leader is both absent and cosmopolitan. We call such commune movements gurucracies. The gurucracy cannot possibly mobilize commitment in the same way that the resident charismatic household can. The gurucracy inevitably contains many fanatical true believers. The charismatic leader's character traits tend to become exaggerated; he becomes endowed with godlike powers much more than does the resident variety. On the other hand, because the members rarely see their leader, there is less chance of disillusionment.

A related problem is the fostering of an elite in each of the communal households that may or may not itself be charismatic but that derives its power and prestige through its privileged contacts with the leader himself. Inevitably, a great many fateful decisions for the commune end up being made by this elite. They represent a source of power that can be abused.

Reflecting the absence of the single charismatic leader, the power hierarchies of absentee charismatic communes tend to be multiheaded. There is usually no single resident who holds unquestioned dominant position. Such a person would obviously be a threat to the absent leader's authority. This is so even when there is a single resident officer.

The Ubiquity of Power

All the communes studied, regardless of ideology, were found to generate a high degree of consensus in ranking themselves within a hierarchy of interpersonal power. With very few exceptions, the power hierarchies generated were stable over time and acyclic in sociometric space. The majority of the members of each commune were ranked into well-ordered hierarchical clusters by the concatenation of dyadic power bonds. It is interesting to note that this was just as true in ideologically egalitarian communes as in nonegalitarian ones.

The nature of a dyadic power relationship is a good deal less intuitive than is that of a dyadic love relationship. A more formal approach was therefore appropriate. We defined interpersonal power primarily through the use of the following question:

> Even the most equal of relationships sometimes has a power element involved. However insignificant it may be in your relationship with the above named person, which of you do you think hold the greater amount of power in your relationship?

In these terms, we can specify the following theoretical framework:

Definition 1: A *power relationship* is defined as the shared opinions of any two members of the same commune as to which of them holds the greater power in their personal interaction.

Definition 2: A *power configuration* of a commune is the set of power relationships for all possible dyads within that commune.

Definition 3: A *power structure* is a transitive ordering (if one exists) of all the power relationships in a power configuration. (Note that it follows from this that, whereas communes must have power configurations, they need not have power structures.)

Theorem: It can be shown that, for any commune, if a power structure exists, it is unique (i.e., it is mathematically impossible to have two transitive orderings that are not isomorphic).

Proposition 1: All charismatic communes have power structures.

Proposition 2: Most noncharismatic communes have power structures.

Proposition 3: The egalitarianism of a commune's ideology has no significant correlation with the probability that the commune has a power structure.

Definition 4: The clarity of a power structure is the ratio of reciprocated to nonreciprocated claim-deference pairs.

Proposition 4: The clarity of charismatic power structures is significantly greater than is that of noncharismatic communes.

The ubiquity of power, in communes, is clearly indicated by the degree to which transitive power configurations are the rule. Only two groups were found that did not have power structures. One of these had one intransitive bond and the other had two. Figures 6-1 and 7-1 illustrate some typical communal power structures. Communal power structures do not, however, tend to have the semilattice or the tree structure that are characteristic of most formal organizations.

Communal power structures do not appear to be artifacts of sociometric data collection techniques. They have measurable associations with behavior and self-perception. The distribution of chores, for example, shows certain interesting patterns of correlation. Those holding intermediate positions in the hierarchy (both dominated and dominating) are workers. They spend a good deal more time than do any other groups doing traditional homemaking jobs such as cooking, housecleaning, and washing dishes. The pattern is similar when we control for sex. Subordinates (those who are dominated by but not dominating at least one person) do fewer household chores than do any other group except for the leaders (those who dominate but are not dominated) who do the least of all. Leaders, however, work the longest hours at the most distinctively communal jobs such as keeping accounts, conveying the communal ideology, and counseling commune members. We can conclude that informal power structures are correlated with a definite division of labor. In terms of labor alone, leaders, workers, and drones seem to characterize the three levels of power. Moreover, this appears to hold true across all ideological types.

FIGURE 7-1.   Some Typical Communal Network Diagrams Illustrating Interpersonal Power

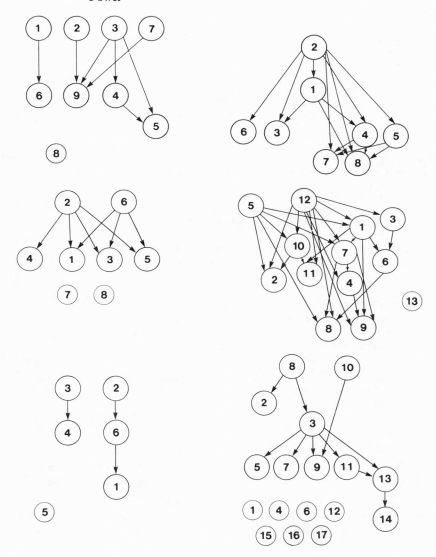

These structural equivalence types distinguish only among kinds of dominance relationships. They do not measure amount of domination. The evidence presented in Table 7-5 shows that the number of other people who dominate one in the interpersonal power hierarchy is associated with low self-esteem, high alienation, and a general feeling of *ressentiment*. These associations hold when ideological type is controlled for.

TABLE 7-5. Correlation of Selected Attitude Scores with Number of People One Is Dominated by in the Commune's Interpersonal Power Hierarchy[1] [2]

Item	Pearson's r
Self-esteem	
I feel that I do not have much to be proud of.	−.17
At times I think that I am no good at all.	−.15
I take a positive attitude toward myself.	.15
No one, with the possible exception of my fellow commune members, is going to care much what happens to me.	−.14
Alienation (standard scales)	
I am skeptical of anything that tries to tell me the right way to live.	.24[a]
Despite what some people say, the lot of the average man is getting worse, not better.	−.31[a]
The fact that this commune functions as well as it does demonstrates that human nature is basically cooperative.	.15
As I view the world in relation to my life, the world completely confuses me.	−.15
With inflation and the control of wages by corporations, there is little possibility that one can control his fate on the economic scene.	−.16
Resentiment	
Some people will be saved and others will not. It is predestined. God knew who would be saved long before we were born.	−.27[a]
There is only one solution to the problems of the world today, and that is Christ.	−.23[a]
The world is basically an evil place.	−.41[a]

[1] A negative correlation means agreement with the item is associated with being dominated by many people.
[2] $N = 272$.
[a] Significant at the .001 level. All others significant at the .01 level.

Being dominant over others shows no such attitudinal pattern. The number of people that one dominates is significantly correlated with two background characteristics, however (being married, being male), and one behavioral trait (time spent doing counseling chores for the commune).

It is interesting to note that, as observed over time, these informal power hierarchies are more stable than are the formal hierarchies that we have been discussing. Formal leadership positions become targets for the accumulated hostilities of communal life and casualties of rapid membership turnover, so that 48 percent of those in formal positions of authority at time 1 (in urban communes) were no longer in these positions one year later. Informal positions of interpersonal dominance, on the other hand are lost at less than half the rate for formal positions (21 percent). Whatever enduring role structure is possessed by communes in the area of power offers more job security through stable network configurations than through the formal hierarchy of offices.

The Elimination of Status

A certain amount of status differentiation is generally assumed to be necessary to maintain any society with some degree of complexity. What amount of status differentiation is necessary to maintain any given society, however, is unknown. Attempts by communist societies to eradicate class and status distinctions have resulted in the emergence of a new class of bureaucratic managers, leaving it unclear as to whether the total amount of social inequality has been reduced or increased.

Equality has been one of the recurrent themes of Western civilization throughout its history. As Norman Cohn has said (1957, p. 195):

> Like the other phantasies which have gone to make up a revolutionary eschatology of Europe, egalitarian and communistic phantasies can be traced back to the ancient world. It was from the Greeks and Romans that medieval Europe inherited the notion of the "state of nature" as a state of affairs in which all men were equal in status and wealth and in which nobody was oppressed or exploited by anyone else; a state of affairs characterized by universal good faith and brotherly love and also sometimes by total community of property and even of spouses.

Every modern revolution has been fought partly to achieve social equality. There have been countless experimental attempts to create small egalitarian communities. Fundamental sources of inequality may perhaps be perceived in the reemergence of status distinctions among small groups of individuals whose aim has been to eradicate such distinctions.

A small community is a primary group in the sense that it contains at least the potentiality of direct personal interaction of each with each. Status inequalities are, therefore, immediately recognizable as avoidance patterns—the archtypical case being the village caste systems in prewar India. Examples of the opposite extreme may be found in some (but not all) American frontier towns (Vogt, 1955, p. 124):

> Although differences in social status exist among the Homesteaders, especially between the "Tobacco Road" fringe and the "acceptable" families in the community, the doctrine of "equality" is firmly held as far as relationships among people within the community are concerned. Everyone is welcome at the dances held in the schoolhouse, where each man is *expected to dance with most if not all of the women present in his own age-grade.* Any family visiting the house of another family at mealtime would be invited to eat. Marriage may take place between any persons of different families in Homestead, and it is believed that each nuclear family within the community should have an equal voice with every other in the management of community affairs. [emphasis added]

The criterion of being expected to dance with every possible partner in one's age grade is as good a definition as any for primary group egalitarianism. Note, however, the allusion to a "Tobacco Road" fringe. This raises the question of whether the egalitarianism of an "in" group always presupposes the exclusion of an "out" group.

Evidence from a block-modeling analysis of the mutual relationships and perceptions of the members of the urban communes indicates that there are pervasive and reasonably stable role avoidance patterns in all of the communes from which such data were collected (Sprague, 1978). The evidence is overwhelming that, from sharing household tasks and child rearing to confiding in and being influenced by, commune members do constantly make distinctions that are consistent across categories and, at least to some degree, translatable into status differentials. As with power, so with every aspect of communal life. As vehemently as commune members deny the existence of differences, the differences nevertheless emerge.

Whether these differences are relevant to the commune members themselves is another matter upon which the evidence is less clear. Certainly there is no general pattern of attitudinal distress signals associated with status exclusion such as we saw earlier associated with power. And those being avoided do not have significantly lower self-esteem than the others. Even the religious and rehabilitational groups, which deliberately seek to impose prestige hierarchies, are at pains to assure that place in these hierarchies does not correlate with degree of integration into the relational networks.

It is often argued that fundamental changes in the role structure of human society are possible but not within a single generation (Bennett, 1975, p. 85). Such changes require not only change in the conscious motivations of adults but a more profound change in the way in which children are socialized. Three generations are the minimum for a true test. The Hutterians become an interesting test case because they have had not three, but over twenty generations in which to accomplish their goals. Still, they find that the necessity for constant struggle has not diminished (Bennett, 1967, pp. 244ff.):

> Hutterites take enormous pains to train their children and themselves in egalitarian patterns and in the repression of self-seeking and other individuating tendencies. Likewise they seek to repress all destructive forms of social cleavage. We must conclude then that in addition to learning something about social uniformity in communalism the Hutterite also learns something about its opposite.

The Hutterians are an example of a commune that has succeeded economically while at the same time successfully deemphasizing individual competition and the need for individual achievement (Bennett, 1967, p. 160):

> The Hutterites seem to feel little need to achieve, but they certainly are given strong incentives to do well for the good of the group. Moreover, they are trained in self-mastery; they are taught to control their impulses and

forego their desires for the good of all. The result is almost a caricature of the classic Weberian type of the Protestant businessman who, ideologically prevented from spending money on his pleasures, reinvests it in his business.

The Hutterian case illustrates the fact that the very strong incentives to produce and, if not to "achieve," at least to perform well can arise in a social system that negates individualism.

Bennett goes on, however, to point out that an infrastructure of covert attitudes concerning man's intrinsic selfishness and individualism coexists in the Hutterian colonies with an official ideological stance of absolute egalitarianism. Quite interestingly he notes that during the early Moravian period of Hutterian history the commune maintained a much larger number of trades, occupations, and professions among its members than it does now, "without any apparent serious tendency towards individual aspirations that posed a threat to communal solidarity. . . . There is reason to believe that the fear of the tendency [toward individualism] may be stronger today" (Bennett, 1967, p. 244). If this is so, it fits what we many times observed among the communes in our own sample: an initial period of success in overcoming the desire for individual status and power, followed by a reversion to the previous state of individualism.

What are some of the bases for the reemergence of status within the commune? Communitarians seem comparatively successful in eradicating status based upon background (or socioeconomic status). More serious and more difficult to eliminate are distinctions based upon seniority, age, skill, and personal influence in decision making. The seniority question has occasioned much debate within communes. The absence of real traditions in most contemporary communes places a premium on the value of the accumulated experiences of those who have been members for a longer time than most. It requires conscious effort on the part of all to avoid making the appreciation of such embodiment of heritage a source of prestige.

Distribution of Income

Primary among the specific role responsibilities of members in all communes except the most anarchistic are those relating to the sharing of work and financial responsibilities. The economic responsibilities of each commune member range from minimal chores related to daily living to lifelong vocations related to an entire way of life. The distribution of expectations along this continuum is determined largely by the extent to which ideology dominates the life of the commune.

Except for extreme anarchistic groups, all communes expect some sharing in the household chores. The extent of work, money and personal investment varies from household to household, depending largely on ideology. Most communes in our urban sample decide upon a certain amount of money to be contributed by everyone. Some negotiate the amount to be contributed depending upon income, ranging from an extreme form of the norm "from each according to his ability and to each according to his need" to a token readjustment of shares based on an attempt to redistribute grossly unequal incomes (Table 7-6).

Some communes get all their income from communal businesses. Members are either paid salaries or given minimal allowances. In the latter case, most purchases of goods and services are done for the entire group by the entire group. This pattern is also found in communes in which members turn over all their income from outside jobs to the household. In communes linked to larger national organizations, a substantial portion of this money may be sent to the national organization. In this situation economic inequalities are cancelled out not only among members of the same commune but among different communes of the same communal federation. However, sizable proportions of the revenues sent to the larger organization are often not redistributed but retained for the larger organization's work of a religious or political nature.

In rural communes we find the same four patterns, but the majority of groups fall into the category of communal business. Usually these businesses are agricultural or horticultural. The most common sources of income in urban communes are salaried jobs held by communal members. Rural communes obtain their income, however, mainly through communal business enterprises or through doles and donations. A certain portion of groups in both categories, however, are supported by one or a few people either living in the commune or in some cases not (Table 7-6).

There is, of course, little motivation for striving in these businesses, especially in communes that have accepted the ideological desirability of a low material standard of living. In this many of them are similar to the nineteenth-century Shakers of whom Nordhoff reported:

> Shakers do not toil severely. They are not in haste to be rich; and they have found that for their support, economically as they live, it is not necessary to make labor painful. Many hands make light work; and where all are interested alike, they hold that labor may be made and is made a pleasure.

As a Shaker spokesman said, "Only the simple labors and manners of a farming people can hold a community together. Wherever we have departed from this rule to go into manufacturing, we have blundered" (Nordhoff, 1875, pp. 141ff., 161).

Economic communism takes two forms in our sample: income redistribution or the investment of the incomes of the members in collectively owned goods or property (with, of course, some correlation between the two). Only a minority of communes practice a total redistribution of incomes. As Table 7-6 indicates, total or substantial redistribution is more prevalent among rural than among urban communes. It is not hard to explain this difference. Rural communal living requires a great deal more cooperation among all members in survival activities than does urban communal living. The members are more

TABLE 7-6. Communitarian Economic Indicators

	Urban		Rural	
	Number	% of Total	Number	% of Total
Distribution of commune income				
Partial income contribution				
Equal shares from individuals	30	50%	7	12%
Unequal shares from individuals	12	20	24	40
Total contribution of individual				
incomes to the group	9	15	10	17
Communal business, no personal				
income	8	15	19	31
Source of communal income				
Communal business	8	14	19	31
Cooperative or partner business	0	0	2	3
Patron or agency	3	5	8	14
Commune-related jobs	1	2	2	3
Regular jobs	42	71	8	14
Doles and donations	5	8	21	35
Basis of economic decision making				
Total communism	14	24	19	31
Substantial communism	10	17	24	40
Minimal communism	27	46	13	22
No communism	8	13	4	7
Total	59	100%	60	100%

dependent upon the commune for support. It is less easy to justify income differences, therefore, in rural settings. Furthermore, far fewer people in rural communes than in urban areas are employed in jobs outside the commune. Therefore, a much higher share of the income to rural communes does not even pass through the hands of individual members before going into the communal treasury.

Political communes and Christian communes practice complete or substantial communism the most frequently, and psychological communes practice it the least. As we saw in Chapter 4, communism of economic life appeared neither to enhance nor impede the commune's chances of survival. In contemporary American society, especially, communal ownership of property does not interfere with the freedom of individual members to withdraw. Neither does it seem a major obstacle preventing people from joining. Communism thus seems more of a way of expressing fundamental values than an economic strategy among contemporary communes. Where the members' values are well expressed by a communistic economic system, there seems to be no particular difficulty in sustaining one.

The possession of individual wealth can be an important factor in determining the degree of subordination of the individual to the commune. When commune members have the opportunity to accumulate capital before joining, and when ideology permits retention of individual bank accounts, the individual is less dependent upon the commune. He or she always retains the option of moving out.

Religious communes, psychological communes, and many political communes justify extensive income sharing ideologically:

> Usually what happens is that everybody tells me what they are making, what their takehome pay is . . . and if someone is doing extra work, like working overtime, that doesn't count. Like my child support is subtracted from my salary, so in other words it is kind of like your takehome. . . . So then—well, Peter doesn't have a salary, so Peter is just given a certain amount of rent . . . a minimum amount . . . some fixed amount that people think is all right. Then what I do is sort of proportion out—like this person makes twice as much as this—and sort of get shares. Then I divide the rent by those shares and proportion it. So I try to proportion it approximately by the various ratios of incomes. Then I read those numbers off, and I say we can make it if we pay this kind of money. Then people say, "I can pay more than that" so then we raise the amount, or "I think that so and so is paying too much" so we lower theirs . . . so we sort of do that until it's arbitrated. . . . We do that whenever situations change. . . . Food is also proportioned, but not as strict as the money.

Other communes, in contrast, may request equal amounts from all members regardless of what price their work commands on the market or the amount of space they occupy in the community. In some extreme cases we find communes that share nothing collectively. For example, in Driftwood, even spices and other kitchen staples are owned individually.

Status Based on Physical Strength

The relationship of power to status within a commune should involve a discussion of force and force threat. Because power relationships in many groups are known to be established in a stable manner on the basis of past instances of force and threat of force, we may not, even in the extended period of field observation, have observed the instances of violent or threatening interaction that may have created a dominance hierarchy. We can, however, map the existing power hierarchy and changes in the power hierarchy, and we can attempt to explain changes of power through examination of the processes of agonistic interaction. Under this rubric we list three overt and four subtle types of interaction. Overt agonistic interaction may consist of (1) aggression, (2) fleeing, or (3) territorial defense. The subtle forms of agonistic interaction may consist of (1) deference, (2) distancing, (3) psychic withdrawal, and (4) status gestures.

Interactions involving force and threat of force are best studied using techniques of direct observation. Because such interactions disturb the cathectic equilibrium, respondents are generally unwilling to recall them during interviews. If they are recalled, it is often impossible for the respondent to separate the event itself from all subsequent interpersonal and communal attempts at reconciliation.

Field observations in rural and urban communes revealed many instances of physical fights. Although no exact tally was kept, a reasonable estimate would seem to be that at least 75 percent of the communes in the study had at least one such fight during the time of the first-wave observation and about 20 percent had them fairly frequently. Contrary to expectation, in few communes were there explicit norms against settling disputes by the use of physical violence.

Although sadism and overt bullying were condemned in all the communes in the sample, the use of force was not especially frowned upon as a means of resolving disputes. Particularly in anarchist communes, the resultant power inequalities were often defended as being more natural, and hence less repressive, than those stemming from institutionalized status differences. This important qualification must be added, however: almost all these communes reserved the right to sit in judgment over the legitimacy of the dispute that resulted in the violence. Sheer coercive physical domination of one person by another was never tolerated. But force and force threat often became salient in cases when the formal exercise of authority was not legitimate. As the commune sat in judgment of such an event, much more attention was given to the reasonableness of the grievances involved and the authenticity of the emotional responses to these grievances than to the appropriateness of the use of physical force to settle the dispute.

Violent actions not involving the use of force against persons were sometimes even more favored. An interesting instance of this type of force, illustrating the subtleties of communal power, occurred in Riverside commune. A woman was having a quiet day working in the kitchen. A man was doing some carpentry work outside the house. The man had a record player near his workplace, with an electrical cord running into the house. He was playing some loud music. The woman came out of the house and turned the volume down by about half. The man said nothing as the woman returned to the house but, after a while, he returned the record player to its original volume. After another while, the woman came out again and turned down the volume, but not by as much as she had the first time. She went back into the house. The man waited for a while and then turned the record player back up to its original volume. The woman then came out with a kitchen knife, cut the electrical cord, and then went back into the house. After a long while, the man repaired the cord and turned the record player back on, but at the volume to which the woman had first adjusted it. Not a word was said during this interchange (nor, as far as we know, after it) by either of the two parties involved or by any of the several onlookers. It was obvious, however, that all were quite pleased both by the nature of the interactions and by the outcome. It seemed to corroborate their ideological belief that formal authority structures can be dispensed with in communes.

Division of Labor

In communes that practice a certain degree of economic redistribution, a structure of dependency may arise in which members who do not have independent sources of income or jobs may provide compensatory services directly to the other commune members or engage in "productive" commune projects to further ideological goals. Thus there may come to be people in charge of what is generally called housework, that is cooking, cleaning, and caring for children. The interpretation given to this structural division of labor generally derives from the ideological disposition of the group. For example, Nova Vita, a therapeutic community, and Love from Above, a spiritual community, both have extensive redistribution systems that exist entirely independently of the productive sphere. The amount of income received or goods enjoyed by an individual commune member has no relationship at all to the amount of money that any one member brings in. Although the two communes are similar in this respect, their interpretations of this economic redistribution make them totally opposed. Members of Nova Vita see the distribution of wealth and the division of labor as a therapeutic device, and it directs all economic behavior accordingly. Love from Above, on the other hand, sees the process as inconsequential to the individual but significant to the goals of the community as a whole. In the latter, economic production and the rendering of support services are both seen primarily from the point of view of the larger spiritual work that they make possible.

Such division of labor that allows the emergence of nonproductive persons in the commune is obviously correlated with commune size. The larger the household, the more extensive the possible division of labor; thus, the larger the household, the more likely a formal structure will be found and the greater the degree of interdependence within this structure. Small communes, on the other hand, tend to rotate work—everyone sharing tasks of income acquisition and household maintenance.

An important aspect of the communal division of labor is the organization of housework. Table 7-7 is a facsimile of a weekly labor schedule used by an ongoing urban commune. Labor credits are assigned to jobs according to principles of equity and supply and demand. Each person is responsible for earning a certain number of labor credits per week (Skinner, 1948). Although this schedule may be a bit more formal than that used in the typical urban commune, it gives a good general impression of the tasks that must be attended to in such a household.

Table 7-8 shows the mean number of hours per week actually spent in various household jobs during the week immediately prior to our first-wave field work. There is no strong pattern of change in the division of labor as one accumulates seniority or as the commune itself gets older. The distinctive pattern of the Eastern religious communes with regard to work should be noted. The most enduring pattern of division of labor is by sex, as we will see in Table 7-10. Communes do better at eliminating other forms of chore inequality than they do with those based upon sex distinctions. In part B of Table 7-8, it can be noted that the variance in time spent doing household chores is generally at a minimum among the recently founded communes and increases with increasing commune duration. This trend holds as well for specific intracommune variances. As in the Israeli kibbutzim, the norm of chore egalitarianism erodes with time.

Many communes do not specify the nature of all simple household tasks in great detail. The commune from which the list shown in Table 7-7 was taken was one with a membership turnover greater than 50 percent per year. Communes with less turnover need not specify job descriptions in such detail because the chores that need to be done are known to all as part of the collective traditions of the commune. Table 7-9 shows the frequency with which patterns of chore organization are found.

Chores, of course, are a major source of conflict within communes. A frequently heard bit of communal wisdom holds that the kitchen is a primary source of all commune disputes. This has been reported also by Rosabeth Kanter and Bennett Berger in various of their independent studies and has been reported as well in connection with the communes in the nineteenth century.

The following quote from an interview is a typical example of such a problem in a semianarchistic commune in which people are expected to do some chores but are never required to do any specific jobs:

> The only problem was between Linda and Joe and Bill because Joe and Bill would go out every morning and leave the dishes in the sink and Linda would end up doing them because she was making her daughter's lunch and there got to be real fights about this. Of course, Joe and Bill could have done their dishes and there wouldn't have been any beef or, it seems to me, Linda shouldn't have gotten that upset about it. But if she had to do them I can see why she got upset. She got really sick of it. She told them a number of times and they still wouldn't do them. Bill, on the other hand, always liked things really neat and always seemed to have a broom in his hand sweeping all around. I didn't even see the dirt. He might sweep in places that I didn't even notice were dirty. He never said anything about it to me so I don't know whether it bothered him or not that I didn't do more around the house.

Most communes have not succeeded in solving the dilemma of reconciling individual freedom and spontaneity with status equality. Role differences among the members of a given commune—that is, workers versus people who stay at home, men versus women, parents versus nonparents, long-term versus short-term members—tend to create status inequities, regardless of egalitarianism and regardless of ideological type.

TABLE 7-7. Labor Schedule for the Week

Job	Credit	Person	Description
Cook	3	M T W T F S	Plan courses so as to serve meal on time. Put away perishables after use. Serve each course in several containers, each to contain the proper serving spoon. Carve meat or fowl. Set pots to soak for dishwasher. Make coffee.
Wash Dishes	2, or 1 each for 2 people	M T W T F S	Wash all dirty dishes, silver, pots and pans, etc., in hot, soapy water. Put each item away in its proper place. Drain or dry all items, especially iron. Clean and straighten up entire kitchen, including table and counters. Sweep floor and mop up puddles. Do not leave scorched pans.
Set table	1/2	M T W T F S	See how many people are signed in. Set table according to the following list, putting perishables on the table just before dinner: Plates, silver, glasses, cups, napkins, salt, pepper, bread, butter, sugar, beer, wine, soda, milk, bottle openers. Salad dressing and soup bowls if applicable.
Serve	1/2 each for two people	M T W T F S	When most people have finished with dinner, clear plates and serving dishes. Serve dessert, coffee, and cream. Clear table. Scrape and organize dishes. Consolidate and put away good leftovers, putting them in plastic containers. Put away butter, milk, etc. Scrub the tables with hot, soapy water. Tidy dining room. Mop up any big messes.
Clean halls and bathrooms	1 1/2 1 1/2 1	3 floor 2 floor 1 floor	Sweep or vacuum halls and baths. Dispose of all trash, bottles, etc. Dust surfaces. Thoroughly clean bathroom fixtures. Clean w.c. with Sani-flush. Mop bathroom floor. Replenish toilet paper and soap. Replace bath mat. Sweep vestibules.

Clean kitchen, dining room and living room	3	Sweep and mop kitchen and dining room twice. Dust and sweep living room. Dispose of all debris. Wax floor occasionally. Return furniture to proper position afterward.
Stairs	2	Sweep twice during week. Dust bannisters once.
Kitchen Sunday	1	Clean kitchen Sunday evening. See Dishwashing.
Put food away	2	Put away food order. Compute and mark prices. Check addition on order slips. Keep stored foods tidy.
Beverages	2	Put milk in refrigerator. Store and replenish beer and soda. Order beverages. Keep tidy. Make sure empties are taken.
Refrigerators	2	Remove contents. Put drip pan under coils and turn box *off*. Sort contents, throwing away all but the best. Wash interior. Replace contents and turn box on. Wash all emptied containers, etc., and clean up any mess.
Stove	2	Remove top, etc., and scour them. Wash entire stove. Remove filter, wash in hot soapy water, and replace. Clean up any mess. Go easy with Easy-off; it's dangerous.
Trash	1	Daily, take out and replace garbage can. Sunday and Wed. nights put cans on sidewalk. Bring in empties. Keep trash storage area neat.
Laundry	1	Wash, dry, and store dish towels, pot holders, bath mats, etc. Clean washer and dryer.
Outside	1	Pick up all trash from front and back yards. Especially, get rid of any junk, broken furniture, etc. Sweep steps.
Maintenance	1	Replace burned out light bulbs. Check for leaky faucets, toilets, etc. Check furnace. Check basement for leaky pipes. Check roof for damage. Report what you can't fix.

Special jobs: Clean and tidy attics and cellars, clean windows.

President, 1; Secretary, 1; Treasurer, 1; Bookkeeper, full; Kitchen Kaiser, full; Labor Czar, 1.

313

TABLE 7-8. Number of Hours Per Week Spent on Communal Chores by Commune Type, Duration, and Member Seniority

A. By Commune Type

Chore	Eastern Religious	Christian	Political	Counter-cultural	Family	Coopera-tive	Psycho-logical	Rehabili-tative	Total
House cleaning									
Mean	3.9	2.9	3.4	2.5	3.8	4.3	2.6	2.7	3.4
S.D.	6.1	3.0	5.9	3.2	6.0	11.3	2.2	5.6	6.0
N	88	35	30	35	30	38	50	6	312
Cooking									
Mean	4.0	3.8	2.5	2.2	3.1	1.4	2.0	13.3	3.1
S.D.	8.0	5.5	2.4	3.1	3.4	1.3	1.7	24.2	6.1
N	86	35	30	35	30	88	50	6	310
Washing dishes									
Mean	2.7	4.1	2.6	2.0	2.4	1.6	1.8	6.0	2.5
S.D.	2.7	11.6	3.2	1.6	1.7	1.4	1.5	11.8	4.7
N	88	35	30	35	30	38	50	6	312
House and car maintenance									
Mean	3.7	4.0	2.5	5.7	1.9	3.1	1.8	2.5	3.3
S.D.	11.6	11.4	6.4	10.4	2.8	6.4	4.4	6.1	8.7
N	89	35	30	35	30	38	50	6	313
Babysitting for communal children other than one's own									
Mean	1.0	2.4	0.8	1.1	2.1	0.3	0.8	—	1.1
S.D.	3.5	7.0	1.8	2.6	3.3	1.0	3.2	—	3.6
N	89	34	30	34	30	38	50	6	311
Laundry									
Mean	1.3	1.4	0.2	0.4	0.3	0.1	0.2	3.3	0.7
S.D.	3.7	2.3	0.8	1.1	0.8	0.4	0.7	8.2	2.5
N	89	35	30	35	30	38	50	6	313

Shopping									
Mean	1.5	1.0	1.2	1.1	1.3	0.7	1.4	0.3	1.2
S.D.	4.6	1.4	2.2	1.2	1.8	1.1	1.8	0.8	2.8
N	88	35	30	35	30	38	50	6	312
Account keeping									
Mean	2.1	0.3	1.5	0.5	0.3	0.3	0.4	—	0.9
S.D.	8.8	0.9	7.3	1.4	1.0	0.6	1.1	—	5.3
N	89	35	30	35	30	38	50	6	313
Keeping communal records									
Mean	1.6	0.7	0.3	0.2	0.1	0.1	0.1	10.3	0.8
S.D.	4.8	1.9	1.0	0.5	0.7	0.4	0.6	18.8	3.9
N	89	35	30	35	30	38	50	6	313
Spreading the ideological message									
Mean	6.6	2.4	10.8	2.1	0.5	0.1	4.1	0.2	4.0
S.D.	12.3	3.1	24.8	5.8	1.3	0.3	10.1	0.4	11.5
N	75	32	30	32	30	37	47	6	289
Counseling									
Mean	2.9	4.5	1.0	2.6	1.7	0.8	3.7	19.0	2.9
S.D.	6.1	6.7	1.8	5.7	2.5	1.4	7.0	18.1	6.1
N	83	35	30	34	30	38	49	5	304

TABLE 7-8. *(continued)*

B. By Commune Duration

Chore	Three Months or Less	Middle Range	1970 or Earlier
House cleaning			
Mean	2.9	3.0	5.1
S.D.	3.2	4.3	8.2
N	44	233	30
Cooking			
Mean	3.0	3.0	4.0
S.D.	4.1	5.4	11.5
N	44	231	30
Washing Dishes			
Mean	2.6	2.6	2.4
S.D.	2.4	5.0	5.4
N	44	233	30
House and car maintenance			
Mean	4.8	2.9	3.3
S.D.	10.4	8.7	6.0
N	44	234	30
Babysitting for communal children other than one's own			
Mean	0.7	1.2	1.0
S.D.	1.7	4.0	2.5
N	44	232	30
Laundry			
Mean	0.5	0.7	1.6
S.D.	1.2	2.2	5.2
N	44	234	30
Shopping			
Mean	1.2	1.3	0.6
S.D.	1.3	3.2	1.0
N	44	233	30
Account keeping			
Mean	0.4	1.1	0.5
S.D.	1.0	6.1	1.1
N	44	234	30
Keeping communal records			
Mean	0.7	0.6	2.5
S.D.	1.7	3.0	8.8
N	44	234	30
Spreading the ideological message			
Mean	1.4	4.5	5.1
S.D.	2.7	12.6	12.0
N	43	216	25
Counseling			
Mean	2.4	2.6	4.5
S.D.	4.6	5.5	6.8
N	43	229	27

TABLE 7-8. *(continued)*

C. By Year of Joining

Chore	1969	1970	1971	1972	1973	1974
House cleaning						
Mean	1.5	6.0	4.9	2.3	3.8	3.2
S.D.	1.9	6.5	6.7	2.6	5.3	6.6
N	4	6	14	29	84	173
Cooking						
Mean	0.5	4.5	2.9	1.8	3.6	3.1
S.D.	1.0	4.5	3.3	2.4	6.8	6.4
N	4	6	14	29	83	172
Washing dishes						
Mean	0.8	1.7	3.1	1.4	2.1	2.9
S.D.	1.0	0.8	2.1	1.0	2.3	6.0
N	4	6	14	29	84	173
House and car maintenance						
Mean	6.0	4.5	4.3	2.5	3.9	2.9
S.D.	7.0	8.6	9.4	9.3	11.9	6.7
N	4	6	14	29	85	173
Babysitting for communal children other than one's own						
Mean	0.5	4.5	1.3	0.4	1.8	0.7
S.D.	1.0	4.3	3.1	1.0	5.5	2.1
N	4	6	14	29	84	172
Laundry						
Mean	0.3	0.3	1.4	0.1	1.2	0.5
S.D.	0.5	0.5	3.2	0.3	3.6	2.0
N	4	6	14	29	85	173
Shopping						
Mean	0.8	0.7	1.1	0.5	1.9	1.0
S.D.	0.5	0.8	1.4	1.2	4.9	1.4
N	4	6	14	29	84	173
Account keeping						
Mean	0.3	0.3	0.5	0.5	1.7	0.7
S.D.	0.5	0.8	1.2	1.4	8.0	4.3
N	4	6	14	29	85	173
Keeping communal records						
Mean	0.3	—	1.6	0.2	1.0	0.8
S.D.	0.5	—	5.3	0.7	2.6	4.6
N	4	6	14	29	85	173
Spreading the ideological message						
Mean	—	1.8	8.3	4.2	2.6	4.6
S.D.	—	2.9	14.4	9.4	6.3	13.6
N	4	6	14	26	77	160
Counseling						
Mean	6.3	4.8	3.2	2.4	4.1	2.2
S.D.	13.0	7.8	3.9	4.6	8.2	5.0
N	4	6	13	28	83	168

TABLE 7–9. Frequency of Patterns of Household Chore Distribution in Rural and Urban Communes

	Urban		Rural	
	Number	% of Total	Number	% of Total
Assigned chores	17	28%	12	20%
Rotated chores	14	23	8	13
Voluntary choice	16	27	25	42
Anarchistic or totally voluntary	10	17	15	25
Other, mixed or don't know	3	5	0	0
Total	60	100%	60	100%

Sex-Role Differentiation

There are significant behavioral and attitudinal differences between the sexes in all of the communes in our study. No commune has come anywhere near to succeeding in abolishing sex-role distinctions, although a number of communes have made this their highest ideological priority.*

Table 7-10 shows the extent of the sexual division of labor for the commune population as a whole. Women spend more than double the amount of time than men do each week (12.3 hours versus 5.7 hours) on cleaning, cooking, and dish washing. The imbalance is even greater with respect to minding other members' children and doing laundry (2.6 versus 1.1). Men spend considerably more time during the week on home and car maintenance, keeping the account books, spreading the communal message, and counseling other commune members than do women. The sexes achieve a roughly equal balance in time spent shopping and time spent answering communal correspondence.

Women in urban communes are employed at outside jobs about as frequently as men are. It is difficult to explain why, if opportunity time is about the same and the ideology supports the eradication of sex role differences in communal work, such pronounced differences should persist.

Although males tended to leave communal living more frequently than females, males, paradoxically, expressed a greater degree of long-range commitment to their communes than did females. There is some evidence that communal living tends to be a more discontinuous experience for women than for men. Men had a higher proportion of use of drugs before joining the commune, for example, but women had a slightly higher proportion than men after joining the commune.

In some of the communes some of the women came to be defined as either mothers or females, but not both. One woman ex-member of a Southern com-

*Bartelt (1978) has presented evidence that the record of contemporary communes gives evidence of even less achievement of sex-role equality than was attained by the communes of the nineteenth century.

TABLE 7-10. Time Spent Per Week in Communal Chores by Sex

Chore	Sex	Mean Hours	Mean Difference Significance (t-test) $(p \leqslant .05)$[a]
House cleaning	Male	2.0	
	Female	4.8	.001
Cooking	Male	1.8	
	Female	4.4	.001
Washing dishes	Male	1.9	
	Female	3.1	.008
House and car Maintenance	Male	4.3	
	Female	2.2	.04
Babysitting for communal children other than one's own	Male	0.7	
	Female	1.5	.05
Laundry	Male	0.4	
	Female	1.1	.002
Shopping	Male	1.3	
	Female	1.1	n.s.
Account keeping	Male	1.1	
	Female	0.7	n.s.
Keeping communal records	Male	0.8	
	Female	0.9	n.s.
Spreading the ideological message	Male	4.9	
	Female	3.1	n.s.
Counseling	Male	3.2	
	Female	2.5	n.s.

[a] N = 313; n.s. = not significant

mune complained in an interview about the negative sexual orientation of her former communal house as being chauvinistic. She said that she had to leave because she had become the only "female" in the house—by definition female meaning free, loose, and sexually available. Two other women in the house were not defined as female—one because she was married and had a child and thus was a mother and another because she was having psychological problems. This woman said:

Whenever a man came over to see me or eat or do something I didn't know if it was my imagination, but [the male commune members] seemed to be very cold to him and gave him dirty looks because I was the only female in the house and this lead to a sense of possessiveness. They expected that this meant bed privileges or something because I think it was that way with some [woman] before and [she] had been sleeping around a lot more. But they couldn't accept the fact that there was a difference and they were just really cold to men that came over. One guy that came over, they just picked on him so much. . . . Jerry came out and said, "Oh, are you coming here to steal our women?"

In a report on a study of California communes Berger et al. (1973) stated that:

The women's liberation movement would probably not approve of the position of women in most communes. . . . With the exception of those religious communes which have a specifically sexist creed, women can be found doing any but the most physically arduous labor, and in several communes we have studied closely women do play important leadership roles, but on the whole they are less ideologically forceful than men and express themselves with generally less authority—although we have encountered important exceptions to this tendency.

Conclusions

Invidious power and status distinctions do not seem to vanish in communes. Where effort is applied to abolishing such distinctions in one area of life, they merely reappear in another area. Anarchistic communes succeed quite readily in abolishing formal authority relations. But differences in interpersonal power, which are universal in communes, soon give rise to new hierarchies. Economic leveling is easily achieved only to give rise to status differentiation in communal work roles. The latter are usually sex linked.

We did not find a single example of a commune without a power hierarchy or of one in which the men did as much of what has traditionally been called "woman's work" as did the women. This does not prove that such a commune might never exist. But it does suggest that the human tendencies toward pecking order and primary process categorization are not among the behavior patterns that can be easily willed away, even by men and women of the most sincere commitment.

We have seen that communes promote neither autonomy nor equality. How then are individual interests protected? The central importance of love in communitarian behaviors and ideologies suggests that we look to generalized altruism as a possible source of such protection. However, as we shall see in the next chapter, this solution raises problems of its own.

It hardly needs saying that such mutualistic communities will also be plagued by conflict. Conflict is at the very heart of life, resulting not simply from the malevolence of others in the struggle for place or portion, but also from the fact that men of the best will in the world seem to suffer incurably, so far as one can tell, from what William James called "a certain blindness" in perceiving the vitalities of others.

Benjamin Nelson

CHAPTER   8

The Problem of Vulnerability

Inequality need not be a bar to the achievement of social structure based on love if the commune members really care about the well-being of one another. After all, few social entities are as unequal in the distribution of power as families; yet families, more than most social groups, attempt to act in behalf of the interests of all of their members. Communes that have failed to achieve either perfect consensus among autonomous wills or perfect equality may still hope to attain to the level of mutual caring and empathy found in successful families. As we have seen, many communes are ideologically committed to more than this, to the goal of becoming better than families at these matters.

We do find examples, both historical and contemporary, of communes' achieving such high levels of mutual caring, sometimes even sustaining them over several generations. The risks of communitarian living, however, are so great, the mutual vulnerability so dangerous, that only the most steadfast have a chance of making it. This steadfastness must be unanimous or nearly unanimous, making the extent of vulnerability that much greater. If even a few break rank and run, no individual person, not even a majority faction, can ensure the success of the commune by keeping faith. Most communes eventually succumb to one of the two pitfalls built into the self-investment scheme discussed in Chapter 6: (1) consensual bankruptcy or (2) the anticipation of consensual bankruptcy.

The dilemma is this: Consensual bankruptcy, in the form of an insurmountable crisis of charismatic legitimacy, can be devastating, not only to the commune but also to the mental health of the commune members. But to the extent that commune members attempt to guard themselves against this danger, they fall prey to the anticipatory danger, the sham communion of pseudo-intimacy. This is the less explosive of the two possibilities but, for social structures whose common coin is love, its effects are equally devastating. Networks of love can turn into networks of hate or indifference regardless of whether commune members make the mistake of risking too much or risking too little.

This is what is so sad about many sincere communitarian endeavors. When one is spending money faster than one is earning it, the path to bankruptcy is plain to see. But one cannot as easily tell when one's social commitment account is being depleted. Experiences of spiritual and emotional renewal are subtle and deceiving. Often the sheer intensity of a renewal of solidarity is greatest as the network of relationships is already entering its death throes. As we saw in Chapter 4, communal love can be a signal of communal decay. The usual guidelines for knowing when to work hard at relationships and when to relax do not seem to apply to communal situations. Nobody intuitively grasps the necessary lead times.

Very aware of the pitfalls, the investment of self in communal organizations is often, nevertheless, seen as worthwhile by the individual member. As an ego renunciation problem, it is perceived as a valid form of yoga—perhaps the most valid for a Westerner with a sense of political and social responsibility—the yoga of interpersonal harmony through renunciation of primary allegiance to the isolated ego. The question of survival or nonsurvival is, in this sense, irrelevant. If we dwell, in this final chapter, on the problems of collective vulnerability, this should in no way be taken as an admonition that life is best lived by avoiding such vulnerability.

Crises of Charismatic Legitimacy

Let us first discuss the more dramatic but rarer of the two problems. A sudden breakdown in the legitimacy of absolute charismatic authority can be a gory sight to behold. This fact, at least, has been firmly impressed upon the public consciousness by the mass suicidal and homicidal ending of the Jonestown commune in Guyana, and will need no further evidence here. This, however, is an extreme example, and, as has been the case with most of the phenomena discussed in this book, we prefer to try to understand the breakdown of charismatic legitimacy not solely in terms of its extreme manifestations but in terms of its variation along a continuum from mild to severe.

All nonroutinized charismatic authority, as Weber (1947, p. 362) has argued, must be continually proven on a personal (i.e., relational) basis to remain legitimate. Charismatic leaders must constantly prove that they are being effective in achieving the commune's ideological goals. For external goals involving the relation of the commune to the outside world, myth may easily be substituted for achievement. As Festinger et al. (1956) and others have shown, even the most tangible failures in the external domain have a way of increasing rather than decreasing charismatic legitimacy. But for internal goals (especially those involving what Parsons would call the integrative and latency dimensions), real achievement is much harder to fake. Commune members rely on the personal experience of communion to convince themselves, first, that the entity to which they have surrendered a portion of their autonomy is real and, second, that their fellow communitarians have not begun to withdraw from it. If the communitarian charismatic leader loses the ability to trigger the communion experience, sooner or later he and the commune are in trouble.

The Experience of Communion

The state of communion is one in which there is no alienation from the collectivity. The group is at one with itself. Any collectivity can experience such a state upon occasion. In Chapter 3 we briefly alluded to decision making under communion as deriving from the intersection of the members' preference sets. In Chapter 4 we discussed its instability as a form of organization. In Chapter 6, communion was again briefly mentioned as one of Kanter's (1972) six commitment mechanisms. These various perspectives all refer to a common core.

Communion is experienced as a shared altered state of consciousness in which the problems of autonomy and inequality are temporarily solved. There are no roles and no directed relationships. The group is experienced as more real than the individual. Such communion experiences are reported from among all eight ideological types represented in our sample of communes. They are also a well-recognized phenomenon in religion and politics, among youth groups, and within many tribal cultures (e.g., Eisenstadt, 1971; Turner, 1969).

It is important to understand the place of communion within the consensus-building process. Communion is the actual medium through which consensus is achieved. A commune that is able to govern itself effectively as a decision-making body is most often the one that can most reliably trigger the state of consciousness known as communion.

The convergence of beliefs, preferences, and judgments that accompanies submission to charismatic authority begins to appear in the state of ordinary individualistic consciousness only very slowly if at all.* The Iowa-bred convert to an Eastern religious commune does not suddenly develop a personal yen for brown rice and a personal distaste for steak and potatoes. Rather, he or she becomes part of a group that collectively prefers brown rice to steak and comes increasingly through relational reinforcement to experience the group will as his or her own, physiologically as well as symbolically. When the convert is off by himself/herself, engaged in his/her own noncommunal activities, with no stimuli of communion around to remind the convert of his or her altered state, it is very easy for that person to fall back into precommunal views. This is why, in some of the more extreme communitarian cults, only the most fully converted are ever allowed even a few moments in such a condition of autonomy.

The importance of constant relational reinforcement is most clearly seen by looking at an example of what can happen when the reinforcement is suddenly, if only briefly, withdrawn. Tex Watson had been a member of the Charles Manson Family for eight months when he was sent on a fund-raising mission that required him to travel alone. (This occurred before any murders had been committed). As he describes the experience (Watson, 1978, pp. 81ff):

> . . . suddenly I was jolted by the realization that for the first time in what seemed like years, I was alone, by myself, not with Charlie or anyone else in the Family. There was just me, Charles Watson, standing on the curb with my thumb out in the bright November sunlight. There was something exhilarating about it. . . . I'd forgotten what it was like to feel the freedom that being on your own, responsible to no one, can give you. . . . What was it that made [the people in the cars going by] look free and alive in a way I wasn't? Suddenly it hit me—they had lives of their own, they could choose. . . . I no longer existed, not in the sense that the people passing me on the street existed, had lives, made choices. Everything had seemed so certain, but now there was panic.

Watson left The Family a month later and drifted back into noncommunal life easily enough, falling in love and living with his woman friend in Hollywood. But too much self had already been invested in Manson and there was nobody around with the skill to deprogram Watson or to help him free himself psychologically:

> Sometimes I felt as though [Manson] were always with me, thinking my thoughts for me—or *his* through me. . . . It was as though Charlie kept pulling me back, slowly but persistently, even though we'd had no contact since I walked out the back door of that Topanga Canyon cabin. I tried to fight it, but it was no use; he wouldn't let go of me. He'd seen the world I was living in and he'd warned me, and I found it just what he'd said it would be. Even though a part of me liked it, enjoyed all the things I'd been

---

*For empirical evidence concerning the process of attitude convergence in the urban commune subsample, see Aidala (1979) and Mannhardt (1979).

denying myself, it wouldn't work—I couldn't make it work. Nine months with the Family had made too deep a mark on me. Finally one day I picked up the phone and called the ranch. Even before I dialed, I think I'd decided to go back to Charlie.

The individual sharing in communion is at a peak of psychic vulnerability. Depending upon whether he chooses as a point of reference the personal self or the collective self, he defines himself as either totally alienated or totally without alienation. In the collective identity that person is safe but feels keenly that, should the collective identity fail him, there is no individual identity to fall back on. From the perspective of the commune this is a desirable situation; the very knowledge of the extent to which self has already been invested becomes the motive to continue to invest self.

Evidence of the importance of communion in the collective decision-making process is seen in the responses of communitarians to the question of what distinguishes genuine consensus from mere unanimity. Across all ideological categories, a unanimous vote unaccompanied by the experience of communion is grounds for suspecting the validity of the underlying consensus. The following is a response of this sort from one of the commune members in our sample:

> By midnight we had all agreed that they should be allowed to stay for a few days at least. Everyone was tired. At an SDS meeting that would have been the end of it. But then Eric said, "You know, I just don't feel right about this." And all of a sudden, its hard to describe, but we all knew exactly what he meant. At least I did and most people said [later] that they felt the same way. . . . We wound up talking until after 4:00 in the morning and we trotted out the whole history of all the decisions we've ever made about letting people in and not letting people in. I found out a lot I didn't know about people's [supposedly forgotten grievances] and we talked about the fears—mine also—about the way the group's changing and how new members affect that.
>
> And, of course, we wound up with the same decision we had at midnight, but what a difference! The first time we were just a bunch of people who had made a decision, and we were dead tired, and nobody wanted to look in anyone else's eyes. But after we'd really talked it out, everyone felt really good about it and really close. . . . Most of us didn't even try to get some sleep but just started making breakfast and getting ready for the day's work.

Another interesting point to note about this example is that the search for communion was not started by the charismatic leader but by one of the more peripheral members. As the informant later went on to say:

> No, I'm not really surprised that it was Eric who started it. You know Eric doesn't usually say much at meetings but he's been around for a long time and he's really tuned in [and he's also] a little paranoid at times. Ray [the charismatic leader] calls him Mr. Gallup because he's always going around asking everybody what they think about different things. . . . It used to bother me but it doesn't as much anymore. Anyway, something

like that would bother Eric more than most of us, but if he hadn't spoken up maybe somebody else would've or maybe Ray would've said something.

The investment of self clearly provokes a widespread need among the members for information about each other's feeling states. Such information exchange is a natural by-product of the achievement of consensus through communion. It need not be facilitated by the charismatic leader, but it is doubtful if it would have occurred at all had the leader been absent. For it to work, commune members must remain constantly vulnerable in their inner most thoughts and feelings and constantly vigilant in probing the vulnerability of the other members. In the most extreme cases, no private cognition, however trivial, can be tolerated.

Charisma and the Brink of Madness

The charismatic commune is a dangerous place in which to live. There is probably no form of social organization in which the participants are more prone to behavioral influences over extended periods of time that go completely counter to actions they would take as isolated individuals. Moreover, the source of influence itself is far from being steady and stable. The alteration of consciousness in communion leads to an increase in charismatic susceptibility. Phenomenologically, members describe their sense of an absorption of intimate feelings by the charismatic leader, who redistributes them to the entire collectivity. But a reinforcement of consensus will not result unless the investment of self, on the part of each individual, is strengthened and charismatic legitimacy thereby affirmed. Identical experiences of communion may give rise to renewal, to malaise, or to insanity.

One of the responsibilities of the charismatic leader is to channel interpersonal commitment safely into consensus. He plays for high stakes both because he is expected to make use of his power to modify the very desires of the participants and because he must also make sure that each member is remaining vulnerable to that power in about the same degree. It is the high degree of personal vulnerability necessary for investment of self in a charismatic community that leads people to require guarantees that the investment level of others is being kept similarly high. A degree of involvement of the leader in the private lives of the followers will be tolerated that otherwise, by associational standards, would constitute intolerable tyranny.

The charismatic leader is not free to deviate in any direction he wishes from generally accepted standards of truth and morality. He must be sure to avoid not only inconsistency but also any radical deviation from the unexpressed latent consensus of the group. A clear example of the interplay between leader and followers in the charismatic process is afforded by an examination of the commune whose ideology Charles Manson transformed from countercultural* to psychopathological (Bugliosi, 1974, pp. 483ff.):

> Those who did join him were not the typical girl or boy next door. Charles Manson was not a Pied Piper who suddenly appeared on the basketball court at Texas State, handed Charles Watson a tab of LSD, then led him into a life of crime. Watson had quit college with only a year to go, gone to California, immersed himself in the selling as well as the using of drugs, before he ever met Charles Manson. Not just Watson but nearly every other member of the Family had dropped out before meeting Manson. Nearly all had within them a deep-seated hostility toward society and everything it stood for which preexisted their meeting Manson. . . . They chose, and Manson chose, and the result was the Family. Those who gravitated to the Spahn Ranch and stayed did so because basically they thought and felt alike. This was his raw material.
>
> In shaping that material into a band of cold-blooded assassins, Manson employed a variety of techniques.
>
> *He sensed, and capitalized on, their needs.* As Gregg Jakobson observed, "Charlie was a man of a thousand faces" who "related to all human beings on their level of need." His ability to "psych out" people was so great that many of his disciples felt he could read their minds. . . .
>
> *Drugs were another of his tools.* As brought out in the psychiatric testimony during the trials, LSD was not a causal agent but a catalyst. Manson used it very effectively, to make his followers more suggestible, to implant ideas, to extract "agreements." As Paul Watkins told me, Charlie always took a smaller dose of LSD than the others, so he would remain in command.
>
> *He used repetition.* By constantly preaching and lecturing to his subjects on an almost daily basis, he gradually and systematically erased many of their inhibitions. As Manson himself once remarked in court: "You can convince anybody of anything if you just push it at them all of the time. They may not believe it 100 percent, but they will still draw opinions from it, especially if they have no other information to draw their opinions from."
>
> Therein lies still another of the keys he used: in addition to repetition, *he used isolation.* There were no newspapers at Spahn Ranch, no clocks. Cut off from the rest of society, he created in this timeless land a tight little society of his own, with its own value system. It was holistic, complete, and totally at odds with the world outside.
>
> *He used sex.* Realizing that most people have sexual hangups, he taught, by both precept and example, that in sex there is no wrong, thereby eradicating both their inhibitions and their guilt.
>
> But there was more than sex. *There was also love,* a great deal of love. To overlook this would be to miss one of the strongest bonds that existed among

---

*Manson's commune is not in the sample. From all published reports, however, it was, in its early stages, virtually indistinguishable from some of the rural communes in our sample that we have labeled countercultural.

them. The love grew out of their sharing, their communal problems and pleasures, their relationship with Charlie. *They were a real family in almost every
sense of that word,* a sociological unit complete to brothers, sisters, substitute
mothers, linked by the domination of an all-knowing, all-powerful patriarch.
Cooking, washing dishes, cleaning, sewing—all the chores they hated at home
they now did willingly, because they pleased Charlie.

He used fear, very, very effectively. Whether he picked up this technique
in prison or later is not known, *but it was one of his most effective tools
for controlling others.* It may also have been something more. As Stanford
University Professor Philip Zimbardo, a long-time student of crime and its
effects, noted in a Newsweek article: "By raising the level of fear around you,
your own fear seems more normal and socially acceptable." Manson's own
fear bordered on paranoia. . . .

He brought to the surface their *latent hatred,* their inherent penchant
for sadistic violence, focusing it on a common enemy, the establishment. He
depersonalized the victims by making them symbols. It is easier to stab a
symbol than a person.

He taught his followers a completely *amoral philosophy,* which provided
complete justification for their acts. If everything is right, then nothing can
be wrong. If nothing is real, and all of life is a game, then there need be no
regret. [emphasis added]

The need for charisma continually to be proved does not disappear even in
the most fully institutionalized communes. Among the venerable Hutterians,
as Bennett has described them (1975, pp. 83, 86), the tension expresses itself
not as psychopathological acting out, as in the Manson family, but instead as
constant gnawing pressure, a warding off of alienation:

If you labor, love, and share long enough, persistently enough, and in the
milieu of unobtrusive leadership and unobtrusive rules of the game, you
will get the idea; that is, "internalize" the habits. You may reserve to yourself these selfish motives and paranoid suspicisions, never really rooting them
out of the lower brain, but at least they are in the basement. *You may need
ways of seeking emotional relief—Hutterites take a lot of [tranquilizers]* —and
the commune may come to have a *slightly skewed, eccentric, moody atmosphere. Lots of colitis.* Not only are the emotions being suppressed, but so is
the guilt and doubt over the inevitable institutionalization of the system. . . .

I am saying that *the commune can be a relief* for people fed up, or unable
to cope with the rat race, and certainly if the Hutterites are typical, *true
mental illness is rare,* but I am also saying that to participate successfully in a
commune, it is *necessary to pay certain social-emotional costs* (Hutterite
psychosomatic illnesses are common). [emphasis added]

The payoff for accepting this tension is a consensual community that (as long
as the legitimacy of the charismatic authority structure continues to be affirmed) allows people a freedom from the ordinary constraints of culture-bound
reality, without denying them an alternative shared reality to cling to.

The Cognitive Dimension of Alienation

In Chapter 6 we defined alienation as an objective state of individuals in relation to the collectivity—a consensual incapacity. But this state can only be experienced by individuals, and, because decision making and the search for consensus are perceived as mental activities, alienation will be experienced as having an important cognitive dimension. This shared cognitive inability to order the world in such a way that collective decisions can be made now demands our attention.

If it is true that individuals invest all or part of their decision-making capacities in the commune, and if it is true, as we have discussed in the preceding section, that communes act as powerful shapers (sometimes even as destroyers) of their members' minds, a possible causal linkage between these two facts should be investigated. Peter Berger (1969, p. 4) provides a framework for such a linkage in his conception of the dialectic process through which meaning systems are created:

> The fundamental dialectic process of society consists of three moments, or steps. These are externalization, objectivation, and internalization. Only if these three moments are understood together can an empirically adequate view of society be maintained. Externalization is the ongoing outpouring of human being into the world, both in the physical and the mental activity of men. Objectivation is the attainment by the products of this activity (again both physical and mental) of a reality that confronts its original producers as a facticity external to and other than themselves. Internalization is the reappropriation by men of this same reality, transforming it once again from structures of the objective world into structures of the subjective consciousness. It is through externalization that society is a human product. It is through objectivation that society becomes a reality *sui generis*. It is through internalization that man is a product of society.

Each commune member carries within him, in Berger's (1969) terms, an internalization of the charismatically objectified communitarian reality. Charisma has built up this reality through the successive imposition of levels of consensual specificity (see Table 6-4) from the ability to distinguish relevant aspects of meaning, to the setting of Cl_{alt}, which imposes an absolute value on the entire system. When charisma fails, the individual is left with an analogue to the classic neurotic situation—an inability to cope with certain aspects of "reality." The fact that the "reality" being threatened is itself a charismatic artifact, and not the "reality" of the mainstream culture, does not make the threat any less stressful for the commune participant.

Now we come to one of the most remarkable and, in many ways, puzzling findings of this entire research.* There is clear isomorphism between the cogni-

---

*Although this aspect of the alienation and charisma model comes near to the end of our exposition, it was, empirically, one of the first dramatic regularities in the comparative

tive aspects of some of the most common neurotic disturbances and the empirical properties of the levels of alienation and charisma, which were outlined in Chapter 6:

Charisma Type	Alienation Level	Cognitive Neurosis
Exemplary	Meaninglessness	Paranoia
Policy	Aimlessness	Obsessive compulsiveness
Executive	Powerlessness	Hysteria
Normative	Normlessness	Impulsiveness
Absolute	Self-estrangement	Submissiveness

In attempting to evaluate the empirical evidence for these statements about the cognitive dimension of alienation, we encounter, in a study like this one, a serious question of validity. The diagnosis of neurotic disturbances of cognition in individuals is a very subtle and tricky business even when attempted by those with psychiatric training. Our evidence is based upon observations by sociologists, none of whom have had psychiatric training. Furthermore, we are not ascribing cognitive neuroses to individuals but are attempting the much more risky procedure of ascribing them to entire sets of emergent roles within collectivities.

Notwithstanding these very real problems, the matter at hand seems far too important to avoid. For one thing, if one grants at least a rough validity to our simplistic social psychiatric diagnoses, the evidence provides some striking corroboration for the theoretical framework developed in Chapter 6. For another, it has potential clinical significance as we shall see in the following discussion. Finally, in the absence of great numbers of people who are trained both in sociological measurement and psychiatric diagnosis, there are necessarily very many areas on the boundary of these two disciplines in which initial exploration will have to be done by the half-ignorant. If the findings presented here prove replicable, even in part, there will certainly be a need for a good deal of more precisely designed interdisciplinary research in this area, on groups in general, not only on communes.

The most basic of the cognitive manifestations of alienation is collective paranoia. It occurs whenever there is a loss of confidence in charismatically defined meanings. Thorn & Thistle, a commune described in Chapter 5, provides a good example of garden-variety paranoia as a crisis of legitimacy. Thorn & Thistle was a minimally charismatic commune. Its charisma was of the type one (exemplary) pattern and was invested not in a single charismatic leader but in a small charismatic group. Self was not invested beyond what was necessary to maintain a structure of shared meanings. The members of Thorn & Thistle themselves often remarked on what they called their "tendency to reinforce

---

observation of commune ideologies to be noted, and it helped to lead us to many of the earlier formulations discussed in Chapters 6 and 7.

each other's paranoia." World, national, and local events would be interpreted as potential threats to the commune's continuing existence. Conversely, disagreements within the commune would be seen as schisms in the revolutionary movement. Even this commune research project was under suspicion as a possible front for FBI or CIA surveillance. None of these paranoid episodes lasted too long or interfered seriously with communal functioning. This type of paranoia contrasts sharply with the virulent paranoia that is the final and often terminal stage of the complete breakdown of absolute charismatic legitimacy, to be discussed shortly.

The next manifestation of charismatic breakdown to be discussed is the obsessive-compulsive response. It is most frequently expected and most frequently found among those communes at a type 2 or policy level of charismatic investment. Policy charisma has to do with the modification of preference orderings. Group marriage communes therefore provide a useful site for examining this form of charismatic breakdown. The potential interference of dyadic preferences with charismatic collective preference orderings makes the need for policy charisma incessant even in communes that are not otherwise charismatic.

The Family (discussed in Chapter 5) is an example of such a group marriage commune. Policy charisma was lodged in a small group of core members, who could always be relied upon to put the overall concept of the group marriage ahead of any specific desires that they or other members had for specific sexual partners. In a crisis, the origins of which are partly obscure, but which had to do both with the legitimacy of homosexual pairings within the group marriage and with the issue of shared responsibility for young children, the core group lost the confidence of the larger collectivity. What happened next is that the commune went on a methods binge. It attempted to substitute for the lost charismatic core with lists, rotation schemes, and mating rituals, which continually grew more cumbersome and elaborate even as they proved unworkable.

Associated with communes that are charismatic only up to the executive level, we find crises of legitimacy taking the form of collective hysteria.* Attention blurs and it is difficult to distinguish events with real consequences from play acting. An example of this kind of crisis was seen at the Ecology commune in New England. Ecology was a countercultural commune led by a single leader who was judged to be charismatic up to the level of decision making. A crisis of legitimacy occurred when the members of Ecology realized, in October, that they had not made adequate preparations for their first communal (and for most also their first rural) winter. Chris, the charismatic leader, was so forceful and self-confident in his speech and in his actions that it apparently never occurred to any of the members to doubt that he had given the matter thought and had made adequate plans. It was not that Chris was incompetent or that he shunned

---

*Shapiro (1965, pp. 122ff.) identifies, in a clinical setting, the cognitive style of hysteria precisely with the co-existence of clearly formed goals and preferences without a clear sense of associated utilities (i.e., costs and benefits).

the responsibility. It was just that he had lived only on the West Coast and was not experienced in preparing for New England winters. The group went through a three-week period of alternating frantic activity and optimistic complacence. Dozens of partial schemes were discussed, often accompanied by dramatic bursts of rhetoric, but nobody seemed to realize that it mattered more that something get done than that the decision be clear. The commune barely survived this crisis and then only by means of a massive infusion of borrowed money.

Among the type 4, or normative charismatic groups, the characteristic crisis of legitimacy is impulsiveness. This kind of crisis was observed at Flowing Water when the old guru died. The death was not unexpected and a competent successor had been chosen and placed in readiness. Nevertheless, there was an interim period before the new leader could really be accepted as and feel the part of *the leader*.

During this interim period, the commune exhibited a number of dramatic symptoms in its collective and individual decision making that are generally associated (e.g., Shapiro, 1965, pp. 134ff.) with an impulsive style of cognition. The commune experienced spiritual forces impelling them to certain activities (e.g., repairing a road) or forms of organization (creating new status distinctions) that were not really called for in terms of the communal agenda. Each decision seemed rational enough in its own terms, but there was no conception of an overall plan. This the old guru had supplied, and impulsive behavior continued until the new guru was able to take over this function.

The cognitive disorder associated with type 5, or absolute, charisma is submissiveness. The common manifestations of this among cult members, the glassy eyes, the hollow beaming smile, are too well known to need examples here. As many accounts of cult experience have indicated (e.g., Edwards, 1979), these exaggerated symptoms of extreme cognitive submissiveness (turning off the mind) are a conditioned response, among cult members, to any challenge to the absolute truth of the cult reality.

Of much greater interest with respect to the type 5 charismatic groups is the process of charismatic unwinding that can be observed as the breakdown of legitimacy spreads from an initial challenge to absolutism, to normative doubt, to doubt about the assignment of utilities, to doubt about the ordering of preferences, and finally to doubt about the construction of meanings. Of course, a charismatic group at any level can experience not merely a simple crisis of legitimacy at its highest-achieved level of self-investment but an unwinding all the way down to loss of shared meanings. But our example is chosen from the type 5 charismatic groups to illustrate the process through all of its stages. In each case observed, the commune did follow the indicated chronology of symptoms, although, in some instances, one or more levels were skipped.

Waystation was a Christian evangelical commune located in a small town on a busy highway. It was dedicated to saving the souls of the many transients who passed through the area. Wayne, the charismatic leader, had a reputation for miracle working with lost souls. About 40 percent of the commune population were such converts. The others were mostly people who had heard Wayne speak or heard about his work and had come to join him.

The crisis of charismatic legitimacy in this commune is unusually clearly demarcated. It began with a rather sudden moody withdrawal of Wayne from the daily commune life. He was said to be depressed about the magnitude of evil in the world and how little one man, even one commune, could do about it. At this time also, in a probably not unrelated incident, Wayne was discovered to be sleeping with one of the recent young female converts—despite the commune's strict rule of celibacy. It is interesting to note that both the leader and the followers were quite defensive about the significance of this discovery and seemed to feel a strong need to justify the action to continue to believe that the leader could do no wrong.

It was at this point that the commune began to develop certain of the signs of becoming a cult. There was vague talk about the need to prepare for a special mission on a large scale that would soon be revealed and a sense that this would be seen to justify special behaviors and normative standards, not usually a part of Christian life. It was at this time also that the glassy eyed, frozen smile look associated with cult experience (Edwards, 1979; Conway and Sigelman, 1978) began to appear on the faces of the Waystation members. In terms of our model, this was a symptom of a crisis of self-estrangement. A sense of legitimate total commitment to the charismatic leader had given way to an artificial forced total commitment, maintained only through adherence to the mind-emptying discipline of submissiveness.

Soon after this, the commune entered an impulsive stage, (associated with the breakdown of normative charismatic legitimacy) as the charismatic consensus continued to unravel. This occurred as the new special mission failed to materialize. The commune went into a period of watching for signs and portents. The environment was scanned for a sense of direction. At one point, the whole commune transported itself to the top of a mountain to await instruction but none was given.

A short hysteric stage, associated with the breakdown of executive legitimacy, followed. Faith in the charismatic leader continued to deteriorate. His ability to engender group consensus even on simple issues came into question. This was a period of stormy emotional outbursts, long meetings, and battles against evil spirits. But the evil spirits, at this stage, were still perceived as coming from outside the commune.

The fourth stage of the charismatic crisis was characterized by an obsessive-compulsive battle against aimlessness. By this time it had become clear to all that the grand mission was not going to materialize. After the drama of the hysteric period, this stage was remarkably quiet and orderly. It was a time of serious long-range planning. Attempts were made to relegitimate the modest work of wayside evangelism by developing comprehensive programs emphasizing efficiency, diffusion of the message, and eventual branching to develop other evangelical missions. The walls of the largest room in the main house were totally covered with some of the most complex charts and organizational plans that we had ever seen, in or out of Washington D.C. There was a crispness and earnestness about all of the commune members. The leader's role was largely instrumental at this time. There was a sense that the crisis was over, that the commune had regained its bearings.

The final (paranoid) stage of the crisis of charismatic legitimacy seemed to develop without warning. Suddenly there was a shared knowledge that there were enemies within. A number of long-term members were expelled, with much emotional agony, at this point, and others became disillusioned and left. The commune dropped all its evangelical work in a frenzied attempt to purify itself.

Ultimately, the commune was saved from self-destruction not through its own efforts but by an accident of history. At just about this time, the charismatic Christian evangelical movement (discussed in Chapter 2) was developing a national organization. There was enough of an overlap between Waystation's ideology and that of this larger nationwide social movement for a federation to take place. Wayne was well able to accept the loss of his absolute authority, which he admitted not having handled very well. He became a valued officer within the larger organization and continued to lead his commune until he was transferred to another assignment.*

Crises of charismatic legitimacy are easier to understand, in terms of our theory, from the perspective of followers than they are from the perspective of leaders. From the point of view of one who has invested a great deal of self into a consensual collectivity embodied in the person of a charismatic leader, there is ample reason to panic when the leader begins to falter. The specific form which this panic takes, collective impairment of cognition especially of the decision-making function, is also quite understandable in light of the importance that reality building and collective decision making have in the genesis of communitarianism. But why do the charismatic leaders seem to buy so thoroughly into the game? To the same extent that commune members come to perceive charismatic leaders as repositories of their invested selves, charismatic leaders come to view their followers as extensions of their own egos and sometimes even physically as extensions of their own bodies. This book offers no explanation for this latter phenomenon, and can only suggest that it might be an important subject for future psychiatric and psychopolitical research.

---

*Although the crisis of charismatic legitimacy at Waystation had a reasonably happy ending, evidence of very similar crises—at the Bruderhof (Zablocki, 1971), Synanon (Ofshe, 1976; Overend, 1978) and Jonestown (Kilduff and Javers, 1978)—indicates that more disastrous outcomes are quite possible. From a clinical perspective, the quiescent crisis of aimlessness is a matter of some concern. This calm before the storm may easily lull the observer if not understood in full theoretical context.

The Organization of Intimacy

The kinds of breakdowns of charismatic legitimacy that we have been discussing, although interesting and important especially for the more long-lived communes, are found only in a minority of our cases. Fewer than 10 percent ($N = 11$) of communes were observed to go through such a crisis during the year separating the first and second waves and less than half presented evidence of ever having experienced such a crisis during their lifetimes.

A more common way of dealing with the problem is to forestall the charismatic crisis by anticipating it. In slightly charismatic communes, this may be accomplished by adopting anticharismatic patterns of dyadic bonding. The relational pattern associated with stability (low cathexis combined with high dyadic partiality) discussed in Chapter 4 is an example of such an adaptation. But in the fully charismatic communes there is no such relatively easy option. The shadow of the threat of charismatic tyranny under which the members live creates an overwhelming need for mutual love. At the same time, the instability of communes, both in membership and in self-investment terms, requires of members the ability to endure the constant making and breaking of relationships impartially and to be protected against the transmutation of love into dominance. The majority of the charismatic communes were found among those with the relational pattern characterized by high cathexis and low dyadic partiality. Under these constraints, in order to ward off crises of charismatic legitimacy, a distinctive style of communitarian intimacy has had to be developed.

The Norm of Amaturity

A distinguishing feature of communitarian intimacy is the deliberate and often principled avoidance of maturity. The word "maturity" is used here to mean having completed natural growth and development, its standard dictionary definition. We do not mean to imply that communitarian behavior and relationships are immature or stunted in development. The avoidance of maturity does, however, imply the persistence of a childlike plasticity of preference among commune members that makes it much easier for them to alienate portions of the decision-making function from themselves to the group and to tolerate high levels of membership turnover.

We prefer to use the term "amaturity" for this deliberate cultivation of unfinishedness. In relationships it generally manifests itself as intense love without long-term commitment. In personal behavior it is neither clearly superior nor clearly inferior to what we generally think of as conventional mature behavior. This seems to be what Erik Erikson (1970, p. 11) has in mind when he says:

> youthful behavior, where it arouses ambivalent fascination, always appears

to be both prophetic—that is, inspired by the vigour of a new age—and retrogressive in as far as it seems to insist on outworn simplicities and to betray astonishing regressions.

Both the experience of alienation and its charismatic resolution are made more palatable by the cultivation of amaturity. Most Americans are socialized to believe strongly in the appropriateness of associational norms to govern group behavior. One feels guilty for not functioning as a good responsible citizen, even though, as we have seen, the citizen role is not appropriate for communitarian life. The norm of amaturity provides justification for relinquishing the citizenly burden of an independent critical judgment. One thereby makes room in one's self for growth and charismatic inspiration. The twentieth chapter of the *Tao Te Ching,* which gives eloquent testimony to this point of view, was prominently posted in a number of the communitarian homes:

> The people in general are happy.
> I alone am tranquil, and have made no sign,
> Like a baby still unable to smile;
> Forlorn as if I had no home.
> Others all have more than enough,
> I alone am always begging for more.
> Others have crisp clear minds,
> My mind is ignorant, the mind of a fool.
> The vulgar are bright,
> And I alone seem to be dull.
> The vulgar are discriminative,
> And I alone seem to be blunt.
> I am negligent as if being obscure;
> Drifting, as if being attached to nothing.
> The people are all busy with important things to do.
> I alone am impractical and awkward,
> A glorious infant, still sucking at the breast.

Evidence for the lack of conventional maturity among commune members may be inferred from the kinds of life activities that they judged problematic and for which they looked to communal living for help. The urban commune members were asked to sort a list of activities by whether living communally made it easier or harder to accomplish them (see Table 8-1). The two at the top of the list and the two at the bottom of the list should especially be noted. They indicate that solving mental or emotional problems and being cared for when physically ill are almost universally valued as advantages of communal living. At the other extreme, being married and being monogamous are among the chief liabilities.

Rates of illness (both mental and physical) are certainly no lower in communal households than they are in nuclear family households. In fact for highly contagious infections (hepatitis, veneral disease) the commune member bears a significantly higher risk than the conventional family member. In listing mental

TABLE 8-1. Percentage of Urban Respondents Who Found That Selected Activities Were Made Easier/Harder by Living Communally

	% Who Found Item Relevant and Who Could Choose	Of Those Who Would Choose, % Who Found Activity		Total Respondents[1]
		Easier	Harder	
Solve mental or emotional problems	90%	96%	4%	450
Be cared for when physically ill	88	97	3	458
Relate to people openly and spontaneously	88	96	4	454
Meet new people	87	93	7	458
Be the kind of person you want to be	81	94	6	447
Find out who you are	80	98	2	449
Meet financial emergencies	80	96	4	455
Find out what you want in life	76	97	3	451
Support yourself financially	75	92	8	458
Pursue a religious discipline	64	87	13	445
Start a new intimate relationship	64	71	29	448
Be single	63	93	7	444
Pursue artistic or scholarly interests	63	62	38	448
Pursue career or profession	56	80	20	451
Raise children	52	76	24	432
End an intimate relationship	45	74	26	448
Work for political change	45	84	16	450
Be married	40	49	51	420
Be monogamous	37	58	42	431

[1] Respondents answered this question selectively, leading to N's varying from a high of 458 to a low of 420. It is quite likely that many of these "no answers" are equivalent to the "not relevant" response. However, because of the ambiguity involved, only those who actually checked "neither or not relevant" were included in the computation.

and physical hygiene as the major advantages of communal living, the members must have something else in mind. The issue is probably dependency. These are mostly young people with a great need to feel independent of childhood roles. But they are not yet able to do without parenting when they are sick or confused. In the family such care is often purchased with the admission of dependency and the acceptance of restrictions. In the commune, members can parent one another and feel safe and loved even while experimenting with freedom and independence.

From an Eriksonian (1963) perspective, most of the first nine items on the list in Table 8-1 have to do with preadult developmental tasks, whereas most of the last nine items have to do with adult or late adolescent developmental tasks. It is clear from the table that commune members find the preadult tasks more relevant and that they are more likely to see the commune as facilitating these tasks than the other tasks.

There is very little ideological variance in these findings.* The members of the political and the rehabilitational communes tend to be a bit more negative on most of the items and the members of the psychological communes tend to be a bit more positive, but in no cases are the rank orderings of the items seriously altered. Note that, on matters of personal identity formation (e.g., find out who you are), almost no one sees the commune as an obstacle to achievement.

Amaturity affects intimate relationships in a variety of ways. Two in particular are important enough and universal enough to require further discussion: (1) the relations between the sexes and (2) the relations between adults and children. With regard to the first, we must be aware that the absence as well as the presence of sexual activity may be significant. Celibacy may be the signal of a brotherly-sisterly incest taboo; promiscuity may be the ritualized manifestation of communion. With regard to adult-child relations, we shall see that the refusal of adults to regard themselves as more mature than and therefore superior to the commune children is responsible for certain paradoxes.

Sexuality and Marriage

There exists no single dominant norm governing sexual relations in communes. Instead, there is a wide variety of patterns ranging from sex with anyone forbidden to sex with everyone required (see Table 8-2). Some form of monogamous pattern is followed by more communes that follow any other single pattern, but this still comprises less than half the communes. Less than a quarter are based upon "official monogamy" in the sense of requiring a marriage license.

---

*The one exception is the middle item, "pursue a religious discipline," which we have not placed in either of the two subsets. For this item, knowledge of ideological type proportionally reduces error in predicting the item response by more than half. For the item "work for political change," a reduction of a fifth can be achieved. For all other items it is negligible.

TABLE 8-2. Sexual Organization of Rural and Urban Communes

Dominant Norm	Rural		Urban		Total	
	Number	% of Total	Number	% of Total	Number	% of Total
Compulsory celibacy	3	5%	5	9%	8	7%
Voluntary celibacy	0	0	7	12	7	6
Licensed monogamy						
Commune approval required	2	3	4	6	6	5
Commune approval not required	8	14	12	20	20	17
Unofficial monogamous marriage with commitment	21	35	9	15	30	25
Shifting sexual relationships	14	24	9	15	23	19
Partial group marriage	9	15	5	9	14	12
Group marriage, all included	1	2	0	0	1	1
Mixed	1	2	8	14	9	8
Total	59	100%	59	100%	118[a]	100%

[a]In two cases, the dominant norm could not be determined.

It is important for most communes to find some way of taming the dyadic sexual bond. Adopting a norm of celibacy is the most direct way of doing this. As Table 8-2 indicates, only 13 percent of the sample communes practiced celibacy at the time of the first wave of the study.* But this figure is misleading in that it fails to take account of the larger number of individual commune members who practiced celibacy as a discipline within communes in which this was not the dominant norm. In three of our communes, celibacy was expected only of the charismatic leader. In one commune, the charismatic leader (and his selected partners) were the only ones allowed to be noncelibate.

Celibacy is a prime example of the kinds of ideological orientation that we discussed in Chapter 6. It is easy to reach consensus on the value of celibacy; it is much less easy to achieve consensus on the practice of celibacy. Three types of social control mechanisms are used to enforce the norm of celibacy. One of the most effective, in communes that are part of federated systems, is the transfer of one of the members of a budding romantic dyad to a different household. This mechanism is particularly effective because the involved parties themselves are generally distressed by their developing sexual attraction and thus become willing self-accusers.

A second control mechanism involves the loss of status. Celibacy is strictly

*All the celibate communes were religious in ideology with one exception, a political commune.

required unless you are married and, if you get married, you are put back a step in the sacral hierarchy. All the voluntarily celibate groups in our sample made use of this mechanism. It usually worked to discourage sexuality while giving the commune members a sense of free choice. Those that did choose to get married often left the commune soon afterward. In a number of instances, couples who were able to stick it out eventually became commune leaders.

A third control mechanism, sometimes used in conjunction with the second, required celibacy only within the commune's physical perimeters. What a person did when away from the commune was his or her own business. In groups with little or no investment of self, such moral dualism represented a recognition that the norms had not been internalized, and it was the least effective of the three mechanisms for controlling sexuality. Members characteristically responded to the inevitable deepening of outside sexual attachments by staying away for longer and longer periods of time, by leaving altogether, or by eventually flouting the rules by bringing the loved one home.

The imposition of a communewide incest taboo is a mechanism for regulating sexuality that is closely related to this third mechanism for enforcing celibacy. Instead of making a distinction between inside and outside, the distinction is made between insiders and outsiders. Much attention has been given to the question of the existence of communitarian incest taboos, especially in the study of exogamic behavior among second-generation *sabras* in the Israeli kibbutzim (Spiro, 1958, pp. 347ff.; Bettelheim, 1969, p. 255; Talmon, 1972, pp. 139ff.). However, in the communes in our sample, the second generation was negligible in magnitude, and the incest taboo was far from universal.

Those communes that supported an incest taboo often did so in self-conscious attempts to make the commune an alternative family. Danziger and Greenwald (1973, p. 24ff.) describe the case of a commune in New Brunswick, New Jersey, that first declared itself to be a family and then decreed that it followed from this definition that any sex between members would be forbidden on the grounds that it would be incest. The handful of other communes that prohibited sex among members (either absolutely or only among the unmarried) usually did so for pragmatic reasons and did not label what they were prohibiting incest. Anticipation of the difficulty of having eventually to live with a former lover was one common reason given for the prohibition. Another was the concern of married couples to avoid sexual competition from singles.

Those communes whose members tried to maintain active sex lives under the constraint of an incest taboo usually found the situation awkward. Women, in particular, complained about logistical difficulties. For both men and women, the membership status of serious lovers who spent a lot of time in the communal home was a serious problem. One commune attempted to solve the problem with a lover's clause, which granted immediate membership to the lover of any member—but this proved to be unworkable. Another commune divided sex partners into three categories: fellow commune members (forbidden), serious lovers (allowed only away from home), and tricks (allowed at home for casual sex only). This system worked to everyone's satisfaction for about a year and a half and then started to deteriorate as lines of demarcation increasingly blurred.

The most interesting thing about all these rules to abolish or limit sexual behavior is the frequency with which they were covertly violated. In 60 percent of the communes with restrictions on sexual behavior, there was at least one (and often several) documented instance of a violation.* Frequently, these involved the leaders of the celibate or sexually restrictive communes. More than just hypocrisy seems to have been at work here. The strong bonds that communal living engenders provide dyadic paths for sexual attraction that even the most ideologically committed found hard to resist.

Many communes have sought not to restrict sexuality but to encourage fuller sexual freedom. As we saw in Chapter 5, images of sexual utopia in which repression disappears and the commune comes to be bound together through mutually harmonious relationships of sexual love are quite common, especially in secular communes, but occasionally in religious communes as well. Sexual repression is often attacked, not only as something harmful in itself, but as the linchpin of the entire repressive capitalist system (Reich, 1970; Marcuse, 1962).

We have already seen, in Chapter 3, that communes do not, in general, tend to wild outbursts of sexual experimentation.† However, Table 8-3 indicates that males respond sexually to the event of joining a commune differently from females. Communal living provides females with an opportunity to "catch up" with males in diversity of sexual experience. In most sexual categories listed in Table 8-3, males had greater proportional experience than females prior to commune membership. But females tended to make up for this gap by greater experimentation after joining. For homosexuality and group marriage in particular, the rates of first female exposure after joining were almost double the male rates.

It should not be thought that women were therefore the chief beneficiaries of communitarian sexual freedom. On the contrary, they often seemed to be its victims. The interlarding of affection with power, which we discussed in Chapters 4 and 7, seemed generally to work against the interests of women. Perhaps it would be more accurate to say that it worked to divide women into two unequal groups: a small minority of the strongest and most self-confident who thrived on sexual freedom and the majority who seemed to suffer because of it.

The relationship between love and power in communes is illustrated by the following excerpt from an interview with a women in a commune in Atlanta:

---

*Because such documentation was understandably hard to come by, it is likely that the actual percentage was much higher.

†In fact both historically and in terms of the data presented in Table 8-3, the modal pattern of sexual experimentation in communes is celibacy.

TABLE 8-3. The Sexual Experimentation of Men and Women as a Function of Commune Membership

Sexual Behavior	Sex	Proportion of All Respondents Who Had Ever Engaged in The Behavior	Proportion of Those Who Had Ever Engaged in the Behavior Who Had Done So Only	
			Before Joining but Not After	After Joining but Not Before
Sexual relations with more than one person at the same time	Men	31%[a]	56%	25%
	Women	32	56	27
Homosexual relations	Men	18	54	19
	Women	17	38	36
An arrangement of open marriage[1]	Men	18	67	14
	Women	18	62	13
Group marriage	Men	4	75	25
	Women	2	60	40
Public nudity	Men	56	43	22
	Women	46	34	24
Celibacy	Men	40	21	43
	Women	38	23	38
Falling in love	Men	89	47	5
	Women	86	42	4

[1] Open marriage refers to a marriage contract in which the partners agree to release each other from the vows of sexual exclusiveness.
[a] Total respondents, N = 542; 298 men and 244 women.

342

I was working with him being a carpenter's helper for a while because I didn't have a job yet. One night a few weeks after I was living there, he came into my room at night and crawled into bed with me, you know, wanted to make love. It completely freaked me out because I really didn't know what to say. He was telling me that we couldn't communicate unless we had sex. You know, the same stuff you hear since you are fifteen, and it's all bullshit. I have heard this for years now. I think I have managed to communicate with men without sex. I really think it's too bad. I don't have sex with women and I communicate with them. I try. But eventually he got the point and left, but after that, maybe it was my imagination, but I think that I really didn't know how to handle the situation. With so many men it is so connected with the ego. If you reject them sexually that means you *reject* them. And how do you tell someone that you might like them even though you don't want to sleep with them? The men here don't seem to really understand that.

We saw in Chapter 7 that no commune was able to overcome the sex-role stereotyping of labor. In emotional matters even more, the traditional association of women with expressive functions prevailed. Note in Table 8-4 the extremely high frequency of females in confiding bonds; females tend to be most chosen as confidantes both of other females and of males. In the same table, it can be seen that the self-attribution of personality characteristics also conforms to conventional sexual stereotypes. A male is more likely than a female to see himself as influential, decisive, charismatic, narcissistic, holy, dominant, and sexy. A female, on the other hand, is more likely to see herself as loving, strong, supportive, intuitive, dependent, passive, and interested both in children and in fixing up the communal house.

The rationale for sexual freedom is that it provides liberation from traditional sex roles. Yet the evidence that we have seen suggests that such liberation has not happened either in the domain of work or in the domain of relationships between the sexes. It may be that it cannot happen in collectivities based upon the investment of self. The logic of sexual liberation requires the radical separation of affection from power. The logic of self-investment, based upon the arguments presented in Chapters 4 and 6, may require that affection and power be predicated upon one another. This is speculative, but, for whatever reason, it was the case that males dominated fellow commune members in the power hierarchies almost twice as often as did females and that females were chosen as most loving almost twice as often as males.

Moreover, marriage within a communitarian context, on the whole, could not be considered to be sexually liberated. There is no evidence in our data that communes promote equality within the marriage relationship. There were twenty married couples for whom relationship data were available. Of these twenty, eleven had no strict power relationship (i.e., strict in the sense that both husband and wife agree on which of them has the power). In all nine cases in which a strict power relationship existed between husband and wife, the husband held the power. Of the remaining eleven couples, the pattern was

TABLE 8-4. Personality Differences by Sex: Urban Commune Members

A. Confiding Relationships by Sex of Chooser and Chosen[1]

		Confidant(e)		
		Male	Female	
Confider	Male	108 (34%)	207 (66%)	315 (100%)
	Female	99 (19%)	412 (81%)	511 (100%)

[1] N = 826 (unit of analysis is the dyad).

B. Differences in Personality Self-attribution by Sex[1]

	% of Each Sex Ascribing Attributes to Themselves	
	Males	Females
Attributes more often chosen by women than men		
Loving	39%	59%
Interested in children	36	52
Strong	32	39
Supportive	49	55
Intuitive	37	41
Dependent	18	22
Interested in fixing up the house	43	46
Passive	20	23
Attributes more often chosen by men than women		
Influential	40	22
Decisive	39	25
Charismatic	21	9
Narcissistic	24	15
Holy	17	9
Dominant	20	16
Sexy	17	15

[1] N = 333.

mixed. In six cases, the male was higher in rank, number of subordinates, or both. In two the female was higher. In the remaining three they were of equal rank.

The entire question of marriage opens up another dimension in the organization of communitarian sexuality. We saw in Chapter 3 that communal living is associated with very high levels of marital dissolution. But, when we reexamine the stability of the marital bond through the prism of our ideological typology, this association no longer appears to be so straightforward. Marriage is the area of life in which the religious communes and the secular communes are most completely set off from each other. Religious communes, where they do not require celibacy, support and strengthen the marriage relationship; secular communes most often undermine and weaken it.

Of the fifty-four legally married couples who were observed in communal living over a full year, seventeen were in religious communes and thirty-seven were in secular communes. Of those in the religious communes, 76 percent remained intact over the year. Of those in the secular communes, only 27 percent remained intact. This cannot be explained by the argument that religious couples leave their communes prior to getting divorced whereas secular divorcing couples remain. The rate at which couples left was almost identical for religious and secular communes, and the scattered ex-member data available on couples indicate that the rate of breakup was higher for the secular than for the religious among those couples who left as well as among those who stayed.

A portion of the observed difference in marital stability between religious and secular communes in undoubtedly due to self-selection. Those with greater commitment to fidelity and other traditional marital values tend to gravitate to religious life-styles and hence to religious communes. For example, in an attempt to measure marital anomie, commune members were asked to agree or disagree with the following statement: "With respect to relations between husband and wife these days there are no clear guidelines to tell us what is right and what is wrong."

Only 11 percent of the members of the religious communes agreed with this statement ($N = 158$). In the nonreligious communes, 59 percent agreed with the statement ($N = 211$). Moreover, these figures were not much changed when only new members of these communes were considered, indicating that this extreme attitudinal difference is something that people probably bring with them to their communes.

However, the difference between marital stability in religious and in secular communes cannot be explained solely in terms of self-selection because this difference is greater than any observed between religious and nonreligious people outside of communal living. A part is probably due to the greater support that religious communes give to marriage. Much of this support was expressed in relational terms. Religious communes tended to treat the married couple as a single sociometric node, an expanded self that was investing its identity in the still larger expanded self of the commune. Secular communes tended to treat the couple as two distinct people who happened to be married. This difference is clearly reflected in responses to two questions that were asked in selected urban communes: In the religious communes, 83 percent of the measured perceptions of married couples saw the husband and wife as rarely or never disagreeing with each other on commune issues. In contrast, only 36 percent of the perceptions of married couples in secular communes fell into this category.

The second question asked, "To what extent are married couples perceived as being part of the commune as a unit as opposed to being members as individuals?" The married couples in religious communes were perceived as being part of the commune as a unit 44 percent of the time versus, in the secular communes, only 11 percent of the time.*

Although most secular communes tolerated marriage, it was not given a great deal of ideological respect, and this was reflected in the attitudes toward marriage expressed by both married and single members of these secular communes:

> I think for me it's unnecessary. Marriage is institutionalized neurosis.

> Marriage is a trap; an artificial commitment toward a limited life-style.

> I wish it could disappear completely. I would discourage someone planning to get married.

> I'm more open to it than ever before but I still doubt I'll get married. I don't think much of my parents' marriage and that makes a difference for me.

> It's unnecessary bondage that limits people's creative, intellectual, and community growth. It's similar to black slavery for women.

> Living here, it's easier not to. My needs get met here or by friends. But there may be a situation to get married for practical reasons.

> It's economically discriminatory and sexist. I lean toward contract marriages.

> I have mixed feelings. I certainly believe in an open marriage relationship.

> For me it's extremely valuable because of the person I'm married to. But I feel a little bad sometimes when I'm with feminists because of course I'm not economically independent.

> I'm dubious about monogamous marriage. I'm curious about group marriage but I'm not ready yet.

A number of secular communes had positive fantasies about group marriage, although few were willing to attempt to act them out. As a form of sexual experimentation at the other extreme in terms of frequency of sexual activity from celibacy, it accomplishes much the same goals from the point of view of community, as Kanter (1972), Noyes (1870), and others have pointed out. Both celibacy and group marriage serve the important function of decreasing the strength of dyadic bonds (see Chapter 4). They also remove the necessity for the individual to juggle nuclear family loyalties as opposed to communal loyalities (Constantine and Constantine, 1973; Ramey, 1972).

The attitudes of the members of the religious communes contrasted sharply with those of the secular:

> It's the greatest thing that ever happened in my life. The Lord intended me to find real happiness and fulfillment. I have no negative feelings about it at all.

---

*N = 124. Unfortunately these questions were not asked in the communes from which the separating couples came, so it is not possible to say what effect these perceptions had on the stability of a specific couple.

It's a holy communion of two people. It's something that shouldn't be broken if at all possible.

I think it would be beautiful to have that commitment. The institution of marriage is falling apart and marriage takes very strong commitment.

If I marry it will be understanding that marriage is for keeps regardless of what happens. Death is the only way to break marriage. But I don't feel obligated to marry.

It's a sacred thing. People are intended to be monogamous.

It's a beautiful thing. It's a trying situation but there is no liberation without labor.

The Lord wants me to stay single for a while. People are complete outside of marriage and should not be coerced.

People wonder why I'm not married. It's a blessing because I don't have to direct myself to a man.

How can I give myself to another if I don't know myself right now.

I'm married to the Guru. I don't need any other kind of marriage.

At their most extreme, religious communes deny their members the right to divorce. Many other religious communes look on such a prohibition with favor but do not feel ready to try it. The surrender of autonomy of the couple to the group is often highly valued by the couple. It provides them with a family security that they could not provide for themselves. It may be one of the most important mechanisms whereby religious communes are able to make the transition from short-term to long-term stability.

Experiments in Parenting

The avoidance of intimacy carries over, in many contemporary communes, to the relationships between parents and children. A widely recurrent pattern takes the form of an insistence that even very young children take responsibility for themselves and their own actions. The following is an excerpt from an interview with a mother of a young preteenage girl living communally:

Q: Has she had sex play with other children?
A: Yes.
Q: Did you do anything about it?
A: No. I've given it a lot of thought. I've made it a point to tell her how I valued my sex life, what I think is a good way to be but I haven't told her not to do it.
Q: What values are those?
A: I think that relationships are important, that two people care about each other. She knows more than I did. I didn't know those kind of possibilities existed. I didn't have any idea that kids could have any kind of sexual contact when I was a kid.

Q; Did it surprise you when she started?

A: It surprised me and made me fell sort of puritanical for a while, then I felt that I wasn't right and I didn't try to put anything bad on her. . . . I'm glad I didn't put any worrisome energy into it or make her feel doubtful.

There is a certain irony in the prevailing *laissez-faire* attitude toward child rearing. In this respect, contemporary communes are very different from most of their older counterparts. Child rearing has often been deemed the best opportunity to engineer consensus. The Hutterites are a good example of this point of view (Bennett, 1967, p. 248):

These thoroughgoing methods produce the Hutterian consensus, an element of conformity in the Hutterian personality that shows up in psychological tests. In the study by Kaplan and Plaut, the "normal" Hutterian personality revealed by projective tests was remarkably homogeneous and had content duplicating the major features of Hutterian culture as viewed from the outside. There was remarkably little difference between individual protocols; and there was "no status differentiations," and little "overt" competitiveness."

The Hutterian expression, "Train the tree when it is young for when it is old it is impossible to bend," is indicative of the extremely rigorous inculcation of ideological values imposed upon children from the earliest ages.

Contemporary communes have often taken the opposite perspective involving a glorification of the child and an involvement in being childlike. One observer reported a large sign hung on the wall of a communal house which read, "Find Out What the Children Are Wondering and Wonder It." This attitude prevails in many of the rural and some of the urban households included in our study.

Some communes adopt formal mechanisms for dealing with shared parenthood (see Table 8-5). Eiduson (1979) found great diversity in the childrearing patterns of the rural communes that she studied and this is also what we found. In some the adults spend time and get great joy from being with the children. The adults obviously feel that the children are an important part of the community, and the children also feel that—as well as being part of the larger community. This is in contrast to many communes in which so much emphasis is placed on adults' being able to spend time for themselves, that the groups sometimes come close to the risk of child neglect.

Another major source of parental uneasiness centered around ideological conflict, especially in communes where not all parents accepted the childlike philosophy of the hippie establishment. The following is an account, by a commune member of the late 1960s, of such a conflict (Gardner, 1970, pp. 18ff.):

Many a group meeting centered around the problem of "the kids." (Before their arrival, we had only one or two infants and a 3-year-old girl.) Because they were breaking out of a sick environment, their parents felt the kids

TABLE 8–5.   Communal Childcare Arrangements

	Proportion of All Communes		Proportion of Only Those Communes that Have Children	
	Urban	Rural	Urban	Rural
No children allowed	28%	5%[a]	—	—
No children present	33	5	—	—
Parents totally responsible for care of their own children	13	10	33%	11%
Cooperative childcare arrangements among individual commune members	17	49	42	54
Communal day care center	6	22	14	24
Extended family[1]	4	10	11	11

[1] In the extended family, all children are related to all communal adults as if the latter were all equally their parents.
[a] N = 120; 60 urban and 60 rural communes.

needed a maximum of patience and love and understanding. Other people felt they needed simply to be treated as human beings and that their mother should not repress the anger and frustration which she obviously felt. Other people were at a loss to give them love, when in fact the only emotions which these kids inspired in most of us were anger and annoyance.

Most of us felt that we should in fact try to let them work through their hang-ups and hopefully eventually come out the other side. Let them yell "penis" and "vagina" at the top of their lungs in order to hear the echo bounce off the mountains. Let them throw Raggedy Ann into the cellar and elaborate upon her tortures while chanting, "No, you *can't* come out of the cellar!" all day long. Maybe we could have managed that all right.

But what no one seemed to be able to endure were the howls and wails which rose from the lungs of one sister after the other, time after time, all day long, and particularly on rainy days of which there were many, locked up with them in the house all day long.

Apparently we just weren't strong enough nor healthy enough ourselves to be able to cope with these children. And their parents, who had had such great hopes of finding in us a healthy environment, soon had to build their own shelter in order to remove themselves from our environment.

On the whole, however, comments from communal parents were favorable about the experience of raising their children collectively. The following is a sampling of quotations from these questionnaires:

This is the best option available for raising children, both emotionally and financially. It gives them a good, healthy environment that you have some control over.

The commune is an excellent place to raise children because there are so many adults here who deal with children in a conscious manner.

The commune provides a calm atmosphere for the children. The presence of different adults helps my children to lessen their attachment to their parents. They also learn the discipline of group life.

There are a lot of warm honest people who are willing to take their share of responsibility for the children.

The commune provides a supportive environment for the kids and for my raising them. They have learned that their actions affect others and they have learned to take responsibility for their actions. They see that different adults have different ways of dealing with anger and frustration and that they can have different ways too.

My child can always find people to relate to her when I'm busy or tired. She learns other people's values.

(Single mother) My daughter receives more male attention than she would at home alone with me.

This is the best place in the world for children. Kids are treated like people in little bodies.

This is a fantastic place for children. I've never seen happier kids. It changes them so much. They become independent and mature. Communal living encourages them to become adults.

The foregoing has suggested an intriguing paradox. The communal parent often seems to combine a highly developed concern and regard for the happiness and welfare of his or her child with an unwillingness to act in behalf of that happiness and welfare. Ideologically, this will often be explained in terms of the principles of Summerhill or of karma or of some combination of the two. In other words, the communal ideology, if it is Summerhillian, will argue that the child is born perfect and becomes corrupted only through the repressive influence of his or her environment (usually meaning adults). The karmic ideology, somewhat more pessimistically, argues that the child is born with hang-ups accumulated from previous lifetimes that he or she must try to expunge during his or her current lifetime. Any attempt at parental interference runs the risk of shielding the child from his or her fate and robbing him/her of his/her opportunity to undo negative karma (karma that perhaps can be undone only through suffering).

These peculiar ideological tenets can be explained in terms of the evolution of adult attitudes toward the child in response to the accelerating pace of social and cultural change. Briefly, this evolution can be conceived of as proceeding through three distinct stages:

1. *Unconscious transmission of the heritage:* During the time when childhood was not yet recognized as a unique psychological category, the child automatically grew into a set of patterns from which there was no expected systematic deviation over a period of many generations. The

parent did not have to *know* how to raise his or her child. He or she need only set the example of his/her own maturity.

2. *The art of or science of child rearing:* This is associated with the period (roughly 1800–1950) when the adult member of the society expected that society to change significantly from one generation to the next, but to do so in a manner that was basically predictable. The success of a child in coping with the problems that were to come in his or her own adult life were then seen as a function of his/her parents' ability to anticipate those problems and prepare him/her adequately for them.

3. *Sacral neglect:* With the postwar generation of parents, we come to a generation that perceives change as happening so rapidly that the parent cannot hope to anticipate the needs of the adult of the future. Along with the abrogation of responsibility of preparing a child for an unknown future, quite naturally goes the hope (expressed however not as a hope but as a conviction) that the nature of this awe-inspiring social change is in fact benevolent. The parent need only stand out of the way.

Sacral neglect implies not the neglect of indifference but the hesitation born of awe. It does not imply that communal parents do not characteristically feed their children well, make provision for their comfort, shelter, and safety, and look after their health. But, in the realm of the emotional and of whatever the commune may regard as spiritual, there is a true dread of assuming responsibility for action.

This attitude is illustrated in the following response of a young commune father:

Q: Are there any exemplary type people you'd like to see him model himself after?

A: No. Because there isn't any model. He's an Aquarian. He's in the year 2000; that's where he comes in. Jesus was about 29 or 30 when he finally decided what to do. . . . When these kids are that age it will be 2001. There is no mold that I have pictured for him because he is going to do something to blow my mind. I can't even picture it.

Families of Limited Liability

There exists no social institution (at least in American society) capable of routinely providing the kind of intimacy that commune members seem to seek. A desire for such intermediate *gemeinschaft* has, in recent years, added to the already existing strains on both neighborhood and family as social institutions without noticeably filling the gap. Without a clear model of what such intermediate *gemeinschaft* should look like, communes often wind up vacillating between ideological images of community and ideological images of family.

In our sample, the family image has generally been the more compelling if for no other reason than the communes' relatively small populations. But communes have, nevertheless, remained genuinely ambivalent toward the family, and this ambivalence is reflected in the difficulty that communes have had in solving the most elementary problems of relationship between the sexes and between the age grades. Janowitz (1967, pp. 210ff.) has shown that the community of limited liability can be a viable social invention in response to some of the contradictions of contemporary life and culture. But the family of limited liability may be a contradiction in terms. At best, such collectivities may survive precariously, from year to year, always on the knife's edge of charisma without ever reaching any permanent equilibrium.

Family Imagery in Communitarian Ideology

Communitarian movements have always had to confront the question of whether, and to what extent, they were families, or took the place of families in their members' lives. But, in this regard, contemporary communes are significantly different from the utopian communities in America during the eighteenth and nineteenth centuries and from the Israeli kibbutzim. The utopias and the kibbutzim strove to develop a familial structure in the hope that this would facilitate the achievement of certain (social, political, and economic) nonfamilial functions. American communes, on the other hand, are looked to by their members for the fulfillment of familial functions without the restrictions of the family structure (e.g., sexual and child-rearing functions without marital and intergenerational responsibilities). The utopias and kibbutzim used family structure to recreate society without impersonality. The communes use voluntaristic structure to recreate family without nuclear dependence.

Rosabeth Kanter has pointed out an important distinction between utopian communities of the nineteenth century and the commune of today (1972, p. 165):

> Whereas communes of the past were described in books about socialism, communism and cooperation, communes today are increasingly discussed in books about family. Communes of the past called themselves "societies" (the Society of Believers, the Harmony Society), indicating their interest in comprehensiveness; today's groups are more frequently called "families" (the Family of Mystic Arts, the Lyman Family).

It is interesting to ask whether such nomenclature reflects a distinct ideological direction.

There are, as we have seen, communes that are expressly extended family oriented. They are self-consciously founded as alternatives to the isolated nuclear family, typically by married or formerly married persons whose previous nuclear family experience was dissatisfying in some regard. The ideologies of such communes are, for obvious reasons, more highly loaded with familial concerns than are the ideologies of communes formed by young single people just out of high school or college. One suspects that growing concern with the decline of the traditional nuclear family has resulted in disproportionate amount of attention paid this type of commune by academic researchers as well as by the American public. But only 11 of the 120 communes in our sample are alternative family oriented.

Yet because a communal group's principal ideological goals are other than family oriented this does not make it incorrect to view communes as extended families. Communes are often spawned by larger religious, social, or political movements. These larger movements have in common major dissatisfactions with contemporary society. But their programs stress the importance of what type of person to be and how to relate to others, as well as how to change society. The establishment of a community of like-minded persons is seen as a means to achieve various internal relational and external institutional goals. What needs to be explained, therefore, about a political commune, for example, is not its political consciousness but its communitarian organization.

As Goode (1964, p. 2) has pointed out, all social movements oriented to large-scale social change devote attention to the family because family patterns are perceived as central elements in any social structure. Thus, whether any commune's specific goals are religious, political, or psychological, we find concern with family forms and relations. In the decade 1965–1975, the relative concern of many religious and political movements with the family increased drastically. For many reasons, some of which were discussed in Chapter 2, family life during this period was seen as highly problematic.

We may ask whether the familial structure assumed by most communes is deliberate or epiphenomenal. The fact that members of a commune share the same household forces them willy-nilly, into some kind of intimacy. Thus many familial concerns are inevitable—for example, the regulation of sexual relations. However, it is significant that commune members deliberately choose to live under conditions of such forced intimacy. Another is that, having chosen to do so, they do not in most instances, adopt the distancing mechanisms that residents in rooming houses (or even coeducational dormitories) use to maintain social distance. It would seem that, at least the intimacy (either sexual or non-sexual) of family is esteemed by communitarians, even if the commitment of family is not.

The sharp distinction that communitarians make between closeness and permanence in relationships is perhaps a key to resolving the ambiguity surrounding communal familism. Communes that have been distinguished as having familial ideologies value interpersonal bonds that are both close knit (in the family sense) and permanent (or at least long term). Many of the others, however, value the former without the latter.

In Chapter 5, it was seen that the most highly esteemed of all instrumental values to communitarians is love. They are one of the few populations for which comparable data are available to rank loving even higher than honesty. In earlier chapters, we have also seen abundant evidence of the importance of dyadic loving relations in communal life. On the other hand, among terminal values, family security was ranked fourteenth out of nineteen. This is a value that almost all other populations rank among the top three (see Table 8-6).

A content analysis of the open-ended responses to questions about the commune members' goals, values, and reasons for joining provides evidence that the urban commune members do not perceive the building of alternative family forms as a primary concern (c.f., Aidala, 1979). However, comparable data for the rural do not exist, and there is reason to believe that alternative family building is of greater importance among the rural communitarians.

Yet we cannot rely entirely on conscious goals and reasons adduced by commune members themselves for participation in a communal household. Whatever their admitted group goals or reasons for joining, we find that a large proportion of commune members feel that the commune is their family. Fifty-nine percent of our sample agree with the statement, "I feel that the people in this commune are my true family." However, recall that in Chapter 4 we saw that response to this question varied considerably by the criterion of whether or not the commune had a charismatic leader. One plausible explanation for this variance is that commune members hold inarticulate and incoherent longings for the commune to become a new kind of family for them. But, without a charismatic leader to give these yearnings meaning and form, the yearnings themselves do not rise to the level of consciousness. Instead, the commune members will act out, unconsciously (and often neurotically), the outmoded role behaviors of their families of origin.

In Conclusion

In these eight chapters we have looked at communes from many perspectives. A good number of intriguing findings have been made and yet much territory has remained unexplored. The task of reducing 120 distinct worlds of meaning to comprehensible and comparable units has necessarily meant ignoring an abundance of interesting material. But the decision to organize our study around the search for consensus has proven a fruitful one. The most general overall finding of this book is that communal systems, in their search for consensus, tend to generate intense networks of interpersonal interaction, which, in the absence of periodic charismatic renewal, tend to be associated with communal instability.

The first two chapters of this book were devoted to locating communes and communitarianism in time and space. Evidence was first presented to show that communes are a recurring historical phenomenon appearing in times and places characterized by a rapid proliferation of meaning systems and choice alternatives. In Chapter 2 we showed that the most recent communitarian movement in the United States is yet another example of this recurrent phenomenon and that, while it has certain unique features of its own, it does not differ from the various communitarian movements of the past more than those movements

TABLE 8–6. Comparative Evaluation of Family Security[1]

Sample Ranking Family Security	Family Security (composite rank)
High	
Age in 30s	1
Whites	2
Poor (income less than $2,000)	2
Age in 20s	2
Age in 70s	2
U.S. males	2
U.S. females	2
Blacks	4
Low	
Homosexuals	12
Catholic priests	12
Seminarians	12
Hippies	14
Communitarians	14

[1] Except for the communitarian data, these ranks were compiled from Rokeach (1972, passim) from data collected at various times in the 1960s and 1970s.

differ from one another. We further saw that the United States, like most complex societies, neither encourages nor represses communitarian experiments. The great bulk of observed commune instability must be attributed to factors within the communes themselves, not to externally imposed repressions or enticements.

Of the many findings presented in Part I of this book, undoubtedly the most significant is the love density (cathexis) effect. This may be summarized as follows: (1) When comparing communes with one another, the greater the proportion of possible relational linkages among members characterized by a loving bond, the more unstable will be the commune; (2) however, when comparing individuals within the same commune, the effect of loving is reversed (i.e., the more loving choices received by a member, the greater the likelihood of his remaining a member); (3) and finally, in communes with resident charismatic leaders, the above relationship between loving and instability does not apply.

It is interesting to note that the relational configurations of the communes allow us to predict their stability over the entire following year. These indicators predict the future state of the commune better than any other set of variables including the expectations of the commune members themselves. This leads us to argue that, in certain types of collectivities, the relational network is so sensitive an indicator of collective sentiment and organizational solidarity that it can give prior warning of structural events that will later be motivated by dispositions that have not yet been consciously articulated by the participant members. Whether relational networks have this capacity only in communes or also in other types of collectivities such as families is an important subject for future research.

The causal mechanism by which cathexis leads to organizational instability in communes seems to be the reduction of interpsychic distances beyond the limits of the humanly tolerable. Our evidence suggests, as have other studies (e.g., Etzioni, 1975, Granovetter, 1973), that too much bondedness can be as harmful for an organization, even for a commune, as too little bondedness. However, as findings in the second half of this book suggest, this leaves communes in a serious bind because the logic of charismatic self investment requires just such a reduction of interpsychic distances. Communes are thus seen to be intrinsically unstable in the absence of either (a) a reliable and replenishable source of charismatic authority, or (b) some internal or external force that functions to hold down the level of cathexis.

The causal mechanism and the causal direction of the association between cathexis and charisma remain a good deal less clear. Various works in progress by Bradley, Mannhardt, and Zablocki may eventually shed some light on this question, although further research is also likely to be needed. A related problem requiring further research involves the role of interpersonal power hierarchies in the charismatic process. We have found that such hierarchies are universal among the communes in our sample but that they tend to overlap with love networks more fully in the charismatic than in the noncharismatic communes. Analysis of later waves of data may help us to determine the actual mechanism by which this occurs.

The major empirical finding presented in Part II of this book concerns the association between charismatic authority and the search for consensus. This finding involves indirect evidence and is thus difficult to summarize. It involves the behavioral orientation of commune members to a nested set of five skills or tasks which are postulated to be necessary for the attainment of consensus. These tasks are: (1) meaning construction; (2) value ordering; (3) the assignment of utilities to outcomes; (4) the development of rules or norms of decision making; and (5) the setting of a standard of comparison whereby the entire communal enterprise can be evaluated against alternative ways of living. It is hypothesized that, in order to achieve these tasks, each one of which is dependent upon the achievement of all those preceding it, commune members invest themselves in the group and this investment forms the basis for charismatic authority.

The existence of this nested set of decision-making skills cannot be demonstrated directly with the data available. Instead, two sources of indirect evidence are tapped to buttress the general ethnographic plausibility of the argument. The first source of indirect evidence is a strong isomorphism between the hypothesized investment pattern and the observed ways in which authority is observed to be centralized and autonomy surrendered in the 120 communes. These were found to fit a Gutman scale of precisely the kind that would have been predicted by our hypothesis. The second source of indirect evidence is again an isomorphism, this time between the set of five decision-making skills and the collective cognitive breakdowns associated with various levels of crisis of charismatic legitimacy. Again it was found that the patterning of these crises was just what would have been predicted by the argument.

By focusing attention on the small group decision-making process, we have come to define alienation differently from many sociologists. Alienation is perceived to originate neither in the relationship of the individual to *a priori* meanings, values, and norms, as many functionalists believe, nor in the reification of the meanings, values, and norms that "man" himself has created, as sociologists of knowledge seem to suggest. People do indeed create their own "realities" but they do so collectively, not individually. It is precisely in this problematic *collective* process of reality construction that the roots of alienation begin and the fundamental link between alienation and charisma must be understood.

We need, in future work, to learn more about the psychological components of charismatic relations. What actually happens to people, cognitively and emotionally, when they invest themselves in a collectivity? What happens to charismatic leaders when their authority begins to be questioned? Swanson (1978, 1978a) in his work on trance states and possession has been pursuing some promising leads in this direction, as have the various researchers attempting to understand the process of deprogramming. But much more remains to be done.

There is an urgent need to understand more about the circumstances in which people turn to charismatic leaders and voluntarily sever their links with the habit of ordinary critical reflection. However, the need is not just to understand why people join and stay in communes. Although communal living remains an option for (in some places) up to two percent of the population, *communitarianism,* defined as communal living in the service of shared ideological goals, has rapidly declined since 1975. Someday it will rise again in another form, as it always has; meanwhile, isolated successful communes will continue to prosper. The urgency of the need to better understand charisma derives from the fact that, while the commune movement has declined, the search for charismatic consensus that engendered it has intensified. It is likely that this search will take ever larger, more institutionalized forms in American society to the increasing peril of our democratic and pluralistic traditions.

Appendix A

Methods of Procedure

The earliest motivation for this study came from a dissatisfaction with the superficiality of survey designs, on the one hand, and with the artificiality of laboratory designs, on the other. The kinds of questions being addressed required an experimental design, not of the classical sort, but one which investigated naturally occurring social experiments in which the phenomena to be observed might do more than merely reflect the experimenter's preconceptions. The commune as such was viewed as a cultural niche of voluntarism, in which the elements of individual and collective choice in social action would not be eclipsed by the overwhelming cultural forces of law and tradition. This it has proved to be. Tapping the potential power of commune-based research, however, has also meant grappling with some unusual obstacles in research design, sampling, data collection, measurement, and analysis.

Research Design

The design for this research evolved and expanded over the years. Originally (1965) there was no more plan in mind that simply to do a grand tour of American communes (after the manner of Macdonald in the nineteenth century), participating fully in their collective lives for as long as possible and recording their experiences especially as these bore on the problems of decision making and collective goal definition. The research was soon given a more specific focus through an involvement with the Haight-Ashbury Research Project and its efforts to learn about the drug use patterns in rural California communes and the relationship of these patterns to social organization and collective behavior. At this time the idea of studying an entire social movement through the intensive investigation of a sampling of its discrete manifestations first took root.

As research data accumulated, two further design considerations became evident: (1) the feasibility and utility of a longitudinal perspective with one-year time intervals and (2) the desirability of attaining a nationwide geographic sample. By 1973, a large systematic mass of data had been accumulated. It was evident by this time that the original hunches were correct—that this was indeed proving to be a strategic research site in which to study fundamental questions concerning individual and collective behavior and social organization.

In 1973, a critical decision was made to double the size of the data base by launching a systematic study of urban communes to parallel the study of rural communes that was still going on. The urban phase of the study was seen as an opportunity to achieve four major goals: (1) to implement the multimethod research strategy pioneered by Lazarsfeld and described by Sieber (1973) in which systematic statistical data are collected to test hypotheses generated by earlier intensive field investigation of the same or similar phenomena; (2) to follow the changing contours of an evolving social movement as it shifted from a primarily rural setting to a primarily urban setting; (3) to add an important new ecological variable to our comparative analysis—the effect of urban versus rural location—on commune organization; and probably most important (4) to introduce for the first time an ability to systematically disaggregate from the commune to the individual as a unit of analysis and also to reaggregate to the level of the sociometric network.

The original research design for the urban phase called for elements both of comparative and quasi-experimental structure (Campbell and Stanley, 1963):

$$
\left.
\begin{array}{ccc}
0 & X_1 & 0 \\
0 & X_2 & 0 \\
\cdot & \cdot & \cdot \\
\cdot & \cdot & \cdot \\
\cdot & \cdot & \cdot \\
0 & X_n & 0
\end{array}
\right\} \quad \text{Treatment groups}
$$

$$
\begin{array}{ccc}
\quad 0 & \quad\quad 0 & \quad \text{Control group}
\end{array}
$$

The design was comparative in that it envisioned examining the effects of n different ideological types of communal living experience over a one-year period as well as a control group that had not lived communally. The design was quasi-experimental rather than truly experimental in that persons were distributed among categories by self-selection rather than by randomization.

This original research design had to be modified in several major ways. Nobody was interested in funding the study of a full-fledged noncommunitarian control group, so this part of the design had to be curtailed. The data, furthermore, ultimately proved to be far too rich to be encompassed within a single dimension of comparison. Although use of the ideological typology proved to be one fruitful way to classify the communes, a number of other criteria proved equally fruitful. The simple comparative structure therefore gave way to a more complex multivariate analytical scheme. Finally, the two waves of research proved to be sufficiently rewarding to justify a continuing interest in the subject. One year after the second wave, a third wave of data collection, on a somewhat reduced scale, was carried out, and the communes have been visited or contacted by mail or phone at one-year intervals since then.

In the absence of a real control group, makeshift controls were utilized wherever possible. An introductory sociology class made up of Columbia and Barnard students (none of whom were living communally) was given the attitude questionnaire (see the subsequent discussion of data instruments) one month after the commune sample received it. Only the questions dealing with attitudes toward one's specific current communal living group were omitted. Responses are given in Appendix B. For some of the background questions and a few of the standard attitude scales, national sample comparisons were also available. In particular, the *NORC General Social Survey* for 1974 and the *Youth in Transition* 1974 follow-up survey were both used in this capacity. Standard background items were deliberately phrased according to NORC format to facilitate such comparisons. However, these merely served to establish a minimal control baseline on selected variables. There was nothing approximating a control panel.

Multiple-Wave Design Aspects

The urban phase of the study best approximates the features of a panel design. By convention, time 0 is always considered to be the month in which the commune was founded. The commune at time 0 is never observed directly but only through retrospective evidence. Time 1 is the month of first formal contact. This varies over many years for the sixty rural communes. For the urban it is either August 1974 or February 1975. Time 2 is always the same calendar month as time 1 but one year later.* Time 3 is one year later than that, and so on.

First-wave data collection was conducted in five of the cities in August 1974[†]; Boston field work was undertaken in February 1975, six months later. The reason for keeping one city out of phase was to control both for seasonal effects and for the effects of specific historical events that might influence changes observed between the 1974 and 1975 waves of data collection. The

---

*In six instances, because of logistical problems, there was a thirteen-month rather than a twelve-month delay between time 1 and time 2. In each successive wave, the actual variance in elapsed time increased.

[†]But preliminary field work in all cases was begun two months earlier.

second wave of data collection began in August 1975 (preceded by spring previews of all groups that had been studied in 1974). Boston again followed six months out of phase, preceded by a winter preview.

No effects attributable to seasonal variation were observed in comparing the winter data from Boston with the summer data from the other five cities. In fact, on almost all structural, behavioral, and attitudinal indicators, the data from Boston were very similar to those of the other cities. Its commune members were better educated, more likely to come from middle-class backgrounds, and more likely to have been born out of state. However, these may well be distinguishing characteristics of the city of Boston as a whole, not particularly of its communes.

Historical effects, on the other hand, may have had a slight effect in changing commune attitudes between August 1974 and February 1975. Boston commune members were much less likely than those in any of the other five cities to "see the world as a basically evil place." Was this due to the fact that, in August 1974, the Watergate crisis was reaching its dramatic climax with the resignation of Nixon, whereas, in February 1975, order was being restored and prison sentences given to high-ranking officials? Perhaps of somewhat more concern for this study is the question of whether the six-month lag was responsible for the markedly lower proportion of Boston commune members' wishing to move to a rural commune. If this is due in part to elapsed time, the fact is significant because it indicates that the rapid decline of the rural communitarian social movement (discussed in Chapter 2) was capable of producing major short-term attitude changes. However, it might simply be the case that Boston, as an attractive city, is much more likely than any of our other cities to produce positive attitudes toward urban communal life. Nothing more definite can be said on this matter.

Hierarchical Unit-of-Analysis Design Aspects

The rural data analysis had clearly shown that the fate of communes must be understood in large part both in terms of their component parts and in terms of the larger human ecology and history in which they are embedded. By the components, we mean not only the individual members but also the relational bonds among the members. Indeed, the rural investigations had clearly shown that, if there was one single most important key for understanding communitarian dynamics, it was to be found in the network analysis of their relationships. By the larger human ecology, we mean to refer not only to relations with the commune's neighbors and the local authorities but also to the historical, ecological, and demographic forces that were and are in the process of transforming the local neighborhoods and larger geographical regions.

For these reasons, the research called for data to be collected with respect to each level of a hierarchy of units of analysis. At the greatest level of disaggregation, the bulk of the data was collected from individuals about individuals.

Immediately above that, data were collected using the dyad as the unit of analysis. Most of this information was gathered from the individual participants in each dyad, but some reflected the observations by others of the dyad. The third unit of analysis was, of course, the commune itself. The fourth was "neighborhood" data in which the census tract for urban and the county for rural communes was the unit. Finally, the region itself (see the section on sampling following) was considered the unit of greatest aggregation on which systematic data were collected.

Multimethod Design Aspects

In one sense the shift from the rural to the urban phase of the study meant a shift from an emphasis on participant observation to an emphasis on survey techniques. However, in another more important sense, the entire study was heavily committed throughout to a strategy of integrating as many methods of investigation as possible. From the very earliest days of the study, it was recognized that participant observation and detached observation were two quite distinct methods, each indispensable in the effort to understand communal life. Structured and unstructured interviews with members, ex-members, and neighbors were seen also as providing unique information. Although the resources available and the antiscientific temper of the times made it impossible to distribute questionnaires, systematic statistical information from individuals was recorded whenever possible. Most important, all these techniques were constantly used to triangulate, to cross-validate findings. Very little confidence was placed in results that could be perceived by only one method.

In the urban phase, questionnaire techniques predominated. But close to 1,500 hours of person-to-person, open-ended interviews were recorded on tape and on interview schedules, and these formed an indispensible part of the data library. Although opportunities for prolonged participant observation were few in the urban phase, these were utilized whenever possible. Detached observation continued, as before, to hold an important place in the research repertoire.

One thing became evident through consistent use of this multimethod strategy: none of these methods was worth overly much by itself for penetrating these private worlds of meaning. Each of the techniques contributed quite a bit of insight, and it was gratifying to see the extent of overlap among them all. But each had its own blind spots and produced its own mirages. For the study presented in this book, any one of the research methods alone would have produced a lot of truth but, if relied upon exclusively, would have presented it indistinguishable from a large amount of error. The amount of error left in the book, although undoubtedly far from negligible, is at least much reduced because of the use of a multimethod strategy.

Urban Phase Research Instruments

The following is a brief description of the basic survey instruments used in the urban phase of the study.*

The Commune-Level Data Protocol. This is a schedule of items that uses the commune as the unit of analysis. The protocol includes fifty-four closed-ended items (such as dates of founding, type of authority, rationality of decision making, economic organization, method of child rearing, type and intensity of ideology, and marital and sexual arrangements) and was filled out by field-workers in cooperation with members of the communes themselves.

Personal Background and Participation (Long Form). The "long form" is a schedule of items that explores in detail the individual's personal biography. The long forms were personally administered by fieldworkers to four or five members of each commune. These interviews took from two to four hours to complete, and they cover, extensively, each respondent's early life, with particular emphasis on the year just prior to joining the commune. The long form also devotes considerable attention to the respondent's current life, present goals, and participation in the ongoing activities of the commune. This schedule is a combination of open- and closed-ended items.

Personal Background and Participation (Short Form). It was recognized, in advance, that not all commune members would have the time or the interest to respond to the detailed questions of the long form. Consequently, a "short form" instrument was developed that contains twenty of the most important closed-ended questions from the long form. The short form comprises the minimal data set desired for each commune member.

Attitude Questionnaire. The attitudes instrument is a set of ninety-nine Likert-type items drawn, for the most part, from standard scales used on national surveys for the assessment of alienation, preference, self-esteem and self perception (see Appendix B). Priority for inclusion in the questionnaire was given to sets of items such as the Srole anomia and Harris Alienation scales, both of which have been widely administered to other, noncommunitarian samples of the national population.

Relationship Questionnaire. This instrument consists of sociometric choice questions in which each individual is asked to respond to a complete set of questions describing his/her relationships with *every other* member of the commune. Selected items from this questionnaire are reproduced on the following pages.

Supplementary Questionnaire. Preliminary analysis of data from the five-city 1974 summer survey indicated that several important areas of communal

*Space limitations prevent facsimiles of these instruments from being presented here. Copies are available upon request from the author.

The Relationship Questionnaire
(selected items)

EXPLANATORY NOTE

The following page in this questionnaire (page 3) is the source of most of the relationship data used in this book. Each respondent received a questionnaire with multiple copies of page 3 inserted in it. A respondent in a commune with a population of nine, for example, would receive a questionnaire with eight page 3's, one for each person other than himself. Each of these page 3's would have one of the commune member's names typed in at the top. Therefore, in completing this questionnaire each respondent supplied us with a page 3 describing his relationship with each other respondent in the same commune.

5. This sheet is about _____

a. How long have you known the above named person?

   Years _____   Months _____

b. In your own words briefly characterize the changes which have occurred in your unique relationship with this person as a fellow commune member over the last twelve months or, if less, for the time you have known each other.

   _____

c. How many hours in a typical week do the two of you spend together just by yourselves? _____

d. If you happen to know it, state what kind of work (his/her) father did while the person named above was growing up. _____

e. Even the most equal of relationships sometimes has a power element involved. However insignificant it may be in your relationship with this person, which of you do you think holds the greater amount of power in your relationship?

   _____

f. If this commune did not exist, would you want to have a close relationship with this person? _____

g. For the list of descriptions below, indicate if the following are involved in your relationship with the person named above by checking the appropriate answer. *Please answer each of the following:*

Work together	Yes_____	No_____	Sometimes_____
Spend free time together	Yes_____	No_____	Sometimes_____
Mind children together	Yes_____	No_____	Sometimes_____
Sleep together	Yes_____	No_____	Sometimes_____
Confide in each other	Yes_____	No_____	Sometimes_____
Loving	Yes_____	No_____	Sometimes_____
Exciting	Yes_____	No_____	Sometimes_____
Awkward	Yes_____	No_____	Sometimes_____
Feel close to each other	Yes_____	No_____	Sometimes_____
Tense	Yes_____	No_____	Sometimes_____
Jealous	Yes_____	No_____	Sometimes_____
Agree on communal policy matters	Yes_____	No_____	Sometimes_____
Feel estranged from each other	Yes_____	No_____	Sometimes_____
Exploitive	Yes_____	No_____	Sometimes_____
Hateful	Yes_____	No_____	Sometimes_____
Improving	Yes_____	No_____	Sometimes_____
Sexual	Yes_____	No_____	Sometimes_____

h. Do you feel that the overall relationship between the two of you is more important to you, or do you feel it is more important to the above named person?

_____ More important to you   _____ More important to him/her

i. In your relationship with this person, does he/she ever act to you as a father or mother, sister or brother, son or daughter, or none of these? _____

j. Although we realize that it may be difficult for you to judge, which of the two of you would you say is held in higher esteem by the communal household as a whole?

_____

For the two questions that follow, please indicate your answer by drawing a vertical line through a point on the scaled line below which best represents how close your opinion is to either of the opposing views given.

k. What role do you think the above named person's presence and action play in the commune's survival?

Endangers the |ıııııııııııııııııı| Is crucial to the
commune's survival   commune's survival

l. Do you feel that this person lives up to the principles of the communal household?

Seldom acts with any |ıııııııııııııııııı| Always acts with
regard for the   high regard for the
commune's principles   commune's principles

6. Who in your communal household:

_____ a. is energetic

_____ b. is innovative

_____ c. The commune seems to work better when he/she is present.

_____ d. knows me in some ways better than I know myself

_____ e. is often aloof

_____ f. has taught me something about how life should be lived

_____ g. is fatherly

_____ h. is motherly

_____ i. The commune seems to feel closer and more together when he/she is present

7. Name the five people who are most significant in your life at the moment, whether or not they are fellow commune members, and describe their relationship to you.

NAME   RELATIONSHIP

1. _____   _____

2. _____   _____

3. _____   _____

4. _____   _____

5. _____   _____

8. The expression of different views and feelings about things generally occurs when a group of people lives, works, or plays together. Although this may not have arisen so far in your relationship with the commune, would you name *two other commune members* whom you feel you would most turn to for support in the event of a disagreement or problem emerging between you and the rest of the commune.

    1. _____

    2. _____

9. Do you hold a position in this commune? If so, what are the duties and responsibilities of this position?

    _____ Hold no position.

POSITIONS HELD   RESPONSIBILITIES AND DUTIES

_____   _____

_____   _____

_____   _____

_____   _____

10. Who is generally recognized as the leader of this commune?

_____

11. Would you please write the name of one commune member who:

_____   has new ideas for the commune.

_____   is able to help resolve relationship problems which emerge between members from time to time.

_____   something important seems lacking in the commune when he/she is not present.

_____   seems to have an inexhaustible supply of love.

_____   is the person whose advice you generally seek when making an important personal decision.

life (e.g., decision making, personal goals and expectations, communal change) invited deeper exploration than that provided in the original five instruments. As a result, a supplementary questionnaire was developed to replace the "short form" and was utilized in the out-of-phase Boston data collection during the winter of 1975. The supplementary questionnaire includes all the items from the short form (so that short-form material is uniform and comparable across all three personal background instruments).

Ex-Members. Because the very nature of communitarianism tends to inhibit the development of firm, long-term personal commitments (see Chapter 4), a high turnover rate was anticipated between wave one and wave two. Follow-up of ex-members, therefore, comprised an important segment of the two-wave research.. During the course of 1975 summer data collection, fieldworkers compiled lists of ex-members, and, in cases where the ex-members could be located within the SMSA, fieldworkers distributed ex-member questionnaire forms to these individuals. In most cases, however, ex-member location procedures took several steps, often involving contact with a member's parents or other relatives living in different states (these contact addresses were obtained from all respondents during the 1974 data collection process). Because of budget and time constraints, it quickly became apparent that not all ex-members could be traced and interviewed. As a result the ex-members were divided into three priority categories, with major search and retrieval efforts being devoted to those with high priority and minimal search and retrieval efforts devoted to those with low priority. In all cases, however, where a respondent could be readily located, no matter what the priority rating, efforts were made to retrieve ex-member information. Completed questionnaires were eventually received from 32 percent of the ex-members. Systematic biases were observed when comparing ex-member respondents and nonrespondents on the basis of their first-wave responses. Those who did not return ex-member questionnaires were quite a bit more radical in their first wave responses than those that did. This must be borne in mind in drawing conclusions from ex-member data.

Sampling

The 120 communes selected for this study cannot, of course, be considered a probability sample of American communes. There was no feasible way to enumerate the population of American communes from which the sample was drawn. Even the total number of communes in this population can only really be estimated to an order of magnitude. Nevertheless, considerable efforts were made to eliminate the known sources of bias that may have skewed the results of previous commune studies. It is probably safe to say that inferences drawn from the results of this study, to American communes in general, will usually be closer to the mark than inferences drawn from any other currently published study. However, the reader interested in drawing such inferences (a concern that has not been central in this book) would do well to take heed of the sampling idiosyncracies described in the following pages.

The Population

In the most general terms, the overall population from which the rural sample was drawn is made up of every rural commune that had all or part of its existence within the continental United States, during the period July 1965 to July 1974. Note that the communes need not have been founded in the United States (although all of them were) or within the specified period (eight were founded earlier). What is meant by "commune" in this regard is discussed in the introduction to this book and should be taken as a restriction on the population as well as on the sample. It would, for example, be incorrect to draw inferences from this study to communes without ideologies or public identities or to those made up of adults of only one sex.

The urban portion of the commune population is restricted to those in existence in July 1974. Unlike the rural sampling, which was done at various times throughout the period, the urban sampling (except for the lagged Boston subsample) was all done within that single month. Whether it is safe to generalize from these to earlier urban communes, or whether those in existence in 1974 had certain distinctive *fin de mouvement* characteristics that made them different, is not answerable within the context of this research. Both the absence of census data and the absence of any federation of American communes contribute to our lack of reliable statistical data concerning the commune movement as a whole.

The Sampling Unit

In the introductory chapter we defined precisely what was to be considered a commune for the purpose of this book. In most instances, this definition was sufficient to allow us to determine unambiguously whether or not a given observable entity was eligible to be included in the sampling frame. However, there were a few cases in which the decision to include or not to include was based on judgments not explicit within our definition.

A decision was made to include all communes in existence during the time of the enumeration even if they were begun in an earlier era. This complicated our attempts to treat the commune sample as part of a single social movement. However, it served to increase the variance in commune duration, which proved to be useful. Because no effort was made to select communes on the basis of founding-year cohort, this decision could have gone either way.

A decision was made to exclude groups of people who had made definite plans to live communally (even if these included formal contractual agreements) but who were not yet doing so. Groups that had occupied the same piece of land as another commune but had revolted from that commune to set up their own were also excluded unless the schism was recognized as permanent by both groups.

A decision was made to treat each household of a multihousehold communal federation as a separate commune. However, in some instances even the definition of what constituted a single household proved ambiguous. Household was defined as a functional rather than as a physical entity. A group owning or renting several separate dwelling units and freely and fluidly distributing its members among them was considered to be a single commune. If interhouse access was not free and fluid but limited in the service of ideological norms, the commune was still treated as a single unit. Examples of the latter were communes with a separate house for the charismatic leader, as a distancing mechanism, or separate houses for men and women or for the fully initiated and the novices. It followed from these decisions that the inclusion of one commune from a communitarian federation did not reduce the probability that another commune from the same federation in another geographical region would also be chosen. This happened in several instances. In one of them, as shall be discussed shortly, it was deliberately contrived to happen.

Selection of Geographical Regions

The commune sample is made up of ten communes from each of twelve distinct geographical areas. Each of the twelve areas is a cluster of contiguous counties. Six of the county clusters are rural and were discovered and delineated through field work. The other six county clusters are urban and follow metropolitan boundaries established by the U.S. Census Bureau.

The six rural areas were chosen because that is where the communes were. Rural communes are more visible than urban communes and they also tend to be less uniformly distributed in space. Through prolonged field work over a period of several years we were able to determine with reasonable certainty the location of the major areas:

Northcoast: *California*—Marin, Sonoma, Mendecino, Humboldt, Del Norte, Lake
Southcoast: *California*—Santa Clara, Santa Cruz, Monterey
Rio Grande: *New Mexico*—Bernalillo, Santa Fe, Rio Arriba, Taos
Colorado—Costilla, Las Animas, Conejos, Rio Grande, Pueblo
Cascade: *California*—Butte, Tehama, Shasta, Siskiyou, Yuba, Sutter
Oregon—Josephine, Jackson, Klamath, Douglas, Lane, Benton, Linn
Taconic: *Vermont*—Addison, Rutland, Bennington, Windham, Windsor, Orange
Massachusetts—Berkshire, Franklin, Hampshire
New York—Dutchess, Green, Columbia, Washington
Appalachia: *Pennsylvania*—Fayette, Green, Somerset

West Virginia—Marshall, Preston, Tucker, Grant, Randolph, Pendelton, Hardy

Maryland—Baltimore, Carroll, Fredrick, Alleghany

Virginia—Rappahannock, Louisa, Rockingham, Page, Madison, Culpepper, Orange, Greene, Albemarle, Nelson, Amherst, Bedford, Roanoke, Pulaski, Montgomery, Wythe, Smyth, Washington

North Carolina—Yancy, Buncombe, Henderson, Transylvania, Jackson, Clay, Macon

Georgia—all counties west of the Chattahoochee and Flint rivers including all counties on north border of state

Tennessee—Johnson, Carter, Unicoi, Greene

Urban communes were to be found in virtually all large- and medium-sized cities and their surrounding suburban areas. Rather than aiming for maximum density of concentration, we aimed to maximize geographical diversity. The U.S. Census Bureau divides the nation into nine major geographical regions. Originally, two of the regions were combined (South Atlantic and East South Central) and the largest Standard Metropolitan Statistical Area from each of the eight regions was selected for study. However, pretests clearly indicated that time and budget constraints would not permit detailed ethnographic and survey analysis of all eight areas. As a result, Chicago and Denver (East North Central and Mountain regions) were arbitrarily dropped from the list and the following six SMSAs remained: Los Angeles, Twin Cities, Atlanta, Houston, New York, and Boston.

The primary reason for selecting cities by arbitrary census definitions was to avoid the regional bias that has affected previous studies of communal life. Because most of the active commune researchers in recent years have been based on the West Coast, a disproportionate amount of research on contemporary communes has focused on communities west of the Mississippi. Although there are probably more communes in the West than in the East, this regional bias in sampling has deprived researchers of important systematic data concerning differences in communal life in different regions of the country.

The Enumeration Stage in the Urban Areas

During a preliminary month of fieldwork in the summer of 1974, fieldworkers in each city compiled a conprehensive* census of communes within the

---

*"Comprehensive" is, of course, a relative term. In some SMSAs, such as Houston and Atlanta, fieldworders felt that they had exhausted the commune population. Every new reference or contact circled back to a previously enumerated group, and, in fact, as the study progressed, no new groups were discovered. In New York, however, "comprehensive" had more to do with the numbers and types of groups unearthed than with the proportion of groups in the universe that had been located. Communal households in New York are so numerous, anonymous, and dispersed that previously unsurveyed groups appeared incessantly throughout the course of the study.

TABLE A-1. Sampling Proportions of Urban and Rural Communes

Areas Studied	Census Region	Census Division	1974[a] Population (millions)	Population Change (1970–1974)[a] (%)	Existence of a Commune Clearinghouse Organization	Est. Number of Communes (during time of study)	Number Located in Commune Census	Number Studied First Wave	Number Surviving, Second Wave
Urban/SMSA									
New York	NE	Mid. Atlantic	9.6	−4.1%	Yes	200–500	72	10	7
Boston	NE	New England	2.9	−0.3	Yes	200–400	180	10	7
Minneapolis –St. Paul	NC	W. North Central	2.0	2.3	Yes	100–150	56	10	8
Atlanta	S	S. Atlantic and E. South Central	1.8	12.2	No	50–75	39	10	9
Houston	S	W. South Central	2.3	14.4	No	50–100	37	10	10
Los Angeles –Long Beach	W	Pacific	7.0	−0.8	Yes	200–500	55	10	7
Rural County Clusters									
Northcoast	W	Pacific	0.7	0.1	Yes	200–400	n.a.	10	8
Southcoast	W	Pacific	1.6	0.2	No	150–250	n.a.	10	6
Rio Grande	W	Mountain	0.4	0.1	Yes	100–150	n.a.	10	9
Cascade	W	Pacific	0.6	0.1	No	100–150	n.a.	10	8
Taconic	NW	Mid. Atlantic, New England	0.6	0.1	No	250–400	n.a.	10	6
Appalachia	S	S. Atlantic and E. South Central	0.9	no change	Yes	300–400	n.a.	10	9

[a]For urban areas, 1975 is used as the base year, instead of 1974, for U.S. census data only.

SMSA. This compilation was achieved through the exploitation of every fore-seeable (and serendipitous) source of commune information. Sensitive to the sampling biases that have plagued most commune research (e.g., undercounting of "nameless" communes, overrepresentation of highly institutionalized groups, underrepresentation of short-lived and nonmiddle-class groups), fieldworkers were instructed to start their census work from a wide variety of different entry points.

The search for communes was, of course, complicated by definitional problems. Many groups that satisfied the study's definition of "commune" did not, in fact, answer to the name of "commune," and, conversely, many groups that called themselves "communes" did not satisfy the definition at all. In explaining their needs to informants, therefore, fieldworkers used the word "commune" with discretion and emphasized instead the ideological, the common residence, and the multiple-person characteristics of the groups that they were seeking.

Sampling of Communes

In the urban areas, after approximately four weeks of field work, the census information from each of the cities was sufficiently complete to permit selection of individual communes to be studied in depth. Although a random sampling of the enumerated universe would have provided the most stringent sampling criterion, much of the representative control of the six-city sample would have been lost by random selection. Instead, the individual communes were selected on the basis of certain key variables such as ideology type, population size, number of children, type of neighborhood, and year founded. In the rare instances where access was flatly denied by a selected commune, the next highest group on the priority list was chosen for study.

There was, however, one significant deviation from the "relevant variables" selection procedure. Early in the fieldwork, a number of nationwide religious cults, organized in the form of federations of communal households (whose members often moved among households in different states), were located. In fact, ten of these cults were identified during the summer field work of 1974, each centering around the veneration of a guru, prophet, or avatar. Because of the obvious sociological and historical importance of these new religious federations, and because of the unique opportunities they provide for cross-regional comparisons among representatives of the same communitarian organization, one cult was selected for study. Representative households belonging to this cult were included in the sample from each of the six cities.

In the rural areas, within each county cluster, ten communes were selected for study. No formal or informal sampling procedures were used because we felt reasonably confident that we were aware of all significant dimensions of variation and could select a sample on general subjective criteria that seemed typical of the larger commune population. Five rural communes refused access and were excluded from the study. In each case a similar commune from the same cluster of counties was selected to replace it.

To the extent that this study attempts to generalize from findings concerning 120 communes to statements about "life in American communes," the representativeness of the sample, it is clear, is up for question. The major problem, however, with assessing representativeness is that there is virtually no information available (other than this study's six-city census) concerning the number or types of communes existing in the United States. The very few systematic studies that have been conducted on communes (e.g., Jaffe, 1975; Kanter, 1974) have been limited to small geographic areas (e.g., New Haven and Boston) and have explicitly excluded from consideration "creedal households" and federations. By excluding religious, spiritual, and political groups (and by concentrating, thereby, solely on "domestic households"), these earlier studies contribute little to an overall estimate of the commune universe.

In summary, the commune sample chosen for this book deviates in many ways from a strict probability sample and requires far more cautious interpretation of specific results. However, it allows us some latitude in making inferences about the population of communes and commune members as a whole, while giving us a greater flexibility than a probability sample would provide.

Selection of Respondents

An attempt was made to study the entire adult (over 15 years of age) population of each of the communes. In the rural groups this was easily accomplished through participant observation, but systematic data were collected from only a small minority. In the urban groups all members were asked to supply basic survey data. However, not all were willing to participate, and not all of those who did participate took part in all aspects of the data collection.

The six survey instruments already discussed were used as indicated. In addition to strictly individual-level data, a complete enumeration of dyadic relationships on a wide variety of relational variables was elicited. Systematic global data concerning leadership, economic organization, marriage, child rearing, decision making, and so on were also collected for all rural and urban communes. Ecological data on each of the communes were collected for the surrounding neighborhood. In the urban communes, the statistical neighborhood used was the census tract; for the rural communes, the entire county.

Data Collection

Because of the wide variety of emotional and rational justifications for denying access to strangers with tape recorders and survey instruments, fieldworkers spent a great deal of time with individual members and with the groups as a whole before they sprang the question of official access. A wide range of objections were voiced by individual commune members:

"This is our home, our family, not some scientific laboratory experiment"; "How can you possibly understand anything about what we're up to with a bunch of printed questions"; "We've been through this before. Some guys came and lived here for almost a month last year and got in everyone's way and asked a lot of questions and said they were writing a book and we have never seen one word of anything they wrote and have never heard from them again"; "A lot of people have been busted around this city lately and I think we'd better keep our mouths shut"; or, "I have a friend who lives in a commune who just lost custody of her child because of it, and I'm not about to put myself in the same position."

But, despite these objections and despite the self-imposed research constraint that the commune *as a whole* must give permission to be studied (although individual members might refuse), only five of the rural and six of the originally selected urban communes denied access. Furthermore, during the course of the first-wave research, none of the rural and only one of the urban groups that had agreed to participate withdrew that agreement (and that one only prohibited questionnaire distribution) once data collection was underway.*

In communes, subject response is much a function of the attitude and manner of approach of the investigators. Commune members are quick to detect and respond negatively to signs of patronizing or stereotyping. The fact that commune members must be approached within their own collectivity makes them especially capable of taking the offensive in such situations. On the other hand, the same commune members will usually respond warmly and generously to research that takes them seriously and that respects areas of privacy. Backstage behavior (Goffman, 1959) must always be recognized as such. Above all, one must respect what the commune is trying to do on its own terms.

The extent of cooperation and the apparent quality of the data collected were, on the whole, quite high. All the rural and urban communes participated in the gathering of the systematic commune-level information. At the individual level there was a more selective but still quite high rate of response. We received personal background data (short or long forms) from 81 percent of the possible urban respondents (N = 667), more than half of whom participated in autobiographical interviews. Relationship data were obtained from 70 percent[†] and attitude data from 60 percent. The lower rate of response to the attitude questionnaire also unfortunately corresponds to a lower quality of data. Enthnographic and interview cross-checks revealed a uniformly high quality to the responses to personal background and relational instruments. These were also

*Others, however, as elsewhere noted, forbade the use of certain specific questionnaires. The attitude questionnaire was most frequently griped about but it was the relationship questionnaire that was most frequently forbidden or restricted.

†Five communes refused to allow the relationship questionnaire to be distributed on principle. If these are excluded from the count, the rate of response is closer to 80 percent in the communes participating. In analyzing the relational data, only those groups (N = 42) with 85 percent or better response rates were deemed complete enough to be included.

generally judged to be relevant by the commune members. The attitude questionnaire met with much greater hostility and probably produced a somewhat higher rate of nonserious response.

From the experiences of the first wave of urban data collection and analysis, it became apparent that certain changes in procedures and instruments would enhance the usability of the second-wave data (always, of course, with an eye toward comparability between first- and second-wave materials). Perhaps the most significant difference between first- and second-wave urban data collection procedures was a difference in emphasis on units of observation. For the second wave, the communal group as a unit of observation and analysis assumed precedence over the individual-level biographical concerns of the first wave.

In two of the cities (Minneapolis and Los Angeles) the 1974 resident fieldworkers, who were, by this time, well known to most of the groups, also conducted the 1975 fieldwork. In Minneapolis, none of the ten groups refused reentry permission. In Los Angeles, two groups refused reentry. One of the refusing groups had also denied access in 1974 for all but tape-recorded interviews. The other group had participated fully in 1974 but did not grant access in 1975.

Problems of Measurement

In ideological communities, things are sometimes different from what they seem and often different from what their members prefer to believe. The usual problems of measurement are thus exacerbated by the problem of having to continually adjust to rapid changes in baseline meaning and value systems. All members of the research team who participated in field work felt the strain of trying to maintain objectivity in the face of so many conflicting claims to absolute wisdom. One succumbed completely and "went native." All the rest of us experienced periodic decompensation in the form of episodes of intense attraction to and/or repulsion from specific communes.

In the face of these kinds of cognitive pressures it seemed to make sense to hold fast to a uniform notion of sociological objectivity. The epistomological canon that governed our efforts to measure what we saw, therefore, was the assumption that all attributes of persons, relationships, and collectivities are variable properties whose presence or absence and magnitude can be determined by means that do not significantly interact with specific settings. This perspective of course blinded us to many important aspects of communitarianism that other studies will have discovered. It did, however, also allow us to generalize, compare, and contrast on a scale that no other study of communes has attempted.

Reliability and Validity

Two kinds of reliability were matters of concern: response stability and intercoder reliability. With respect to the first, attitude and relationship responses were particularly open to question. The test-retest reliability of the attitude questionnaire was measured on a group of college students with a 48-hour interval between tests.* On no item did more than 10 percent of the students shift from agreement to disagreement or vice versa, and for a majority of items there were no such shifts. However, higher rates of shift, up to 25 percent, were recorded when a shift was defined as any change along the five-point Likert scale. Shifts into and out of the no answer/no opinion category were particularly frequent. The attitude items should be considered, at best, of marginal reliability. The stability of the relational responses was harder to check, requiring as it did a test group of people who knew each other quite well. The only test-retest reliability check done on this instrument used the commune project office staff, tested in the morning and again in the afternoon. Almost no shifts were observed between tests, indicating a reasonable level of stability. However, more work on this instrument needs to be done.

Intercoder reliability was more of a problem, particularly for the global-level urban commune data recorded in the field. For such judgment items as ideological intensity and rationality in decision making, for example, it was difficult to get a farflung staff of fieldworkers to apply common yardsticks. In the end, after many hours spent in long-distance telephone conferences, only a series of around-the-country tours by the core staff (Zablocki, Bradley, and Aidala) to visit, at least briefly, virtually all the urban communes, assured a degree of data comparability that we felt we could live with. There is still, however, undoubtedly more error of this kind left in the urban data than in the rural, where at least a single person's judgment prevailed.

Evidence for measurement validity was provided by the multimethod approach to data collection as we discussed earlier. In general, the survey measures of key concepts converged quite well with nonsurvey measures. Specific validation problems are best discussed in terms of the specific concepts for which the problems emerged. The following are some of the more important examples:

1. *Relational measures:* At the dyadic level, relationship questionnaire items converged with field observations and the opinions of interviewees. But, to the extent that these responses were used to trace a network of an entire commune, the data were quite vulnerable to incompleteness of response. For this reason, for commune-level network indicators such as love density, only those communes with 85 percent or more responses on the questionnaire were included (N = 42). This was all the more necessary because, unlike the other questionnaires, the probability of filling out a relationship questionnaire was judged to be far from independent of one's position in the network.

2. *Power:* The evident validity of our naïve measure of interpersonal power was quite surprising. The indicator was based upon a single question asking each respondent to evaluate his or her relative power with respect to each other commune member. A *strict* power relationship was said to exist between A and

---

*Many of the items, of course, were parts of standard scales with well-established levels of reliability and validity.

B if *A* claimed power over *B* and *B* acknowledged *A's* power over *B*. A *relaxed* power relationship was said to exist if *A* claimed power over *B* and *B* did not claim power over *A,* or if *B* acknowledged *A's* power over *B* and *A* did not deny having power over *B*. Both measures produced revealing network diagrams, with almost no intransitive cycles. However, the strict measure was the one actually employed in this book. Neither measure attempted to determine degree of power, consistency of power, or the areas of life in which the power was exercised.

3. *Dyadic cathexis:* The most important of the relational measures used in this book is dyadic cathexis—a measure of the love between the two parties that comprise any dyad. Each person was asked to evaluate his or her relationship with each other person in the commune with respect to a number of relational attributes or "loadings." One of these was *love* (yes, no, or sometimes). A loving bond was said to exist between person *A* and person *B* if and only if *A* and *B* both replied "yes" to the love question about each other. At the group level, cathexis was defined as the density of loving bonds, the proportion of all possible dyads in the commune for which there was a loving bond between the members. This measure of cathexis varied in the communes studied during the first wave from 10 percent to 100 percent.

The love density measure of cathexis correlates positively with all other measures of positive affect density (e.g., improving, exciting) and negatively with measures of negative affect. The positive correlation between cathexis and membership turnover discussed in Chapter 4 holds, although not quite as strongly, when alternative measures of positive affect are substituted for love density.

4. *Negative cathexis:* This was originally conceived as the mirror image of dyadic cathexis. The measure to be used was the proportion of dyads that mutually responded "yes" to the question about *hatred*. However, too few respondents answered this way to provide us with a variable with a reasonably wide range. This remained a problem when "sometimes" responses were grouped with "yes" responses. In order to pick up a wide range of differences in the expression of negative affect, we had to go to a composite measure. A bond of negative affect was said to exist between the members of a dyad if each member of the dyad responded "yes" or "sometimes" to *any one of* the following descriptions of the relationship: *hateful, jealous, awkward, tense,* or *exploitative*. Our measure of negative cathexis is undoubtedly a lot less valid and pure than our measure of positive cathexis.

5. *Dyadic partiality:* Four measures were used, at one point or another in the study, to ascertain the extent to which commune members singled out one another for a special relationship. It was, of course, important to keep this measure free of overlap with measures of emotional attraction or repulsion or with measures of deference or respect. The research design originally called for using the amount of time that any two people spent together, just by themselves, as an indicator of dyadic partiality. But this was found to be a variable

that was highly constrained by factors having nothing to do with partiality. A useful substitute measure was found in the question, "If the commune did not exist, would you want to have a close relationship with this person?" However, unfortunately, that question was not asked of many of the early respondents in the first wave.

The measure finally used in this book was again a composite measure but one, unlike negative cathexis, that seemed to converge well with field work observations of dyadic partiality. The two components of our index of dyadic partiality are significance and intimate knowledge. The first was determined by asking each person to list the five most significant people in his or her life (in or out of the commune). This was the only question asked in which the respondents were forced to be selective by being limited in the number of names they could list. The second was determined by asking each person if he or she were aware of each other person's father's occupation. Informal discussions with a number of social psychologists indicated that this was a good way of distinguishing people who had spent some time talking with each other about themselves from those who had not. A dyadic relationship of partiality was said to exist if and only if each member of a dyad listed the other as one of his or her five most significant others and if each member also indicated awareness of the other's father's occupation. Density of partiality ranged among the communes from 0 percent to 33 percent.

6. *Disintegration:* Defining communal disintegration involves three distinct issues: loss of domicile, loss of members, and loss of corporate identity. Each has something to do with disintegration, and each may vary independently of the others. This problem has plagued commune archivists for over a hundred years (Nordhoff, 1875; Bushee, 1905; Wooster, 1924; Deets, 1939; Bestor, 1950; Kanter, 1972; Okugawa, 1974), leading to substantial discrepancies in historical statistics. For the purposes of this study, loss of members is clearly the most important criterion. However, even a complete loss of membership was not by itself deemed sufficient to define a commune disintegration. We define a disintegration to have taken place whenever at least two out of the following three events take place in a year: (1) 100 percent membership turnover, (2) change in or loss of domicile, (3) abandonment of corporate identity. Although this definition is somewhat arbitrary, it did sort out the problem cases nicely, sorting them into the categories that seemed intuitively right.

7. *Ideology:* Our definition of ideology in Chapter 5 is fairly straightforward. What may not be as straightforward is our insistence on treating ideological intensity as a variable property of any collectivity. This has led us to treat under the same rubric totalitarian cults at one extreme and groups of people gathered together to share a more relaxed and pleasant life-style at the other. The underlying conviction has been that the advantages of being able to treat ideological intensity as a continuum far outweigh the advantages of being able to rigidly separate groups that are organized according to ideological principles from groups that are organized in some other manner.

8. *Alienation:* Two very different measures of alienation were used in this book. In Part I, we stayed pretty close to Seeman's (1972) multidimensional operational definition, putting particular emphasis on the dimensions that he calls *meaninglessness* and *cultural estrangement.* Alienation of commune members was determined through standard scales and questionnaire items and cross-validated through interviews and observations. In Part II, beginning in Chapter 6, a theoretical rationale was developed for a quite different conception of alienation having to do with the loss of consensus. Only construct validity is offered in evidence for the appropriateness of this definition. A great deal of work remains to be done in exploring its convergent and discriminatory properties. An advantage of this conception is that it is likely to allow us to discriminate better than do traditional conceptualizations between alienation and related concepts such as stress, misery, and anomie. However, the proposed definition may not converge so well with traditional definitions of alienation, and the question of whether this is good or bad is a matter to be debated.

The Measurement of Charisma

The most difficult of all our validation problems had to do with the measurement of charisma. As with alienation, this has been a key research concept for which this book has proposed a radical departure in conceptualization, a departure whose utility only future research can establish. But, in the case of alienation, there were at least well-established measures against which our new measure could be contrasted. Charisma has been a concept, on the other hand, which no one has seemed to know how or on what level to measure. There has even been doubt as to whether or not it is appropriate to measure it at all. The very ideas that charisma can exist in a secular-rationalist society, that it can exist in nonreligious contexts, that it can be found in small communities, are by no means universely accepted. An association, in the minds of some, of charisma with "greatness" has led to questioning the validity of attaching the label to some of the admittedly small-time operators at the heads of certain communes. This research has, nevertheless, remained committed to the assumption that charisma is a variable property of any social system in which there is personal identification of one's self with a consensus-building authority structure. The results of the research have strengthened our belief in this assumption.

Five distinct methods, of widely varying usefulness, were used to locate charismatic leaders and charismatic situations. The least face valid of these was a self-reporting system in which each person declared whether or not he or she was charismatic. There was little overlap between the list of self-reported charismatics and the opinions of either fellow commune members or fieldworkers. A second method was reputational; it counted the votes received from fellow commune members as to one's personal charisma. Although this possessed greater face validity and convergent validity than did the first measure, it still suffered from great variation in interpretation, especially across ideological categories. The meaning of the term charisma to the commune members themselves is, of course, a topic worthy of investigation in its own right (Sprague, 1978; Bradley, 1979). But its use is not appropriate in the current study.

Although the self-reporting and reputational methods were useful in establishing initial lists of potential charismatic candidates, the final determination of charismatic leaders and charismatic communes was based upon the following three methods of measurement: (1) directed interviews asking for evidence of charismatic contexts, (2) nondirected interviews in which such situations or persons were spontaneously mentioned, and (3) direct observations of decision making and the distribution of authority.

As described in Chapter 6, these led to our being able to locate thirty-one charismatic leaders in forty-four communes, eight situations of less charisma, three situations of routinized charisma, eight situations in which a degree of charisma was vested not in a single leader but in a nucleus or core of members, and fifteen situations judged potentially charismatic. In addition, five examples were found of individuals who might have been charismatic leaders in other settings but who were not able to secure any sort of following in their own communes. At least two of these later went on to become charismatic leaders of other communes.

Again, as with alienation, the major source of validity for our classification comes from the place of the concept within the larger theory. An important independent source of empirical validation may be seen in the nesting of concentration of authority along exactly the unidimensional continuum predicted by the theory. In contrast to the situation with respect to alienation, there are probably more serious problems remaining with the discriminant aspect of the validity of this concept than with its convergence with other measures. In particular, more work needs to be done to avoid dangers of overlap with the following concepts: authority in general, expressive leadership, and moral leadership.

Analysis of Data

In a comparative study, one is forced to reduce much of the richness of the phenomena being investigated to gross statistical terms. But this reduction, although aesthetically costly, is intellectually rewarding. We have seen that the emergent properties of the communal bond, at the dyadic and composite levels, assert themselves with convincing authority, just because the entities being studied are so ethnographically rich in observable social events. The convergence between statistical findings and qualitative observations enhances our confidence in both.

Qualitative evidence plays three distinct roles in this study: (1) to generate hypotheses, (2) to explore aspects of communitarianism not amenable to quantification, and (3) to validate, through postcorrelative means, quantitative findings. The largely qualitative rural research proved to be an abundant source of hypotheses, many of which have been successful in predicting urban communal behavior. As a parallel technique, qualitative analysis has been particularly valuable in the analysis of deviant cases. Particularly for the hypotheses of the form "X, Y, and Z will (or will not) occur unless charisma (or some other force) intervenes," the analysis of relationships that do not follow the pattern of the majority of groups in the sample has been particularly instructive. Finally, qualitative corroboration has been useful in the interpretation of findings in a number of quantitative areas, particularly the following: changes in self-esteem and self-perception over time; changes in alienation both from the commune and from the larger society over time; reasons for and proximate causes of the decision to join a commune; and reasons for and proximate causes of the decision to leave.

Prior Effects

The research is not designed as a before-and-after study, but as a comparison at two points in time. No attempt was made to design any retrospective measures of respondents' alienation upon first joining the commune. Such data would be highly suspect. Lack of a true time 0 is something of a drawback from a clinical point of view. We have not been able to estimate for the therapist the probable effect of sending a patient off to live in a commune for a year. This would have been possible if we had altered the design to include only communes that were just getting started or only members that had just joined ongoing communes, or a combination of these. We would have paid for this clinical gain with higher sampling costs and a reduced number of communes in the sample. Even from the clinical point of view, this design would miss any effects that typically occur after the first year of communal life, effects that prior research indicates are often significant.

But from a scientific point of view, there is no harm in lacking a true time 0, unless the assumption is made that significant changes occur early and that cases with prior commune history will have washed out with respect to measurable change. This is extremely unlikely to be true. All prior evidence suggests that the communal living experience is one of continual change. Aside from their intrinsic interest as social experiments, this is why communes constitute such a fine strategic research site for the study of attitudinal (and behavioral) change. Our problem turned out to be quite the opposite: so much change on so many of the variables simultaneously, that the causal patterns were detectable only to a limited degree and only as a result of very careful analysis.

Effects of Membership on Behavior and Personality

One of the most difficult problems facing sociology is the measurement of social system effects on behavior (e.g., Coleman, 1972; Duncan and Featherman, 1973). The problem becomes even more complicated when there is concern not only with behavioral change, but with attitudinal or personality change as well (Bohrnstedt, 1969; Lazarsfeld, 1972; Wiggins, 1973). The problem of isolating the magnitude of behavioral and attitudinal change actually brought about by the commune experience itself is only partly resolvable.

We can identify at least seven possible effects that could bring about an observed difference between commune members and noncommune members on a particular attribute.

These effects are the following:

1. *The joiner effect:* Difference attributed by propensity to seek communal living correlated with the magnitude of the variable.
2. *The stayer effect:* Difference brought about by the differential probability of those high in the variable to stay on, so that, over time, those lower in the particular variable selectively weed themselves out or are weeded out by the group.
3. *The exposure effect:* The possibility that the difference comes about not by a differential propensity to join but, rather, by what happens to the individual after he or she joins the commune. Exposure effects can be of many kinds. The simplest would be directly proportional to the amount of time spent in the commune. It is more likely, however, that a more complex contextual type of exposure effect would operate insofar as the degree to which exposure effects affect the given variable might be determined by the distribution of that variable among the other commune members.
4. *The zeitgeist (or period) effect:* The effect of the historical times in which the communes are living, the *zeitgeist* effect, would have to operate in conjunction with one of the other types of effects, and it is not so much an explanation per se as a possible confounding influence on joiner-stayer-exposure effects, as are the next two types.
5. *The ecosystem effect:* The differential effect of the period as mediated through the surrounding environment—for example, the economic growth of Houston, the stability of Minneapolis, and decline of New York during the year of the study.
6. *Cohort effects:* The effect attributable to growing older.
7. *The recruitment effect:* Similar to a joiner effect, but stemming from the differential screening of applicants by the commune.

To analyze the source of differences in specific attributes among these various effects, we have had to make use of both cohort and panel aspects of the research design. Here the fact that communes are not made up of groups of individuals who all joined at exactly the same time was put to use. If they had been, it might have been impossible to distinguish between joiner and exposure effect. But we have in any commune a variety of exposure times ranging from new members with exposure time of virtually zero to founders whose exposure time is equal to the life of the commune. By seeing the extent to which the difference between the magnitude of the trait among members and the magnitude of the trait among noncommune members vanishes when we look at the subset of new members, we can get some clue as to the possibilities of there being a joiner effect or at least eliminate the stayer effect as a sole explanation of the phenomenon. In a similar manner, the use of panel data helps to distinguish between joiner and equivalent effects, but is open to possible confusion by the period effect and also, of course, by an age effect. For those attributes for which we have noncommunal data, as well as communal data, at both points in time, the problems of a period effect are vastly reduced. Simply by correlating the attribute with age among all members of the sample, we get some measure of the degree to which there is confounding by a birth cohort.

For example, a *zeitgeist* effect has certainly contributed to the cessation of participation in political demonstrations and riots on the part of the commune members. For some attributes, the different amount of time spent precommunally and communally determines the opportunity to engage in these activities, and such opportunity is the important intervening variable. Of course, there is a great deal of variation among commune members, and the ratio of communal time to precommunal time ranged among our subjects from a low of one month to eighty years up to a high of twenty years to zero in one of the few cases of a sabra commune member in our sample.

Statistical Tests of Significance and Size of N

Two related points should be made regarding tables in this book that display relations among variables measured at the individual and/or dyadic levels of analysis. It will be noted that tests of significance for these relationships are sometimes not given. It will further be noted that the overall N, the number of units on which the association is based, ranges over a wide number of values.

The decision to omit significance tests in some instances was made because there are times in this book when the object of data presentation is to display patterns with specific commune populations, not to draw more general inferences. Significance tests are used to determine the probability that an association found in a sample will also be present in the population from which the sample was drawn, and they are not appropriate in all data analytic contexts. Although significance tests have other uses, in particular to help relate strength of association to degrees of freedom, the multilevel design of the study would have made such usage possibly misleading. For example, the number of dyads in a group of any size is much larger than the number of individuals, and if the number of dyads were used to estimate degrees of freedom,* tables involving dyadic measures would show far greater spurious significance. Since, for the most part, in these instances where we dispensed with significance testing, only

*See, however, Laumann and Pappi, 1973, for a discussion of the arguments against asserting such an equivalence.

very strong relations were reported, it was felt that such information could be conveyed most economically with the help of a few qualifying adjectives (e.g., strong, weak, negative, marginal) rather than with the formal apparatus of statistical testing.

The reader will note variation in the size of N from one table to the next. This has to do with the problem of shifting levels of analysis but even more so with the fact that multiple instruments were used, each with its own response rate, and that individuals tended to respond selectively even to items within the same instrument. Finally, for particularly important variables, missing questionnaire data were often "filled in" through information obtained *en passant* in the course of taped interviews. Tables based upon small N's should not be considered to be based upon subsamples of the entire case base. They are merely based upon data not collected from all cases.

With regard to the number of cases when the commune is the unit of analysis, a few additional points should be made. When N = 120, the full sample of rural and urban communes has been included, missing values being duly noted. When N = 60, the full sample of urban communes is always to be assumed unless the table specifically states otherwise. When N = 40 (plus or minus 1 or 2), the subsample of urban communes for which full relational data are available is to be assumed.

Relational Perspective

An innovative feature of this book is its attempt to explain group-level phenomena in terms of relational variables. This has made the analysis more complex than it would have been had only individual attributes been used. But the results strongly support the contention that, at least for some kinds of collectivities, the dynamic forces at work are to be found among, rather than within, the individual participants.

The network perspective reduces individuals to points or circles and relationships to lines, in the hope of gaining geometrical and algebraic insights into complex patterns of human interaction. In recent years there has been a flurry of methodological development in the field of network analysis (Davis, 1970; Holland and Leinhardt, 1974, 1976; Alba, 1975; White et al., 1976). However, these very real methodological innovations have, thus far, been long on promise and short on significant concrete findings.

The techniques of network analysis have suffered over the years from a procrustean persistence in putting them to use in situations to which they are not applicable. In this book, significant results are achieved with sociometric techniques because they are applied to a subject matter in which interpersonal relationships are of the utmost importance.

A number of distinct sources of evidence led us to the relational perspective. Ethnographic accounts, both of urban and rural communal life, have consistently indicated that the events of communal living are best explained as changes in the patterns of attracting and repelling, dominating and deferring, interacting and abiding. These relationships make up the daily life of communes. Furthermore, retrospective accounts of communal schisms, while generally expressed in ideological terms, have left the impression that the root of most schisms can be traced to relationships.*

On the other hand, the shortcomings of sociometric analysis are well known. Infield (1947), one of the earliest sociological researchers of contemporary communes, was well aware of their suitability for sociometric analysis. However, the 1940s and 1950s afforded neither technical facilities for multiplex analysis† nor data bases for systematic comparison. Where such technical facilities and data have been available, chiefly in experimental laboratories and primary school classrooms, significant, although rather unexciting, results have accrued. Both in methodology and in theory, sociometric analysis has consistently failed to live up to its high promise over the years.

We had reason, however, to expect that an application of network analysis to communes would provide a different and more satisfactory result. There were a number of reasons for this optimism. One is that communes are small but sufficiently complex, well-bounded, social networks providing an opportunity for complete sociometric enumeration. Of course, no commune in the study consisted of a completely closed sociometric structure, and some communes had at least as many sociometric bonds linking them to the outside society as they had bonds linking the members to each other. However, to a much greater extent than perhaps any other contemporary social collectivity, it is possible to think of communes as self-contained relational structures and commune members as bundles of group-defined roles.

Insufficient attention has been paid to distinguishing situations likely to produce significant sociometric effects from those in which relationships have been effectively neutralized as constraints upon action (e.g., well-run bureaucracies). Relational information can easily be obtained from any collectivity no matter how banal the interactions among the members of that collectivity may be. For example, consider people riding up together in an elevator. All will be capable of responding honestly to a question asking them which three others in the elevator they feel closest to. Such information may even produce intriguing sociometric patterns, but the power of indices derived from these

---

*It may be significant in this regard that most commune respondents who expressed an opinion on the matter thought that the relationship questionnaire was by far the most relevant of the survey instruments used.

†Very recent advances in computer techniques for subgraph enumeration (e.g., Holland and Leinhardt, 1974) and structural equivalence classification by block modeling across multiple networks (White et al., 1976) provide at least a beginning of a method for coping with the rapid increase in number of cases when one moves from the individual to the dyadic level, to the triadic level, and beyond. Many graph-theoretical theorems of interest to the student of social structure, however, remain probably solvable but unsolved at this writing.

patterns to explain social organization or behavior has understandably been quite limited.

At least four stringent requirements must be met for any collectivity before we should expect that its network traces will be significant in predicting group structure and future behavior.

1. *Complete enumerability:* Open-ended networks present intractable difficulties in that an enumeration of all members cannot be made. We are not suggesting that sociometric techniques cannot be useful in describing large populations. Granovetter (1973) and Laumann and Pappi (1973) provide two recent examples of how this may be done. However, to make use of the explanatory power of the contents of social relationships requires either the gathering of data on all possible dyadic pairs (as we have done) or the solution by statisticians of the problem of sampling from networks.

2. *Structural involution:* This consists of a high ratio of in-group to out-group relationships. Although there is no such thing in contemporary society as a completely involuted collectivity of any size, we should expect our results to be necessarily limited in power any time that successive concatenations of network linkages continue indefinitely to incorporate larger and larger collectivities and do not at some point begin to curl back upon themselves.

3. *Salience:* Relationship per se should be important to the members of the collectivity. In general, we should expect to find that the degree to which the content of the relationships is important to the individuals determines the extent to which relationships in and of themselves will be important determinants of organizational behavior.

4. *Situation specificity:* Relationships have the property of lying dormant much of the time and becoming active only when events occur that require noninstitutionalized or antiinstitutional responses. The frequency of such events will be directly proportional to the importance of the relationships themselves in explaining behavior.

Once satisfied that a phenomenon is one that is likely to be explained relationally, it is then necessary to choose a relational perspective (i.e., structure or process) and a relational unit of analysis (i.e., dyad, triad, or larger subnetwork).

The Relationship as Structure

There are two ways of looking at networks of relationships in communes. A relationship may be looked at as a conduit for transactions that occur between two or more individuals. Or, as has been done in this book, relationships may be thought of as structures having a reality and life of their own, independent of the individuals who occupy their nodes.* We assumed that the relationships being investigated actually did exist and that they had a determinable structure that could change or remain stable but that existed in space and time. It is, however, equally legitimate to look at relationships as conduits for transactions that take place among people. The relationship itself, in either case, cannot of course be directly observed. We obtained, as in the individual level of analysis, only a report or an account of what the relationship was like. Yet we may be on more solid ground than in traditional survey analysis in having two reports of each relationship—one from either side. Furthermore, in the commune study, there has been strong and consistent ethnographic cross-validation of the sociometric findings.

Relational Effects

Information concerning all possible dyad relations among members of each commune was transcribed on a computer-analyzable file. Each variable in the file corresponds to one directed observation about one dyad (e.g., Betty's observations about her relationship with Peter concerning the variable "loving"). Data for the relational file were gathered for the two time periods and include the following kinds of information:

1. relationship information (e.g., is this specific relationship loving, improving, tense, awkward);
2. behaviors information (e.g., who in the commune cleaned the kitchen this week);
3. characteristics information (e.g., who in the commune is loving, supportive, charismatic, decisive).

Through a system of flags, it is possible to determine whether or not a respondent failed to complete a questionnaire and/or did not answer the questions for the specific alter and whether the individual (1) has remained in the commune for both time periods, (2) left the commune after the first time period, or (3) entered the commune in the second time period.

This file can be analyzed through the use of standard statistical packages. In addition, Fortran programs were developed specifically to transform the dyad relationships into sociometric matrices. Other programs, developed both in-house and elsewhere, can be used with the matrices to perform various sociometric analyses, for example, triad census counts (Holland and Leinhardt, 1970), and measures of hierarchy.

---

*This is a different kind of reification from the more common kind, which makes individuals the units of analysis.

Choice of Dyad as the Relational Unit

The relational unit of analysis throughout this book has been the dyad. The dyad is the smallest possible relationship. We have no direct data on triads. Triadic data must be built up out of dyadic components. For analysis of triadic censuses built up out of the dyadic components of these communes, see Bradley (1979). In a similar manner, larger subnetworks up to and including the entire commune as a network can be built up out of dyadic units. Each dyadic datum has been created from two bits of information reported independently by each participant in each possible dyadic configuration. Thus, when we look at triadic configurations (A, B, C) such as transitivity, the survey data to be examined will consist of information about each triad's three component dyads (AB, AC, BC).

Communal relationships, as we have seen, are often highly cathected (i.e., highly charged with sentiment). The degree of cathexis in a commune is important in determining whether the relational position of individuals in a network will explain much about their behavior or will explain little. Communes are kinds of organizations, unlike business organizations, where the relationships tend to be salient, noninstitutionalized, and charged with affect.

The previous emphasis in network analysis (e.g., Davis, 1970; Hallinan, 1974) on situations of low emotional cathexis (e.g., school classrooms) might well explain the greater sparsity of significant findings and correlations. The intrinsically dyadic nature of communal relationships points to another reason for focusing upon pairs (Bennett, 1975, p. 73):

> The point is that communalism is never total—humans are not ants—but must always be adjusted to specific ideologies and to certain regularities in human psychology and social life. Clearly, sexual experience and love have a strong dyadic character—it is impossible to thoroughly communalize them, despite the kibbutz attempt or the myths of "primitive sexual communism." For bioemotional reasons, the cathexis is largely limited to two persons at any one time.

Appendix B

Attitude Scores
and Tables

TABLE B-1. Attitude Items: Urban Commune Members and College Student Control Group

Item	Commune Mean ($N = 398$)	Columbia-Barnard College Student Control Group Mean ($N = 26$)	Mean Difference Significance (t-test) ($p \leqslant .05$)
Sometimes I believe in God and sometimes I don't.	3.87[a]	3.69[a]	–
Raising children is important work.	1.20	1.27	–
On the whole, I am satisfied with myself[4]	2.02	2.58	.03
I prefer rock music to classical music.	2.91	2.65	–
Nowadays, a person has to live pretty much for today and let tomorrow take care of itself.[2]	2.76	3.73	.001
Spontaneity is often an excuse for irresponsibility.	3.41	3.16	–
Communes with a formal structure tend to stifle creativity among their members.	3.56	NA	–
In spite of what some people say, the lot of the average man is getting worse, not better.[2]	2.86	3.08	–
Over the past few years, blacks have gotten more than they deserve.	4.47	4.50	–
I am able to do things as well as most other people.[4]	1.81	2.04	–
It's hardly fair to bring a child into the world with the way things look for the future.[2]	3.96	4.00	–
Every able-bodied male should willingly serve for a period of time in his country's military service.	4.50	4.28	–
I feel left out of things around me.[1][2]	4.20	3.96	–
Some people will be saved and others will not. It is predestined. God knew who would be saved long before we were born.	3.85	4.42	–

NA – Not available.

Statement			
I feel that the people in the commune are my true family. [6]	2.38	NA	—
While man has great potential for good, society brings out primarily the worst in him.	3.01	3.24	—
Despite the great diversity of religious orientation that currently abounds, it is still possible for the sincere seeker to separate truth from illusion.	1.86	1.92	—
With respect to relations between husband and wife these days, there are no clear guidelines to tell us what is right and what is wrong.	3.28	3.48	—
I am convinced that working slowly for reform within the American political system is preferable to working for a revolution.	3.00	2.16	.002
There is only one solution to the problems of the world today, and that is Christ.	3.36	4.00	—
The people running the country don't really care what happens to people like myself. [1] [2]	2.55	2.25	—
Most people in this commune are more inclined to look out for themselves than to consider the needs of others. [6]	4.01	NA	—
I take a positive attitude toward myself. [4]	1.77	2.13	—
An urban communal household is better than nothing, but I would eventually prefer to live in a rural commune or a rural intentional community.	3.08	NA	—
If my country had been destroyed, I still would not push the button to wipe out the attacking enemy nation.	1.90	2.04	—
The rich get richer and the poor get poorer. [1]	2.31	2.46	—
A solution to many of our society's current problems is to build communitarianism into a widespread social and political movement.	2.95	NA	—

393

TABLE B-1. Attitude Items: Urban Commune Members and College Student Control Group *(continued)*

Item	Commune Mean (N = 398)	Columbia-Barnard College Student Control Group Mean (N = 26)	Mean Difference Significance (t-test) (p ≤ .05)
There is not much that I can do about most of the important national problems we face today.	3.31	2.54	.01
I feel that there is a great distance between me and the other commune members. [6]	4.44	NA	—
If people worked hard at their jobs, they would reap the full benefits of our society.	3.97	3.46	.05
The present condition of society makes doing unto others as you would have others do unto you impractical.	4.15	3.28	.001
A good teacher is one who makes you wonder about your way of looking at things. [3]	1.88	1.81	—
I would definitely prefer living in the country to living in [name of city]. [7]	2.08	3.42	.000
Most people in [name of city] are more inclined to consider the needs of others than to just look out for themselves. [5] [7]	3.82	3.92	—
If you're not careful, the average person that you meet in [name of city] will take advantage of you. [5] [7]	3.39	3.58	—
No one in [name of city], with the possible exception of my fellow commune members, is going to care much what happens to me. [5] [7]	3.92	NA	—
[Name of city] is such a large place that a person like myself has almost no chance to make his views known to the powers that be. [7]	3.19	2.92	—

Statement			
The fact that [name of city] is able to function as a city as well as it does demonstrates that human nature is basically cooperative. [5][7]	2.83	3.35	—
Events in [name of city] are so chaotic that long-range urban planning is simply an exercise in futility. [7]	3.26	3.58	—
I have very definite, established goals in life that I intend to pursue at all costs.	2.45	3.23	—
Once you've experienced what it really means to be united with a group of people, you can never again be content with a noncommunal way of life.	3.10	NA	—
Politics nowadays is so complicated that I would have difficulty classifying myself as a liberal, or a conservative, or a moderate.	3.01	2.85	—
I think it's healthier for children to grow up in a communal household than in the household of a nuclear family.	2.38	NA	—
A man who is ready to die for his country deserves the highest honor.	4.03	3.23	.000
There are so many interesting things to do in the world, I can't see how people narrow themselves to a single lifelong occupation.	2.80	2.85	—
It is possible to get a relevant and valuable education at many American universities, provided that you are willing to study hard.	2.76	1.85	.001
The fact that this commune functions as well as it does demonstrates that human nature is basically cooperative. [6]	2.45	NA	—
I would rather be a child than an adult.	3.82	3.83	—

TABLE B-1. Attitude Items: Urban Commune Members and College Student Control Group *(continued)*

Item	Commune Mean (N = 398)	Columbia-Barnard College Student Control Group Mean (N = 26)	Mean Difference Significance (t-test) (p ≤ .05)
I prefer a dinner of brown rice and organically grown vegetables to a steak dinner.	2.66	4.00	.000
All in all, I am inclined to feel that I am a failure. [4]	4.60	4.46	—
As I view the world in relation to my life, the world completely confuses me.	4.09	3.62	—
A person who leads an even, regular life in which few surprises or unexpected happenings arise really has a lot to be grateful for. [3]	4.02	3.62	—
The only way to be happy living communally is to live from day to day and to be prepared for anything to change at any time.	2.73	NA	—
Sometimes I don't care whether I get anywhere in life or not.	3.69	3.69	—
There's a person in this commune who seems to have an inexhaustible supply of love.	2.33	NA	—
With inflation and the control of wages by corporations, there is little possibility that one can control his fate on the economic scene.	3.09	2.69	—
Grading college papers according to the truth of what has been expressed in them is unfair because all truth is relative.	3.24	3.04	—
I would hate missing a commune meeting more than I would missing a day's work.	2.87	NA	—

Statement			
I am sure that I would rather have children than not have children.	2.33	1.92	—
It is good to live in a fantasy world every now and then.	2.86	1.84	.000
A good job is one in which what is to be done and how it is to be done are always clear.[3]	3.44	3.32	—
I think that there is a very good chance that I will still be living communally ten years from now.	2.39	NA	—
I feel that I do not have much to be proud of.[4]	4.13	4.12	—
I like parties where I know most of the people more than ones where all or most of the people are strangers.[3]	2.25	2.23	—
I certainly feel useless at times.[4]	3.16	3.04	—
I have a hard time getting my opinions to count for anything in this commune.	4.32	NA	—
There are odd moments now and then when I suspect I might go to pieces.	3.22	2.69	—
In order to get ahead in the United States today, you are almost forced to do some things that are not right.	3.17	3.12	—
While I am working, I usually look forward to quitting time.	3.26	2.31	.000
The average university student nowadays is just a cog in a giant machine.	2.69	2.35	—
At times I think I am no good at all.[4]	3.72	3.69	—
I am proud of my work.	2.01	2.04	—
The world is basically an evil place.	4.04	4.12	—
By getting married, a person gives up a lot of power over the direction his life will take.	3.39	3.23	—

TABLE B-1. Attitude Items: Urban Commune Members and College Student Control Group *(continued)*

Item	Commune Mean ($N = 398$)	Columbia-Barnard College Student Control Group Mean ($N = 26$)	Mean Difference Significance (t-test) ($p \leqslant .05$)
This country would be better off if religion had a greater influence in daily life.	2.72	3.08	—
Every now and then I can't seem to make up my mind about things.	2.33	1.92	.01
Concerning man's freedom to make his own choices, I believe man is more or less bound by limitations of heredity and environment.	3.48	2.42	.000
I prefer alcohol to marijuana.	3.36	2.56	.002
People who have the power are out to take advantage of us.[1]	2.68	2.24	—
For myself, communal living is not an end in itself but a means of achieving certain goals.	1.89	NA	—
I would rather be married than single.	3.02	2.52	—
To be willing to have one's own opinions changed by the influence of others is a sign of weakness.	4.35	3.92	—
I feel that I'm a person of worth, at least on an equal basis with others.[4]	1.45	1.24	—
I have to admit that the people whom you find living in communes tend to be less competent in practical matters than the average person I know not living communally.	4.20	NA	—
I feel that I have a number of good qualities.[4]	1.51	1.28	.03

Statement			
Every now and then I lose my temper when things go wrong.	2.16	2.47	—
No one in this communal household is going to care much what happens to me.[6]	NA	4.64	—
I wish I could have more respect for myself.[4]	3.17	3.12	—
You can never achieve freedom within the framework of contemporary American society.	3.62	3.44	—
Whenever I fail, I have no one to blame but myself.	2.19	2.42	—
There is really no such thing as a problem between people that can't be solved.[3]	2.96	2.26	.01
What I think doesn't count very much.	4.12	4.10	—
My work days are usually more exciting and enjoyable than my weekends.	3.85	3.70	—
I believe that forgotten childhood experiences have an effect on me.	2.24	1.97	—
If I went to the university for further education, I would have great difficulty deciding what field of study to concentrate in.	3.52	3.61	—
I am one who never gets excited when things go wrong.	4.31	3.92	—
I would like to help bring about a world in which most people live in communes or intentional communities.	NA	2.82	—
I am skeptical of anything that tries to tell me the right way to live.	2.31	2.91	.04

399

TABLE B–1. Attitude Items: Urban Commune Members and College Student Control Group *(continued)*

Item	Commune Mean (N = 398)	Columbia-Barnard College Student Control Group Mean (N = 26)	Mean Difference Significance (t-test) (p ≤ .05)
To understand other members of this commune, words usually aren't necessary.[6]	3.13	NA	—

[a] All items were scored on a five point Likert scale: 1 = strongly agree, 2 = slightly agree, 3 = neutral or no opinion, 4 = slightly disagree, 5 = strongly disagree.

[1] Item is part of the Harris alienation scale.

[2] Item is part of the Srole anomia scale (Robinson and Shaver, 1973, p. 256).

[3] Item is part of the Budner Intolerance of ambiguity scale (Robinson and Shaver, 1973, p. 401).

[4] Item is part of the Rosenberg self esteem scale (Robinson and Shaver, 1973, p. 81).

[5] Item is part of an urban trust scale based on Rosenberg's faith in people scale (Robinson and Shaver, 1973, p. 612).

[6] Item is part of a communal trust scale based on Rosenberg's trust in people scale (Robinson and Shaver, 1973, p. 612).

[7] For comparison purposes, commune means in this table were computed for New York commune members only (N = 63).

TABLE B-2. Comparative Analysis of Items Comprising the Rosenberg Self-esteem Scale

	Samples of Adult Males only — Percentage Responding in Highest Self-esteem Category				Mean Scores for Commune Members Present and Responding Both Waves Only							
	Urban Communes 1974	Youth in Transition 1974	Pearlin Study 1972	Kohn Study 1964	All Stayers 1974	All Stayers 1975	Freshmen[1] 1974	Freshmen[1] 1975	Sophomores[2] 1974	Sophomores[2] 1975	Veterans[3] 1974	Veterans[3] 1975
I feel that I'm a person of worth, at least on an equal basis with others.	69%	61%	71%	44%	1.4	1.7	1.3	1.6	1.4	1.7	1.7	1.6
I feel that I have a number of good qualities.	65	47	70	NA	1.4	1.6	1.4	1.6	1.4	1.6	1.4	1.4
All in all, I am inclined to feel that I'm a failure.	76	NA	72	NA	4.6	4.6	4.7	4.8	4.5	4.5	4.7	4.4
I am able to do things as well as most other people.	42	43	57	29	1.7	2.0	1.5	2.0	1.9	2.2	1.9	1.7
I feel that I do not have much to be proud of.	52	36	68	NA	4.2	4.3	4.2	4.4	4.2	4.2	4.4	4.2
I take a positive attitude toward myself.	51	36	56	30	1.7	2.0	1.5	1.7	1.9	2.0	2.0	2.3
On the whole I am satisfied with myself.	43	NA	47	NA	1.8	2.2	1.6	2.0	2.0	2.3	1.9	2.3
I wish that I could have more respect for myself.	29	NA	58	23	3.1	3.4	3.3	3.4	3.0	3.6	3.0	3.1
I certainly feel useless at times.	29	NA	50	20	3.2	3.3	3.1	3.1	3.3	3.7	3.5	3.1
At times I think that I am no good at all.	46	34	71	37	3.8	4.0	3.7	3.9	3.7	4.1	4.1	4.1
Total	246	1620[a]	2300[b]	3087[c]	76	76	31	31	29	29	16	16

NA – Not available.

[a]Same mean age as commune members in 1974.
[b]Chicago area.
[c]Sample of Americans in civilian occupations.

[1]Freshmen are stayers who had been members 6 months or less at time 1.
[2]... Sophomores are stayers who had been members between 6 and 18 months at time 1.
[3]Veterans are stayers who had been members more than 18 months at time 1.

TABLE B-3. Percentage of Attitude Items for Which Responses Vary Significantly by Ideological Type

	Total Number of Items Asked	% Significant .0001 or More	
		Number	% Significant
Attitudes about religion	5	5	100%
Attitudes about political issues	11	9	82
Attitudes toward communal living	6	4	67
Attitudes about human nature	5	3	60
Attitudes about respond-ent's city	7	4	57
Attitudes toward present communal living situation	7	4	57
Attitudes about work and career	8	4	50
Attitudes about university, education	4	2	50
Attitudes about self	20	8	40
Attitudes toward marriage and family	6	2	33

References

Adams, Bert N.
    1974   "Birth Order: A Critical Review," *Sociometry* 35(3): 411–439.
Adams, Grace, and Edward Hutten
    1942   *The Mad Forties*. New York: Harper.
Adler, Nathan
    1972   *The Underground Stream: New Life-Styles and the Antinomian Personality*. New York: Harper Torchbooks.
Aidala, Angela
    1976   "Attitudes of Commune Members toward Themselves, Communes, and Society." New York: Urban Communes Research Project Working Paper.
    1977   "Ideology in Communal Groups: A Shared Search for Family?" Chicago: Presented at meetings of the American Sociological Association.
    1979   "Ideological Systems: A Longitudinal Study of Norms, Values, and Ideology in Communal Living Groups." Ph.D. dissertation, in progress. New York: Columbia University.
Aiken, M., and J. Hage
    1966   "Organizational Alienation: A Comparative Analysis," *American Sociological Review* 31(4): 497–507.
Alba, Richard D.
    1975   *The Intersection of Social Circles: A New Measure of Social Proximity in Networks*. New York: Herbert H. Lehman College, City University of New York and Bureau of Applied Social Research, Columbia University.
Albert, Robert
    1953   "Concept of Cohesiveness," *American Journal of Sociology* 59: 231–243.

Albertson, Ralph
    1936   "A Survey of Mutualistic Communities in America," *Iowa Journal of History and Politics* 34(October): 375–445.
Alfred, Randall H.
    1976   "The Church of Satan," in C. Glock and R. Bellah (eds.), *The New Religious Consciousness*. Berkeley: University of California Press.
Allardt, E.
    1971   "Alienation," in J. Israel (ed.), *Alienation: From Marx to Modern Sociology*. Boston: Allyn & Bacon.
Almond, G.
    1954   *The Appeals of Communism*. Princeton, N.J.: Princeton University Press.
Altman, Israel.
    1979   "Islamic Movements in Egypt." *Jerusalem Quarterly* 10: 87–105.
Alyea, Paul and Blanche R.
    1956   *Fairhope, 1894–1954*. University: University of Alabama Press.
Andrews, E.
    1953   *The People Called Shakers*. New York: Dover Press.
Andrews, Kenneth and D. Kandel
    1979   "Attitude and Behavior: A Specification of the Contingent Consistency Hypothesis." *American Sociological Review* 44(2): 298–310.
Apsler, A.
    1974   *Communes through the Ages*. New York: Messner.
Arensberg, Conrad
    1961   "The Community as an Object and Sample," *American Anthropology* 62(2): 186–202.
Armytage, W. H. G.
    1961   *Heavens Below*. London: Routlege & Kegan Paul.
Arnold, David O. (ed.)
    1970   *The Sociology of Subcultures*. Berkeley, Calif.: Glendessary Press.
Arnold, Eberhard
    1965   *Love and Marriage in the Spirit*. Rifton, N.Y.: Plough.
Arnold, Emmy
    1963   *Torches Together*. Rifton, N.Y.: Plough.
Aron, Raymond
    1962   *The Opium of the Intellectuals*. New York: W. W. Norton.
Arons, Stephen
    1971   "Values Embodied in Law Relating to Education, Family, and Child-rearing." Honolulu: Presented at the American Psychological Association meeting, September 1.
Arrow, Kenneth J.
    1963   *Social Choice and Individual Values*, 2nd ed. New Haven, Conn.: Yale University Press.
Asch, S. E.
    1951   "Effects of Group Pressure upon the Modification and Distortion of Judgments," in H. Guetzkow (ed.), *Groups, Leadership, and Men*. Pittsburgh: Carnegie Press.

Atcheson, R.
1971   *The Bearded Lady.* New York: John Day.
Austin, Barbara L.
1971   *Sad Nun at Synanon.* New York: Pocket Books.
Bachman, Jerald G.
1970   *Youth in Transition. The Impact of Family Background and Intelli-
        gence on Tenth-Grade Boys.* Vol. 2. Ann Arbor: Institute for Social
        Research, University of Michigan.
——, R. L. Kahn, M. T. Mednick, T. N. Davidson, and L. D. Johnston
1967   *Youth in Transition. Blueprint for a Longitudinal Study of Adoles-
        cent Boys.* Vol. 1. Ann Arbor: Institute for Social Research, Univer-
        sity of Michigan.
——, S. Green, and I. D. Wirtanen
1971   *Youth in Transition. Dropping Out – Problem or Symptom?* Vol. 3.
        Ann Arbor: Institute for Social Research, University of Michigan.
——, P. O'Malley, and J. Johnston
1978   *Adolescence to Adulthood: Change and Stability in the Lives of
        Young Men. Youth in Transition.* Vol. 6. Ann Arbor: Institute for
        Social Research, University of Michigan.
Baden, John, and Richard Stroup
1972   "Choice, Faith, and Politics: The Political Economy of Hutterian
        Communes," *Public Choice* 212(Spring): 1–11.
Bahr, Howard M.
1973   *Skid Row: An Introduction to Disaffiliation.* New York: Oxford
        University Press.
Baker, Elsworth F.
1967   *Man in the Trap: The Causes of Blocked Sexual Energy.* New York:
        Macmillan.
Baker, Russell
1970   "Observer: Lord Sean's Wives and Fellow Husbands," *The New York
        Times Magazine* April 5.
Baltzell, Digby E.
1968   *The Search for Community in Modern America.* New York: Harper
        & Row.
Banfield, Edward
1958   *The Moral Basis of a Backward Society.* Glencoe, Ill.: Free Press.
Bannester, E. Michael
1969   "Sociodynamics: An Integrative Theorem of Power, Authority,
        Influence, and Love," *American Sociological Review* 34(June):
        374–393.
Barnett, Larry
1972   "The Rural Ideal in American Society and Its Influence on Attitudes
        towards Population Limitation," *The Journal of Biosociological
        Sciences* 4: 235–246.
Bartell, Gilbert D.
1971   *Group Sex: An Eyewitness Report on the American Way of Swing-
        ing.* New York: Signet.
Bartelt, Pearl W.
1978   "Gender Differentiation in Utopian and Communal Societies." San

Francisco: Presented at the Seventy-third annual meeting of the American Sociological Association.

Baskir, Lawrence M., and William A. Strauss
1978   *Chance and Circumstance.* New York: Knopf.

Beame, Hugh, et al.
1973   *Home Comfort.* New York: Saturday Review Press.

Becker, Gary
1976   *The Economic Approach to Human Behavior.* Chicago: University of Chicago Press.

Beech, R., and A. Schoeppe
1970   "A Developmental Study of Value Systems in Adolescence." Miami Beach, Fla.: meetings of American Psychological Association.

Belcher, John C.
1967   "The One-Person Household: A Consequence of the Isolated Nuclear Family?" *Journal of Marriage and the Family* 29(3): 534–540.

Bell, Daniel
1960   *The End of Ideology.* New York: Free Press.
1973   *The Coming of Post-Industrial Society: A Venture in Social Forecasting.* New York: Basic Books.

Bellah, Robert N.
1970   *Beyond Belief.* New York: Harper & Row.
1976a   "New Religious Consciousness and the Crisis in Modernity," in C. Glock and R. Bellah (eds.), *The New Religious Consciousness.* Berkeley: University of California Press.
1976b   "The New Consciousness and the Berkeley New Left," in C. Glock and R. Bellah (eds.), *The New Religious Consciousness.* Berkeley: University of California Press.

Belov, Fedor
1955   *The History of a Soviet Collective Farm.* New York: Praeger.

Bengston, V., and J. Starr
1975   "Contrast and Consensus: A Generational Analysis of Youth in the 1970's," in Robert Havighurst and Philip Dreyer (eds.), *Youth: The Seventy-fourth Yearbook of the National Society for the Study of Education.* Chicago: University of Chicago Press.

Bennett, John W.
1967   *Hutterian Brethren: The Agricultural Economy and Social Organization of a Communal People.* Stanford, Calif.: Stanford University Press.
1975   "Communes and Communitarianism," *Theory and Society* 2: 63–94.

Bennis, Warren, and Philip E. Slater
1968   *The Temporary Society.* New York: Harper & Row.

Bensman, Joseph, and Michael Givant
1975   "Charisma and Modernity: The Use and Abuse of a Concept," *Social Research* (Winter): 570–614.

Berger, Bennett M.
1967   "The New Morality?" San Francisco: Presented at the Plenary Session of the Society of Social Problems, August 27.
——, et al.
1971   "Child Rearing Practices of the Communal Family," in J. Skolnick (ed.), *Families in Transition*. Boston: Little, Brown.
——, Bruce Hackett, and R. Mervyn Millar
1972   "The Communal Family," *Family Coordinator* 21(October): 419–427.
——, Bruce Hackett, and R. Mervyn Millar
1973   "Supporting the Communal Family," in Rosabeth M. Kanter (ed.), *Communes: Creating and Managing the Collective Life*. New York: Harper & Row.
——, and Bruce Hackett
1974   "On the Decline of Age Grading in Rural Hippie Communes," *Journal of Social Issues* 30(2): 163–183.
Berger, Peter L.
1963   "Charisma and Religious Innovation." *American Sociological Review*, 28(6): 940–950.
1969   *The Sacred Canopy: Elements of a Sociological Theory of Religion*. Garden City, N.Y.: Anchor Books.
1970   *A Rumor of Angels*, Garden City, N.Y.: Anchor Books.
1979   *The Heretical Imperative*, Garden City, N.Y.: Anchor Books.
——, Brigitte Berger, and Hansfried Kellner
1973   *The Homeless Mind: Modernization and Consciousness*. New York: Random House.
——, and Thomas Luckmann
1966   *The Social Construction of Reality*. Garden City, N.Y.: Doubleday.
Bestor, A. E., Jr.
1950   *Backwoods Utopias: The Sectarian and Owenite Phases of Communtarian Socialism in America, 1663–1829*. Philadelphia: University of Pennsylvania Press.
1953   "Patent-office Models of the Good Society: Some Relationships between Social Reform and Westward Expansion," *American Historical Review* 58: 515–526.
Bettelheim, Bruno
1969   *The Children of the Dream: Communal Childrearing and American Education*. New York: Macmillan.
Bierstedt, Robert
1954   "The Problem of Authority" in *Freedom and Control in Modern Society*. Morroe Berger, T. Abel and C. Page (eds.), New York: D. VanNostrand, Inc.
Bikle, George B., Jr.
1971   "Utopianism and the Planning Element in Modern Japan," in David Plath (ed.), *Aware of Utopia*. Urbana: University of Illinois Press.

Birnbaum, Norman
   1962   *The Sociological Study of Ideology, 1940–1960: A Trend Report and Bibliography.* Oxford: Blackwell (International Sociological Association of UNESCO).
Bishop, Claire
   1950   *All Things Common.* New York: Harper & Row.
Black, Duncan
   1958   *The Theory of Committees and Elections.* Cambridge: Cambridge University Press.
Blasi, Joseph R.
   1978   *The Communal Future: The Kibbutz and the Utopian Dilemma.* Norwood, Penn.: Norwood Editions.
Blau, Peter
   1955   *The Dynamics of Bureaucracy.* Chicago: University of Chicago Press.
   1964   *Exchange and Power in Social Life.* New York: Wiley.
——, and W. Richard Scott
   1962   *Formal Organizations: A Comparative Approach.* San Francisco: Chandler.
Blauner, Robert
   1964   *Alienation and Freedom.* Chicago: University of Chicago Press.
Bloesch, D.
   1964   *Centers of Christian Renewal.* Philadelphia: United Church Press.
Blumer, Herbert
   1953   "Collective Behavior," in A. M. Lee (ed.), *Principles of Sociology.* New York: Barnes and Noble.
Bohrnstedt, George
   1969   "Observations on the Measurement of Change," in E. Borgatta (ed.), *Sociological Methodology, 1969.* San Francisco: Jossey-Bass.
Boissevain, J., and J. C. Mitchell
   1973   *Network Analysis: Studies in Human Interaction.* The Hague: Mouton.
Boocock, Sarane S.
   1974   "Youth in Three Cultures." Paper prepared for special issue of *School Review,* November.
Boorman, S. A. and H. White
   1976   "Social Structure From Multiple Networks, II. Role Structures," *American Journal of Sociology* 81(6): 1384–1446.
Bord, Richard
   1975   "Toward a Social Psychological Theory of Charismatic Social Influence Processes," *Social Forces* 53(March): 485–496.
Bradley, Ray
   1979   "Pyramids of Power and Communion: The Structural Properties of Charismatic Communes," Ph.D. dissertation, in progress. New York: Columbia University.
Briggs, K.
   1977   "New Religious Movements Considered Likely to Last," *The New York Times,* June 22, p. A15.

Brody, Richard, and Benjamin Page
 1973   "Indifference, Alienation, and Rational Decisions: The Effects of Candidate Evaluations on Turnout and the Vote," *Public Choice* 15(Summer): 1–17.
Broom, Leonard and P. Selznick
 1968   *Sociology.* New York: Harper & Row.
Brown, L. Dave and Jane C.
 1973   "Group Process in an Urban Commune," in Rosabeth M. Kanter (ed.), *Communes: Creating and Managing the Collective Life.* New York: Harper & Row.
Brzezinski, Zbigniew
 1970   *Between Two Ages: America's Role in the Technotronic Era.* New York: Viking.
Buber, Martin
 1949   *Paths in Utopia.* Boston: Beacon Press.
Buchanan, James M., and Gordon Tullock
 1962   *The Calculus of Consent.* Ann Arbor: Ann Arbor Paperbacks, University of Michigan Press.
Buder, Stanley
 1970   "Pullman: Town Planning and Social Control in the Gilded Age," in Raymond A. Mohl and Neil Betten, (eds.), *Urban America in Historical Perspective.* New York: Weybright and Talley.
Bugliosi, Vincent, with Curt Gentry
 1974   *Helter Skelter: The True Story of the Manson Murders.* New York: W. W. Norton.
Bushee, Frederick A.
 1905   "Communistic Societies in the United States," *Political Science Quarterly* 20(December): 625–664.
Calverton, V. F.
 1941   *Where Angels Dared to Tread.* Indianapolis: Bobbs-Merrill.
Campbell, Donald T., and Julian C. Stanley
 1963   *Experimental and Quasi-Experimental Designs for Research.* Chicago: Rand McNally.
Cancian, Francesca
 1975   *What Are Norms? A Study of Beliefs and Action in a Maya Community.* Cambridge: Cambridge University Press.
Cantril, Hadley
 1941   *The Social Psychology of Social Movements.* New York: John Wiley.
Caplow, Theodore
 1968   *Two against One: Coalitions in Triads.* Englewood Cliffs, N.J.: Prentice-Hall.
 1973   "Goals and Their Achievement in Four Utopian Communities," in Rosabeth M. Kanter (ed.), *Communes: Creating and Managing the Collective Life.* New York: Harper & Row.
Carden, Maren Lockwood
 1969   *Oneida: Utopian Community to Modern Corporation.* Baltimore, Md.: Johns Hopkins University Press.

410   References

Case, John and R. Taylor
    1979   *Co-ops, Communes and Collectives.* New York: Pantheon Books.
Cavan, Sherri
    1971   "Hippies of the Redwood Forest." San Francisco: Unpublished, Scientific Analysis Corporation, October.
    1972   *Hippies of the Haight.* Saint Louis: New Critics Press.
Chafee, G.
    1958   "Isolated Religious Sects as an Object for Research," *American Journal of Sociology* 35: 618–630.
Chomsky, Noam
    1969   "Linguistics and Politics," *New Left Review* 57(September–October): 21–34.
Clark, B. Stephen
    1972   *Building Christian Communities.* Notre Dame, Ind.: Ave Maria Press.
Clark, E. T.
    1949   *The Small Sects in America.* Gloucester, Mass.: Peter Smith.
Cochrane, R.
    1971   "The Structure of Value Systems in Male and Female Prisoners," *British Journal of Criminology* 11: 73–79.
Cohn, Norman
    1957   *Pursuit of the Millennium.* New York: Essential Books.
Coleman, James S.
    1957   *Community Conflict.* Glencoe, Ill.: Free Press.
    1961   *The Adolescent Society.* New York: Free Press.
    1963   "Comment on 'On the Concept of Influence,'" *Public Opinion Quarterly* 27(1): 63–82.
    1966   "Foundations for a Theory of Collective Decisions," *American Journal of Sociology* 71(May): 615–627.
    1971a   "Community Disorganization and Conflict," in Robert K. Merton and Robert Nisbet (eds.), *Contemporary Social Problems.* New York: Harcourt Brace.
    1971b   *Resources for Social Change.* New York: Wiley-Interscience.
    1971c   "Clustering in *N* dimensions by use of a system of forces," *Journal of Mathematical Sociology* 1(January): 1–47.
    1972   *Transcendent Corporate Actors.* Mimeo.
    1973   "Loss of Power," *American Sociological Review* 38(1): 1–17.
    1974   *Youth: Transition to Adulthood.* Chicago: University of Chicago Press.
Conkin, Paul K.
    1964   *Two Paths to Utopia.* Lincoln: University of Nebraska Press.
Constantine, Larry and Joan M.
    1973   *Group Marriage.* New York: Collier Books.
Conway, Flo, and Jim Sigelman
    1978   *Snapping.* Philadelphia: J. B. Lippincott.
Copans, Stu, and David Osgood
    1972   *The Home Health Handbook.* Brattleboro, Vt.: Stephen Greene Press.

Coser, Lewis A.
  1974   *Greedy Institutions: Patterns of Undivided Commitment.* New York: Free Press.
Cox, Harvey
  1977   *Turning East: The Promise and Peril of the New Orientalism.* New York: Simon & Schuster.
Cross, Frank Moore, Jr.
  1961   *The Ancient Library of Amran: A Survey of Ten Dead Sea Scrolls and the Community Which Owned Them.* Garden City, N.Y.: Anchor Books.
Cross, Whitney R.
  1965   *The Burned-over District: The Social and Intellectual History of Enthusiastic Religion in Western New York, 1800–1850.* New York: Harper Torchbooks.
Culpepper, Robert H.
  1977   *Evaluating the Charismatic Movement.* Valley Forge: Judson Press.
D'Andrade, Roy
  1965   "Trait Psychology and Componential Analysis," *American Anthropologist* 67: 215–228.
Danziger, Carl, and Matthew Greenwald
  1973   *Twenty Four Alternatives: A Look at Unmarried Couples and Communes.* New York: Institute of Life Insurance.
Davidson, Sara
  1973   "Hippie Families on Open Land," in Rosabeth M. Kanter (ed.), *Communes: Creating and Managing the Collective Life.* New York: Harper & Row.
Davidson, Terrence N.
  1972   *Youth in Transition. Evolution of a Strategy for Longitudinal Analysis of Survey Panel Data.* Vol. 4. Ann Arbor: Institute for Social Research, University of Michigan.
Davies, James C.
  1962   "Toward a Theory of Revolution," *American Sociological Review* 27(February): 5–19.
  1965   *The Early Christian Church.* New York: Holt Rinehart & Winston.
Davis, James A.
  1961   *Great Books and Small Groups.* New York: Free Press.
  1970   "Clustering and Hierarchy in Interpersonal Relations: Testing Two Graph Theoretical Models on 742 Sociomatrices," *American Sociological Review* 35(October): 843–851.
deCoulanges, Fustel
  1956   *The Ancient City.* New York: Doubleday.
Deets, Lee Emerson
  1942   "Data from Utopia." New York: Hunter College, mimeo.
Delespesse, Max, and Andre Tange
  1967,   *Communauté Humaine: Des Communautaires Temoignent.* Paris:
  1971   Fleurus. 2 vols.

deLint, Jan E.
   1966   "A Note on Smart's Study of Birth Rank and Affiliation in Male
            University Students," *Journal of Psychology* 62(2): 177–178.
Dember, William N.
   1964   "Birth Order and Need Affiliation," *Journal of Abnormal and Social
            Psychology* 68(5): 555–557.
Demerath, N. J., and Victor Thiesen
   1966   "On Spitting against the Wind: Organizational Precariousness and
            American Irreligion," *American Journal of Sociology* 71(May):
            674–687.
Demos, John
   1970   *A Little Commonwealth: Family Life in Plymouth Colony*. New
            York: Oxford University Press.
Diamond, Sigmund
   1958   "From Organization to Society: Virginia in the 17th Century,"
            American Journal of Sociology 63(5): 457–475.
——, (ed.)
   1963   *The Creation of Society in the New World*. Chicago: Rand McNally.
Diamond, Stanley
   1957   "Kibbutz and Shtetl: History of an Idea," *Social Problems* 5(2):
            71.
Diamond, Stephen
   1971   *What the Trees Said: Life on a New Age Farm*. New York: Dell.
Doll, Eugene
   1951   "Social and Economic Organization in Two Pennsylvania German
            Religious Communities," *American Journal of Sociology* 57:
            168–177.
Donham, Parker
   1970   "Town Wants Commune Closed," *The Boston Globe*, October 12.
Dore, Ronald
   1959   *Land Reform in Japan*. London: Oxford.
Dornbusch, Sanford
   1954   "The Military Academy as an Assimilating Institution," *Social
            Forces* 33(May): 316–321.
Dorner, Peter
   1977   *Cooperative and Commune*. Madison: University of Wisconsin
            Press.
Dow, T. E., Jr.
   1969   "The Theory of Charisma," *Sociological Quarterly* 10(Summer):
            306–318.
Downs, Anthony
   1957   *An Economic Theory of Democracy*. New York: Harper.
Downton, James V., Jr.
   1979   *Sacred Journeys: The Conversion of Young Americans to Divine
            Light Mission*. New York: Columbia University Press.
Doyle, Leonard, J. (trans.)
   1948   *St. Benedict's Rule for Monasteries: St. John's Abbey*. Collegeville,
            Minn.: Liturgical Press.

Dreyer, Philip H.
  1975   "Sex, Sex Roles, and Marriage Among Youth in the 1970s," in
           Robert J. Havighurst and Philip Dreyer (eds.), *Youth: The Seventy-
           fourth Yearbook of the National Society for the Study of Educa-
           tion*. Chicago: University of Chicago Press.
Duncan, Otis D., and David L. Featherman
  1973   "Psychological and Cultural Factors in the Process of Occupational
           Achievement," in A. S. Goldberger and O. D. Duncan (eds.), *Struc-
           tural Equation Models in the Social Sciences*. New York and Lon-
           don: Seminar Press.
Duparc, Pierre
  1968   "Confraternities of the Holy Spirit and Village Communities in the
           Middle Ages," in Fredric Cheyette (ed.), *Lordship and Community
           in Medieval Europe*. New York: Holt Rinehart & Winston.
Durkheim, Emile
  1949   *The Division of Labor in Society*, George Simpson (trans.). Glencoe,
           Ill.: Free Press.
  1951   *Suicide*. Glencoe, Ill.: Free Press.
Eaton, Joseph
  1952   "Controlled Acculturation: A Survival Technique of the Hutterites,"
           American Sociological Review 17: 331–340.
——, and S. Katz
  1942   *Research Guide on Cooperative Farming*. New York: H. W. Wilson.
——, and Robert Weil
  1955   *Culture and Mental Disorder: Comparative Study of the Hutterites
           and Other Populations*. New York: Free Press.
Edwards, Christopher
  1979   *Crazy for God*. Englewood Cliffs, N.J.: Prentice-Hall.
Eiduson, Bernice
  1979   "The Commune Reared Child," in S. Noshpitz (ed.), *Basic Hand-
           book of Child Psychiatry* (vol.1). New York: Basic Books.
Eisenstadt, Samuel N.
  1968   *Max Weber on Charisma and Institution Building*. Chicago: Univer-
           sity of Chicago Press.
  1971   "Sociological Analysis and Youth Rebellion," in *From Generation to
           Generation: Age Groups and Social Structure*. New York: Free
           Press.
Ellul, James
  1964   *The Technological Society*. New York: Knopf.
Ellwood, Robert S., Jr.
  1979   *Alternative Altars: Unconventional and Eastern Spirituality in
           America*. Chicago: University of Chicago Press.
Engels, Frederick
  1942   *The Origin of the Family, Private Property, and the State*. New
           York: International Publishers.
  1959   "Socialism: Utopian and Scientific," in Lewis S. Feuer (ed.), *Marx
           and Engels: Basic Writings on Politics and Philosophy*. Garden
           City, N.Y.: Doubleday.

414   References

Erasmus, Charles J.
    1977   *In Search of the Common Good: Utopian Experiments Past and Future.* New York: Free Press.
Erickson, William
    1973   "Social Organization of an Urban Commune," *Urban Life and Culture* 2(July): 231–256.
Erikson, Erik
    1968   *Identity: Youth and Crisis.* New York: W. W. Norton.
    1970   "Reflections on the Dissent of Contemporary Youth," *International Journal of Psychoanalysis* 51: 11–22.
Etzioni, Amitai
    1957   "Solidaric Work-Groups in Collective Settlements," *Human Organization* 16: 2–6.
    1968   "Basic Human Needs, Alienation and Inauthenticity," *American Sociological Review* 33(December): 870–885.
    1969   "Reply to Nettler," *American Sociological Review* 34(August): 553ff.
    1972   "The Search for Political Meaning," *Center Magazine* 5(March–April): 2–8, 11.
    1975   *A Comparative Analysis of Complex Organizations,* exp. ed. New York: Free Press.
Fairfield, Dick
    1971   *Communes, U.S.A.* San Francisco: Alternatives Foundation.
    1972a   "Communes Europe," in *The Modern Utopian.* San Francisco: Alternatives Foundation.
    1972b   "Communes Japan," in *The Modern Utopian.* San Francisco: Alternatives Foundation.
Fararo, Thomas
    1973   *Mathematical Sociology,* New York: Johy Wiley.
Faris, Robert
    1964   *Handbook of Modern Sociology.* Chicago: Rand McNally.
Fernandez, James
    1978   "Passage to Community: Encounter in Evolutionary Perspective," in Kurt Back (ed.), *In Search for Community.* Boulder, Colo.: Westview Press.
Ferriss, Abbott
    1970   *Indicators of Change in the American Family.* New York: Russell Sage Foundation.
Festinger, Leon, et al.
    1950   *Social Pressures in Informal Groups.* Stanford, Calif.: Stanford University Press.
    1952   "Some Consequences of Deindividuation in a Group," *Journal of Abnormal Social Psychology* 47: 382–389.
    1956   *When Prophecy Fails.* New York: Harper.
Feuer, Lewis
    1962   "What is Alienation? The Career of a Concept," *New Politics* 1 (Spring): 116–134.

Flynn, Thomas
1974   *The Charismatic Renewal and the Irish Experience.* London: Hodder and Stoughton.
Fogarty, R. S.
1972   *American Utopianism.* Itasca, Ill.: Peacock Publishers.
Forsyth, Sondra, and Pauline Kolenda
1966   "Competition, Cooperation, and Group Cohesion in the Ballet Company," *Psychiatry* 29(2): 123–145.
Freilich, Morris
1963   "Toward an Operational Definition of Community," *Rural Sociology,* 28: 117–127.
French, David and Elena
1975   *Working Communally: Patterns and Possibilities.* New York: Russell Sage Foundation.
Freud, Sigmund
1971   *Group Psychology and the Analysis of the Ego.* New York: Bantam Books.
Friedell, Morris
1967   "Organizations as Semilattices," *American Sociological Review* 32(1): 46–54.
Friedland, W.
1964   "For a Sociological Concept of Charisma," *Social Forces* 43(October): 18–26.
Friedrich, Carl S.
1959   *Community.* New York: Liberal Arts Press.
Fugitt, G. V.
1971   "The Places Left Behind: Population Trends and Policy for Rural America," *Rural Sociology* 36(December): 449–470.
Galaskiewicz, Joseph
1976   "Social Networks and Community Decision Making." Ph.D. dissertation. Chicago: University of Chicago.
Gans, Herbert J.
1962   *The Urban Villagers: Group and Class in the Life of Italian Americans.* New York: Free Press.
1967   *The Levittowners: Ways of Life and Politics in a New Suburban Community.* New York: Vintage Books.
1968   *People and Plans: Essays on Urban Problems and Solutions.* New York: Basic Books.
1974   *More Equality.* New York: Vintage.
Gardner, Hugh
1973   "Crises and Politics in Rural Communes," In Rosabeth M. Kanter (ed.), *Communes: Creating and Managing the Collective Life.* New York: Harper & Row.
1978   *The Children of Prosperity: Thirteen Modern American Communes.* New York: St. Martin's Press.
Gardner, Joyce
1970   "Cold Mountain Farm," New York: unpublished.

Gaskin, Stephen
    1974   *Hey Beatnik! This Is the Farm Book.* Summertown, Tenn.: Book
            Publishing Co.
    1976   *This Season's People.* Summertown, Tenn.: Book Publishing Co.
Geertz, C.
    1964   "Ideology as a Cultural System," in David Apter (ed.), *Ideology &
            Discontent.* New York: Free Press.
Glick, Paul C.
    1975   "Some Recent Changes in American Families," *Current Population
            Reports,* Series P–23 (52), U. S. Bureau of the Census.
——, and Robert Parke, Jr.
    1971   "Prospective Changes in Marriage and the Family: Trends in Mar-
            riage and Stability of Marriage," in Bert N. Adams and Thomas
            Weirath (eds.), *Readings on the Sociology of the Family.* Chicago:
            Markham.
——, and Arthur J. Norton
    1977   "Marrying, Divorcing, and Living Together in the U.S. Today,"
            Population Bulletin 32(5).
Glock, Charles Y.
    1976   "Consciousness among Contemporary Youth: An Interpretation," in
            C. Glock and R. Bellah (eds.), *The New Religious Consciousness.*
            Berkeley: University of California Press.
——, and Robert Bellah (eds.)
    1976   *The New Religions Consciousness.* Berkeley: University of Cali-
            fornia Press.
Goffman, Erving
    1959   *The Presentation of Self in Everyday Life.* Garden City, N.Y.:
            Doubleday.
    1969   *Strategic Interaction.* Philadelphia: University of Pennsylvania Press.
Goldstein, L.
    1974   *Communes, Law, and Commonsense.* Boston: New Community
            Projects.
Gollin, Gillian Lindt
    1967   *Moravians in Two Worlds.* New York: Columbia University Press.
Goode, William J.
    1957   "Community within a Community: The Professions," in David
            Minar and Scott Greer (eds.), *The Concept of Community.* Chicago:
            Aldine.
    1959   "The Theoretical Importance of Love," *American Sociological Re-
            view* 24(February): 38–47.
    1964   *The Family.* Englewood Cliffs, N.J.: Prentice-Hall.
    1965   *After Divorce.* Glencoe, Ill.: Free Press.
    1972   "The Place of Force in Human Society," *American Sociological
            Review* 37(October): 507–519.
    1978   *The Celebration of Heroes.* Berkeley: University of California
            Press.
Goodman, Paul
    1959   *The Empire City.* Indianapolis: Bobbs-Merrill Co.

——, and Percival Goodman
1960   *Communitas: Means of Livelihood and Ways of Life.* New York: Vintage Books.

Goren, Arthur A.
1970   *New York Jews and the Quest for Community: The Kehillah Experiment, 1908-1922.* New York: Columbia University Press.

Gouldner, Alvin W.
1960   "The Norm of Reciprocity: A Preliminary Statement," *American Sociological Review* 25(April): 161-179.

Granovetter, M. S.
1973   "The Strength of Weak Ties," *American Journal of Sociology* 68 (May): 1360-1380.

Gray, Donald J., and Allan H. Orrick
1966   *Designs of Famous Utopias.* New York: Holt Rinehart & Winston.

Grierson, D.
1971   *Young People in Communal Living.* Philadelphia: Westminister Press.

Gross, Neal, and William E. Martin
1952   "On Group Cohesiveness," *American Journal of Sociology* 57: 546-564.

Gustaitis, Rosa
1969   *Turning On.* New York: Macmillan.

Hague, W.
1968   "Value Systems and Vocational Choice of the Priesthood." Ph.D. dissertation. Alberta, Canada: University of Alberta.

Hallberg, Gunilla and Goran
1973   "A Swedish 'Big Family,'" in Rosabeth M. Kanter (ed.), *Communes: Creating and Managing the Collective Life.* New York: Harper & Row.

Hallinan, Maureen
1974   *The Structure of Positive Sentiment.* Amsterdam: Elsevier Publications.

Handlin, Oscar and Mary F.
1971   *Facing Life: Youth and the Family in American History.* Boston: Little, Brown.

Hare, A. Paul
1973   "Group Decision by Consensus," *Sociological Inquiry* 43(1): 53-77.

Hargrove, Barbara
1976   "Church Student Ministries and the New Consciousness," in C. Glock and R. Bellah (eds.), *The New Religious Consciousness.* Berkeley: University of California Press.

Havighurst, Robert J.
1975   "Youth in Social Institutions," in Robert J. Havighurst and Philip Dreyer (eds.), *Youth: The Seventy-fourth Yearbook of the National Society for the Study of Education.* Chicago: University of Chicago Press.

418   References

——, and Philip Dreyer
1975   "Youth and Cultural Pluralism," in Robert J. Havighurst and Philip Dreyer (eds.), *Youth: The Seventy-fourth Yearbook of the National Society for the Study of Education*. Chicago: University of Chicago Press.

Hawthorne, Nathaniel
1852   *The Blithedale Romance*. New York: W. W. Norton.

Hayden, Dolores
1976   *Seven American Utopias*. Cambridge, Mass.: M.I.T. Press.

Hayden, Tom
1977   "Writing the Port Huron Statement," in Lynda R. Obst (ed.), *The Sixties: The Decade Remembered Now by the People Who Lived It Then*. New York: Random House.

Heberle, Rudolf
1951   *Social Movements: An Introduction to Political Sociology*. New York: Appleton-Century-Crofts.

Heckman, John
1973   "Cambridge Commune: The Cat Is Everyone's," in Rosabeth M. Kanter (ed.), *Communes: Creating and Managing the Collective Life*. New York: Harper & Row.

Hedgepeth, William, and Dennis Stock
1970   *The Alternative: Communal Life in New America*. New York: Macmillan.

Heider, Fritz
1958   *The Psychology of Interpersonal Relations*. New York: Wiley.

Heinz, Donald
1976   "The Christian World Liberation Front," in C. Glock and R. Bellah (eds.), *The New Religious Consciousness*. Berkeley: University of California Press.

Hennacy, Ammon
1964   *The Book of Ammon*. Salt Lake City: author.

Henner, Martin
1976   "Legal Responses to the Communal Living 'Family,'" New York.

Hernes, Gudmund
1976   "Structural Change in Social Processes," *American Journal of Sociology* 82(3): 513–547.

Hershberger, Ann
1973   "The Transiency of Urban Communes," in Rosabeth M. Kanter (ed.), *Communes: Creating and Managing the Collective Life*. New York: Harper & Row.

Hicks, George
1971   "Utopian Communities and Social Networks," in David Plath (ed.), *Aware of Utopia*. Chicago: University of Illinois Press.

Hill, Michael
1973   *A Sociology of Religion*. New York: Basic Books.

Hillery, George A.
1968   *Communal Organizations*. Chicago: University of Chicago Press.

1971 "Freedom and Social Organization: A Comparative Analysis," *American Sociological Review* 36(February): 51–65.

Hinds, William A.
1971 *American Communities.* New York: Corinth (first publ. 1908).

Hine, R. V.
1973 *California's Utopian Colonies.* New York: W. W. Norton.

Hobsbawm, E. J.
1959 *Primitive Rebels: Studies in Archaic Forms of Social Movement in the 19th and 20th Centuries.* Manchester: Manchester University Press.
1975 *The Age of Capital: 1848–1875.* New York: Scribner's.

Hochschild, Arlie Russell
1973 *The Unexpected Community.* Englewood Cliffs, N.J.: Prentice-Hall.

Hoffer, Eric
1966 *True Believer.* New York: Harper & Row.

Holland, Paul, and Samuel Leinhardt
1970 "A Method for Detecting Structure in Sociometric Data," *American Journal of Sociology* 76(November): 492–513.
1973 "The Structural Implications of Measurement Error in Sociometry," *Journal of Mathematical Sociology* 3: 85–111.
1976 "Local Structure in Social Networks," in David R. Heise (ed.), *Sociological Methodology 1976.* San Francisco: Jossey-Bass.

Hollenbach, Margaret
1973 "Relationships and Regulation in 'The Family' of Taos, New Mexico," in Rosabeth M. Kanter (ed.), *Communes: Creating and Managing the Collective Life.* New York: Harper & Row.

Holloway, Mark
1966 *Heavens on Earth: Utopian Communities in America, 1680–1880.* London: Turnstile Press.

Homans, George
1950 *The Human Group.* New York: Harcourt Brace.
1961 *Social Behavior: Its Elementary Forms.* New York: Harcourt Brace.

Hong, Lawrence
1978 "Risky Shift and Cautious Shift: Some Direct Evidence on the Culture-Value Theory," *Social Psychology* 41(4): 342–346.

Horowitz, Irving Louis
1978 *Science, Sin, and Scholarship: The Politics of Reverend Moon and the Unification Church.* Cambridge: M.I.T. Press.

Horton, Lucy
1972 *Country Commune Cooking.* New York: Coward, McCann & Geoghegan.

Hostetler, John A.
1963 *Amish Society.* Baltimore, Md.: Johns Hopkins University Press.
1974a *Hutterite Society.* Baltimore, Md.: Johns Hopkins University Press.
1974b *Communitarian Societies.* New York: Holt Rinehart & Winston.

Houriet, Robert
1971 *Getting Back Together.* New York: Coward, McCann & Geoghegan.

Howard, Nigel
1971   *Paradoxes of Rationality*. Cambridge, Mass.: M.I.T. Press.
Huxley, Aldous
1965   *Brave New World, and Brave New World Revisited*. New York: Colophon Books.
Infield, Henrik
1942   "Social Control in a Cooperative Society," *Sociometry* (August): 258–271.
1947   *Sociometric Structure of a Vets Coop Land Settlement*. Sociometry mono. 15. New York: Beacon House.
1949   "The Sociological Approach in Research on Cooperation," *Rural Sociology* 14(2): 157–171.
1954   *People in Ejidos*. New York: Praeger.
——, and Ernest Dichter
1943   "Who Is Fit for Cooperative Farming?," *Applied Anthropology* (January–March): 4–16.
——, and J. Maier
1950   *Cooperative Group Living*. New York: Henry Koosis.
Israel, Joachim
1971   *Alienation: From Marx to Modern Sociology*. Boston: Allyn and Bacon.
Israel, Matthew L.
1973   "Irritations and Jealousies," in Rosabeth M. Kanter (ed.), *Communes: Creating and Managing the Collective Life*. New York: Harper & Row.
Jacobs, Ruth Harriet
1971   "Emotive and Control Groups at Mutated New American Utopian Communities," *Journal of Applied Behavioral Science* 7(March–April): 234–251.
Jaffe, Dennis
1975   "Couples in Communes." Unpublished Ph.D. dissertation, Yale University.
James, Bartlett B.
1899   *The Labadist Colony in Maryland*. Baltimore, Md.: Johns Hopkins University Press.
Janowitz, Morris
1953   *A Community Press in an Urban Setting*. Chicago: University of Chicago Press.
1959   *Sociology and the Military Establishment*. New York: Russell Sage.
1978   *The Last Half-Century*. Chicago: University of Chicago Press.
Jerome, J.
1974   *Families of Eden*. New York: Seabury Press.
Johnson, Benton
1963   "On Church and Sect," *American Sociological Review* 38(4): 539–549.
Johnson, Gregory
1976   "The Hare Krishna in San Francisco," in C. Glock and R. Bellah (eds.), *The New Religious Consciousness*. Berkeley: University of California Press.

Johnston, Lloyd
  1973   *Drugs and American Youth: A Report from the Youth in Transition Project.* Ann Arbor: Institute for Social Research, University of Michigan.
Jones, Maxwell
  1953   *The Therapeutic Community.* New York: Basic Books.
Kagan, Paul
  1975   *New World Utopias: A Photographic History of the Search for Community.* New York: Penguin.
Kahn, Herman
  1977   Untitled talk presented at Alternatives to Growth 1977 Conference. Houston, Texas.
Kanter, Rosabeth Moss
  1972   *Commitment and Community: Communes and Utopias in Sociological Perspective.* Cambridge, Mass.: Harvard University Press.
  1973a   "The Family and Sex Roles in American Communes," in R. M. Kanter (ed.), *Communes: Creating and Managing the Collective Life.* New York: Harper & Row.
  1973b   "Structure, Functions, and Impact of Urban Communes." Progress Report to the National Institutes of Mental Health.
  1973c   *Communes: Creating and Managing the Collective Life.* New York: Harper & Row.
  1973d   "Utopian Communities," *Sociological Inquiry* 43(3-4): 263-290.
  1974   "Urban Communes and Family History." Denver, Colo.: Presented at annual meeting of Organization of American Historians, April 20.
  1976   *Work and Family in America.* New York: Russell Sage Foundation.
——, and Marilyn Halter
  1973   "Dehousewifing women, Domesticating Men: Equality between the Sexes in Urban Communes." Montreal: Presented at the Annual meeting of the American Psychological Association.
——, D. Jaffee, and K. Weisberg
  1975   "Coupling, Parenting, and the Presence of Others: Intimate Relationships in Communal Households," *The Family Coordinator* 3(October): 433.
Katz, E.
  1971   *Armed Love.* New York: Holt Rinehart & Winston.
Kaufmann, Walter
  1971   "The Inevitability of Alienation," in R. Schacht (ed.), *Alienation.* Garden City, N.Y.: Doubleday.
Keim, Albert
  1975   *Compulsory Education and the Amish.* Boston: Beacon Press.
Kelman, Herbert C.
  1958   "Compliance, Identification, and Internalization: Three Processes of Attitude Change," *Journal of Conflict Resolution* 2(March): 51-60.
Keniston, Kenneth
  1964   *The Uncommitted.* New York: Dell.
Kephart, William
  1976   *Extraordinary Groups: The Sociology of Unconventional Life-styles.* New York: St. Martin's Press.

Keyfitz, Nathan
  1966   "Population Density and the Style of Social Life," *Bioscience* 14
          (February): 98–104.
Killduff, Marshall, and Ron Javers
  1978   *The Suicide Cult: The Inside Story of the People's Temple Sect and
          the Massacre in Guyana.* New York: Bantam Books.
Killian, Lewis
  1964   "Social Movements," in Robert E. L. Faris (ed.), *Handbook of Mod-
          ern Sociology.* Chicago: Rand McNally, pp. 426–455.
Kinkade, Kathleen
  1973   *A Walden Two Experiment.* New York: William Morrow.
  1974   "Power and the Utopian Assumption," *Journal of Applied Be-
          havioral Science* 10(3): 402–414.
Klapp, Orrin E.
  1969   *Collective Search for Identity.* New York: Holt Rinehart & Win-
          ston.
Klassen, Peter James
  1964   *The Economics of Anabaptism, 1525–1560. Studies in European
          History III.* The Hague: Mouton.
Koch, H. W.
  1975   *The Hitler Youth.* London: Macdonald and Janes.
Kramer, Wendell B.
  1955   "Criteria for the Intentional Community." Unpublished Ph.D. thesis.
          New York: New York University School of Education.
Kriyananda
  1968   *Cooperative Communities: How to Start Them and Why.* San Fran-
          cisco: Ananda Publications.
Laing, R. D., et al.
  1966   *Interpersonal Perception: A Theory and Method of Research.*
          London: Tavistock.
Lamott, Kenneth
  1973   "Doing Their Thing at Morning Star," in Rosabeth M. Kanter (ed.),
          Communes: Creating and Managing the Collective Life. New York:
          Harper & Row.
Lane, Ralph Jr.
  1976   "Catholic Charismatic Renewal," in C. Glock and R. Bellah (eds.),
          The New Religious Consciousness. Berkeley: University of Cali-
          fornia Press.
Lanternari, Victor
  1963   *The Religions of the Oppressed: A Study of Modern Messianic
          Cults.* New York: Knopf.
Laslett, P. (ed.)
  1972   *Household and Family in Past Time.* Cambridge: Cambridge Uni-
          versity Press.
Laumann, E. O.
  1973   *Bonds of Pluralism.* New York: John Wiley.
——, and F. U. Pappi
  1973   "New Directions in the Study of Community Elites," in *American
          Sociological Review* 38(April): 212–230.

Lazarsfeld, Paul
 1972   "The Problem of Measuring Turnover," in P. Lazarsfeld, A. Pasa-
         nella, and M. Rosenberg (eds.), *Continuities in the Language of
         Social Research.* New York: Free Press.
——, and Robert K. Merton
 1954   "Friendship as Social Process: A Substantive and Methodological
         Analysis," in Morroe Berger, Theodore Abel, and Charles H. Page
         (eds.), *Freedom and Control in Modern Society.* New York: Octa-
         gon Books.
——, Bernard Berelson, and Hazel Gaudet
 1955   "The Process of Opinion and Attitude Formation," in Paul Lazars-
         feld and Morris Rosenberg (eds.), *The Language of Social Research.*
         Glencoe, Ill.: Free Press.
LeBon, Gustave
 1952   *The Crowd.* London: Ernest Benn (first publ. 1896).
Levine, Saul V., et al.
 1972   "The Urban Commune: Fact or Fad, Promise or Pipe Dream."
         Unpublished paper.
LeWarne, Charles
 1975   *Utopias on Puget Sound: 1885–1915.* Seattle: University of Wash-
         ington Press.
Lichtheim, G.
 1965   "The Concept of Ideology," in *History and Theory* 4: 164–195.
Liebow, E.
 1967   *Tally's Corner.* Boston: Little, Brown.
Lifton, Robert Jay
 1961   *Thought Reform and the Psychology of Totalism.* New York:
         W. W. Norton.
 1971   *History and Human Survival.* New York: Vintage Books.
Lipset, Seymour M.
 1975   "Social Structure and Social Change," in Peter Blau (ed.), *Ap-
         proaches to the Study of Social Structure.* New York: Free Press.
——, et al.
 1956   *Union Democracy.* New York: Free Press.
Litwak, E., and I. Szlenyi
 1969   "Primary Group Structures and Their Functions," *American Socio-
         logical Review* 34: 465–481.
Lofland, John
 1966   *Doomsday Cult: A Study of Conversion, Proselytization and Main-
         tenance of Faith.* Englewood Cliffs, N.J.: Prentice-Hall.
——, and Rodney Stark
 1965   "Becoming a World Saver: A Theory of Conversion to a Deviant
         Perspective," *American Sociological Review* 30(December): 862–
         875.
Loomis, Mildred
 1965   *Go Ahead and Live.* New York: Philosophical Library.
Love, Joseph
 1971   "Utopianism in Latin American Cultures," in David Plath (ed.),
         Aware of Utopia. Urbana: University of Illinois Press.

Luce, R. D.
 1959 *Individual Choice Behavior: A Theoretical Analysis.* New York: John Wiley.
Lüschen, Gunther, and Gregory Stone (eds.)
 1977 *Herman Schmalenbach on Society and Experience.* Chicago: University of Chicago Press.
MacIver, Robert
 1937 "Social Cohesion in the Utopian Communities," in *Society: A Textbook in Sociology.* New York: Farrar & Rinehart.
Manheimer, Dean I., et al.
 1974 *Prospectus for a Study of Transient Youth.* Institute for Research in Social Behavior.
Mannhardt, Michael
 1979 "Structural Properties of Stable Groups." Ph.D. dissertation, in progress. New York: Columbia University.
Mannheim, Karl
 1936 *Ideology and Utopia: An Introduction to the Sociology of Knowledge,* Louis Wirth and Edward Shils (trans.). New York: Harcourt Brace.
Manuel, Frank E.
 1962 *The Prophets of Paris.* Cambridge, Mass.: Harvard University Press.
——, (ed.)
 1966 *Utopias and Utopian Thought.* Boston: Houghton Mifflin.
——, and P. Fritzie
 1966 *French Utopias: An Anthology of Ideal Societies.* New York: Free Press.
 1979 *Utopian Thought in the Western World.* Cambridge, Mass.: Harvard University Press.
March, James G., and Herbert A. Simon
 1958 *Organizations.* New York: John Wiley.
Marcus, John T.
 1961 "Transcendence and Charisma," *The Western Political Quarterly* 14(1): 236–241.
Marcuse, Herbert
 1962 *One Dimensional Man.* Boston: Beacon Press.
Mariampolski, Hyman
 1975 "The Decline of Sexual Egalitarianism on the Kibbutz." Working paper. Lafayette, Ind.: Purdue University.
Marks, John
 1979 *The Search for the Manchurian Candidate.* New York: Times Books.
Masling, Joseph
 1965 "Birth order and the need for affiliation," *Psychological Reports.* 16(2): 631–632.
Maslow, Abraham H.
 1962 *Toward a Psychology of Being.* Princeton, N.J.: D. Van Nostrand.
 1964 *Religions, Values, and Peak Experiences.* Columbus: Ohio State University Press.

1965   *Eupsychian Management: A Journal.* Homewood, Ill.: Irwin-Dorsey.

McCarthy, Mary
1963   "The Oasis," in *Cast a Cold Eye.* New York: Harcourt Brace.

Mead, George Herbert
1934   *Mind, Self, and Society.* Chicago: University of Chicago Press.

Mead, Margaret
1937   *Cooperation and Competition among Primitive Peoples.* Boston: Beacon Press.
1957   "Towards More Vivid Utopias," *Science* 126 (November 8): 957–961.

Meadows, Paul
1944–45 "Movements of Social Withdrawal," *Sociology and Social Research* 29(September–October): 46–50.

Melville, Keith
1972   *Communes in the Counterculture: Origins, Theories, Styles of Life.* New York: William Morrow.

Merton, Robert K.
1936   "The Unanticipated Consequences of Purposive Social Action," *American Sociological Review* 1(October): 894–904.
1959   *Social Theory and Social Structure.* New York: Free Press.

Merton, Thomas
1969   *Mystics and Zen Masters.* New York: Dell.

Messer, Jeanne
1976   "Guru Maharaj Ji and the Divine Light Mission," in C. Glock and R. Bellah (eds.), *The New Religious Consciousness.* Berkeley: University of California Press.

Messinger, Sheldon L.
1955   "Organizational Transformation: A Case Study of a Declining Social Movement," *American Sociological Review* 20(January): 3–10.

Mills, Richard
1973   *Young Outsiders.* London: Routledge & Kegan Paul.

Monsour, Karen, and Beth Stone
1974   "The Hawaii Trip: A Study of a Segment of American Youth," *Psychiatric Annals* 4(6): 340–356.

Morris, Charles
1956   *Varieties of Human Values.* Chicago: University of Chicago Press.

Morrison, Peter A.
1971   "The Propensity to Move: A Longitudinal Analysis." Report prepared for Department of Housing and Urban Development.

Morse, F.
1971   *Yankee Communes.* New York: Harcourt Brace.

Moynihan, Daniel P. (ed.)
1969   *Maximum Feasible Misunderstanding.* New York: Free Press.

Murdock, Iris
1958   *The Bell.* New York: Viking.

Musgrove, Frank
1974   *Ecstasy and Holiness, Counterculture and the Open Society.* London: Methuen.

1975   "Dervishes in Dorsetshire: An English Commune," *Youth & Society* 6(June): 449–480.

Myers, D. G., and H. Lamm
1976   "The Group Polarization Phenomenon," *Psychological Bulletin* 83: 602–627.

Nadel, S. F.
1957   *The Theory of Social Structure*. New York: Free Press.

National Opinion Research Center
1974   *General Social Survey*. Chicago.

Neal, A., and S. Rettig
1967   "On the Multidimensionality of Alienation," *American Sociological Review* 32(February): 54–64.

Nearing, Helen and Scott
1970   *Living the Good Life*. New York: Schocken.

Needleman, Jacob
1970   *The New Religions*. Garden City, N.Y.: Doubleday.

Nelson, Benjamin
1959   "Community—Dreams and Realities," in Carl Friedrich (ed.), *Community*. New York: Liberal Arts Press.

Nettler, G.
1957   "A Measure of Alienation," *American Sociological Review* 22: 670–677.

Neusner, Jacob
1972   *Contemporary Judaic Fellowship in Theory and in Practice*. New York: Ktav Publishing House.

Newcomb, T. M.
1961   *The Acquaintance Process*. New York: Holt, Rinehart, and Winston.

Nisbet, Robert A.
1953   *The Quest for Community*. New York: Oxford University Press.
1966   *The Sociological Tradition*. New York: Basic Books.

Nordhoff, Charles
1965   *The Communistic Societies of the United States; from Personal Visit and Observation: Including Detailed Accounts of the Icarian and Other Existing Societies, Their Religious Creeds, Social Practices, Numbers, Industries, and Present Condition*. New York: Schocken Books (first publ. 1875).

Noyes, J. H.
1870   *History of American Socialisms*. New York: Hillary Press.

Noyes, Pierrepont
1937   *My Father's House: An Oneida Boyhood*. New York: Farrar & Rinehart.

Nozick, Robert
1975   *Anarchy, the State, and Utopia*. New York: Basic Books.

Obst, Lynda R. (ed.)
1977   *The Sixties: The Decade Remembered Now by the People Who Lived It Then*. New York: Random House.

Ofshe, Richard
1976 "Synanon: The People Business," in C. Glock and R. Bellah (eds.), *The New Religious Consciousness.* Berkeley: University of California Press.
Okugawa, Otohiko
1974 "19th Century Communitarian Societies: A Social Movement." Unpublished. Pittsburg: Department of Sociology, University of Pittsburgh.
1980 "Annotated List of Communal and Utopian Societies," in Robert Fogarty (ed.), *Dictionary of American Communal and Utopian History.* Westport Conn.: Greenwood (forthcoming).
Olson, Mancur, Jr.
1968 *The Logic of Collective Action: Public Goods and the Theory of Groups.* New York: Schocken Books.
Ooms, Herman
1975 *Charismatic Bureaucrat: A Political Biography of Matsudaira Sadanobu 1758-1829.* Chicago: University of Chicago Press.
Overend, William
1978 "What Is Happening inside Synanon," *Los Angeles Times,* January 31, IV, p. 2.
Packard, Vance
1972 *A Nation of Strangers.* New York: David McKay.
Pappenheim, Fritz
1968 *The Alienation of Modern Man.* New York: Modern Reader Paperbacks.
Park, Robert E.
1952 *Human Communities.* New York: Free Press.
1972 *The Crowd and the Public and Other Essays.* Chicago: University of Chicago Press.
Parsons, Talcott
1937 *The Structure of Social Action.* New York: McGraw-Hill.
1960 "Pattern Variables Revisited: A Response to Robert Dubin," *American Sociological Review,* 25(4): 467-483.
1967 "Introduction to Max Weber's *The Sociology of Religion,*" in *Sociological Theory and Modern Society.* New York: The Free Press.
——, and R. Bales
1955 *Family Socialization and Interaction Process.* Glencoe, Ill.: Free Press.
——, R. Bales, and E. Shils
1953 *Working Papers in the Theory of Action.* Glencoe, Ill.: Free Press.
Pease, W. and J.
1963 *Black Utopia.* Madison: State Historical Society of Wisconsin.
Peters, Victor
1965 *All Things Common: The Hutterian Way of Life.* New York: Harper & Row.

Piazza, Thomas
  1976   "Jewish Identity and the Counterculture," in C. Glock and R. Bellah
          (eds.), *The New Religious Consciousness*. Berkeley: University of
          California Press.
Pittel, Stephen M.
  1968   "The Current Status of the Haight-Ashbury Hippie Community."
          Unpublished paper.
Plant, James S.
  1950   *The Envelope: A Study of the Impact of the World upon the Child*.
          New York: Commonwealth Fund.
Plath, David W.
  1966   "The Fate of Utopia: Adaptive Tactics in Four Japanese Groups,"
          American Anthropologist 68(October): 1152–1162.
  1971   *Aware of Utopia*. Urbana: University of Illinois Press.
  1973   "Modernization and the Establishment of Communes in Japan," in
          Rosabeth M. Kanter (ed.), *Communes: Creating and Managing the
          Collective Life*. New York: Harper & Row.
Poll, Solomon
  1962   *The Hassidic Community of Williamsburg*. New York: Free Press.
Price, James L.
  1977   *The Study of Turnover*. Ames: Iowa State University Press.
Pritchard, Linda K.
  1976   "Religious Change in Nineteenth-century America," in C. Glock and
          R. Bellah (eds.), *The New Religious Consciousness*. Berkeley:
          University of California Press.
Pulkingham, W. G.
  1972   *Gathered for Power*. New York: Morehouse-Barlow.
Rabin, A. I.
  1958   "Infants and Children under Conditions of Intermittent Mothering,"
          American Journal of Orthopsychiatry 28(3): 577–586.
  1965   *Growing Up in the Kibbutz*. New York: Springer Publishing.
Raimy, Eric
  1979   *Shared Houses, Shared Lives*. Los Angeles: J. P. Tarcher, Inc.
Ramey, James W.
  1972   "Communes, Group Marriage, and the Upper Middle Class," *Journal
          of Marriage and Family* 34(November): 647–655.
  1975   "Legal Regulation of Personal and Family Life-styles." New York:
          Presented at Fourth International Conference on the Unity of the
          Sciences.
Rand, Christopher
  1967   *Los Angeles: The Ultimate City*. New York: Oxford University
          Press.
Rank, Otto
  1914   "The Myth of the Birth of the Hero," *Nervous and Mental Diseases*
          18.
Reed, Roy
  1973   "Conformity Backfires for a Commune," *The New York Times*,
          September 22, 1973, p. 33.

Reich, Wilhelm
1970   *The Mass Psychology of Fascism.* New York: Farrar, Straus and Giroux.
Restle, Frank
1961   *Psychology of Judgment and Choice.* New York: John Wiley.
Rexroth, K.
1975   *Communalism: From its Origins to the 20th Century.* New York: Seabury Press.
Richardson, J.
1976   "Commune Typologies: A Critique and Discussion." Tempe, Ariz.: Presented at Western Social Science Meetings.
Rickman, John
1957   *A General Selection from the Works of Sigmund Freud.* Garden City, N.Y.: Doubleday.
Riesman, David
1950   *The Lonely Crowd.* New Haven, Conn.: Yale University Press.
Rigby, Andrew
1974   *Alternative Realities: A Study of Communes and Their Members.* London: Routledge and Kegan Paul.
Riker, William and P. Ordeshook
1973   *An Introduction to Positive Political Theory.* Englewood Cliffs, N.J.: Prentice-Hall.
Roberts, Ron E.
1971   *The New Communes.* New Jersey: Prentice-Hall.
Robinson, John, and Philip Converse
1972   "Social Changes Reflected in the Use of Time," in Angus Campbell and Philip E. Converse (eds.), *The Human Meaning of Social Change.* New York: Russell Sage Foundation.
Robinson, John and Philip Shaver
1973   *Measures of Social Psychological Attitudes.* Ann Arbor, Mich.: Institute For Social Research.
Rokeach, Milton
1968   *Beliefs, Attitudes, and Values.* San Francisco: Jossey-Bass.
1969   "Religions, Values, and Social Compassion." *Review of Religious Research* 11(1): 24–39.
1973   *The Nature of Human Values.* New York: Free Press.
1974   "Change and Stability in American Value Systems: 1968–1971," *Public Opinion Quarterly* 38(19): 224–238.
——, et al.
1971   "The Value Gap between Police and Policed," *Journal of Social Issues* 27: 155–171.
Rosenfield, Eva
1951   "Social Stratification in a 'Classless' Society," *American Sociological Review* 16(March): 766–774.
Rosner, Menahem
1973   "Direct Democracy in the Kibbutz," in Rosabeth M. Kanter (ed.), *Communes: Creating and Managing the Collective Life.* New York: Harper & Row.

Rossi, Peter H., Richard A. Berk, and Bettye K. Eidson
1974   *The Roots of Urban Discontent, Public Policy, Municipal Institutions, and the Ghetto.* New York: Wiley-Interscience.
Roszak, T.
1969   *The Making of a Counterculture.* Garden City, N.Y.: Doubleday.
Rothchild, John, and Susan Wolf
1976   *The Children of the Counterculture.* Garden City, N.Y.: Doubleday.
Sanders, Ed
1971   *The Family.* New York: E. P. Dutton.
Sapir, Edward
1924   "Culture, Genuine and Spurious," *American Journal of Sociology* 29: 401-429.
Schaaf, V. T.
1925   *The Rule of St. Benedict.* London: Chatto and Windus.
Schacht, Richard
1971   *Alienation.* Garden City, N.Y.: Doubleday.
Schachter, Stanley
1959   *The Psychology of Affiliation: Experimental Studies of the Sources of Gregariousness.* Stanford, Calif.: Stanford University Press.
Scheff, Thomas
1967   "Toward a Sociological Model of Consensus," *American Sociological Review* 32(1): 32-46.
Schiffer, Irvine
1973   *Charisma: A Psychoanalytic Look at Mass Society.* New York: The Free Press.
Schmalenbach, Herman
1961   "The Sociological Category of Communion," in Talcott Parsons et al. (eds.), *Theories of Society.* Vol. 1. New York: Free Press.
Seeman, Melvin
1967   "On the Personal Consequences of Alienation in Work," *American Sociological Review* 32(April): 273-285.
1972   "Alienation and Engagement," in Angus Campbell and Philip E. Converse (eds.), *The Human Meaning of Social Change.* New York: Russell Sage Foundation.
1975   "Alienation Studies," in *Annual Review of Sociology.* Palo Alto, Calif.: Annual Reviews.
Selznick, Philip
1957   *Leadership in Administration.* Evanston, Ill: Row, Peterson.
Sen, Amartya
1970   *Collective Choice and Social Welfare.* San Francisco: Holden-Day.
Sennett, Richard
1978   "Destructive Gemeinschaft," in Kurt Back (ed.), *In Search for Community.* Boulder, Colo.: Westview Press.
Shapiro, David
1965   *Neurotic Styles.* New York: Basic Books.
Shepard, Herbert A.
1965   "Changing Interpersonal and Intergroup Relationships in Organiza-

tions," in James G. March (ed.), *Handbook of Organizations*. Chicago: Rand McNally.

Shey, Thomas
1977   "Why Communes Fail," *Journal of Marriage and The Family* 39 (August): 605–613.

Shils, Edward
1965   "Charisma, Order, and Status," *American Sociological Review* 30 (April): 199–213.
1968   "Charisma," in *The International Encyclopedia of the Social Sciences*. Vol. 2: 386–390. New York: The Free Press.

Sieber, Sam
1973   "The Integration of Fieldwork and Survey Methods," *American Journal of Sociology* 78(May): 1335–1359.

Simmel, Georg
1955   *Conflict and the Web of Group Affiliation*. Glencoe, Ill.: Free Press.
1964   "On the Significance of Numbers for Social Life," and "The Secret Society," in Kurt H. Wolf (ed.), *The Sociology of Georg Simmel*. New York: Free Press.

Simmons, J. L.
1966   "Some Intercorrelations among 'Alienation' Measures," *Social Forces* 44(March): 370–372.

Skinner, B. F.
1948   *Walden Two*. New York: Macmillan.

Sklare, Marshall
1971   *America's Jews*. New York: Random House.

Skolnick, Arlene S. and Jerome H. (eds.).
1971   *Family in Transition*. Boston: Little, Brown.

Slater, Philip E.
1963   "On Social Regression," *American Sociological Review* 28(June): 339–364.
1966   *Microcosm: Structural, Psychological, and Religious Evolution in Groups*. New York: John Wiley.
1970   *The Pursuit of Loneliness*. Boston: Beacon Press.

Smart, Reginald
1965   "Social-group Membership and Leadership and Birth Order," *Journal of Social Psychology* 67(2): 221–225.

Smelser, Neil
1962   *Theory of Collective Behavior*. New York: Free Press.

Smith, Ewart E., and J. D. Goodchilds
1963   "Some Personality and Behavior factors Related to Birth Order," *Journal of Applied Psychology* 47(5): 300–303.

Snyder, Gary
1969   *Earth House Hold*. New York: New Directions.

Sorokin, P.
1950   *Explorations in Altruistic Love and Behavior*. Boston: Beacon Press.

Speck, Ross V.
1972   *The New Families: Youth, Communes, and the Politics of Drugs*. New York: Basic Books.

Spiro, Melford E.
    1956   *Kibbutz: Venture in Utopia.* Cambridge, Mass.: Harvard University
            Press (also Schocken paperback).
    1958   *Children of the Kibbutz.* New York: Schocken Press.
Sprague, Charles
    1978   "The Structure of Interpersonal Attribution." Ph.D. dissertation,
            in progress. New York: Columbia University.
Statistical Abstracts of Israel
    1974   Jerusalem, Tel Aviv: Central Bureau of Statistics.
Stein, Barry A.
    1973   "The Internal Economics of Communes," in Rosabeth M. Kanter
            (ed.), *Communes: Creating and Managing the Collective Life.* New
            York: Harper & Row.
Stein, Maurice
    1959   *The Eclipse of Community.* New York: Harper & Row.
Stinchcombe, Arthur
    1968   *Constructing Social Theories.* New York: Harcourt Brace.
Stoner, Carroll, and J. Parke
    1979   *All Gods Children: The Cult Experience – Salvation or Slavery?*
            New York: Penguin Books.
Stouffer, S. A., et al.
    1949   *Studies in Social Psychology in World War II. Vol. 1. The American
            Soldier during Army Life.* Princeton, N.J.: Princeton University
            Press.
Sugihara, Yoshie, and David W. Plath
    1969   *Sensei and His People: The Building of a Japanese Commune.*
            Berkeley: University of California Press.
Sullivan, Joseph F.
    1979   "A Law Limiting Unrelated Persons in Housing Is Overturned in
            Jersey," *The New York Times,* July 31, p. 1.
Sundancer, Elaine
    1973   *Celery Wine: The Story of a Country Commune.* Yellow Springs,
            Ohio: Community Publishing.
Suttles, Gerald D.
    1972   *The Social Construction of Communities.* Chicago: University of
            Chicago Press.
Swanson, Guy E.
    1960   *The Birth of the Gods.* Ann Arbor: University of Michigan Press.
    1978   "Travels Through Inner Space: Family Structure and Openness to
            Absorbing Experiences," *American Journal of Sociology* 83 (January): 890–919.
    1978a   "Trance and Possession. Studies of Charismatic Influence," *Review
            of Religious Research* 19 (Spring) 253–278.
Talmon, Yonina
    1972   *Family and Community in the Kibbutz.* Cambridge, Mass.: Harvard
            University Press.
Thibaut, John, and Harold Kelley
    1959   *The Social Psychology of Groups.* New York: John Wiley.

Thompson, Hunter
  1972   *Hell's Angels: A Strange and Terrible Saga.* New York: Random House.
Thrupp, Sylvia (ed.)
  1962   *Millennial Dreams in Action.* The Hague: Mouton.
Tilly, Charles
  1974   *An Urban World.* Boston: Little, Brown.
Titmuss, Richard M.
  1971   *The Gift Relationship: From Human Blood to Social Policy.* New York: Vintage Books.
Tobey, Alan
  1976   "The Summer Solstice of the Healthy-Happy-Holy Organization," in C. Glock and R. Bellah (eds.), *The New Religious Consciousness.* Berkeley: University of California Press.
Tobias, Andrew
  1973   "Someday We May All Live in Lefrak City," *New York,* March 12, pp. 38–42.
Toch, Hans
  1965   *The Social Psychology of Social Movements.* Indianapolis: Bobbs-Merrill.
Tocqueville, Alexis de
  1945   *Democracy in America.* New York: Knopf.
Todd, Richard
  1970   "Walden Two? Three? Many More?," *The New York Times Magazine,* March 15, pp. 24–25, 114–126.
Toennies, Ferdinand
  1957   *Community and Society,* Charles P. Loomis (trans). East Lansing: Michigan State University Press.
Toffler, A.
  1971   *Future Shock.* New York: Basic Books.
Treiman, Donald J.
  1977   *Occupational Prestige in Comparative Perspective.* New York: Academic Press.
Tucker, Melinda
  1972   *Coming of Age in Topanga.* Unpublished paper.
Tucker, Robert
  1968   "The Theory of Charismatic Leadership," in *Philosophers and Kings: Studies in Leadership, Daedalus* 12(3): 731–756.
Turk, Herman
  1971   "Task and Emotion, Value and Charisma: Theoretical Union at Several Levels," in Herman Turk and Richard Simpson (eds.), *Institutions and Social Exchange.* New York: Bobbs-Merrill.
Turner, R. and L. Killian
  1957   *Collective Behavior.* Englewood Cliffs, N.J.: Prentice-Hall.
Turner, Victor
  1969   *The Ritual Process.* Chicago: Aldine.
Tyler, Alice Felt
  1962   *Freedom's Ferment: Phases of American Social History from the*

Colonial Period to the Outbreak of the Civil War. New York: Harper Torchbooks.

U.S. Bureau of the Census

    1972a   "Characteristics of American Youth: 1971," *Current Population Reports,* Series P-23, No. 40. Washington, D.C.: Government Printing Office.

    1972b   *Statistical Abstract of the United States: 1972.* 93rd ed. Washington, D.C.: Government Printing Office.

U.S. Department of Commerce

    1972a   "Population Characteristics," *Current Population Reports,* Series P-20, No. 237 (July). Washington, D.C.: Government Printing Office.

    1972b   "Farm Population of the United States: 1971," ERS, P-27, No. 43, (May). Washington, D.C.: Government Printing Office.

    1973   "Population Characteristics." *Current Population Reports,* Series P-20, No. 246 (February). Washington, D.C.: Government Printing Office.

U.S. Department of Housing and Urban Development

    1963   "Land-Use Intensity," *Land-Planning Bulletin,* No. 7 (September). Washington, D.C.: Government Printing Office.

U.S. News and World Report

    1975   October 20, p. 2.

Vallier, Ivan A.

    1959   "Production Imperatives in Communal Systems: A Comparative Study with Special References to the Kibbutz Crisis." Ph.D. dissertation. Cambridge, Mass.: Harvard University.

Vanek, Joann

    1974   "Time Spent in Housework," *Scientific American* 231(November): 116–120.

Vernon, Philip E., and Gordon Allport

    1951   *A Study of Values.* Boston: Houghton Mifflin.

Vesey, L. R.

    1973   *The Communal Experience.* New York: Harper.

Vidich, Arthur J., and Joseph Bensman

    1960   *Small Town in Mass Society.* New York: Doubleday.

Vidich, Arthur J., Joseph Bensman, and Maurice R. Stein (eds.)

    1964   *Reflections on Community Studies.* New York: John Wiley.

Vogt, Evon A.

    1955   *Modern Homesteaders.* Cambridge, Mass.: Harvard University Press.

Wagner, Jon

    1975   "Male Supremacy: Its Role in a Contemporary Commune and Its Structural Alternatives." Dekalb, Ill.: Presented at Conference on Communes: Historical and Contemporary, Northern Illinois University.

Wallis, Roy

    1977   *The Road to Total Freedom.* New York: Columbia University Press.

Warren, Carol A. B.
1974   *Identity and Community in the Gay World.* New York: John Wiley.
Warren, Roland L.
1970   "Toward a Non-Utopian Normative Model of the Community," *American Sociological Review* 35(April): 219–227.
Waters, Frank
1942   *The Man Who Killed the Deer: A Novel of Pueblo Indian Life.* Chicago: Swallow Press.
Watson, Tex
1978   *Will You Die For Me?* Old Tappan, N.J.: Fleming H. Revell.
Weber, Max
1946a "Science as a Vocation," in H. H. Gerth and C. Wright Mills (eds.), *From Max Weber.* New York: Oxford University Press.
1946b "The Sociology of Charismatic Authority," in H. H. Gerth and C. Wright Mills (eds.), *From Max Weber.* New York: Oxford University Press.
1946c "The Protestant Sects and the Spirit of Capitalism," in H. H. Gerth and C. Wright Mills (eds.), *From Max Weber.* New York: Oxford University Press.
1946d "Religious Rejections of the World and Their Directions," in H. H. Gerth and C. Wright Mills (eds.), *From Max Weber.* New York: Oxford University Press.
1947   *The Theory of Social and Economic Organization.* A. M. Henderson and Talcott Parsons (trans.). Glencoe, Ill.: Free Press.
Weiner, Irving and David Elkind
1972   *Child Development: A Core Approach.* New York: John Wiley.
Weiss, M.
1974   *Living Together.* New York: McGraw-Hill.
Weller, Leonard
1964   "The Relationship of Birth Order to Cohesiveness," *Journal of Social Psychology* 63(2): 249–254.
Wenner, Kate
1973   "National Builders in Tanzania," in Rosabeth M. Kanter (ed.), *Communes: Creating and Managing the Collective Life.* New York: Harper & Row.
Westhues, Kenneth
1972   "Hippiedom 1970: Some Tentative Hypotheses," *Sociological Quarterly* 13(Winter): 81–89.
White, Harrison C., et al.
1976   "Social Structure from Multiple Networks. I. Block Models of Roles and Positions," *American Journal of Sociology* 81(January): 730–780.
Whitney, Norman
1966   *Experiments in Community.* Wallingford, Penn.: Pendle Hill.
Wiggins, Lee M.
1973   *Panel Analysis: Latent Probability Models for Attitude and Behavior Processes.* San Francisco: Jossey-Bass.
Williams, Julia
1939   "An Analytical Tabulation of the North American Utopian Com-

munities by Type, Longevity, and Location." Unpublished M.A. thesis. Vermillion: University of South Dakota.

Willmott, Peter, and Michael Young
1973 *The Symmetrical Family.* New York: Pantheon.

Wilson, Bryan R.
1959 "An Analysis of Sect Development," *American Sociological Review* 24(February): 1-15.
1975 *The Noble Savages: The Primitive Origins of Charisma and Its Contemporary Survival.* Berkeley: University of California Press.

Wilson, Robert G.
1963 *Soviet Communes.* New Brunswick, N.J.: Rutgers University Press.

Wish, Harvey
1970 "Urbanism and the Church," in Raymond Mohl and Neil Betten (eds.), *Urban America in Historical Perspective.* New York: Weybright and Talley.

Wooster, Ernest
1924 *Communities of the Past and Present.* New Llano, La.: Llano Cooperative Colony Press.

Worsley, Peter
1968 *The Trumpet Shall Sound.* New York: Schocken Books.

Wright, Charles R., and Herbert H. Hyman
1958 "Voluntary Association Memberships of American Adults," *American Sociological Review* 23(June): 284-294.

Wuthnow, Robert
1976a *The Consciousness Reformation.* Berkeley: University of California Press.
1976b "The New Religions in Social Context," in C. Glock and R. Bellah (eds.), *The New Religious Consciousness.* Berkeley: University of California Press.
1978 *Experimentation in American Religion: The New Mysticisms and Their Implications for the Churches.* Berkeley: University of California Press.

Wynne, Lyman C., et al.
1958 "Pseudo-Mutuality in the Family Relations of Schizophrenics," *Psychiatry* 21(May): 205-220.

Yablonsky, Lewis
1965 *Synanon: The Tunnel Back.* New York: Macmillan.
1968 *The Hippie Trip.* New York: Pegasus Press.

Yankelovich, Daniel
1972 *The Changing Values on Campus.* New York: Washington Square Press.
1974 *The New Morality: Profile of American Youth in the Seventies.* New York: McGraw-Hill.

Yaswen, Gordon
1973 "Sunrise Hill Community: Post Mortem," in Rosabeth M. Kanter (ed.), *Communes: Creating and Managing the Collective Life.* New York: Harper & Row.

Yinger, J. Milton
    1960   "Contraculture and Subculture," *American Sociological Review* 25 (October): 625–635.
Yinon, Yoel, and Aharon Bizman
    1974   "The Nature of Effective Bonds and the Degree of Personal Responsibility as Determinants of Risk Taking for Self and Others," Bar Ilan U, Ramat-Gan, Israel: Bulletin of the Psychonomic Society.
Yorburg, Betty
    1973   *The Changing Family.* New York: Columbia University Press.
Young, Marguerite
    1945   *Angel in the Forest.* New York: Charles Scribner's Sons.
Young, Pauline
    1932   *The Pilgrims of Russian Town.* Chicago: University of Chicago Press.
Zablocki, Benjamin D.
    1970   "The Social Structure of Drug-based Communes." Unpublished paper.
    1971   *The Joyful Community.* Baltimore, Md.: Penguin. (Republished in 1980 by University of Chicago Press.)
    1972   "Anarchy and Decision Making in the Contemporary Commune." Vienna: Presented at the seminar on Decision Making in Nonvoting Groups of the Institute of Advanced Studies.
    1972a   "Some Models of Commune Integration and Disintegration." Presented at the annual meeting of the American Sociological Association.
    1972b   "Communal Child Rearing in Comparative Perspective." Presented at the annual meeting of the American Psychological Association.
    1973   "Communes, Planning, and the Future of Community in America." Symposium presented at the annual meeting of the American Sociological Association.
    1974   "The Use of Crisis as a Mechanism of Social Control," in George Zollschan and Walter Hirsch (eds.), *Social Change: Conjectures, Explorations, and Diagnosis.* Cambridge, Mass.: Schenkman.
    1975a   "Alienation and Charisma in a Context of Decision Making." Chicago: Presented at the annual meeting of the Public Choice Society, April.
    1975b   *Alienation and Investment of Self in the Urban Commune.* Project Report to National Institute of Mental Health, Washington, D.C.
    1975c   "The Implementation of Child Care: The Interplay of Forces Shaping the Development of Day Care as a Social Institution in Six American Cities." New York: Bureau for Applied Social Research.
    1978   "Communes, Encounter Groups, and the Search for Community," in Kurt Back (ed.), *In Search for Community.* Boulder, Colo.: Westview Press.
——, and Rosabeth M. Kanter
    1976   "The Differentiation of Lifestyles." *Annual Review of Sociology.* Palo Alto, Calif.: Annual Reviews.

Zald, Mayer, and Roberta Ash
    1966   "Social Movement Organizations: Growth, Decay and Change,"
            Social Forces 44(March); 327–340.
Zaretsky, Irving I. and Mark P. Leone (eds.)
    1974   *Religious Movements in Contemporary America.* Princeton: Prince-
            ton University Press.
Zorbaugh, Harvey W.
    1929   *The Gold Coast and the Slum.* Chicago: University of Chicago
            Press.

Name Index

Subject Index

443

3